ISBN 978-1-5284-4166-7
PIBN 10919152

1 MONTH OF
FREE
READING

at
www.ForgottenBooks.com

By purchasing this book you are eligible for one month membership to ForgottenBooks.com, giving you unlimited access to our entire collection of over 1,000,000 titles via our web site and mobile apps.

To claim your free month visit:
www.forgottenbooks.com/free919152

THE
PARLIAMENTARY REPORTER,

OR

DEBATES & PROCEEDINGS

OF THE

House of Assembly,

OF

PRINCE EDWARD ISLAND,

FOR THE YEAR 1885,

BEING THE

Third Session of the Twenty-Ninth General Assembly.

CHARLOTTETOWN:
GEORGE W. GARDINER, BOOK & JOB PRINTER, QUEEN SQUARE.
1885.

SESSION 1885.

WEDNESDAY, March 11, 1885.

AT three o'clock, p. m.; His Honor the Honorable Andrew Archibald Macdonald, Lieutenant Governor of the Province of Prince Edward Island, was pleased to command the attendance of Mr. Speaker and the Members of the House of Assembly, at the Bar of the Legislative Council Chamber.

The House accordingly appeared before His Honor, when he was pleased to make a speech to both Houses of the Legislature.

Honorable Members of the House of Assembly having then returned to their seats,—

Hon. Mr. SULLIVAN presented to the House a Bill to be intituled "An Act respecting procedure in the Supreme Court and Court of Chancery," and the same was received and read a first time, and ordered to be read the second time to-morrow.

Mr. SPEAKER reported that when the House did attend His Honor this day in the Council Chamber; His Honor was pleased to make a speech to both Houses of the Legislature,—a copy of which he had, for greater accuracy, obtained—as follows:

SPEECH:

Mr. President and Honorable Gentlemen of the Legislative Council:

Mr. Speaker and Gentlemen of the House of Assembly:

It is with much pleasure that I meet you at this time for the transaction of the public business, and thus inaugurate my official intercourse with the representatives of the people of my native Island.

You will, I feel confident, unite with me in the expression of deep thankfulness to Almighty God for the many favors of the year that is past. Although, in some respects, the harvest was not so abundant as in other years, yet no cry of distress has been heard; while the steady advance which our people are making in material prosperity, the undisturbed public health and the general contentment that prevails, are blessings for which we cannot be too heartily thankful and which it is our duty to acknowledge with feelings of the most sincere gratitude.

Soon after my appointment, I had the pleasure of assisting at the opening of the General Exhibition which was held in Charlottetown last autumn, as well as of the County Exhibitions at Georgetown and Summerside, and I was much gratified at the excellent displays there presented of the fruits of our husbandry and the skill of our artisans. It is indeed pleasing to notice, year after year, the advancement which is being made by our farmers in the science of agriculture, as well as by other classes of the community in various manufactures and industries. The progress which has been made in Stock-raising has been rapid, yet substantial, and the business is one which, if carefully pursued, is destined to prove highly lucrative. Our horses have attained an enviable reputation in the neighboring Provinces and New England States, and it is gratifying to observe so many of our people evincing a determination still further to improve on the high character established, by importing, at considerable cost, strains of some of the best blood which can be obtained in the mother country and United States. It is sincerely to be desired that our success in farming and stock-raising may serve to foster in our young men a taste for agricultural pursuits and induce more of them to apply themselves to so honorable and remunerative an occupation.

I regret to say that the question of our communication with the Mainland in the winter season, still remains in a most unsettled and unsatisfactory condition. Notwithstanding the express terms of the compact under which this Island entered the Confederation and the frequent representations which have been made by the Provincial Government and Legislature, as well as by our representatives in the Federal Parliament, the Province is still unprovided with efficient and continuous steam service for a very considerable portion of the year. The sad disaster in January last, by which so many lives were imperilled and from which such serious results have arisen, is much to be deplored, and it is earnestly to be hoped that it may awaken in the General Government a sense of the responsibility they incur by neglecting to carry out their solemn obligation. Such action as the Provincial Government propose in the matter will, in due course, be submitted to you.

*Mr. Speaker and Gentlemen of the
House of Assembly:*

The Accounts for the past year will be presented to you. The

Estimates for the current year's expenditure, which have been carefully prepared with a view to economy and general efficiency, will also be laid before you.

Mr. President and Honorable Gentlemen of the Legislative Council:

Mr. Speaker and Gentlemen of the House of Assembly:

Since the last Session further negotiations were carried on with the Dominion Government upon the subject of the Piers, resulting, I am happy to inform you, in the removal of the stipulation attached by that Government to the vote by Parliament for the structures assumed as of Federal importance.

Not only has the amount appropriated been paid into the Local Treasury but a further sum has been placed in the estimates of this year to reimburse this Province for certain other piers. Papers on the subject will be laid before you.

Several measures, calculated to advance the welfare of the Island, and promote the efficiency of the public service, will be submitted for your consideration.

In committing to you the work of the Session I rely with confidence upon your patriotism and zeal; and I ask at your hands that co-operation and support without which I cannot hope satisfactorily to discharge the highly important duties which have been entrusted to me. May your deliberations be conducted under the Divine guidance, and may they contribute to the happiness of those in whose interests you are here assembled.

The following committees were then appointed, viz :—

To prepare Draft Address in reply to His Honor the Lieutenant Governor's speech,--Messrs. Mackay, Bentley, Gillis, Holland, Blake, A. Martin, McDougall.

Public Accounts,—Messrs. Bentley, Blake, John McLean, Alex. Martin, Richards, Beer, Farquharson.

To keep up good correspondence with the Legislative Council,— Hon. Messrs. Sullivan, Prowse, Lefurgey, Campbell; Mr. Yeo, Mr. Perry.

To examine Bills to be engrossed,—Honorable Mr. McLeod, Mr. Holland, Honorable Mr. Gordon, Mr. Perry, Mr. D. C. Martin.

Private Bills,—Hon. Messrs. McDonald, Ferguson, Arsenault; Mr. Beer, Mr. Farquharson.

To receive Tenders for Journals, —Hon. Messrs. Ferguson, Prowse; Mr. McLaren.

On expiring Laws,—Hon. Messrs. Sullivan, McLeod; Mr. D. C. Martin.

To revise Journals—Hon. Messrs. Campbell, McDonald; Mr. Sinclair.

On motion,—

Resolved, That a copy of the Journals of this House be sent up to His Honor the Lieutenant Governor each day, as soon as may be after the adjournment.

On motion of Hon. Mr. Sullivan, seconded by Hon. Mr. Ferguson, and carried unanimously,—

Resolved, That Messrs. Isaac Oxenham and George F. Owen be appointed Reporters to this House during the present Session.

House adjourned until three o'clock to-morrow afternoon.

I. O.

THURSDAY, March 12.

MR. SPEAKER in the chair.

Mr. MACKAY, Chairman of Special Committee appointed to prepare an Address in answer to the Speech with which His Honor the Lieutenant Governor opened the present Session, presented the following

DRAFT ADDRESS :

To His Honor the Honorable Andrew Archibald Macdonald, Lieutenant Governor of the Province of Prince Edward Island, etc., etc., etc.

May it please your Honor:

We, Her Majesty's loyal subjects the House of Assembly of Prince Edward Island, thank your Honor for the speech with which you have been pleased to open the present Session.

We have much pleasure in congratulating your Honor in this your inaugural interview with the representatives in Parliament of this your native Province.

We unite with your Honor in expressing our deep thankfulness to Almighty God for the many favors bestowed on this Island during the past year, although the harvest has not been so abundant as in some previous years, yet no material distress has been experienced, and we are glad to know that the people of this Province are steadily advancing in prosperity, for which we unite with your Honor in expressing sincere gratitude.

We are much gratified to know that the General Exhibition held in Charlottetown, as well as the County Exhibitions held in Georgetown and Summerside, have proved so successful, and that our farmers and manufacturers are making such rapid and substantial progress; that our horses are much prized in the neighboring provinces and in the Eastern States, and that so many of our people are showing a determination of further improving the high character already attained by importing some of the best animals which can be obtained for breeding purposes. It is to be hoped that our success in stock raising and farming may foster a taste in the young men of this Province for agricultural pursuits.

We very much regret that communication between this Island and the Mainland in winter still remains in an unsatisfactory condition, notwithstanding the frequent representations which have been made by the Government and Legislature of this Province, as well as by our Representatives in the Federal Parliament. The efficient and continuous steam service promised under the Terms of Confederation are still unfulfilled, and we trust that the sad disaster which took place last January in attempting to cross at the capes may impress the General Government with the necessity of their carrying out their solemn obligation. We will be prepared to con sider any measures which the Government of this Province may submit on the question.

We thank your Honor for the assurance that the accounts for the past year will be laid before us, and that the estimates for the current year will be submitted, and we will cheerfully vote such sums as may be required for the public service.

We are pleased to learn that your Honor's Government have, during the recess, been in negotiation with the Federal Government on the question of the piers, and that the result has been the removal of the stipulation attached to the vote by Parliament for the structures considered of Federal importance, and that a further sum has been placed in the estimates of this year to reimburse this Province for certain other piers, and that papers on the subject will be submitted to us.

Any measures calculated to advance the welfare of this Province will receive our earnest consideration.

We assure your Honor that we will apply ourselves with diligence to the work of the Session, and trust that our deliberations under Divine Providence will result in such measures as may contribute to the interest of the Province.

Received and read, and made an order of the day for to-morrow.

A message was received from the Legislative Council through John Ball, C. L. C., intimating that a committee had been appointed to keep up a good correspondence between the two branches of the Legislature.

Mr. PERRY asked whether copies of the Draft Address would be furnished to members of the Opposition.

Hon. Mr. SULLIVAN said that copies of the Address would be furnished honorable members of the Opposition this evening.

Hon. Mr. FERGUSON, chairman of the committee appointed to receive Tenders for printing and binding the Journals of the House for the present Session, presented the report of said committee. On the recommendation of the committee, the tender of Peter McCourt, being the lowest, was accepted.

Hon. Mr. PROWSE, chairman of the committee appointed to receive Tenders for printing the Debates of the House for the present Session, presented a report, and moved that the Tender of G. W. Gardiner be accepted.

Mr. PERRY said he hoped the reports would be published in book form earlier in the recess than had been the case last year. The first thing honorable members saw when they came to attend this

House was a pile of books containing the reports of the previous Session, and they had no time to examine them in order to ascertain if they were correct. He understood that two gentlemen, whose names are well known in this House and the province, had last session been appointed to report the debates of this House, but the book he now held in his hand, and which purported to be the Parliamentary Reporter for 1884, was not signed by both these gentlemen. True it is that the name of Isaac Oxenham is legible enough, but he would leave it to honorable members to decipher the name of the other. He found on hastily glancing over this book that many mistakes had been allowed to creep into it. While he believed that the Reporters had satisfactorily performed their part, many grievous errors could be seen in this book; and he believed if honorable members had an opportunity of carefully examining it all through many other misprints could be detected.

A committee had been appointed last session to look after these reports, but after waiting twelve months, honorable members find that great errors are allowed to appear in the printing.

He hoped this session that the reports would be reported properly, extended properly, and printed properly.

He did not blame the Government so much as the committee who had been appointed to attend to this matter.

Hon. Mr. SULLIVAN said Reporters sometimes made mistakes in reporting the speeches of honorable members, but the honorable member for Tignish should not forget that honorable members themselves sometimes make mistakes. No doubt errors often crept into the reports of the proceedings of this House through typographical errors; but it was pretty difficult to take up any book without finding some misprint.

Such mistakes will happen where even more care is taken in revising the work than is usually given to publications of this kind.

Of course it was their duty to see that this work was done as well as possible, so that a record should be obtained of the speeches of honorable members. It would be supposed that more care would be taken in the Legislative Council to see that the debates of that body were properly reported, but a great many serious errors might also be noticed in the reports for last session of that august body.

In the address upon winter communication, which had been passed by both branches of the Legislature, and which was a very important document indeed, he (Mr. S.) noticed that the whole meaning of one of the paragraphs of that address had been entirely changed. Instead of saying that the neglect of the Dominion Government to carry out our terms of union was *inexcusable*, the report said that their neglect was "excusable." Now this is a very serious mistake, as it altered entirely the view the Legislature had taken of this matter.

As, no doubt, it is a typographical error, he only mentioned it to show how liable errors of this kind are to creep in.

Mr. D. C. MARTIN said he noticed that West River had been substituted for Flat River on page 401, in his speech on packet service to Wood Islands, Belle Creek and Flat River.

Mr. BEER said the Reporter was no credit to either the Legislature or the printer. It not only had mistakes, but is partly unreadable, especially on page 49, where the impression is so faint that without spectacles it is almost impossible to decipher it.

On page 423, on the Bill respecting the City Council, he noticed a serious omission in the speech of the honorable senior member for the city. It said, "Honorable Mr. McLeod thought there would be ample time to-morrow to," and turning over the page the next thing we see is "Motion put and carried." If any person had taken upon himself to leave out part of these proceedings he thought it was a breach of privilege. In another place, page 418, the honorable senior member for the city is reported as saying, "In 1886, when $19.00 of debentures fall due, they will require to get this power that is now asked for." He (Mr. B.) did not think that was a correct report of what had been said. Again the honorable junior member for Souris is reported as saying

as follows, "Mr. John McLean said he was not against the Bill, but supposing their indebtedness is $100.00, they would only have to collect $20,000.00 of an assessment in order to meet the requirements of their Act of Incorporation."

He (Mr. B.) would protest against honorable members being so misrepresented. There are a great many other places where serious misprints occur. He also noticed that they had some new members in this House with whom he was not acquainted. He might instance "Mr. McLdod and Mr. Meer." It showed that some other method should be adopted. The committee appointed last session were to pay the Reporters if their work was delivered to the printers within six weeks from the close of the session, and he (Mr. B.) presumed that had been done, or the Reporters would not have been paid. He did not see why the reports had not been furnished to honorable members before the opening of this session. If additional time is given the printer it is unfair to other persons who would, in all probability, tender at much lower rates if they knew that so long a time would be given them to perform their contract.

Hon. Mr. SULLIVAN said the mistake mentioned by the honorable member for Southport did not occur in the copy he (Mr. S.) had received. The remarks of the honorable senior member for Charlottetown on pages 423 and 424 appeared to read all right.

The copy the honorable member had must have been specially prepared for him.

Hon. Mr FERGUSON said the errors that occurred in last session's Reporter showed the necesof the Reporters being afforded an opportunity of reading the proof of these debates, before they were inserted in the Parliamentary Reporter. He was, however, afraid that some one had been playing a practical joke on his honorable colleague, as the books on this side of the House did not seem to contain the mistakes complained of.

His honorable colleague in this matter reminded him of a story he (Mr. F.) had heard of a clergyman who was in the habit of giving out the first hymn that caught his eye on opening his hymn book. On one occasion a wag had inserted between the leaves of the old gentleman's book the words of a song which commences in the following manner:

"Old Grimes is gone .
That good old man " &c.

The book naturally opened at this place. Noticing something peculiar in the piece, he turned to the title page, but on finding it to be a copy of the revered hymns of John Wesley he said, "Well I never went back on Wesley's hymns in my life and I am not going to do it now." And so it is with his honorable colleague, the Reporter in his hands contains extraordinary mistakes that are not in the copies other honorable

members have, and perhaps some person had been playing a practical joke on him.

Motion put and carried.

House adjourned until to-morrow afternoon at 3 o'clock,

G. F. O.

FRIDAY, March 13th.

Mr. SPEAKRE in the chair.

Hon. MR. FERGUSON stated that he held in his hand a letter from Peter McCourt, addressed to the Clerk of the House declining to furnish security for the contract of printing the Journal of the present session. He therefore moved that the Tender of G. H. Haszard: being the next lowest for the performance of the work, be accepted.

Motion put and carried.

House adjourned for one hour.

EVENING SESSION.

Mr. SPEAKER in the chair.

The order of the day, viz. House in Committee of the whole, to take into consideration the Speech with which His Honor the Lieutenant Governor opened the Session, having been read.

Mr. McKAY moved that the House do now go into the Order of the Day, and said that in doing so he wished to make a few remarks on the matters alluded to in the Speech with which His

Honor had been pleased to open the present Session. It is a source of gratification to the House and the country generally that a native of this Province occupies a seat as head of the Local Execu tive, and Representative of Her Majesty the Queen. His Honor is the third Islander who has occu pied that position, and from our knowledge of his public acts in the past, we have good reason to believe that he will fill it with credit to himself and to the Province. His Honor has filled many public positions to the entire satisfaction of the people. Under these circumstances, he (Mr. Mc-Kay) felt happy in congratulating His Honor on his appointment to the position he now occupies. The second paragraph expresses deep thankfulness to Almighty God for the many favors of the year that is past. It is a duty incumbent upon this House and upon our people to be thankful to the Giver of all good for the blessings received from Him, and to ask for His guidance in the future. The most civilized and progressive countries in the world are those which acknowledge God's goodness toward them, and the more earnestly they do so the greater the blessings they receive. We as a people, have great cause to be thankful for the blessings of the past year. Few countries are more highly favored with peace and contentment than our own little Island. The harvest of last year was not as large in some cases as in previous years. The wheat crop was, however, a very good one. A large quantity of flour is generally imported into this Province, but last year's crop of wheat was sufficient for home consumption. The oat crop is not so much depended on as in former years, but that of last year was in excess of the crop of 1883. The yield of potatoes was much smaller than usual, but owing to the higher prices obtained for what we had to dispose of, the deficiency was fully made up A large quantity was shipped to other markets. It was true that speculators in this article lost some money, but our farmers did not suffer thereby. The Hay crop was housed in much better condition than usual, and the quality was excellent, although the tonnage produced per acre was not quite so large as in some former years. The prices obtained for it in the market were good, consequently no loss will be sustained. When our farmers prosper and improve their financial position, all other classes of the community are benefited. Our artizans and manufacturers are making steady advances, and are gradually reaching independence and opulence. The large amount now on deposit in the Savings Banks affords evidence of prosperity. The large number of circulars from the Auditors office which are passing through our country Post Offices, and addressed to people of all classes in the community shows that our whole population is steadily advancing in wealth. In fact no Province of the Dominion excels our own with respect to the amount on Deposit, in proportion to population. The next paragraph relates to Exhibitions. This is a matter in which our farmers are now deeply interested, and in which they take an active part. The grants in aid of County Exhibitions have been productive of great good. These Exhibitions bring farmers together from all parts of the Province, and benefit them by the intercourse they have with each other and by the friendly rivalry thus brought about. This causes a desire everywhere to produce the very best Stock, Grain, and Roots, and to excel in every department of farm work. Our exhibits are, therefore, steadily improving,—more particularly those of Stock. Our Horses are in great demand for exportation, and are greatly prized in other places, particularly cart horses and roadsters, which have a high character in the other Provinces and the United States. Dealers in horses come here and purchase any particular kind of horses they require. The owners of the best breeds are sure to obtain their prices. This is the strongest inducement to obtain the best stock from which to breed. Some brood mares which have been imported for breeding purposes have proved of great value in improving our stock. These, with the large number of stud horses now in the Province, have made the Island to become noted for its superior stock of horses. Some years ago the Government were accused of keeping the best horses on the stock farm, where the great majority of our farmers were unable to avail themselves of the services of those animals. Owing to this, these

horses were allowed to pass into private hands, and the requirements of the country are more fully met. He always thought it a mistake to keep too many horses on the stock farm, as their services were not available to the great majority: The present system is found to work much better than the old one The supply of good horses is now simply a matter of money and business. Enterprising men import the best breeds in their own interests as well as those of the country. A large importation of horses by the Government would discourage private speculators who would feel that Government had a monopoly of the business and that there was no room for competition. Under such circumstances, it is far better to leave the matter entirely in the hands of private individuals, who will be very careful to import only such animals as will meet the wants of the country.

The next paragraph refers to continuous communication with the Mainland in the winter season. This is a question which has engaged the attention of the Legislature of this Province for some years past. In 1880 this House took strong action with reference to it, and since then, several debates have taken place, in the course of which honorable members have expressed their opinions pretty freely on the matter. Our winter communication is, however, still in a most unsatisfactory condition. Honorable members, while discussing this question, should not allow local political matters to influence their minds, but should all unite to take such action as they find necessary for the public good. The whole of our people are interested in having the Terms of Confederation fully and completely carried out, and it, therefore, becomes the duty of all to throw aside party jealousies and demand the fulfilment of these Terms. When we accepted the Terms of Confederation, the Dominion Government bound themselves to provide for this Province continuous steam communication with the Mainland winter and summer, but, although we have formed part of the Dominion of Canada nearly twelve years, our winter communication is still in the same condition as it was thirty or forty years ago, during the greater part of the season. The couriers are still obliged to cross the Straits by dragging ice-boats over the cakes of ice and rowing through the intervening spaces of water. The hardships endured by them in the performance of this work are very great. One of the reasons which induced the people of this Province to accept the Terms of Confederation was the provision made therein for keeping up uninterrupted communication with the Mainland winter and summer. We thought that the Dominion was a large country with ample means, and that it was in a much better position to undertake the winter service than the separate Government of this small Province. This was a strong inducement to our people to accept the Terms of Confederation. But those Terms have never been carried out, and the result is that a loss has been sustained by this Province, which figures can-

not clearly show. We contend that the Dominion Government contracted with us at the time of union to give us continuous communication winter and summer, and that they have neglected to fulfil that contract. It is not for us to point out to them how the work should be done. Let them see to that, and find out how to accomplish what they undertook to perform. We have a right to enforce the fulfilment of the Terms of Union to the letter. It is true that the *Northern Light* has assisted in improving the situation, but, after all, what has she done towards continuous communication in winter? For several weeks she has been jammed up in the ice at Georgetown. As an experiment she has been of some service, but we require a much heavier boat built expressly for the route, and one in which the lives of passengers would be safe. It is generally understood that the Captain of the *Northern Light* has received instructions from the Department of Marine not to imperil the lives of those under his care, and not to force the boat into positions of danger. If that boat were suitable for the service required, there would be no such risk to be run, and she could be driven through the ice wherever and whenever required. He contended that we have a right to demand the strict fulfilment of the Terms of Union in reference to this, as well as to other matters. It is true that Sir John's Government has done more than that of McKenzie, but neither of them has been as energetic in carrying out this service as should have been the case. The sad accident which took place on the Capes route this winter may be the means of awakening the Dominion to a sense of their duty with reference to this important matter. That accident nearly became a fatal one, and only through the mercy of Divine Providence were any of the twenty-one men who were exposed on the ice through a whole winter's night in the very severest part of the season, spared to tell the tale of their sufferings. Had they passed a second night in the Gulf, very few of them could have survived. Some of those unfortunate men were on a business trip, and had hope of a quick passage across the straits, but, instead of attaining their object, were maimed for life. Who can tell the loss sustained by those men? In addition to the danger to life, we must consider the loss sustained by our commercial men in being cut off during so many mouths of the year from trading with the sister Provinces, and the rest of the world. Let us, as a people, unite as one man ni demanding the fulfilment of the Terms of Union to the very letter. If we cannot obtain justice at the hands of the Dominion Government, let us lay our case before the Imperial Parliament.

The next paragraph refers to the Public Accounts and Estimates, and the following one to the Piers question. We are informed that during the recess, the Local Government have been in communication with the Government of the Dominion, with reference to the amount due this Province for its piers. During last session the

Opposition in this House declared that the Local Government would never obtain any portion of the money without giving a receipt in full for the amount offered us for all our claims. These predictions have proved to be wrong, and we are now informed that the conditions attached to the vote of last year by the Dominion Parliament have not been exacted, and that not only has that amount—about $54,000—been paid, but that a further sum has been placed in the estimates of the Dominion Parliament, this year, to re-imburse this Province for certain other piers. When the Local Government made the demand for compensation for our piers, a portion of the Local Press admitted the validity of their claim, but he was sorry to say that another portion of it strove to prevent the accomplishment of their object, and when it found that a large part of the money had actually been paid over to this Province, it made an attempt to cartoon the honorable Leader of the Government! This Press was owned by a company which came to this House last session asking to be incorporated under a title that would lead people to suppose that they had a monopoly of the printing and publishing business of this country, calling themselves the "Island Printing and Publishing Company." A leather medal should be struck off and tendered to the Artist of the *Patriot* for his ability in the art of cartooning. The reputed editor of that paper is an ex-Governor, Privy-Counsellor, and one of Leaders of the Opposition Party of this Province. What is the object of that gentleman'? To throw ridicule on the efforts of the Government to obtain from the Government of the Dominion compensation for the money expended on our piers since Confederation. But the cartoon was a complete failure, and had it not been for the name printed in full below, no one would have known that it was intended for the Premier of this Province—Honorable Mr. Sullivan. Would the Opposition in this House attempt to follow the course pursued by the Organ of their party, and attempt to throw ridicule upon the action of the Government in obtaining our just rights from the Government of the Dominion? Let them avow their principles with respect to this question. On April 23rd, 1883, just after the Local Government had made a demand for the amount due us for our piers, the *Patriot* contained the following:

"Mr. Sullivan may bounce as he pleases about the certainty of the Local Government receiving $35,000 from Ottawa for Piers during the current year; but he has not shown on paper the first syllable of a promise of a single dollar on their account. Mr. Ferguson though one of the delegates, was a good deal weaker on the refund question than his leader. He thought that at any rate the Local Government would receive the amount expended on those structures, reports on which were already in the Dominion blue books. We suppose he meant those piers for which the delegates asked a "*payment on account*". The sum expended on these struc-

tures since Confederation, we understand was only some $16,000 and if this amount be all the Government will receive as a refund for piers for this year, the condition of the Province will be deplorable at the end of the year. The Leader of the Government based his defence chiefly on the economy of the Government. He said he did not care though there was a deficit, as long as the Government could show that they had exercised a proper care over the expenditure. This is a most extraordinary view to take of the functions of a Government."

The same paper on February 7th 1884 said:

"It is no wonder frequent begging excursions are made to Ottawa. Our readers will not have forgotten the "three jolly beggars" who visited the Capital last winter, and threatened to stay there until they got "a payment on account." It will also be remembered that in due course they returned with their pockets full— of promises and void of cash. Now we learn the Premier is in Ottawa on the same business, and whether he returns empty or not, it matters little to him. He will be dined and wined, and will return shouting, "Great is Sir John!" Why? Because there is a judgeship in the distance. This is the way we are being ruled by the Tories. We have this only to add, that unless a sudden stop is put to the foolish extravagant policy of the men now in office, we see nothing ahead but taxation, and plenty of it. That this inevitable result may be avoided, must be the wish of every lover of our native Isle."

This is a specimen of the principles of the Organ of the Opposition on this important matter. He would now compare the position of the present Local Government with that of their predecessors in office—the Davies Government. In August, 1876, a General Election took place, when a very strong party was returned to power, and Mr. Davies took charge of the ship of state as Leader of the Government. The only question which had been submitted to the people was that respecting Education. The old system had been in operation a long time, and many reforms were needed to make it efficient. At the General Election alluded to, promises were exacted from every candidate respecting the school question, and a majority was returned to sustain unsectarian schools. But Mr. Davies was not satisfied with passing a new School Act, he went on to change every portion of the civil service of the Province. The result was that he declared himself unable to carry out the changes inaugurated without increased taxation. Said he, "We have given the country a new School Act, the working of which will cost more money; we have raised the salaries of the public officials, and must have more money to meet the increased expenditure." Some of his supporters told him that if he went on in that way, the country would not bear him out, and at the end of a year and a half he began to see that their statements were correct.

Several Conservative members of that Government soon found that matters were getting worse instead of improving, and that unless Mr. Davies went in for economy and retrenchment they would be obliged to sever connection with him. They at length did so, and from East Point to West Cape there was a howl of indignation against that Government, because of the heavy taxes people had to pay, while they received no corresponding returns for them. The result was that the then Government were forced to resign, and the present party came into power in the spring of 1879. The present Government had promised to reduce the taxes, and also the salaries of the public officials. When they had fully examined the state of the Public Finances, they found that not only had the late Government taxed the country very heavily, but that the latter had left a deficit of over $60,000. They at once reduced the cost of maintaining the Civil Service, and repealed the Assessment Act as soon as they found themselves in a position to do so. The result is that we are now free from all direct taxation. In fact we are freer from taxation than any country in the civilized world. When Mr. Davies came into office there was a small land tax, but even that has been swept away. The present Government soon found that the Dominion Government owed this Province a considerable sum of money to which we were justly entitled, and that it was their duty to press our claims for it. They accordingly declared that they would not tax the people until our claims against the Dominion Government were paid. But what does the *Patriot's* cartoon say? It says "tax the people, instead of going to Ottawa for moneys due this Province." Now, he (Mr. Mackay) believed that when the people see that local taxation is really necessary, they will be prepared to pay it; but until then there will be opposition to direct taxation. We have received about $54,000 for our piers, and have been promised about $24,000 or $25,000 more, that is about $80,000 in all. Was it not better for our people to obtain our just dues from the Dominion Government and use them for legitimate purposes than to tax the people to that extent? The Government have been charged by the Opposition with being too economical, too penurious; but the charge was disproven by the facts. He had travelled over the country a good deal, and he thought the people would acknowledge that our roads and bridges were never in better condition than at present. (Opposition members, "No, no.") He maintained that on travelling through the country our roads and bridges would be found to be generally good. It is true that at certain seasons it is useless to expend money on the roads, and their condition at such times is never good. But in ordinary weather they are in good condition. All this has been accomplished at a very moderate cost. Not only has our Government succeeded in obtaining from the Dominion Government the amount of $80,000, but, for all time to come, they have handed over to the latter the maintenance of the wharves and piers, thus relieving us of a heavy item of expenditure and of taxation. The *Patriot* endeavors to show that it will be of no advantage to us to be relieved of our piers, as the Dominion Government will charge heavier rates of wharfage than ever before, and we shall be obliged to pay back, in this way, more than the amount we receive. But what are the facts? The wharves taken charge of by the Dominion Government have been put in very good repair, and instead of increased rates of wharfage being demanded, not one cent had been asked for the use of the wharves. The people have appreciated the action of the Local Government in this matter of handing the piers over to the General Government, and wherever a constituency has been opened, they have received a strong support. No means have been left untried to secure support for the Opposition, but they have been in vain. We frequently hear the Opposition party claiming to be the patriots of this country. Well, love of country is a very fine thing, and is very much talked of now-a-days, but are the Opposition true to their professions in respect? While our Local Government were pressing their claims for compensation for our piers, what did Mr. Davies, the most prominent Opposition representative in the House of Commons, do? He rose on the floor of the House and asked the question whether the Nova Scotia and New Brunswick piers were not also to be taken over by the Dominion Government. We thus find that the man who was returned to the House of Commons to defend our interests, and prevent, as far as possible, the necessity for direct taxation, was prepared to damage the claims of the Local Government to the utmost possible extent. Where is the patriotism of such men? They go to any length to serve the interests of their party in opposition to the best interests of their country. There was another clause of the speech to which he would direct the attention of the House, viz., the last. His Honor expresses the desire that the House will assist him by its co-operation and support, without which he cannot hope satisfactorily to discharge the highly important duties which have been entrusted to him. The people, also, expect the House to study their interests with diligence and attention, and to enact such measures as will prove to the general advantage of the country. It will be the duty of every honorable member around the Board to throw aside party prejudices and to unite in the interests of all classes of people whom he represents. Were any mistake made in the management of public affairs, it might be the cause of running the country into difficulties which would require many years to get rid of, and to reach the position previously held. Every honorable member should interest himself in seeing that the public moneys are properly expended, and that all legislation is in the best interests of the country.

MR. BENTLEY seconded the motion of the honorable member for the Second District of Queen's County, that the House do now go into the Order of the Day for the consideration of the Draft Address in answer to the Speech with which His Honor the Lieutenant Governor opened the present Session, and said that it must be a subject for congratulation to every honorable member of the House that a native of this Island, in whose integrity and ability we have the fullest confidence, has been elevated to the position of representative of Her Majesty the Queen in this Province. Others who were also natives of this Province have filled the same position with credit to themselves and to the country. He agreed with the statement contained in the first paragraph that we should unite in an expression of deep thankfulness to Almighty God for the many favors of the past year. Although the harvest had not been so abundant as in some previous years, it was sufficient to meet the wants of our people. A partial failure of the crops is not felt to such an extent as in former times, when farmers depended upon one or two productions of the soil. Our farmers have made great progress within the past fifteen years, and they now occupy a more independent position. The progress made may not have been so rapid as in some countries, but the improvements have been substantial, and we are in a better position than many other parts of the world. A few days ago, he read an account of the condition of the farmers in one of the Western States of the Union, stating that they had to sell their wheat for twenty-seven cents per bushel, and that they were combining to break up certain rings among the buyers, which they supposed kept down the prices. Looking at great and wealthy England at the present time, we see a sad state of things among the working classes, which are in a far worse condition than the same classes among ourselves. So far as our Exhibitions were concerned, he thought they had been a great success, and had done much towards improving the agriculture of the country. Our farm stock has been vastly improved, and in many instances would do credit to any country in the world. In Dominion Exhibitions held in some of the Provinces, we have carried off a large amount in prizes, and have made the Island famous for its superior stock. He would be glad to see the Government bring down in the estimates a larger grant for those Exhibitions, if they could see their way clear to do so, as greater encouragement is given to our farmers and artizans through them than in any other way. Considering our very limited revenue, however, the Government had done well in this respect. The sum of $2,000, for the whole Island, when divided into so many prizes, as is usual, seems small; but we hope in the course of a few years to be in a better position. One result of the improvement in our cattle and horses is that they stand very high in the neighboring Provinces. It is a great pity that a larger number of thoroughbred cattle was not purchased and distributed and

sold through the Province, as a great deal of interest is now being taken by our farmers in thoroughbred stock. The raising and fattening of the very best breeds of stock will, in future, prove to be one of our best local resources. At present some of our cattle are very inferior, and should be got rid of. In fact, our farmers have hitherto had but very limited means of improving their breeds of cattle, and it requires a considerable time to effect a complete and radical change. There is no doubt, however, that feeding stock is the best and most remunerative kind of business in which our farmers can engage, and that it will soon be one of the principal sources of money making in this Province. Private interprise in the importation of horses has done very much of late for the improvement of the various breeds. It would be well for the Government to encourage it by every means in their power, as the returns to the Province for money expended in this way will be a hundred fold. It is also the duty of the Government to encourage our home manufactures. It is true we have comparatively few of them, but they are of great benefit to us. We have some cheese factories which are doing very much good. Our cheese, butter and cloth factories should receive every possible encouragement, as they are all assisting our farmers and helping to build up the country. If some plan could be devised by which greater encouragement could be given to factories it would result in great good. Larger prizes at our Exhi-

B

bitions, or Bounties, would be money well expended, as it would yield an ample return. If the number of factories could be increased it would be so much better for the country. Our hides and wool are sent away in large quantities to the other Provinces. This is a wrong state of affairs, as these articles should be all used up in home manufactures. The Province is small, but if anything could be done to encourage those manufactures, it would prove a real benefit to the country. The next clause refers to the important subject of winter communication with the Mainland. The agreement made by the General Government with this Province when we accepted the Terms of Confederation has never been carried out. We are not asking the Dominion Government for any favor in reference to this matter; we simply ask for the fulfilment on their part of the Terms of Union, to which they themselves were a party. He thought it right that we should understand our true position with respect to the Dominion. The more we examine and inquire into this matter the more we shall find that we have a right to press our claims for the fulfilment of the Terms of Confederation with respect to winter communication. An opinion appears to prevail throughout the larger Provinces that this Province has been a cause of loss rather than gain to the Dominion, as a whole, and that we are causing a drain upon its resources every year. This opinion seems to have originated with the Honorable Edward Blake. We

find in the *Hansard* for the House of Commons for the year 1880, in a debate on the subject of "Supply," the following remarks by Mr. Blake, on page 1460:—

" I have an interesting table of the results as to the collection and distribution of our revenue for the first ten years after confederation Now, Sir, assigning to each Province the revenue derived from it, as shown by the public accounts and charging each Province with its local services and with such parts of the federal services as are by the public accounts distinguished and assigned to the separate Provinces, the results are as follows : We collected in all $198,-000,000; we spent in all, $189,-350,000, leaving a surplus of $8,650,000. The receipts from Manitoba were $876,000; the distinguished expenditure, $1,599,-000 ; the deficit on this head $722,000. For P. E. Island the receipts were $1,599,000; the expenditure, $2,624,000; the deficit, 1,027,000."

The honorable gentleman went on to show that the whole of the money for the Public Works of the Dominion came from the Provinces of Ontario and Quebec, being careful not to make a distinction between the amount received from the Provinces of Ontario and Quebec separately, as he knew very well the Dominion customs returns show a much greater amount of duties received from Quebec than from Ontario— Montreal and Quebec being the principal ports of entry.

In this statement, Mr. Blake endeavors to show that after the

Island entered Confederation we had cost the Dominion Government more than one million dollars over and above the amount we had contributed to the General Revenue.

A little further on, on page 1461, Mr. Blake spoke as follows: "I freely admit that several of them (the Provinces) are heavier contributors per capita than some of the larger Provinces are, yet not adequate contributors to revenue; on the contrary, they are heavy drains on the revenues of Canada, and it will be further seen that the bulk of the expenditure—I may say every shilling of the expenditure on the Northwest and on the Pacific Railway—is contributed by the Province from which I have the honor to come."

We find, further, that the subject was continued by the members from British Columbia, especially Mr. DeCosmos, who used tables making comparisons between the duties paid by this Province since Confederation, and also by the other Provinces, greatly to the disadvantage of this Island; and these expressions and statements seem to have passed uncontradicted. In looking over this matter, he (Mr. Bentley) was of opinion that we, in this Province, contribute to the Dominion Treasury a much larger amount, yearly, than we receive therefrom, and we have a right to know whether such statements as those, used by Mr. Blake and others, are facts. He believed that they are not, and he (Mr. Bentley) would endeavor to show that Mr. Blake's statements would not stand investigation.

The principal portion of our imports are, of course, from the other Provinces of the Dominion, upon which we pay the duty indirectly, but which does not appear to our credit in the customs returns, because of the duty having been first paid on such imports at the ports of entry, and credited to those respective ports, but which is, nevertheless, added to the price of the goods, and paid again by the purchasers, and ultimately by the consumer. The direct duties paid by our merchants have been decreasing ever since we entered Confederation. Previous to that date, viz., in 1872, our custom duties received by the Local Government here amounted to $304.-377.48, but have dwindled down to $166,988.42 in the year 1883. The diminution is not owing to our importing less than formerly, for we actually import immensely more. It is caused by our importing from the Dominion instead of directly from abroad, or from foreign countries. In order to ascertain the facts of the case as nearly as possible, we must go back for some years and make an approximation. During the ten years previous to Confederation, he found that our imports had increased 100 per cent., and our exports nearly as much. Our imports in 1862, were £211,240 18s. 6d., sterling, and in 1872 they were £446,989, sterling. Our exports in 1862 were £150,549 2s. 1d., sterling, and in 1872 they were £437,548, sterling. Our duties increased from £27,983 12s. 2½d. in 1862, to £93,654, sterling, in 1872.

The average duties during the last year before we went into confederation were about 13½ per cent.; but they have since been increased to an average, for this Island, of about 27 per cent., in 1882, on all goods imported from foreign countries to this Island both dutiable and free. Now, if our imports had not increased at all during the past twelve years, our duties would amount to something over $600,000 under the present tariff; but he believed that our imports had increased 100 per cent. since Confederation, or at the same rate of increase as during the ten years previous to that date. Such being the case, our duties must now amount to over $1,000,-000. But after making due allowance for goods imported from the other Provinces which were the manufacture of the Dominion, we can fairly claim that our dutiable imports have increased at least 50 per cent. since Confederation, which, with the increased tariff would bring our duties up to about $900,000. He felt sure that although that sum did not appear to our credit in the Dominion returns, the Dominion has received annually from this Island, indirectly, the whole of that amount. And what do we receive from the Dominion in return? After a careful computation, and giving the Dominion credit for all we receive, he found the amount to be above $414,000. This includes revenue and payments received from every possible Dominion source. In this amount he allowed a loss to the Dominion in running the Island Railway of an average of $75,000

yearly; expense of collecting custom duties, $20.497.13; cost of Light Houses, construction and maintenance, etc. He took the year 1883 and picked out every item charged against this Province. The expense connected with running the *Northern Light* in that year was $19,680.97, and the receipts from passengers and freight $7,303.26, leaving a deficit of $12,377.71, the whole of which he charged to this Island. The subsidy to the summer boats for carrying mails, viz., $13,730, he found was all charged to this Island; but this amount could not all be fairly charged to this Province, as it is as much benefit to the other Provinces as to us. The half, therefore, of the subsidy paid to steamers for carrying mails he credited to the Dominion. The same remark would apply to the *Northern Light*, but he charged the whole cost of running her to this Province. To this must be added the salaries of the Lieutenant Governor, the Judges of the Supreme and County Courts, and the sessional allowances to all our representatives in the Dominion Parliament; also, the loss of the Dominion on the postal service of this Island; cost of all public buildings, breakwaters, etc., etc. Add, also, the interest on the $800,000 granted us for the purchase of proprietary estates, and also on the extra $100,000 which we cannot draw from capital. Also, the yearly subsidy to this Province on account of population, legislation, etc, and the amount received by our fishermen as fishing bounty. But this amount he spread over the ten years since entering Confederation as it had only been received for the last year or two. The whole amount received from the Dominion in 1883 was about $414,000, but from this. we have a perfect right to deduct $50,000—being the interest on the one million dollars which we certainly should have received as our share of the fishery award, and which we would have received if we had not been in Confederation. Deducting that sum from the total amount, we have $364,000 as the amount received from the Dominion in the year 1883, which, he supposed, could be taken as an average since entering Confederation. There may be some small items not included in this computation, which might possibly bring the amount up to $400,000, but the latter would be the very outside figure. Now, the duties paid on goods imported into this Province are more than double that amount, and, therefore, we are contributing to the revenue of the Dominion more than double the sum we receive in return yearly. If this matter were placed before the Dominion Government in a proper way, he thought they would see the great injustice with which they have dealt towards this Province. The idea seems to prevail at Ottawa that we are a constant loss instead of gain to the Dominion, which is far from being the case. Also, at the time we entered Confederation the debt of the Dominion was not nearly as great as it is at present. We are also bearing our share of the interest of the money expended upon the Railways and Canals of the other Provinces. During the year 1884, the amount expended upon Dominion Railways for construction, maintenance, and repairs was $19,226,798. And on canals there was a direct loss of $1,803,611.10. What was our share of this loss? It is true that we had a branch line of Railway to Cape Traverse, but we are required to pay the interest on the construction of the whole of our main line of Railway, as it is a charge against the Province. This interest is deducted every year from the amount due us from the Dominion Government. Looking at this matter, he thought we were suffering a great injustice at the hands of the General Government. Our Railway is a feeder of the Intercolonial, and materially contributes to the tariff on that road. We, therefore. contribute very considerable to the receipts of the Intercolonial. The Dominion Government have been granting large subsidies to various Railway Companies in the other Provinces, amounting to millions of dollars, to which we contribute our proportionate share. The Railway from Gravenhurst to Callander, 110 miles in length, was subsidized by the Acts of 1882-83 to the extent of $12,000 per mile, or to a total of $1,320,000. There were, also, subsidies of various sums, from $3,200 to $12,000 per mile, granted to a large number of what cannot be called anything but local roads in the different Provinces of Ontario, Quebec, Nova Scotia and New Brunswick during the past few years as shown by the Report of the Minister of Railways. He noticed that that gentleman spoke very disparagingly of this Island Railway, giving as his opinion that there was not much chance of improvement with respect to its returns. This was, no doubt, owing to a misapprehension of the facts of the case. Looking at the sad disaster which occurred on the Straits this winter to our couriers, we had a right to conclude that it was a matter for regret that this Province, which is in all respects a partner, and an equal with the sister Provinces, has to suffer all the inconvenience from the old mode of conveyance of mails and passengers across the Straits, adopted by a past generation thirty or forty years ago. If this Island were not small, the inconvenience would not have been endured until the present time. He hoped our Local Government would press our claims in reference to this matter. We should not rest satisfied with anything less than the complete fulfilment of the Terms of Union. We have no right to acknowledge that continuous steam communication with the Mainland cannot be kept up winter and summer. The Dominion Government entered into an agreement to keep up that communication, and held it out to us as an inducement to enter Confederation. We accepted their offer as part of the Terms of Union, and they should be compelled to fulfil their contract. If justice is not meted out to us without delay, our Government should apply to the Imperial Parliament for the fulfilment of the Terms of Union. Our people would bear them out in doing so, even if some expense were incurred thereby. The poor men who suffered on the occasion referred to, deserve our warmest sympathy. The couriers did their duty manfully and well, and should receive full credit for their noble conduct. The fact that they discharged their duty under the most trying circumstances, and brought the mails and passengers entrusted to their care safe to land, showed that they were faithful to the last. He hoped the matter would not be lost sight of by the Dominion Government, as some of the men are now crippled for life, and will not be in as good a position as formerly to earn their livelihood. The Dominion Government should reward them for their faithfulness and humane conduct under the most trying circumstances.

With respect to the piers question, he felt inclined to give the Government credit for bringing it to a successful issue. It was scarcely to be expected that the Dominion Government would pay over to this Province every dollar asked as compensation for the piers. The fact that they had refunded to us the greater portion of the money showed that our Local Government had pressed our claim pretty strongly. The result has been that this Province is relieved of a heavy annual expense in keeping up and maintaining its piers, and we should give the Government due credit for what they have done. If Ontario, Quebec, New Brunswick, or Nova Scotia were in our position with respect to winter communication and the non-fulfilment of the Terms of Union, they would have had the matter settled long ago, but on account of our small area, isolation, and small representation, the General Government have deemed the matter of little importance. It now becomes us to be alive to our interests, and to press for the fulfilment of the Terms of Union. We have large claims upon the General Government for the loss we have sustained by their neglect, which, if properly pressed, and if secured, would relieve our people for many years to come from direct taxation. He believed that our railway should be taken over by the Dominion Government as the piers had been, and the interest on the cost of construction which is now withheld paid to us annually.

Mr. FARQUHARSON.—Honorable E. Blake introduced a resolution into the Dominion Parliament making provision that we should be allowed a portion of the cost of our Railway, but Messrs. Hackett and McDonald voted against it.

Mr. BENTLEY thought there must be some mistake about this matter on the part of the honorable member.

Hon. Mr. FERGUSON said that Mr. Blake never mentioned the Island in his proposal.

Mr. BENTLEY said that the honorable member for West River would have the fullest opportunity to make a statement with reference to this matter. All the Representatives of this Province in the Dominion should stand by each other in securing for us our rights in reference to the Railway and all other questions. They should constantly look after our best interests, no matter what party is in power. Their motto should be "country first, and party afterwards." Even if they all combined for the benefit of this Province, their voice and influence would be none too strong. They should assist our Local Government in its endeavors to secure our rights, instead of throwing obstacles in the way. They are sent there to further our interests and not to balk the efforts of the Local Government in our behalf.

I. O.

___

FRIDAY, March 13th.

Mr. PERRY said at this late hour he had no desire to make a long speech, especially as his honor the Speaker did not feel very well. Honorable members had been waiting since ten o'clock this morning to have an opportunity of criticising the Address in answer to the Speech of His Honor the Lieutenant Governor, but it was not until nearly nine o'clock this evening that the Government got ready to proceed with this matter. He (Mr. P.) was well pleased and amused at the lengthy and rambling speech of the honorable member from Rustico, who had given them so much information, and who had told them that they had all the wisdom of the Province. The honorable member had also referred to the cartoon and the *Patriot* newspaper, but he (Mr.

P.) did not see how these matters affected the subjects mentioned in the Address, which were the matters that this honorable House were now discussing. Honorable members should stick to the point when addressing the House, and not wander all over the world in order to find matter to abuse their opponents. The honorable member for Kensington had given them a great many figures, and, no doubt, these would be a great source of information not only to honorable members, but to the people of this Province as well. He (Mr. P.) had been looking at the speech several times while the last two honorable members had been speaking and had noticed that it was very well printed on very good paper, and was much better than either the paper or printing of the Parliamentary Reporter for last Session. In reference to the first paragraph he felt proud that a native of the Province had again been selected to fill the honorable position occupied by our present Governor, and he hoped that we always might have men who were natives of this Island occupying this office. In the year 1854, when he (Mr. P.) was first returned to a seat in this House, his friend the Lieutenant Governor was also returned as one of its members. He had watched the public actions of His Honor since then, and had always found him faithfully attending to the duties of a patriot and lover of his country. This is the third time that a native of the Province had been selected to occupy this honorable position, and as we had plenty of good men yet, he trusted

this rule would be followed in the future.

In reference to the second paragraph of the Address, he was amused to hear his honorable friend from Rustico, who told them that the oat crop last year was better than it was the year before, notwithstanding the Governor's Speech told them that the crops were not so good as they had been in former years. Is he so unpatriotic as to ask them not to believe what such high authority had told them? The honorable member cannot be so great a "lover of his country" as the honorable Commissioner of Crown Lands or he would not have said so. Perhaps the honorable Commissioner of Crown Lands is better paid and has more reasons for being a lover of his country. He (Mr. P.) would like to ask what we have to thank the Government for, if we had a good crop? What have they done towards improving our condition? Have they made any movement asking for a Reciprocity Treaty with the Americans? We find lots of petitions being circulated asking the Dominion Government to increase the fishery bounty. The poor fishermen know that the Dominion Government are the cause of the $2 a barrel duty on their fish being imposed, and they wish to get a higher bounty to make up what they will loose on the price of their fish. It was thought that after the Presidential Election that negotiations would have been inaugurated between the two countries, but Sir John said, "Let the Americans approach us first." Knowing we are the weaker party,

had said, and would warn them to beware of that gentleman. Before the session was over he also intended putting a notice in the Order Book asking how often the Commissioner of Crown Lands was absent from his office. He (Mr. F.) also seemed to have an idea that he had all the wisdom of his constituents, and was constantly travelling from one end of the Province to another, lecturing on "Love of Country" and other subjects. If there was no work for him to do in his office he should resign and not be taking the people's money without giving any value for it.

In reference to the paragraph on winter communication, he was very sorry it was so weak, although no doubt it was written by the "Minister of War." If it had not been for the sad accident, which they all must greatly deplore, it is not likely even this most important matter would have been alluded to, and no doubt it is the cause of the Dominion Government being called upon to fulfill the Terms of Union. If he understood rightly, the Government had done nothing during the recess in this matter, for they had announced no correspondence with either the Dominion or Imperial Governments. There is nothing about the $5,000,000 that was demanded last session as compensation for nonfulfilment of the Terms. They had no correspondence to submit on this matter and as they had stultified themselves by not taking any action, after passing in both Houses the Address that last year had been agreed to without opposition, be-

fore voting that this Address do pass, the House would be asked to vote on an amendment to this part of it. The Joint Address last year said as follows : "And they, therefore, claim as due to the present time the sum of $5,000,000, to which they consider this Province justly entitled."

How far are they towards getting the $5,000,000 that is there asked, for? Going on further it said: "The Legislature trust that this most important matter, which they now, for the last time, bring under the notice of the General Government may immediately engage their attention, and that a favorable answer will be accorded without delay, otherwise the Legislature desire that the Government of the Province invoke the interference of Her Majesty the Queen by laying a statement of the grievances complained of at the foot of the Throne."

He (Mr. P.) would like to ask the Government if they had done what they were, by that Address, directed to do? They were told in the Speech that the Dominion Government had taken no action, and he would like to know what the members of the Government were paid $1300 a year for, besides free passes, if it was not to attend to the business this Legislature committed to their charge. In 1884 they were told to do this work and by not attending to it they have made a sad mistake. The men of Murray Harbor, of Cape Traverse and many other sections of this Province will find out that these Ministers did not do their duty. They should be able to tell honorable members of this House that during the recess they had corresponded with the Dominion Government in referrence to this matter, and failing to receive satisfactory answers, they had laid the matter at the foot of the Throne. He knew that they had not done so, for if they had, it would have been mentioned in the Speech. The Opposition will bring in an amendment regretting that no action had been taken on this most important question. If the Government are sincere in looking for the rights of the people they should not have allowed the $24,000, that they are to receive on account of Piers, to be the means of shutting their mouths, and of risking the lives of the people, as the accident this winter had so plainly demonstrated. It was time they shook the dust of their feet and left their offices for better men. If he was reported correctly the people would know that the Government had neglected their duty in this most important matter. The paragraph reads as follows:—

" I regret to say that the question of our communication with the Mainland in the winter season, still remains in a most unsettled and unsatisfactory condition. Notwithstanding the express terms of the compact under which this Island entered the Confederation, and the frequent representations which have been made by the Provincial Government and Legislature, as well as by our representatives in the Federal Parliament, the Province is still unprovided with efficient and continuous steam service for a very considerable portion of the year. The sad disaster in January last, by which so many lives were imperilled, and from which such serious results have arisen, is much to be deplored, and it is earnestly to be hoped that it may awaken in the General Government a sense of the responsibility they incur by neglecting to carry out their solemn obligation. Such action as the Provincial Government propose in the matter will, in due course, be submitted to you."

What did the Government do? Can they show one single correspondence with the Dominion Government on this matter? If they had, why did they not mention it in the Speech The paragraph gave the Government credit, but as far as honorable members knew nothing had been done. They were told last session that the resolution demanding compensation should have been brought in earlier in the session, but it was not brought up until the last day, and they hazarded delaying our claim of $5,000,000 by so doing. But it appears that after they had the resolution authorizing them to press our claim they have delayed it again by doing nothing in the matter. The efficient steam service promised us is still unfulfilled and if it were not for the disaster at the Capes this winter nothing would be done about it this year. In one way the disaster was a god send, for without a serious accident of this kind nothing would be done while these men remain in power. The Address said we will be prepared to consider any measures which the Government of this Province may submit on this question. What measures can they bring on? He wondered at the honorable members for Charlottetown, and others, saying we can compel the Dominion to fulfill our terms by enacting laws to that effect. They may pass resolutions but that is all the good they can do.

The next paragraph says, " We thank your Honor for the assurance that the accounts for the past year will be laid before us, and that the estimates for the current year will be submitted, and we will cheerfully vote such sums as may be required for the public service." Of course the accounts will be presented to us, but he (Mr. P.) was afraid that, when we overhaul them, they will not be very satisfactory. The paragraph respecting the Piers said "that a further sum has been placed in the estimates of this year to re imburse this Province for certain other Piers, and that papers on the subject will be submitted to us." There is some hope that $24,000 additional of pier money will be obtained this year, and as the Government only expected $21,000 from this source last year, they had secured more than they expected. This money is not voted to build new piers, it is only a refund of money expended by the Local Government in former years, and they should have got interest for the many years this money had been paid out. It is said that the Opposition did not look for this money and were derelict in there duty, but his honor the Leader of the Government said

last year that the Opposition had plenty of money when they were in power, and it was not until this party came into office that the Government had to go looking for windfalls. He (Mr. P.) contended that, if the honorable Leader of the Government was correct in his estimates last year, if they got $53,000 that was voted, and $21,000 that they expected, they should show a surplus, and the Speech should announce it. Instead of a surplus he believed they had spent $100,000 of capital in three years, besides getting the roads repaired by Statute Labor; and had run the Province into debt $30,000 or $40,000 He assumed they had run the Province in debt because the *Presbyterian* had sounded the alarm and said the Prince of Wales College must go and taxation be again imposed. This honorable House had the right to assume that with the $24,000 they had obtained this year the Government should have a surplus, if our affairs have not been badly managed. The estimates last year supposed they would receive $54,000 from the Land Office, but he (Mr. P.) believed they had not received $40,000, hardly enough to pay the officials. The honorable Leader of the Government said last year, "Now, he had shown that the estimated expenditure for the year is $249,379.94, and he had also shown how the Government expect to meet that expenditure. It is, of course, impossible to foretell what may happen during the year, but the Government have no reason to doubt that payments expected by them will be made before the close. Should their expectations be verified there will be a considerable surplus." If they obtained all they expected, they must show a surplus. If they do not he would not give much for their veracity. He wanted to remind the House that the Speech showed neglect of honorable members in not mentioning these matters to which he had alluded. Although the crops were not good last year the people are easily satisfied, and if the people are not satisfied it is because they know that the Government had not brought the matter of winter communication before the Dominion Government as they had promised. He hoped the Government would hold out their time but as they had not one scratch of a pen to show that they had done there duty, and had not done what the people expected they would, they will get their condemnation. Are they going to ask again that our Terms of Union be fulfilled after the Address last year authorizing them to lay the matter at the Foot of the Throne if our just claims were not acceded to ?

The honorable member for Rustico had gone over a lot of ground, but when he found fault with Mr. Davies he should not forget that he found fault with his own actions. He now supports the opponents of Mr. Davies, and blames him for actions that were approved of by the honorable members for Murray Harbor, Summerside and Georgetown.

The Fishery Award question is said, by the Government party, to be dead, but he (Mr. P.) thought we ought to have obtained some of that money. He expected the honorable member for Rustico would have told them that the Government had intended to introduce a resolution asking the Dominion Government to pay us our share of this money. There is a great deal of humbug connected with getting the bounty for fishermen, and as there often was more expense attending the obtaining of the several amounts than they were worth, it looked very like a bribe. On the eve of an election, no doubt, some other dodge will be adopted, but the people's eyes are now open and they will tell the honorable member for Rustico that he is not the only man in that respectable district who has wisdom.

He would not further trespass on the patience of the House, but would leave the task of furthering criticizing the Address in the hands of abler men.

Motion put and carried.

The House accordingly resolved itself into a Committee of the whole for the consideration of the Draft Address in answer to the Governor's Speech at the opening of the session.

MR. HOLLAND in the chair.

The first two paragraphs of the Address were severally read and agreed to.

On the third paragraph being read,

Mr. BEER moved that Mr. Speaker take the chair, and that the chairman report that some progress had been made, and ask leave to sit again.

Mr. Sinclair said it would be better to adjourn until to-morrow, as it was now nearly twelve o'clock.

Mr. McKay said it was just as well to finish the Address to-night as in all probability, the first of next week would be lost owing to Tuesday being St. Patrick's Day. If the matter was deferred a great deal of time would be lost, and he did not see any reason why they should not spend two hours and have the several paragraphs discussed. While he was willing to let the Opposition have every opportunity to discuss the matters in the Address he thought it could be finished this evening.

Hon. Mr. Sullivan said he did not see why the several paragraphs of the Address should not be proceeded with, as every opportunity had been given the Opposition to put forth their views.

Hon. Mr. Ferguson said it was not customary to spend much time discussing the Speech without some great constitutional questions were embodied in it, and there was no need of delaying the business of the session on the present occasion.

Motion put and lost.

On fourth paragraph being read,

Mr. Beer said that while there was a good deal in this paragraph that honorable members could agree to, he for one did not think the Government had given that encouragement to the improvement of our stock, especially horses, that they should have done. Owing to the Government not doing justice in this matter, and from their being remiss in their duty, the people had to take the matter in their own hands. They had no stud horses on the Stock Farm, and only a few mares could be seen there. The Government should not take credit for what is being done to improve our Agriculture. By not importing more horses they had forced private parties to take the risk of doing so. The honorable member for Rustico had claimed credit for the Government's inaction in this matter, but he (Mr. B.) considered they should be censured for not importing any stock last year, especially as the Stock Farm stock is getting less every year. At the meeting of the Dairymen's Association last evening, the President complained of the Speech not making some allusion to the dairy interests of the Province, and found it necessary to arraign the Government for not taking more interest in this most important industry. If the Government had the interests of the farmers at heart, reference would be made to the manufacture of cheese in this Province, as it had reached respectable proportions; and a Farmer's Government should have referred to butter also.

We want other breeds of cattle imported, breeds more adapted to the production of milk than those we had, and he (Mr. B.) believed we should get the milking strain of Shorthorns, which had proved the best in the world. Some strains of the Shorthorn breed are good for beef and others for milk, and it is the duty of the Government, at any cost, to import several head of the milking strain of these cattle. He (Mr. B.) would support them in asking for such a grant.

Mr. BLAKE said the paragraph before the Committee refers to the Exhibitions that had been held last October. The General Exhibition held in Charlottetown last year had been one of the most successful that had been held for many years. Great improvement in the stock exhibited could be noticed, yet not so much as ought to be from the efforts put forth by the Government to encourage this most important industry. While some parties had made creditable efforts to improve the quality of our stock a great many had not done so. The Government had done a great deal to encourage stock raising by importing many valuable animals, and no doubt would continue to do so. There was a great difference of opinion respecting the different kinds of stock. Some say the Shorthorn cattle are not the best for milk, and Jerseys, Holstiens and others have their supporters, but he believed the Shorthorns, both for beef and milk, were the most profitable for this Province.

In reference to the cattle on the Stock Farm, while some of them were good milkers, others were not adapted for milking purposes. There was a great difference of opinion existing between the gentlemen who attended the meeting of the Dairyman's Association last night. The President was in favor of Jerseys, but he (Mr. Blake) did not believe it would be to the interest of the Island to import them. The best stock for this Province is those suitable for milk and beef. Cattle that will milk fairly well, and afterwards make a good quality of beef, are the best stock for us to import. Records of different kinds of stock had been kept, and it has been found that the Shorthorns, when tested fairly, were the best, and had taken the prizes on all occasions. The Government had employed the best gentlemen they could get, such as Messrs. Longworth, Gardiner and others, and had imported the best animals they could obtain. He was glad the honorable member for Southport was in favor of the Shorthorn cattle, but it was very difficult to get the milking strain of that breed as they were very highly prized The Government, by keeping Shorthorn and Ayrshire cattle on the Stock Farm, had provided for the improvement of our stock, both for beef and milk, and they were right to wait until the claims of the different breeds had been settled, before expending large sums for the purchase of animals that were not the best. He differed with the honorable member respecting the horses on the Farm. Stud horses did better in the hands of private individuals as they required particular attendance and good handling. The last stud horse sold from the Farm only brought $750, but after he left the Farm he improved so much that after being a short time in private hands he brought $2,200. It is hard to look after these animals, and no doubt it was the particular attention this horse received, after going into private hands, that increased his value.

When horses are in private hands people from different sections of the Province have a better opportunity of profiting by their services, and they thus do more good than if kept on the Stock Farm. Our horses have a good character both in the United States and the Dominion. He had heard American horse buyers say, "There are no horses like Island horses," and the excellent prices that are obtained for good animals encourage their production. He (Mr. B.) was glad to see private individuals importing animals of this discription, and the Government might encourage such enterprize, but the time was not far distant when plenty of the best stock will, by private parties, be imported into the Province. He hoped the horses coming in the future would be of the best stock, so that the very good name we have obtained may be maintained. Our horses brought a lot of money into the Island last year, and a great deal of it came through the excellent reputation we have obtained at the Dominion Exhibitions, where our stock competed. The Government deserve credit for sending our stock to these exhibitions. If we had not exhibited at these exhibitions our horses would not be so well advertised to the people of the United States and the Maritime Provinces.

Our cattle, he was sorry to say, are not improving as they ought. Our farmers keep too many on their farms for the amount of feed they have. He had often wondered why they keep so many, as it is better to keep ten animals well, than twenty which are not half fed.

He was glad to see the Dairyman's Association, and similar societies taking the matter up and discussing the best modes of improving our system of farming, and he hoped the Government would grant any money required for this purpose, as in no better way could it be expended

G. F. O.

Mr. FARQUHARSON said that it appeared to him that the Government had never expended a single dollar excepting in cases where they could see their way clear to get it back again. Private individuals have had to take the matter of securing superior stock, for breeding purposes, into their own hands, and do the best they can, independently of the Government. When strangers inquire for our Stock Farm, they are told that there is little or no stock there worth seeing. This is not what the people of this Province have a right to expect in reference to this matter. A private speculator imports a superior breeding horse, and those who want his services, frequently do not know where to find them. The Government found out there was no money for the Treasury in the Stock Farm, and allowed most of the stock to pass into the hands of private parties. He thought this the wrong course to pursue, and that we should not look at the direct returns, so much as to those which come indirectly. It appeared that they expected to get back to the Treasury every dollar expended. They profess to wish to make this country a desirable place for our young men to settle in. If they encouraged the importation of the best breeds of stock, and the best seeds, and the manufacture of butter and cheese, they would do much to attain that object; but this has not been done. They have done nothing whatever for the encouragement of our home manufactures. What have they done during the past five or six years towards securing for our agriculturists a good market ; to which to export their surplus produce? Were it not that we have a free port of entry for out pioduce on the other side of the Atlantic, where would we be?. .Our farmers would be almost paupers; Do the people of Ontario care whether or not we receive ten cents per bushel for our potatoes? Can the Government show any correspondence with the United States, having for its object the obtaining of Reciprocity with that country, for the benefit of this Province? They say that they are powerless to secure anything for us in that direction; but, if there is any one thing more than another in which we are interested as a people, it is Reciprocity. Can they show a

telegram or communication bearing upon that matter? The fact is, they have done little or nothing to encourage Agriculture and manufactures in the Province.

Hon. MR. FERGUSON said that the subjects referred to in the paragraph under discussion were very important. He regretted that the last speaker, the hon. member for West River, had went so far as to censure the Government for not attempting to provide a market for the surplus Agricultural produce of this Province. The hon. gentleman must know that the Local Government have not the slightest thing in the world to do with such matters, and that they would not be permitted to interfere with it. They have their own proper sphere in which to act and in that alone it was their duty to move. It would show a great lack of intelligence on their part to interfere with the work allotted to the General Government of the Dominion. All that the hon. member said on that subject was, therefore, beside the mark, and does not come within the pale of intelligent and enlightened discussion. The hon. gentleman censured the Government for not having maintained on the Stock Farm, a larger number of horses for breeding purposes. Now, the policy pursued by the Government in regard to that matter, will bear the fullest investigation. They found that the horse business on the Stock Farm had become utterly demoralized. There were outstanding dues for horse service for years and years which it became almost impossible to collect. Another fact was that private enterprise was entirely prevented from importing and maintaining the best breeds of horses, owing to the extent in which the Government engaged in it As soon as he (Mr Ferguson) became one of the Board of managers, he saw that it was the interest of the Government to sell the horses, and not to travel stud horses at all. That was carried out, and the horses then upon the Farm passed into the hands of enterprising farmers and others. The result of the Government's policy in reference to this matter was that within the past five years no less than seventeen highly bred Stallions have been imported into this Province through private enterprise alone. Had it not been for the action of the Government in selling off the horses on the Stock Farm there is good reason to believe there would not have been one Stallion imported during the five years. Of the seventeen horses alluded to, ten were heavy draft horses, four were roadsters and three were blood horses. In fact, the Island has rushed to the front in the importation of highly bred horses. Taking the above facts in connection with the encouragement given by the Government to the Exhibitions, he thought our position in that respect a very good one. The hon. member for West River seemed to think that the object of the Government in connection with the running of the Stock Farm was to make the Accounts for Expenditure and Receipts square with each

other. Well, he (Mr. Ferguson) pleaded guilty to the charge of endeavoring to do this, for he thought it would be a poor example to our farmers if the one Farm managed and controlled by the Government was sinking year after year from $1,500 to $3,000. He wished to show that by good management of the Farm, it could be made self-sustaining; and the result of last year's experience has proved that the Government were nearly correct in that opinion. There were only two horses on the farm when the present Government came to power, and they are still in the country. So far as the horned cattle are concerned, a large number of them have been sold and distributed through the three counties. The cattle now on the farm are larger and better animals than were formerly kept there, and every animal is of pure breed. Private enterprise has taken charge of the horse business, and he wished it was as active with reference to horned cattle; but unfortunately this was not the case. For this reason, the Government should continue to import a stock of the very best horned cattle for the farm, and also improve the strains at present there. There is much truth in the statement that the Durham cattle are among the best for the farm; but a good many of them have been selected from herds kept for the purpose of making beef. The milking strains have been almost killed out of some of the best breeds, but there are still strains of Durhams where the old milking qualities have been maintained in full vigor. If a good Durham bull were imported, whose progeny had strong milking qualities, good milkers could be obtained. More attention should be given to strains of Durhams with milking qualities.

Mr. BENTLEY agreed with the honorable Commissioner of Public Lands in regard to the importation of stallions by private enterprise, instead of by the Government. If any particular breeds of horses, not imported by private individuals, were thought necessary, the Government might undertake to import them. But were the Government to undertake the importation of stallions now, after private enterprise had done so much, the people generally would not thank them for it, as it would do more harm than good. In the distribution of horned cattle, much good has been done by the Government, especially by the sale of thorough bred bull calves. In reference to heifers, so little has been done that the results are scarcely perceptible. A sum of money expended in the importation of some pure bred heifer calves and cows would be well spent. A few thorough bred cows had been sold from the Stock Farm but they were looked upon as inferior; — the reason for this he did not know. He had often been curious to know what was done with the thorough-bred heifers raised on the Stock Farm. There are generally some twenty or thirty calves. What is done with them? The importation of a few thorough-bred short horned

heifers would result in much good. He hoped this matter would receive the fullest consideration.

Paragraph agreed to.

The paragraph on Winter communication was then read.

Mr. BEER said that this paragraph was really the only important one in the Speech and should receive a good deal of consideration. The honorable member for Rustico acknowledged that the steamer *Northern Light* had done some good. This was an important admission from the Government side of the House. It was lately discovered that the vessel did much better by running stern foremost. His honorable friend admitted that she did well for a few years, but that during the past few years she did nothing worthy of mention. The captain has been charged by the Dominion authorities to run no risks except on his own personal responsibility. The boat is said to be in an unfit condition for the work required of her. Who is responsible for this? It cannot be the Government that purchased her and placed her on that route, for she proved herself at that time fully equal to the work she was required to perform. If the boat is unsafe, the Dominion Goverment are certainly deserving of censure. He thought something a good deal stronger than the present paragraph should be placed in the Address with respect to this matter. The Committee who prepared the Address were letting down the Dominion Government much too easily with reference to our Winter communication with the main.

land. A sad accident had occurred, which might have proved fatal, owing to the general Government's turning a deaf ear to our claims with respect to the Terms of Union. Our last appeal was disregarded, and he wished to know why the Local Government had not followed it up by carrying the matter to the foot of the Throne. The people have a right to hold them as well as the Dominion Government responsible for the non-fulfilment of the Terms of Confederation, as it was their duty to press this question to the fullest extent of their ability, and to leave nothing undone in their efforts to secure to us our rights. Had they laid our grievance before the Imperial Government, it is not probable the sad accident alluded to, would have happened; and our Winter communication with the mainland would have been in a far more satisfactory condition than at present. He did not altogether agree with the action of one of our Representatives in the Dominion House of Commons, a few days ago, in pointing out to the General Government what is best to be done to secure for us what we require in reference to this matter That is a question which belongs wholly to the Dominion Government, and not to us. He saw no promise in the Speech of any papers likely to be brought down, which will show what the Government have been doing in connection with this matter, during the recess. They were too late in their present proposition; this action should have been taken long

ago, and he had to express his disapprobation of the manner in which they had neglected our interests in reference to it

Paragraph agreed to.

The next clause, referring to the Public Accounts of the past year, and the Estimates of the present year, was then read.

Mr. BEER agreed with the Paragraph, but if the Government do not take a different course from that pursued by them in the past, he would not feel disposed to vote them such sums as they may propose for the Public service. They have not expended sufficient money on our Public Works. He would be only too glad to give his vote for a sufficient sum for the proper maintenance of that service; and he hoped the Government would be prepared to bring in an Estimate that would meet the Public requirements in reference thereto.

Paragraph agreed to.

On motion, Mr. Speaker resumed the Chair; and the Chairman reported the Address agreed to.

The remaining clauses of the Draft Address were then severally read and agreed to.

Ordered, That the Address be engrossed, and that the same Committee who prepared it, be a Committee to wait on His Honor the Lieutenant Governor to ascertain when he will be pleased to receive the same.

House adjourned until ten o'clock, on the forenoon of the 14th.

I. O.

SATURDAY, March 14.

Mr. SPEAKER in the Chair.

THE ADDRESS.

Mr. McKAY, from the Special Committee appointed to wait on His Honor the Lieutenant Governer, to know his pleasure when he would be attended by the House with their Address in reply to the Speech with which His Honor was pleased to open the Session, reported that His Honor would receive the Address in the Library, at half-past one o'clock this after noon.

The hour appointed by His Honor the Lieutenant Governor to receive the Address of the House in answer to the Speech at the opening of the Session having arrived, Mr. Speaker and the House went up and when they returned,—

Mr. SPEAKER reported that the House had attended upon His Honor and presented their Address, to which His Honor had been pleased to make the following reply:

Mr. Speaker and Gentlemen of the the House of Assembly:

I thank you for your dutiful Address.

I am quite assured you will apply yourselves dilligently to the duties of the Session, and that measures calculated to advan:e the welfare of the Province will receive your careful attention.

THE CHARLOTTETOWN MUTUAL FIRE INSURANCE COMPANY.

A Petitton of B. Heartz, L. L. Beer, Owen Connolly and others, was presented to the House by the Honorable Mr. McLeod, and the same was received and read, setting forth that the Petitioners are desirous of forming a Company for the purpose of insuring property against Fire, and praying that they may be incorporated under the name of the "Charlottetown Mutual Fire Insurance Company."

Ordered, That the said Petition be referred to a Special Committee to examine the same and report thereon by Bill or otherwise.

Ordered, That Honorable Mr. Macleod, Honorable Mr. Prowse and Mr. Blake do compose the said Committee.

Hon. Mr. McLEOD from the last preceding Committee appointed, presented to the House a Bill as prepared by the Committee to be intituled "An Act to Incorporate the Charlottetown Mutual Fire Insurance Company."

Hon. Mr. MACLEOD moved that the Bill be referred to the Special Committee appointed to report on every Private Bill to examine the same and report thereon.

Mr. BEER said it was understood last Session, that in future, private Bills should be printed before coming under the consideration of the House.

Hon. Mr. SULLIVAN said no doubt it would be a great advantage to have Bills printed. The writing was often not legible and honorable members had difficulty in understanding the nature of the measures they were asked to legislate upon. He was afraid, however, that those promoting these Bills might think it a hardship if they were required to do this, as the House might not take any proceedings on them after being presented.

Hon. Mr. MACLEOD said promoters of Bills might be asked to be familiar with the rules of the House, but as there was no rule of the House requiring that these Bills be printed before being presented, it would be unfair to ask them to do so in this case.

Hon. Mr. SULLIVAN said that the printing of these Bills should be under the control of the House and parties interested in them should be required to deposit an amount equal to the cost of having them printed, which the Private Bill Committee could order if it was considered desirable to do so. Under the present rules the Private Bill Committee can tax a Bill $100 or any other amount they think necessary to cover the expense of making it law.

Hon. Mr. PROWSE did not approve of the course recommended by his honor the Leader of the Government. If Bills had to be printed after being referred to the Private Bill Committee, it would delay the business of the House. If the rule is adopted that all Bills shall be printed the public will know it, and Bills will be printed before the Session commences. If it was thought advisable to make it a rule of the House he had no objections.

Mr. PERRY said he did not see how the views of the honorable member for Southport could be carried out, as short Bills would cost a great deal more if they had to be printed before coming into this House. It was not advisable to discourage the formation of companies as we had far too few of them. Public Bills of importance should be printed, as honorable members would then have a better opportunity of studying them, but he did not think it fair to cause these short Private Bills, many sections of which are common to the general Act for Incorporating Private Companies, to be printed. The Private Bill Committee had the power to have any Bill of importance printed and he thought it would be unfair to make a rule of the House that all Bills should be printed.

Hon. Mr. FERGUSON said in general Private Bills are alike and it would be harsh to ask them to be printed before we look at them. Sometimes Bills of a semi-public nature such as the Waterworks Bill of last Session are presented, and in that case he would approve of them being printed. It is, however, in the province of the Private Bill Committee to report that such a Bill shall be printed and he would advise that that Committee be the judge of what should be printed.

Mr. BEER said he believed it would facilitate the business of the House to have all Bills printed, but as the Private Bill Committee had it in their power to have this plan adopted he would leave it to them to have it carried out.

Mr. BENTLEY said notice should be given if the House intended to follow out this rule. It will add greatly to the cost of Bills if they all had to be printed. He did not think any obstacles should be placed in the way of these companies.

Motion put and carried

House adjourned until Monday next, at the hour of three o'clock in the afternoon.

G. F. O.

MONDAY, March 16.

In the absence of Mr. Speaker at half-past three o'clock in the afternoon, a quorum not being present the Clerk adjourned the House until to-morrow at three o'clock in the afternoon.

G. F. O.

TUESDAY, March 17.

MR. SPEAKER in the Chair.

There not being a quorum present, Mr. Speaker adjourned the House until to-morrow, in the afternoon at 3 o'clock.

WEDNESDAY March 18.

Mr. SPEAKER in the Chair.

Hon. Mr. SULLIVAN a member of Her Hajesty's Executive Council, delivered to Mr. Speaker a message from His Honor the Lieutenant Governor. Said message was read, all the members of the House being uncovered, transmitting to the House Copies of Despatches having reference to the presentation to Her Hajesty the Queen of the Joint Address of condolence from the two Houses of the Legislature, on the death of His Royal Highness the Duke of Albany.

Ordered, That said Despatches do lie on the Table.

Hon. Mr. SULLIVAN a member of Her Majesty's Executive Council, also delivered a message from His Honor the Lieutenant Governor, transmitting to the House copies of Despatches and other Documents having reference to the maintenance by the General Government of efficient Steam communication between this Island and the mainland, under the Terms of Confederation.

Moved by Hon. Mr. SULLIVAN, seconded by Hon. Mr. FERGUSON,

Resolved That said Despatches and papers do lie on the table.

Mr. PERRY thought the honorable Leader of the Government should have named the day on which these Papers were to be considered. The subject of Winter Communication with the mainland is a very important one, and a day should be fixed for its full consideration. He made these remarks because the usual course pursued by the Government for the past few years had been to allow papers relating to this subject to lie on the table until nearly the close of the Session, thus allowing the most important business to lie over to the last. The people's representatives had a right to discuss this question, and to know whether or not the Government had been attending to the interests of the country, with respect to it. He was sorry to say that the matter had been too frequently slighted and passed over as of little importance, and this is why h had asked that a day be fixed for its full discussion. To lay these papers on the table, without naming a day for their consideration by the House, was not treating them with that attention which they deserved. A service involving the safety of passengers and mails in the passage across the Straits is one of the most important in this Province. Perhaps the Government may, at any time, be prepared for a full discussion of this matter, but honorable members, generally, have not been so fortunate as to be conversant with all the correspondence, in reference to it, and expect all the information which the Government can supply in connection therewith. It is not right, therefore, to go into its consideration on too short notice. The Opposition should have at least a week's notice of the day on which the subject will be taken up, and there is no reason why it should not be given. He, therefore, moved that the papers just read do not le on the table but that they be made the Order of the Day for Tuesday next.

Mr. Yeo seconded the motion of the honorable member for Tignish, and said that as this was a very important matter to the House, it should be taken into consideration at as early a day as convenient. Generally speaking, in past Sessions the question was laid over until very late, and most all other businesss was disposed of. Honorable members were then anxious to return to their homes, and too little time was given to the discussion of it.

Hon Mr. Sullivan was not surprised at the motion of the honorable member for Tignish, but he was astonished at the action of the honorable Leader of the Opposition in seconding it. The former professed to be so anxious to expedite the public business that he moved to have the consideration of the most important matter postponed for a week! It was probable the honorable member had a few qualms of conscience with respect to the part he had played in regard to it. Although the honorable gentleman had occupied a seat in the Dominion House of Commons for five years, he never once raised his voice effectively in favor of any improvement in our means of Winter communication. But, now, when the honorable member is a thousand miles away from the seat of Government he makes a great deal of noise about this matter. When the question comes up for the consideration of the House, he (Mr. S.) hoped it will be discussed without any political feeling or Party bias, in order to secure a complete settlement of your claims, and the fulfilment of the Terms of Confederation. It is, therefore, to be regretted that the honorable member for Tignish made this extraordinary motion. The Government are anxious that no delay should take place in considering this matter, and in order that it may have precedence over every other question, have brought down and laid on the Table of the House all the Despatches and papers in connection with it. He did not hesitate to say that this was more important than any other question now before the country, and for this reason, the Government have taken the earliest opportunity afforded them of bringing it to the attention of the House. But what is there in the Documents now laid before the House to elicit any new discussion on this question? One of the enclosures in this message from His Honor is a copy of the Address transmitted last Session to Ottawa; and another is the Minute of the Executive Council of this Province dated 20th February last, forwarded to the Dominion Government. That minute sets forth nothing new that can be said on the subject. The only new point which might be noticed is one which the honorable member for Tignish has never yet discovered, namely, the fact that no provision has ever been made by the Dominion Government for the conveyance of a single passenger across the Straits by the ice-boats between the Capes! The contract with the couriers simply requires the carriage of the mails between the Island and the mainland; so that any passenger who ventures to cross the Straits by the the ice-

boats, does so at the risk of his life. The couriers may refuse to convey any passenger who presents himself for crossing. This is an important matter, and it has been brought to the notice of the Dominion Parliament. This question of Winter Communication has been brought before the House at as early a day as possible, and it is the intention of the Government to move for its consideration at a very early date. We have twice appealed to the Dominion Government for the fulfilment of the Terms of Confederation in reference to continuous communication with the mainland in Winter, and it is not the intention of the Government to make another appeal to that quarter. The Address of last Session and the Minute of the Executive Council were both forwarded to Ottawa without any satisfactory result; and the only means of redress now left us, as a Province, is to Petition Her Majesty the Queen to have the Terms of Confederation with the Dominion carried out, and to have this Province indemnified for the loss sustained by it owing to the non-fulfilment, by the Dominion Government, of those Terms. This is all the Legislature can do, or that any Parliament can do to secure our rights with respect to this matter. He proposed, therefore, to bring down to the House, an Address to Her Majesty on this subject, for its approval; but it is necessary that a Resolution making provision for such an Address be tabled for twenty-four hours, before it can be introduced. It is intended to give honorable members ample time to consider this matter. Although the Government had shown a disposition to do this, the Opposition complained that the question was dealt with in too much hurry. He would venture to say that when the question comes up for discussion, they would not advance a single idea not already in the possession of the House. The papers on the Table require no consideration. The Despatches from the Dominion Government simply acknowledge the receipt of the Address and Minute of Council. He felt sure that the course now proposed by the Government would commend itself to every honorable member of the House. It is our duty to demand that the Dominion Government shall fulfil the compact entered into at Confederation, so far as it is possible to fulfil it; and it is a duty from which the Government have no intention of flinching.

Mr. FARQUHARSON said that the Leader of the Government appeared surprised at the action of the Opposition in reference to this matter; but the honorable gentleman must recollect that the question was not introduced for discussion, last Session, until the second last day of that session, although the Government had promised to go into its consideration at an early day.

Hon. Mr. SULLIVAN said that the Government would bring up this matter for discussion in due time; but the Legislative Council had not yet presented their Address in answer to His Honor's Speech; and no joint action with them could be taken until they did so.

Mr. FARQUHARSON had been in the House long enough to discount the statements made by the honorable Leader of the Government. The motion made by the honorable member for Tignish that the question be considered by the House on a day fixed for that purpose was moved in order that it may not be postponed until the last day of the session, as was the case in a years gone by. It appeared that the Address of both branches of the Legislature was forwarded to Ottawa, and that its receipt was duly acknowledged, but the whole of last Summer had passed away without their taking any further action with respect to the matter. Was this performing their duty to the country? He thought not. On the 28th February last, they framed a Minute of Council and forwarded it to Ottawa, but had it not been for the sad accident on the Straits, a little before that date, it is not probable that the Minute alluded to would ever have been made. Nothing can be obtained from the General Government without persistent and repeated efforts. It is necessary to go again and again. The matter of Winter communication is one of vast importance to this Province; but have the Government attended to it as they should have done? If we look at the records of 1881, 1882, 1883, 1884, we shall find that important questions such as the Fishery Award and Winter communication were laid over until the very last days of those Sessions, and received but scant consideration. He never could understand why. Under these circumstances, he thought the Opposition should not be found fault with for asking that a day be named for the consideration and discussion of the Papers relating to Winter communication. It appears that the Government ask to be indemnified for the loss sustained on account of the non-fulfilment of the Terms of Confederation, to the extent of five million dollars. The amount is below the sum we should receive on that account. The Dominion have acted shamefully towards this Province in the matter of Winter communication, and have a right to remunerate us for our loss. We are not begging for money; we simply ask for our rights. The very price paid for this Province on its entering Confederation has been refused us; and the lives of our people and the safety of our mails are endangered by the passage across the Straits between the Capes in an open boat! It appears that it rests entirely with the couriers themselves to say whether they will convey a solitary passenger across the Straits in the ice-boats or not! He thought the amendment quite in order.

Hon. Mr. CAMPBELL said that the question of Winter Communication was a very important one and should not be discussed in a party spirit; but it appeared to him that certain honorable members of the Opposition could not approach it otherwise. It was true that during one or two Sessions, the matter was allowed to lay over until near the close, but that did not show that it was unimportant. The memorial of the Legislature last Session went up to Ottawa in good time to be dealt with. The honorable member for West River was at one time a member of a Local Government, which did nothing to secure to us our just claims from the Dominion, either in reference to Winter communication or any other question. Did the honorable gentleman make any effort to protect the rights of our people, or to secure for them the fulfilment of the Terms of Confederation? If any member of the House at that time wanted to raise a storm, he had only to complain that the McKenzie Government had not fulfilled the terms of Confederation as they should have done. The present Government had not been at all backward in pressing our claims as a Province upon the General Government; but how had they been treated by the Opposition when endeavoring to secure compensation for the piers? The honorable member for West River was the man who declared he was ready to take the responsibility of whatever appeared in the columns of the *Patriot* newspaper, and the aim of that paper, from the first was to obstruct the Government in securing for this Province the amount due for its piers. It is well known that the present Opposition Party, when in power, never could secure a single dollar of the moneys due this Province from the Dominion on any special claim for our rights. It now appears that the honorable member for West River is prepared to back up the honorable member for Tignish; in endeavoring to thwart the efforts of the Government to secure the fulfilment of the Terms of Confederation with reference to Winter communication with the mainland. The Government have done all that lay in their power to secure justice from the Dominion Government with respect to this matter; but they cannot take the Minister of Marine by the throat and compel him to grant what we ask. It is now, therefore, our duty to present an Address to Her Majesty the Queen, praying her to have the Terms of Confederation fulfilled, and to grant us compensation for our loss in connection with this matter since Confederation. It was to have been expected, under such circumstances, that all shades of politicians would have united and met the Government in a proper spirit for the purpose of assisting them in securing for this Province that which would benefit its whole population; but it appears that the honorable members for West River and Tignish have no other wish than to benefit their party for the time being.

Mr. SINCLAIR said that if he understood the motion of the honorable member for Tignish, it was not made for the purpose of postponing the consideration of the question of Winter Communication; on the contrary, the hon-orable gentleman desired to prevent the postponement of the matter, as had been the case in the past, until near the close of the Session. He (Mr. S.) thought it was the duty of the Government to inform the House when the question would be brought up for discussion, and fix a day for that purpose. He could prove that the Government were charging the Opposition with doing what they had never done. The Opposition had never endeavored to thwart them in their efforts to procure from the Dominion Government compensation for our Piers An important question, such as that of Winter Communication with the mainland should come up for discussion on a day appointed for that purpose, of which due notice should be given. It is well-known that it was a common practice of late to postpone the consideration of the most important questions until near the close of the Session, and if a different course is pursued in the present case, it will be an unusual one. In his opinion, the compact entered into by the Dominion Government with reference to continuous Steam communication between this Province and the mainland, had been entirely abrogated or broken through. Under such circumstances, the proper course to pursue is to lay our case before Her Majesty the Queen. His desire was to approach the consideration of the matter in a proper spirit, and he thought the House should know when it is to come up for discussion, in order that honorable members may be prepared to discuss it in an intelligent and proper manner.

Hon. Mr FERGUSON said that if he understood the situation aright, the Opposition were very desirous of making a little cheap popularity out of this matter, and to make believe that they are more anxious to do something for the improvement of our present means of Winter communication than the Government themselves are. As the Opposition are anxious to have a discussion on this question at this early stage of the proceedings, he thought it necessary to say a word or two as to the duty of the two political parties in reference to it. What was done to secure our rights by the two honorable members on the other side of the House who occupied seats in the House of Commons for a period of five years? Could those honorable gentlemen show that they ever brought this question to the notice of the House of Commons with the view of having the Terms of Confederation fulfilled? What were the facts? The old *Albert* was placed by the Mackenzie Government on the Georgetown and Pictou route, and those honorable members as well as the other members of the present Opposition would almost take a person by the throat if he insinuated that the Terms of union were not being completely carried out by the employment of that boat; and afterwards of the *Northern Light*. The fact is, the honorable members alluded to—the honorable member for Tignish and the honorable member for Strathalbyn

—never mentioned the matter in the House of Commons during the five years they represented this Province in that House. When the Opposition held the reins of power in this Province, did they ever make any effort to remedy our grievances in reference to this matter? What was their position in the Local Legislature and at Ottawa? Oh, those dear good men who composed the Mackenzie Administration were not to be disturbed at all in reference to such little questions as this matter of Winter communication! But the present Government have taken a different course. They say that the Dominion Government were a contracting party in agreeing to the Terms of Confederation, and that they are bound to fulfil those terms. This is their position, and the Opposition will vote for their measures when the latter are brought down. Honorable members opposite in one breath tell the Government that they are delaying the consideration of this matter too long, and in the next breath, they say that they want proper notice of the day when the question will come up, in order that they may have time to prepare for it. By referring to the Journals of the House, it will be found that there is scarcely an instance where the late Government when in power, brought down a notice of this kind so early in the Session as in the present case. The Government have shown their hand in reference to this matter at as early a day as was possible, in the best interests of the country. There is no doubt that the Leader of the

Opposition would have acted quite differently had not his Lieutenant taken his present course. But the latter never opens his mouth without putting his foot in it! The result was that the hon. member's colleagues had either to back him up or leave him in the lurch. In view of the fact that the Opposition had all the Correspondence on this question before them on the table, and, the greater portion of it printed, he was surprised that they had not shown better taste than to have raised the present discussion.

Mr D. C. MARTIN was surprised at the action of honorable members on the Government side of the House with respect to this question. They appeared to lose all interest in it, in order to attend to that of party politics. This question of Winter communicatson is a highly important one to people of this Province, and one in which all are interested. He therefore thought that a day should be appointed for its consideration, and full and free discussion. This was the course pursued in the Dominion Parliament in such cases. Questions of this kind are there made the order of the day for a day named. If this Province is entitled to be compensated for its loss on account of the non-fulfilment of the Terms of Confederation, to the extent of five millions of dollars, it was certainly right and proper that the Government should name a day for the consideration of this matter. When the honorable Commissioner of Crown lands gets up to make a speech on such a question as, this, he should show the House a good example in the manner with which he deals with it. The honorable gentleman asserted that the party to which the Opposition belong never did anything to secure to this Province its rights in the matter of Winter communication. The very contrary was the fact, as they were the only party that ever did anything at all in that direction. First the *Albert*, and afterwards the *Northern Light* was placed on the route between Georgetown and Pictou. What has the present Dominion Government done to provide for us continuous Steam communication between this Province and the mainland? Absolutely nothing! He thought a day should be fixed and set apart for the discussion of this most important question, and that the matter should be approached by both parties in a proper spirit and free from all party prejudice.

Mr. JOHN MACLEAN was very much surprised at the action of the Opposition in raising this discussion at this stage of the proceedings in reference to the Documents now before the House. He had expected that they would have been pleased to assist the Government in carrying on the business of the country in a satisfactory manner, that they would throw no obstacles in the way of a full and fair discussion of this most important question, and that they would not oppose any measure until they had good reason to do so. He would move that the hon.

orable member for Tignish have leave to withdraw his motion.

Hon. Mr. PROWSE said that it appeared to be a very difficult matter to satisfy the Opposition. Some of them complained that the discussion did not come on soon enough, while others thought it would take place too early, and that they would be unprepared for it. Their fears were altogether groundless. The people expect the Government to do their duty, and the latter intend to do it in reference to this, as well as all other matters. He was glad to see that this question had become a live one. Honorable members of the Opposition and their supporters had ridiculed the Government because they had not pointed out to the Dominion Government what they should do to improve our means of Winter communication with the mainland. But the Local Government said: "No; that is not our business; our duty is to see that the Terms of Confederation are carried out; the Dominion Government may do so at an expense of only a dollar if they can; but if it costs them millions, those terms must be carried out." If the choice of a route were left to local parties, each would be found to have predilections in favor of some particular place; some gentlemen of the Opposition for instance, favored the Georgetown and Pictou route, others the Capes route, and others the West Point and Richibucto route. To attempt to dictate to the General Government as to the route to be chosen, or the means of fulfilling

the Terms of Union, would only defeat the object we have in view, as we would be told that we ourselves are divided in opinion on the matter. On the whole, he thought we were more justified in agitating for a tunnel than any particular route by steamboat. He believed that according to the terms of the compact made at Confederation, the Dominion Government would never be able to carry them out by navigation; nevertheless, it is for them to find a way of doing so, and not for us. Some of the most eminent men in the Dominion, to day, agreed with him in that opinion. No less a personage than the Archbishop of Halifax had stated through the press that before the end of the present century we shall have continuous steam communication with the mainland either by a tunnel or a bridge across the Strait.

Mr. BLAKE seconded the amendment of the honorable junior member for Souris, (Mr. J. Maclean) and said that he regretted that this very important question could not be discussed without party bias and party references. It had been agreed by both parties that we have not been properly treated by the Dominion Government with respect to our means of Winter communication with the mainland. Neither of the two political parties had performed their duty towards us in regard to this matter. This question was one of the most important ever discussed in this House, and should be dealt with in a manner which would show that we, as a people, are alive to that fact. Last Session, when an Address to His Excellency the Governor General, was passed by both branches of the Legislature, it was agreed by both sides of the House, that every effort should be made by both of our local parties to have this great question satisfactorily settled. In addition to this, public meetings had been held a short time ago in Charlottetown, Summerside, and other places, protesting against the manner in which this Province had been treated in reference to this matter, and urging the fulfilment by the General Government of the terms of Union. At these meetings, party feeling was cast aside, and it was resolved that all would unite for the general good, to attain the object so much desired by the people of this Province. He fully agreed with the statement made by the honorable member for Murray Harbor, that this House should not point out the means by which the Terms can be carried out, but should leave that matter to be decided by the Dominion Government themselves. He had always been of opinion that those terms could never be thoroughly carried out by means of steamboats; and as to a tunnel, the cost would be too great for the Dominion Government to entertain it. It may be said that before the century is out, a tunnel or bridge may be constructed across the strait; but he did not think the General Government would undertake so expensive a work. Up to the present time, the Dominion Government did not seem to have come to any conclu-

sion with reference to this matter, and had merely informed us that the question was "under consideration" and would be acted upon in due time. He (Mr. Blake) thought the time had arrived for laying this matter at the foot of the Throne, as sufficient time had elapsed since Confederation, for the Dominion Government to fulfil the terms of union. Great credit is due the Local Government for the proposal, they now make to the House in this respect. He felt confident that the appeal to the Imperial Government would secure to us our rights in reference to this matter. We, as one of the two great contracting parties of the union, have had to carry out our portion of the terms, and there is no doubt the Imperial Government will insist that the Dominion Government shall fulfil their contract with us. One of the greatest inducements held out to us to enter Confederation was that we should have continuous steam communication with the mainland Winter and Summer; because we had some experience of the difficulties to be encountered and overcome. Owing to the neglect of the General Government with respect to the Winter service, one of the most unfortunate accidents that ever occurred in the Straits took place during the present season. Twenty-one men very nearly lost their lives in an attempt to cross to the mainland. Perhaps this may be the means of awakening the Dominion Government to a sense of their duty to us in reference to this matter, and to remedy the grievance complained of. In fact they have already intimated to our representatives in the Parliament of the Dominion, that they have sent down an Engineer to report as to the best means of keeping up continuous communication with the mainland in Winter. That official, he (Mr. B.) believed, was on the Island at the present time. He was quite satisfied that the Government would bring this matter up for discussion at an early day, and therefore hoped the honorable member for Tignish would obtain leave to withdraw his motion.

Mr. FARQUHARSON said that if the statement of the honorable member for Murray Harbor to the effect that he was of opinion that the terms of union in respect to winter communication could not be fulfilled by means of navigation, should reach the Dominion Government, it would operate against us, and injure our case. The honorable member went so far as to say that he thought the terms could only be fulfilled by the construction of a tunnel or a bridge across the Straits. This was wrong, as it was confining our request to the four corners of something we know they will not undertake. In fact, such language was absurd, and no sensible man would talk in that way. The honorable member had discovered that he was in company with the Archbishop of Halifax, in entertaining that opinion, and had to inform the House of the fact. It appeared that there was not a member on the Government side of the House who would not echo

every word uttered by Sir John in reference to this matter, although the Dominion Government gave them a slap on the face every time they appealed to Ottawa. They still declare the members of that Government to be the right men in the right place. It is well-known that the steamer *Northern Light* had been denounced by Sir John's Government as a useless old boat; and that owing to the way she had been handled, she had proved almost a complete failure. If Mr. McKenzie were in power, he would be honest enough to do something more than has been done.

Hon. Mr. PROWSE. What did Mr. Mackenzie say with respect to this Province ? It was this : "I think we have done very well for Prince Edward Island, and that we have carried out the terms of Union." Yet the honorable member for West River declared that gentleman would ' have "done better for us" than Sir John had done! If we suggest the means of carrying out those terms, and those means should prove a failure, our mouths would be stopped, and we could not make a demand. If we suggest the proper course to pursue, we should suggest something that would be sure to prove a success, if properly carried out. The only sure means of winter communication with the mainland would be either a bridge or a tunnel. If the Dominion Government find it impossible to fulfil their compact at Confederation, they should come to us with a proposition, or ask us what compensation we will take in lieu of the fulfilment of the terms. This was his position on this question, and he did not think it unreasonable, or impossible to be met A compact was made with British Columbia that a railway should connect that Province with the rest of Canada, and that it should be completed within ten years after the union, and commenced within two years. British Columbia enforced the fulfilment of those terms by carrying her case to the foot of the Throne, and the result was that the Canada Pacific Railway was built at a cost of one hundred millions of dollars. If that Province could enforce the fulfiment of the Terms of union with the Dominion, there was no reason why our terms could not be carried out by the construction of a tunnel costing only one tenth of the amount paid for the Pacific Railway. So far as the *Northern Light* is concerned, she has done some service as well as injury to this Province. She is at present hemmed up in Georgetown harbor, by a barrier of ice which cannot be broken through, while for the past two weeks the straits in the direction of Pictou are quite navigable for any ordinary steamer of less power than she has. He was not here as a supporter of Sir John's Government or of any political party, but as a Representative of the people of this Island. He maintained that the instructions given to the captain of the *Northern Light* by the Marine Department were such as no ship owner would give to a commander of one of his vessels. Those instructions

were to the effect that the captain would be held responsible for any risk he would run with the vessel, in taking her into positions of danger, if any lives were lost or propey injured. If such instructions were given to the captain of any ordinary vessel, he would at once refuse to navigate her. The consequence was that the greatest care has been taken of the *Northern Light* up to the present time; and it was never discovered until the present winter that she made better progress through the ice, stern foremost than in the usual manner. We should wake up and demand the entire fulfilment of the terms of union, no matter in what way the General Government accomplish it. He, for one, would never demand the fulfilment of those terms by means of navigation, and the Dominion Government would never, through his advice, spend their money in attempting to do so.

Mr. PERRY said that whatever line of action the Opposition pursued, they understood one another, but he was sorry to say that there was a great diversity of opinion in the Government ranks on this very important question. The House had been informed by the honorable member for Murray Harbor that it is impossible for the Dominion Government to fulfil the terms of union except by means of a tunnel or a bridge across the Straits. And the honorable junior member for Charlottetown stated that he never expected to see either a bridge or a tunnel, as those works would be too costly for the Dominion Gov ernment to undertake. He did not know whether or not the honorable member had been instructed to make such a statement as that in this House; but there was no doubt it was reported, and would in due time reach Ottawa, and perhaps weaken our case. From these conflicting statements, it appeared that the Government and their supporters were divided on this matter. He was sorry that they had placed themselves in such a position, but he was pleased to see the discussion take the range it had. What had the Government been doing for the whole of the past year with respect to this question? Absolutely nothing. The honorable Leader of the Government, asked what the honorable member for Tignish ever did while representing a constituency of this Province in the House of Commons, to have the terms of union fulfilled with respect to winter communication. If the honorable gentleman would refer to the records of that House for the Sessions of 1875, '76, '77 and '78, he would find that he (Mr. P) had brought this matter prominently before the Dominion Parliament, and that the steamer *Northern Light* was placed on the route. But what had the friends of the present government at Ottawa done during the seven years they have been in power, since 1878? Nothing. When the Government charge the Opposition with making this a political question, they assert what is not correct. He for one, was desirous to have the matter discussed apart from all party politics,

in order that the rights of this Province may be secured. H l l not the slightest intention of e — barassing the Government w th respect to it. The Opposition had a right to ask that a day be appointed for the consideration of this question, and therefore his motion was perfectly in order. He hoped the discussion would take place within a reasonable time, in order that the matter might be dealt with on its merits.

Hon. Mr. LEFURGY said that it appeared to him that the Opposition were determined to find fault with the actions of the Government, no matter what the latter did. Why did they ask that a day be appointed for the discussion on this matter of winter communication? They seemed prepared to go into it at one, and professed to understand the situation far better than did the government themselves. There seemed to be a difference of opinion as to the best way of effecting steam communication with the mainland in winter; but the better way was to let the Dominion Government decide that matter for themselves. He thought both parties should unite and demand the complete fulfilment of the terms of union. No honorable member should take advantage of a discussion on this question to commence cavilling at the actions of any particular government. One thing is clear, and that is that the terms of union have not been carried out, and that neither the Mackenzie nor Sir John Government have done their duty. He thought, however, that the present Dominion Government had done better for us than the other. The honorable Leader of the Government deserved a great deal of credit for his action with respect to the Piers question. We are to receive about $80,000 in all and the matter is not settled yet; there is a number of Piers still to be arranged for. The Dominion Government agreed to undertake certain duties, and they must fulfil their contracts. We must also be compensated for the loss sustained by the non-fulfilment of the terms of union, whether that loss is one million or five millions of dollars.

The maendment to the amendment was then put and carried, the House dividing as follows :

YEAS : Honorables Messrs. Sullivan, Fergusor, McLeod, Arsenault, Campbell, Lefurgey, Prowse, Macdonald, Gordon ; Messrs. Mackay, Bentley, John Maclean, Macdougall, Alex. Martin, Gillis, Blake,—16.

NAYS : — Messrs. Perry, Yeo, Hooper, Matheson, Farquhaáson, D. C. Martin, Sinclair, Maclaren, —8.

The main motion was then put and carried unanimously.

Hon. Mr. MACDONALD, from the Special Committee on Private Bills, and to whom was referred the Bill to be intituled : "An Act to Incorporate the Charlottetown Mutual Fire Insurance Company," to examine the same and report thereon, presented to the House their report that said Bill was of a private nature and liable to fees, and that thirty dollars be charged.

Ordered, That the Report of the Committee be adopted, and that the Bill be read a second time to-morrow.

House adjourned until to-morrow at three o'clock in the afternoon.

I. O.

THURSDAY, March 19.

Mr. SPEAKER in the chair.

CHARLOTTETOWN MUTUAL FIRE INSURANCE COMPANY.

On motion the Bill intituled "An Act to incorporate the Charlottetown Mutual Fire Insurance Company" was read the second time.

Hon. Mr. MACLEOD said in moving that the House do now go into Committee of the whole, for the consideration of the aforesaid Bill, it was customary to give some explanation of the nature of the Bill that was to be considered. The present Bill was for the purpose of establishing a Mutual Fire Insurance Company. At present there is no such company on the Island as all the companies now doing business are foreign companies. In his opinion it was time such a company was established. In 1849, a Mutual Fire Insurance Company had been establish d which did business on exactly the same principles as the one now proposed by this Bill. Although that company had done business for a number of years, no call had been made on the shareholders, nor was any call made until they had suffered a loss of $28,000 or $30,000 by a large fire that swept away a great amount of property in the city. Notwithstanding this great loss only one call had been made on the Shareholders, and when it was considered desirable to wind up the business of the incorporation, the sum of $14,000 had been divided among the Shareholders, after paying all the losses that had been sustained. It was a great pity the former company had been dissolved, for if it had continued, it would not only have made money for the shareholders, but would have saved a large amount to the citizens in general. If that company had continued we could get insurance effected at about one per cent. instead of paying four or five per cent. as had be to paid to day. Foreign companies have a monopoly of the Fire Insurance business and have adopted a scale of rates a great deal higher than should be charged, and we have to pay double what we had to do some time ago. It is time some company stepped in and remedied this state of affairs. The great trouble is that Foreign companies employ so many agents, who being paid by commission on the amount of premiums they collect, are induced to accept risks that should not be taken, whereby the losses of the companies are greatly increased. If a conservative company was established that would be careful to select only good risks the rate of insurance to those in a mutual company like the one now contemplated would be lessened. The

Bill, as introduced, only contemplated doing business in Charlottetown and Royalty, but now it is considered advisable to alter it, so that risks can be taken in any part of the Province, and it is proposed to amend the Bill for that purpose. Gentlemen in Prince and King's County may wish to take risks in this company and become shareholders and it is thought advisable to have the Bill framed so as to allow them to do so. The provisions of the Bill are identically the same as those of the former Mutual Fire Insurance Company Act. He would briefly refer to some of the more important clauses of the Bill. It provides for the appointment of seven directors who shall be directors of the Company for the year after it commences business. The members of the Company shall be all those who take risks in it. After the first year the members or shareholders of the Company shall elect the directors for the ensuing year. It provided that in case an extraordinary fire occurs, the shareholders shall be liable to a call or assessment of five per cent. of the amount they have insured and that only one such call shall be made in any one year. Thus the shareholder's utmost loss is the amount paid as premium and the assessment of five per cent. It will, however, be only in case of an extraordinary calamity that any calls or assessments will be required as the premiums will meet all ordinary losses. When it is considered that the old Fire Insurance Company only had to make one call in all the years they did business and that that call was necessitated by the great fire that swept away a large portion of the city, it will be seen that no great risk will be incurred by those who insured in this company. The bill also contained the usual provisions for holding real-estate mortgages and other securities to a certain figure. It is not advisable to give corporations the power of acquiring all the property in the province and this provision should be inserted in all bills of this nature. There are provisions for determining what shall constitute a quorum and other details necessary for the successful working of such companies. Every risk has to be submitted to the board of Directors and if accepted by them, a policy may then be issued. The gentlemen who will constitute the first Board are all good business men, and, no doubt, will carry on the business of the company for the first year in a careful manner. The next year the appointment of the Directors will be in the hands of the shareholders and it will then be to their interest to see that competent men are selected.

Motion put and carried.

The House accordingly resolved itself into the said Committee.

Mr. John Maclean in the chair.

On the first clause being read:

Hon. Mr. MACLEOD said he would move that the clause be amended by inserting the words "the Province of Prince Edward Island" in place of the words "Charlottetown, Common Lots, and Royalty."

On motion clause as amended agreed to.

On third clause being read.

MR. BENTLEY said he would like to know if a person insuring in this company was liable for five per cent. of the amount of his policy besides the premium that would be yearly charged to him. He believed it was a good thing for the Island to establish a company of this kind, as it would likely cause other companies to lower the rate of premium they will charge in the future, but he was afraid, if this clause was included in the Bill, that very few persons would be disposed to do business with the Company. He was not in favor of this part of the Bill.

Hon. Mr. MACLEOD said the last speaker did not seem to understand that this was a Mutual Fire Insurance Company and that no shares had to be purchased by the shareholders. If it was a stock company, the shareholders would have to pay into the funds of the company the amount of their shares, but in this company the shareholders pay for no stock. If ordinary losses occur they are paid out of the amount received from premiums only. If a very large fire occurs by which a large amount of the property insured in this company is destroyed, then five per cent. of the amount at risk can be claimed from those who are insured. In all probability the ordinary loss will be paid by the premiums. The old Fire Insurance Company only made one small call of one per cent. after paying a loss of $28,000, notwithstanding they did business for thirty-one years; and when the company was wound up $14,000 had been divided among the shareholders. This clause did not mean that a man shall pay five per cent. each year, but was only a provision that in case of a serious calamity, means should be forthcoming to meet the loss. The directors will look out that no large amount of insurance is effected in any one block. From the names of the directors he would not anticipate any great loss.

Hon. Mr. PROWSE said the object of the Bill was very good and likely the passing of it will have a good effect. During the last few years Insurance premiums had gone up one hundred per cent. without any sufficient reason. We know that a large number of companies are desirous of doing business and their agents are anxious to get a large number of risks. They employ everyone and any one to canvass for them, and in consequence many risks of a poor class are taken. In this way many losses are met with, and in consequence, those who want legitimate insurance have to pay a greater amount than they otherwise would have to do. He had

been told that it cost forty per cent. of the Premiums to pay the working expenses of these companies. A great part of these expenses should be saved by the establishment of this company. The old company only charged one half per cent. and during the years he (Mr. P.) had been insured in it he had no call to pay. The call was a very necessary part of the Bill as by it every insurer became a shareholder. Instead of paying their shares in money. they are allowed to retain their capital until a heavy loss occurred and even then the greatest amount they will have to pay will be five per cent. of the amount they had insured. If the company is well managed, there is no doubt, but it will bring down the cost of insurance.

Hon. Mr. FERGUSON said he was glad to see this Bill coming before the House as it was a general complaint that the rate of insurance was too high. The old company that had formerly done business had a wholesome influence on the business of the Island and no doubt this company would have an equally beneficial effect. The bill, however, should be amended so that the Government might be enabled to insure the Stock Farm buildings, the Asylum, Government House and other property in their possession. The Bill required that security should be given to the person insuring either by warrant of attorney. or other means, that the call of five per cent. when made would be paid, and he thought it desirable that some person on behalf of the Government, should be authorized to give this security.

Mr. SINCLAIR said he considered that those who insured would not be so safe as the company. The company are the insurers, and if he understood the matter aright, all the insured can make the company pay is the five per cent. of their policies. He did not think this was enough security. There are names among the directors that would induce people to insure and one fire might sweep away all the capital of the company and these men would only be liable for five per cent. of their insurance. He thought the people of the country should be protected and it was their duty as legislators to see that no bills were passed that would cause suffering. At present insurance in the country is not high as it can be obtained for one and a half per cent. for three years which is not an exhorbitant rate. And the companies now doing business not only had a large paid up capital, but had to deposit in the Dominion Treasury at Ottawa, large sums of money to secure the payment of any losses that occurred. The House would never legislate properly until Bills of this kind are printed, as honorable members cannot vote conscientiously on them, when they do not understand their nature

Mr. FARQUHARSON said if the honorable member insures for $1,000 he would be liable for five per cent. of it, if the premiums received by the company would not cover the losses they sustained. It looked a small security in case of a large fire, but those who insured were aware of this when they accepted the risk. When men insure in this company they get a rate at least one half less than they now had to pay in Charlottetown, and if a great calamity occurred, there was a chance of securing a fair share of profits. The bill contained a provision for dividing these profits and parties insuring will no doubt get their insurance at a great deal less than they now have to pay. A great many citizens are willing to come into this company and the premiums will amount to a considerable fund, and if ordinary care is taken there is no risk of any call being made on the shareholders. The old company insured at half of one per cent. and had a considerable surplus, and now that foreign companies had trebled this rate, no doubt plenty of risks of the very best character can be obtained.

Dr. GILLIS said as this call of five per cent. could only be made once in each year and as the formation of such a company would have a great effect on other companies doing business in the Province, he believed that it was right and proper that this Bill should be passed. If care was taken in accepting only good risks, no heavy losses might occur for many years.

Hon. Mr. PROWSE said he would like to know what provisions are made in this measure for dividing any profits that may be accumulated from the payment of premiums? As it is a mutual company every one who insures had a right to a share of the profits, and he thought it only proper that all those who had been insured should have a share when the profits were divided. The profits may go on accumulating for years and a set of rascally directors may refuse to continue the insurance of men who had been paying into the funds of the company for a long time in order that they might not be eligible for a share of the accumulated profits. The profits might in this way be divided among those who did not pay towards them.

Mr. FARQUHARSON said as only those who remain in the company are liable for the five per cent. call, that he did not see how those who withdrew from it, could claim any share of the profits that might accrue. He would like to see the interests of those who had to go out of the company secured, but he did not see how it could be done.

Hon. Mr. MACLEOD said the man who dropped out of the company cannot expect a share in profits that may accumulate after he had left it. The profits that accumulate while a person is in the company will be distributed among the shareholders as dividends, part of which he will receive. The directors are only appointed for the management of the company and not for the purpose of winding it up, a matter which will be altogether in the hands of the

company. Due notice must be given to the shareholders to attend any meeting for such a purpose and in this way no shareholder can be defrauded.

Hon. Mr. PROWSE said a person may have $10,000 of insurance for a number of years and the directors may then say that they are not disposed to carry his risk any longer. This person after paying in a large amount to the funds of the company may be deprived of any share of the accumulated profits that he has directly contributed to. Every man who insures has a direct interest in the affairs of the company and some means should be adopted by which the interests of such a case as he had instanced would be secured.

Hon. Mr. MACLEOD said he observed that there was a provision in the Bill incorporating the old company that the Government could insure in it, and he would move that a similar clause be added to the Bill under consideration.

Mr. SINCLAIR said it was the duty of Legislators to see that Bills passed are prepared carefully. If this amendment is inserted in this Bill great loss may be occasioned some future government. Suppose the Government insure public property in this company and after a time another lot of men are selected to conduct the affairs of the Government, this company may refuse to accept the risks of the new Government, and the country will lose any share of profits that may have accrued while the public property was insured. This clause may be used to further party interests and he would not approve of it.

Hon. Mr. MACLEOD said it was not likely that any directors of the company would refuse good risks in order to shut men out of the company who had been insured in it. If the shareholders find the directors acting so unfairly, it will be easy for them to dismiss the directors and elect new ones.

Mr. A. MARTIN said he thought the profits that accrued should be divided at stated periods By this means all persons who insured in the company would have an opportunity of receiving a share of the profits that accumulated during these periods, and while they were insured.

Mr. BENTLEY said that he understood that the person who insured in this company would get a share of the dividends each year while he was a member of the company. After a member leaves the company he cannot expect to get a share of any profits that afterwards may be made. As he now understood the Bill, the five per cent. clause was a very good one, as it gave every person who insured, an interest in the proper working of the company.

Clause as amended agreed to.

The clause of the bill, referring to meetings of the company having been read.

Hon. Mr. MACLEOD said the Bill contained provisions for holding the annual meeting of the company once a year, but a special meeting can be called by twenty-five policy holders, and notice calling said meeting can be given by publishing the time and place and purpose of meeting in some newspaper for blank number of days. He thought fourteen days would be short enough notice to give of such meetings and would move that the blank be filled with the word fourteen.

Motion agreed to.

Clause agreed to.

On motion Mr. Speaker resumed the chair and progress was reported, and leave obtained to sit again.

House adjourned until to-morrow afternoon at three o'clock.

G. F. O.

FRIDAY, March 20.

A petition from James A. Macleod, Donald MacNeill, George Henderson, and others, Trustees of the Free Church of Charlottetown, was presented to the House by Hon. N. McLeod, and the same was received and read, praying that An Act be passed, vesting certain lands and property in John D. Macleod, of Charlottetown, in fee simple.

Ordered, That said petition be referred to a Special Committee, to report thereon by Bill or otherwise, and that Honorable Mr. MacLeod, Mr. John Maclean and Mr. Blake do compose the said Committee.

Hon. Mr. MACLEOD from the last preceding Committee appointed, presented to the House a Bill as prepared by the Committee, to be intituled "An Act to enable the Minister and Trustees of the Free Church Congregation, in the City of Charlottetown, to sell certain Lands," and the same was received and read the first time, and referred to the Private Bill Committee to examine the same and report thereon.

On motion of Honorable Mr Macleod, the House resolved itself into a Committee of the whole to take into further consideration "An Act to incorporate the Charlottetown Mutual Fire Insurance Company."

Mr. John Maclean in the chair

A clause having been read:

Hon. Mr. MACLEOD said that this clause would limit the power of persons who insured very heavily in this company; and prevent them from having a preponderating influence. Under this Bill, no party will have more than four votes. It would be better not to give any person too many votes, in order that he may not be inclined to wind up the affairs of the company too soon.

On motion, the clause was agreed to.

The remaining clauses of the Bill were severally read and agreed to, without debate.

On motion, Mr. Speaker resumed the Chair, and the Chairman reported the Bill agreed to.

Ordered, That the said Bill be engrossed, and that it be read the third time to-morrow.

Hon. Mr. SULLIVAN, a member of Her Majesty's Executive Council, presented to the House by command of His Honor the Lieutenant Governor,—

The Report of the Provincial Auditor on Public Accounts of the Province of Prince Edward Island for the financial year ended 31st December, 1884.

Ordered, That said Report be referred to the Committee on Public Accounts.

Hon. Mr. FERGUSON, a member of Her Majesty's Executive Council presented to the House, by command of His Honor the Lieutenant Governor,—

The Report of the Commissioner of Crown and Public Lands for the year 1884.

Ordered, That said Report be referred to the Committee on Public Accounts.

Hon. Mr. SULLIVAN, a member of Her Majesty's Executive Council, presented to the House by command of His Honor the Lieutenant Governor,—

The Report of the Trustees and Medical Superintendent of the Prince Edward Island Hospital for the Insane, for the year 1884.

Ordered, That said report do lie on the table.

Hon. Mr. Sullivan a member of Her Majesty's Executive Council, delivered to Mr. Speaker a message from His Honor the Lieutenant Governor, and the said message was read by Mr. Speaker, all the members of the House being uncovered, and is as follows:

A. A. MACDONALD, Lieut. Governor.

The Lieut. Governor transmits estimates of the sums required for the service of the Province for the current year, and in accordance with the provisions of the British North America Act, 1867, and recommends these estimates to the House of Assembly.

Government House,　　}
　　March 19, 1885.　　}

Ordered, That the accompanying Estimates do lie on the table.

House adjourned until to-morrow forenoon at ten o'clock.

I. O.

SATURDAY, March 21.

Hon. Mr. MACDONALD from the Private Bills Committee, to whom was referred the Bill intituled "An Act to enable the Ministers and Trustees of the Free Church

Congregation in the City of Charlottetown, to sell certain lands," reported that the Bill was of a private nature and recommended that a fee of Twelve Dollars be charged.

Report adopted.

Mr. A. MARTIN in accordance with notice placed on the Order Book asked the honorable Commissioner of Public Works to lay on the Table of the House a return or statement of all the expenditure by the Government in connection with the Southport Ferry from the year 1869 to 1884, both inclusive.

Hon. Mr. CAMPBELL said the report asked for by the honorable junior member for Belfast was being prepared. It would take some time to get the report ready, but as soon as the Secretary of his department could get the report ready, it will be presented.

A petition of J. M. Sutherland, L. L. Beer, W. A. Weeks and other shareholders of the Charlottetown Woollen Company was presented to the House by the Hon. Mr. Campbell, and the same was received and read, praying for an Act to empower them to increase the capital stock of said company from time to time or all at one time until it shall reach the sum of one hundred thousand dollars.

Ordered, That said petition be referred to a Special Committee to examine the same and report thereon by Bill or otherwise.

Ordered, That Honorable Mr.

Campbell Mr. McKay and Mr. Blake compose said Committee.

Hon. Mr. Campbell, from the last preceding Committe appointed, presented to the House a Bill as prepared by the Committee, to be intituled ". An Act to amend An Act to incorporate the Charlottetown Woolen Factory Company, and the same was received and read the first time, and ordered to be relerred to the Special Committee on Private Bills, to examine the same and report thereon.

TELEPHONE COMPANY.

A petition of Charles Palmer, B. Rogers, M. Macleod and others, was presented to the House by Mr. Sullivan, and the same was received and read, praying for An Act to incorporate the Telephone Company of Prince Edward Island.

Ordered, That said petition be referred to a Special Committee to examine the same and report thereon, by Bill or otherwise.

Ordered, That Honorable Mr. Sullivan, Honorable Mr. Prowse and Hon. Mr. Gordon compose said Committee.

Hon. Mr. SULLIVAN from the last preceding Committee appointed presented to the House a Bill, as prepared by the Committee, to be intituled ". An Act to incorporate the Telephone Company of Prince Edward Island," and the same was received and read the first time, and ordered to

be referred to the Special Committee on Private Bills to examine the same and report thereon.

ACT RESPECTING PROCEDURE IN SUPREME COURT AND COURT OF CHANCERY.

The Order of the Day for the House in Committee on the second reading of the Bill to be intituled, "An Act respecting procedure in Supreme Court and Court of Chancery," having been read.

Hon. Mr. SULLIVAN moved that the House do now go into the Order of the Day and said the Bill before them only contained a few simple provisions which are considered desirable in order to facilitate and expedite proceedings in the Supreme Court and Court of Chancery. At present parties suing on Notes of Hand, bills of exchange or other documents of this kind are met with pleas that the defendant did not make the note or did not endorse or accept the Bill of Exchange, although none of these claims have any foundation in fact. By means of such pleas the trial of the suit may be put off for some time, and it has often been found that these pleas are only mere subterfuges to keep the creditor out of his rights. It is often found that the debtor who puts in these false pleas, makes away or disposes of all his property during the time the suit is pending whereby the creditor loses not only his just claim but also the costs. The object of the several provisions of the Bill are not to take away any rights that the debtor now has, but to require, that when sued, the defendant shall make an affidavit before a Judge setting forth the particulars of his defence and the reason why he will contest the Plaintiff's claim, when such is done, it will be for the Jury and Court to decide on the merits of the case. Another provision is to remedy the following grievance. A firm can sue for any amount owing them and the party sued may set forth his statement, but need not set up any objection to the names of the parties composing the firm, or that there are more parties in the firm than mentioned in the summons and may by doing so put the Plaintiff to great costs. This clause provides that if such a defense is to be made, that the party making it will be required to make an affidavit that this is his objection to the claim and by doing so, will enable the firm to have satisfactory evidence of the names of the parties who compose it or to withdraw the suit without additional cost. At present parties doing business have hardly any protection. When they come to realize their debts they are met with pleas of this nature by which the collection of their claims are deferred until the debtor has an opportunity to make away with all his property, when the creditor is set at defiance. It is desirable that the procedure of our Courts should not be made a means by which honest men can be defrauded out of their just rights.

Motion carried. House resolved itself into a committe of the whole.

Mr. Holland in the chair.

Mr. D. C. MARTIN said a similar Bill to the one under consideration was before the House last session, and was framed entirely in the interest of foreign corporations. He felt sure this Bill was not a judicious one. Although the clause under consideration was not very objectionable, the Bill contained a clause requiring a man to swear to what he had no means of proving or of knowing whether he was right or not. That clause was against the interests of the poor man, as it changed the course of procedure now adopted.

Hon. Mr. SULLIVAN said the clause under consideration was identical with the one passed last year, after considerable discussion and as the honorable member said it was not objectionable, he considered it would expedite the business of the House, if objections were only taken to such clauses as were objectionable.

Mr. FARQUHARSON said he did not see anything objectionable in this clause. If a man contracts a debt, he ought to pay the party with whom he contracts it. We often see that companies are formed such as John Smith & Co., and after a time John Smith goes out, and yet the name is continued. People give the company credit because John Smith is a good man, although he may have no interest in the firm bearing his name. He (Mr. F.) considered that such companies should be compelled to set forth all the names of the partners, and provision should be made in this Bill that they do so.

Hon. Mr. SULLIVAN said no doubt there was considerable in what the honorable member said, but we have a law on our statute book already that met the case. This law required that all firms should register the names of their several partners before they could collect their debts. It is the business of the man who gives credit to see that John Smith and Company are solvent and no law we can make will suit the case better than the present law of partnership. The clause under consideration is to meet another case. Suppose the Charlottetown Woolen Company or the Amherst Boot and Shoe Company gave credit and the person to whom they do so comes and says he did not owe them, and he can set them at defiance, until he puts his property out of the way. Then he will come into court and say the Company had not carried out the provisions of their act of incorporation. This clause provides, that if such a defense is intended to be set up, it must be put forward at once and can not be brought in afterwards. Of course the plaintiff would have to prove his claim in the ordinary way even though no such objection was put in by the defendant.

Mr. D. C. MARTIN said the clause was objectionable because by it, it would not be necessary to prove to partnerships. Suppose a party signed a note in favor of the Charlottetown Woolen Company and is sued for it by persons representing themselves as such company and judgment is given against him, and afterwards suppose the real company sue for the debt, the person may have to pay the debt twice. This clause by requiring the defendant to make an affidavit before putting in his defence, was against the interest of the defendant.

Hon. Mr. SULLIVAN said the clause was very plain. Suppose a company brings an action against John Smith, he pleads he never contracted any debt. When the case came to be tried, the defendant may then say that the corporation had no power to sue, and may gain further time, while the evidence necessary to prove the right of the company to sue is forthcoming. Now this clause said that if the defense he intends setting up is of this nature, that it must be set forth at first and not brought in afterwards. If you are sued by a company, and put in a defense that the company had no power to sue, it is all right, for then the company will be prepared to prove their right to take the action. This clause only provides that the defendant shall set forth what the defense really is. If he makes objection to the corporation, either to its composition or conduct, it must be put forth along with any other defence that will be set up. It is the same as in the School Act where the party sued had to set forth the particulars of his defence so that the Trustees might know on what grounds the action is defended. The only difference this clause will make is that the Plaintiff will know if the defendant means to take up this defence. In case it is not set up, all the company will have to do will be to set up a *prima facie* case, and prove that the goods or value was delivered.

Clause agreed to.

Another clause being read.

Mr. D. C. MARTIN said this was the objectionable clause of which he had spoken, as it necessitated an affidavit on the part of the defendant and is drawn up in the interest of Foreign corporations. It puts the defendant on his defence in a matter that at present the plaintiff had to prove. The defendant had to swear that these parties who are suing him, do not compose the company, before he can put in his defence, although it may be altogether of a different nature. If I sign a note to J. Jones & Co., J. Smith may claim to be one of the firm, and sue for the amount of it, and if the firm did business outside of the Island, I have to swear that he is not one of the firm before I can plead.

Hon. Mr. SULLIVAN said it was not so at all. All corporations must produce *prima facie* evidence of their claim. Every defence a party had could be set up. All the rights the defendant had at present could be maintained and continued without this Bill, and this provision was only intended to expedite the business of the

Courts. Suppose the Firm that is sueing changes its partners, has the buyer a right to turn round and say that the firm has no right to sue because it was not composed of the same partners as when the debt was contracted or not exactly as represented in the summons. The debtor may leave this defence to the very last in order to practise dishonesty and if so inclined, there is nothing at present to prevent him doing so. A similar law to this one exists in Ontario, Nova Scotia, New Brunswick and in almost every civilized country where no bankrupt law is in force.

Mr. D. C. MARTIN said we had a law requiring parties composing a firm to prove their partnership, but this law changes that excellent provision. Why should a debtor be placed in a worse position? According to this Act the defendant had to swear that the plaintiff was not the party legally authorized to sue, instead of the plaintiff having to swear that he was the proper party.

Mr. FARQUHARSON said it was evident that this Bill was not in the interest of local companies, who were registered, but in the interest of foreign companies who were not registered. He did not think a man should be exempt from debt because the plaintiff cannot prove that he is a regular member of a corporation, but it should be provided that the person suing should prove that he was the proper person to bring the action and recover the debt.

On motion Mr. Speaker resumed the Chair, and progress was reported and leave given the Committee to sit again.

Hon. Mr. SULLIVAN a member of Her Majesty's Executive Council, presented to the House by command of His Honor the Lieutenant Governor a Report of the Public Schools of Prince Edward Island for year 1884.

Ordered, That said report do lie on the table.

Hon. A. J. MACDONALD from the Private Bills Committee and to whom was referred the Bill intituled "An Act to amend the Act to incorporate the Charlottetown Woolen Company" reported that the Bill was of a private nature and recommended that ten dollars be charged.

Report adopted.

Hon. A. J. MACDONALD from the Private Bills Committee and to whom was referred the Bill intituled "An Act to incorporate the Telephone Company of Prince Edward Island," reported that the Bill was of a private nature and recommended that Twenty-five dollars be charged.

Report adopted.

Hon. Mr. SULLIVAN moved that the Bill intituled "An Act to incorporate the Telephone Company of Prince Edward Island," be read the second time on Monday.

Motion put and carried.

Hon. A. J. MACDONALD for Non Commissioner of Public Works moved that the Bill intituled "An Act to amend the Act to incorporate the Charlottetown Woolen Company," be read the second time on Monday.

Motion put and carried.

Hon. Mr. MACLEOD moved that the Bill intituled "An Act to enable the Minister and Trustees of the Free Church Congregation in the city of Charlottetown to sell certain lands," be read the second time on Monday.

Motion put and carried.

House adjourned until Monday afternoon at three o'clock.

G. F. O.

MONDAY, March 23.

On motion of the honorable Mr. Campbell seconded by Mr. Blake, the Bill to be intituled "An Act for the Incorporation of the Charlottetown Woolen Company," was read the second time, and committed to a committee of the whole House.

The House accordingly resolved itself into the said committee.

Mr. ALEX. MARTIN in the Chair.

The first clause having been read.

Hon. Mr. CAMPBELL remarked

that the Company had been incorporated with a Capital Stock of $10,000; and now, wished to increase the latter to $100,000.

Hon. Mr. Prowse said that a former Woolen Manufacturing Company, occupying the same premises were obliged to close up their business but this company were desirous of extending theirs. The National Policy had, no doubt, been the cause. It was time for the honorable member for West River to make a recantation of his principles in that respect.

Mr. Farquharson thought the National Policy had ruined thousands of persons in the Dominion. Manufacturing operations are, in many cases, dying out, and our business men are suffering. The National Policy had nothing whatever to do with this Company's operations. Many industries are prospering in spite of the National Policy. The honorable member for Murray Harbor was a manufacturer, and he (Mr. F.) would venture to say that he was making no more money out of it than out of the Moncton Lock Factory.

Hon. Mr. Campbell thought the prosperity of this company was very largely owing to the National Policy. The old company went to the ground for want of protection. He understood that the present Editor of the *Patriot* was the organizer of that company, and that it died a natural death. He was free to admit that the new company was under much better business management than the old one had been. How many Starch Factories had we in the Province previous to Confederation? Not one!

Mr. Farquharson.—Starch in the United States is worth about $75 a ton, but we have to pay about $40 per ton duty to get it there. It is admitted free of duty into Free Trade England, however.

Hon. Mr. Prowse said that the honorable gentleman who had just sat down was protected in this country to the extent of two cents per pound duty, on starch. He (Mr. P.) was very well satisfied with the Starch Manufacturing Business, and believed that it will succeed in this country. The National Policy has caused a large amount of money to be invested in manufacturing, which otherwise would be lying idle. This Woolen Company is doing a great deal of good, as it converts the raw material into manufactured goods, and gives employment to a large number of people. He believed that it showed the good effects of the National Policy more than any other business in this Dominion

Clause agreed to.

On motion, Mr. Speaker resumed the Chair; and the Chairman reported the Bill agreed to, without any amendment.

Ordered, That the said Bill be engrossed; and that it be read the third time to-morrow.

Mr. BEER, according to previous notice on the Order Book, asked the honorable Commissioner of Public Works when he expected to lay on the table of the House the Report of the Public Works Department.

Hon. Mr. CAMPBELL expected to be able to do so to-morrow.

Mr. FARQUHARSON according to previous notice placed by him on the Order Book asked the honorable Commissioner of Public Works to lay on the table of the House a detailed account, to date, of all contracts entered into by tender or otherwise since 31st December, 1884, and the amount for which each contract was let; also, the contracts (unfinished) carried forward from last year, and the amounts due on them; also the amount of work done on the Public Works since 31st December, 1883, and not tendered for or sold by public auction.

Hon. Mr. CAMPBELL said that so far as the first part of the honorable member's question was concerned, the papers would be laid on the table of the House as soon as possible. The reply as to unfinished contracts will be contained in the Report of the Department when laid on the table of the House. The detailed statement asked for in the latter part of the question cannot be furnished before the last of April, as its preparation involves a large amount of work. If the honorable member would divide his question, and ask for each item separately,

answers could be given on some of them within a week or ten days. Some contracts are as low as one dollar, while others are over $10. By asking for the latter class, the honorable member would obtain an earlier reply.

Mr. FARQUHARSON had asked a question, and had a right to receive a reply. A large sum of money was spent for work done by the day, without tender or sale of any kind. He would therefore ask a return of all payments over ten dollars at least.

Hon. Mr. CAMPBELL —Would the honorable member name the particular works of which he wants a Return? If he would do so, a return would be furnished at once, as he (Mr. C.) had nothing to conceal.

Mr. BEER said that the honorable member for West River had asked a reasonable question, and if the Secretary of Public Works had not time to prepare it, help should be afforded him for that purpose. Many questions will yet be asked before the House rises, and the Opposition expect replies within a reasonable time.

Hon. Mr. PROWSE said there appeared to be a sort of mania on the other side of the House, for asking questions. The same thing prevailed among the Opposition in the House of Commons at Ottawa. Members there had asked questions, the preparations for Replies to which cost considerable sums of money, yet many of the papers containing those Replies had never been opened after being laid on the table. The honorable Commissioner of Public Works had, in the present case, made to the honorable member for West River a very fair offer, to facilitate the preparation of the answer to the latter's question.

Mr. D. C. MARTIN said that a question of the same nature as that now asked by the honorable for West River was asked last year, and a similar fuss was made about giving a reply. The Opposition were entitled to a full answer to all such questions. If the Assistant in that Department had not time to prepare answers, help should be afforded him. The Opposition could not vote intelligently on such matters, without the information sought.

Hon. Mr. FERGUSON said that some honorable members had asked questions without having a very definite idea of what they were asking for. In some cases, they had little idea of the expense and trouble entailed upon a Public Department to furnish the information asked for. And if assistance were called in to help to prepare the papers required, it is probable that honorable members of the Opposition would be the first to find fault. The honorable member now asked for something that would necessitate going into the Returns of every Supervisor in the Province, in order to obtain a reply thereto. In fact, to obtain that Reply would involve an amount of labor altogether unreasonable to impose upon the Public Works Department. That honorable gentleman should put his question in such a form that a reply could be given within a reasonable time. But the object evidently was to have an opportunity to say that the Government refused to give the information asked for.

Hon. Mr. CAMPBELL did not want to shirk this question. He was anxious to supply all the information asked for, in a proper manner. Under the Statute every Supervisor is allowed to expend ten per cent. of the money entrusted to him for expenditure, by private contract, without tender or sale by auction. In order to ascertain the answer to a part of the question of the honorable member for West River, it would be necessary for him (Mr. C.) to call before him every Supervisor in the Province and ask him how much of the work supervised by him was sold without Public Auction. How unreasonable such a request! Let the honorable gentleman name three, four, six, or ten contracts of any Public Works in this Province for which he wants a return, and it will be cheerfully furnished. He knew the honorable member's object, and would defy him to show any mismanagement.

Mr. FARQUHARSON thought that the Returns of the Supervisors should show what he had asked for.

Mr. MACKAY thought it would

be a very laborious task to answer the question of the honorable member for West River. If the honorable gentleman wanted the details of any particular contract or contracts, why did he not ask for them ? If, in order to obtain a reply to the honorable member's question, a vast amount of hard labor would be required, the House may be prorogued before it could be given. Let the honorable member ask the question in such a way that a Reply could be given him without entailing so much labor. He would support his honorable colleague in asking for any information which will conduce to the interests of the people of this country. If, however, it would take weeks to prepare the documents asked for, he did not think the question should be entertained.

Hon. Mr. CAMPBELL said that if he understood the question, the desire of the honorable member for West River was to ascertain how much work in his Department was performed by the day, instead of being let by Public Auction. This information would be supplied within one week.

On motion of Honorable Mr. Sullivan, the Bill intituled " An Act to incorporate the Charlotte town Mutual Fire Insurance Company," was read the third time and passed.

House adjourned until to-morrow forenoon at ten o'clock.

I. O.

TUESDAY, March 24.

MORNING SESSION.

Mr. Speaker in the Chair.

An Act to further amend An Act respecting the Garnishment of Debts.

Hon. Mr. SULLIVAN having obtained leave, presented to the House a Bill to be intituled " An Act respecting the Garnishment of Debts," and the same was received and read the first time, and was ordered to be read a second time to-morrow.

CHARLOTTETOWN WOOLLEN COMPANY.

On motion of Mr. Campbell " An Act to amend the Act to incorporate the Charlottetown Woollen Company was read the third time and passed.

On motion of Honorable Mr. Sullivan the House resolved itself into a committee of the whole for the purpose of further considering the Bill intituled " An Act respecting Procedure in the Supreme Court and Court of Chancery.

Mr. JOHN MACLEAN in the Chair:

The clause under consideration having been read.

Hon. Mr. PROWSE said it appeared extraordinary that every Session Bills to regulate the Procedure of the Supreme Court are passed. It seemed that the more bills that are passed the more that are wanted. What the people wanted was equity and not law, and he did not see why the rules and regulations of the Courts should not be left to the Judges. These amendments entail large expenditure and cost the poor people of the country large sums of money. There is too much expense put upon the people.

Mr. SINCLAIR said the honorable Leader of the Government almost promised last year, to have Bills coming before this House printed. Every year there are lots of Lawyer's Bills submitted some of which were of very questionable benefit. He considered last session that the Bill introduced by the senior member for the city was among this class and after seeing it in print he was confirmed in his opinion that it was an injurious Act. Bills are introduced and honorable members not being very well acquainted with their provisions do not like to go against what the lawyers say in reference to them. He did not think judgment should be passed before the evidence was heard. The least thing honorable members could get was that those bills should be printed, when honorable members would be accountable for what was legislated on. When a chairman of committee did not read distinctly, it was impossible to understand the nature of the clause they were asked to legislate on.

Hon. Mr. MACLEOD said the honorable member for Springton had referred to the Bill passed last Session known as the " Chancery Act 1884." There was nothing objectionable in that measure for a number of tedious suits that had been hanging for years had been brought to a termination through its operation. It was scandalous the way chancery suits had been allowed to drag from year to year. The practice in Prince Edward Island in reference to suits in the Chancery Court was like the practice in England one hundred years ago and required amendment and it was found that the Bill passed last year worked admirably. Some provisions of it that had been alluded to in the Press, might not be beneficial, but no harm had yet arisen from them. The clause of the Bill under discussion provided that when a party signed a note and wished to contest the payment of it, he had to make an affidavit before he could get an order from a Judge of the Supreme Court to allow him to put in his defence. He (Mr. McL.) did not approve of the clause as it would involve considerable expense on the part of the defendant, who would have to employ an attorney to draw such affidavit and to get the Judge's order. He believed it would be prejudicial to the poorer classes both in town and country. Although it was the law in other provinces we could get along very well without it.

Hon. Mr. SULLIVAN said he would explain the necessity of the clause. As the law is at present any firm or individual may hold a note, and issue a writ against the party making it The party may say he never made the note or put in any other defence, which might occur to his imagination. The plea that the defendant never made the note is a very common one and the process of trial is often postponed indefinitely. When the plaintiff at last obtains a judgment, he finds the defendant has disposed of his property. He (Mr. S.) knew of hundreds of such cases since the bankruptcy law had been repealed. This clause could not injure the party sued for at present the procedure in practice allows Lawyers to put off the case, whereby the Plaintiff often had to pay large amounts of costs incurred on both sides. These costs are incurred by delaying the trial. If the defendant has a good defence he has the same right of putting it in as he had now. The only change is that the defendant shall show that he has a good defence and wishes to go to trial. You cannot get any snap judgment through the passing of this clause of the Bill and he did not see any injury that would accrue from it. It will hasten the time in which honest debts can be collected. There is a considerable amount of suing both in the County and Supreme Courts and this clause will be an advantage to both the debtor and creditor as it would save large amounts of costs.

Mr. D C. MARTIN said the only objection to this clause was that the debtor had to make an affidavit and the Plaintiff was not required

to do so. If the creditor had to make an affidavit that the debt was due before getting a writ, it would not be so unfair. Everything is in favor of the creditor in this clause and it was not reasonable that such should be the case. At present the debtor had only to put in his defence and the creditor had then to prove his case and if no defence is put in can get judgment in eight days. There is nothing in the clause to prevent the defendant doing away with his property as even if it is passed the debtor will have sixteen days to put his property out of the reach of his creditor.

Mr. SINCLAIR said debtors did not always lose the cases they contested as they often had good cases and gained their suits. By this clause the defendant is put to double expense and had to stand a trial afterwards

Hon. Mr. FERGUSON said if the defendant had a good case, he could get the costs incurred, paid by the creditor. All this clause required was that the debtor made an affidavit, and proved that he had really a good defence.

Mr. BLAKE said the law at present was in favor of the dishonest man. If you take an action to recover a debt, the debtor can delay proceedings, and when you finally get the case tried and recover judgment you find that all the property had been done away with. If any obstacles are placed in the way of honest men collecting their debts it is a mistake. The laws are made for honest men, but unfortunately dishonest ones take advantage of them. He was not acquainted with the law, but would be sorry to see anything passed by this Legislature that would be against the interests of honest men. Bills of this nature should be printed before coming before the House so honorable members could understand them, but from what he understood of the clause under consideration, he did not think any hardship would arise from it.

Mr. SINCLAIR said at present a creditor can take a debtor before the courts, but by this clause the debtor had first to go before a judge before he can defend his case in the Courts. If a creditor sues it should be sufficient for both parties to have an opportunity of being heard when the case came to trial. The more this clause is examined the worse it appeared as it actually strikes at "Magna Charta" the great bulwark of the liberties of British subjects. This Bill gives the Judge power to determine whether the defendant had a good case or not. Every person should be allowed to go to our courts with his defence. The operation of this clause will occasion additional expenses, and whether the defendant gained or lost, the parties would be charged heavy costs.

Mr. FARQUHARSON said at present the defendant had to put in his defence within eight days and he did not understand the honorable senior member for Belfast when he said the debtor had sixteen days to do away with his property. It may work injuriously to cause some to comply with this clause but it will work beneficially for a great many who are foolish enough to incur heavy expenses in putting off the trial of their cases. He agreed with other honorable members that these Bills should be printed so their nature could be understood.

Hon Mr. MACLEOD said he did not consider this Bill hard to understand. As the Law now stands the defendant can put in his defence within eight days and he may have different objects in doing so. Under this clause he must put in his plea in eight days and at the end of another eight days he must put in his real defence, and prove to the satisfaction of the Judge that it is a valid one. This may be a great hardship to a poor man, who has a complicated defence. It will cost him a considerable sum to have it properly done, and it will often prevent the poor man from doing so. This clause constitutes the Judge both judge and jury and it is not desirable to do so. The clause said the affidavit can be made before a Commissioner for taking affidavits, but it is a well known fact, that the great majority of the commissioners are not qualified to draw up such an affidavit properly. The defendant often pleads a set off that the Judge would not accept but which the jury might consider a good defence. If the Judge is arbitrary he can refuse to give the order to enable the defendant to plead his case before a jury and great hardship may be caused. Many e ences against suits can not be set out by a poor man at short otice. There are various reasons why a promissory note can not be collected. Suppose a man joined another person in making a note or endorsed the note to a third party, and that he had an idea that the plaintiff had given additional time to the maker of the note, and in consequence that he was not liable to pay it. At present he puts this in for his defence and at the Court calls the maker of the note and other witnesses to prove this fact, and gets an opportunity to show that he is not liable. This clause would take away this privilege, unless he made an affidavit to what perhaps he was not very sure about. He knew that some are not scrupulous about making affidavits but the honest man would through this clause be most liable to suffer. It is customary to put off trials for want of evidence and people do not often hesitate to make an affidavit in order to do so, but it was not right to require persons to make affidavits to facts they were not very sure about. He had heard of a party who being anxious to have a trial put off was told that it would be necessary to make an affidavit that additional evidence was required in order to do so. When the party was told this, he said "fill up the necessary affidavit and I will swear to it." You can sue now in any County for debts contracted within the province and the business of the courts was not

often unnecessarily delayed. If a man chooses to put away his property he can do it in sixteen days as easily as he can do it in two months and the passing of this clause will not enable creditors to secure their debts any better than they can at present.

Mr. BEER said it appeared that when lawyers differed the clients had to pay the costs. Judging from what had been said respecting the clause under consideration, he thought it would work injuriously.

Hon. Mr. SULLIVAN said notwithstanding all that had been said against this clause he considered it a most equitable provision. He would again read the clause so honorable members would understand that no privilege will be taken away by its operation. All it necessitated was that the defendant had to swear that he had a good defence, and it would not be necessary for him to be prepared with witnesses at that time. It seemed to him that it was most equitable and it gave the defendant sixteen days to put in his defence. He could not see where any hardship would arise from this provision. It should not be forgotten that often honest poor people are the plaintiffs in cases of this kind and may be set at defiance by a party who by putting in the customary pleas can defer the case for a long time. The hardships talked of would be as often on one side as the other. This clause will not be so good for the lawyers as the present practice, as not so many defences will be put in after it came into operation and the lawyers will get less to do. This Bill had been passed by this House last year and he did not see why this clause was more objectionable now than it had been then. There is no law but will sometimes create hard ships, nevertheless all laws should be for the greatest good to the greatest number of people. If it took away any right he would not advocate it. It only provided that if a man had no defence, it should appear at the first and not be left until heavy expenses had been incurred. If the defendant had a good defence or even a defence of any kind, it was necessary that he should put it forth and make an affidavit that he contested the suit for these reasons.

Mr. BEER said the case instanced by the honorable senior member for the City was very much to the point. This clause would prevent such defences being put in, and would, no doubt, be the cause of hardship.

On motion of Honorable Mr. Mr. Macleod the clause was disagreed to.

On motion of Honorable Mr. Sullivan Mr. Speaker resumed the Chair.

House adjourned for one hour.
G. F. O.

AFTERNOON SESSION.

Hon. Mr. SULLIVAN pursuant to notice given to him on the Order Book, moved that the House do now resolve itself into a Committee of the whole to take into consideration the expediency of introducing a Bill to improve and consolidate the Laws relating to Bills of Sale; and said that a Bill similar to the present one was introduced in 1883, and also in 1884, but the Legislative Council refused to pass it, being, he understood, under some misapprehension with reference to it. This is a public Bill, and he hoped no honorable member would regard it as affecting himself individually. On the contrary, all should divest themselves of all private feelings in regard to it, and treat it as a public measure. The law now in force relating to Bills of Sale was passed in 1860, and works injuriously to both Debtors and Creditors. At the present time, there are in the Protbonotary's Office no less than 19,000 Bills of Sale, and in the other two Counties there is also a large number. In examining these, it is impossible for any one to say what portion of the amount for which they were given is due. The Bill now before the House will provide that within a reasonable time the creditor shall certify whether all, or a certain amount is due, or whether the Debt has been paid. At present, when a Sheriff goes and levies upon some property, and he is told that there is a Bill of Sale upon it, he has to take the responsibility and run the risk of being prosecuted, if he levies upon it. Now, that is not a position in which the law should allow the Sheriff to be placed. It is, therefore, proposed that after a certain period, every person who holds a Bill of Sale, shall forfeit the amount due upon it, and that it shall be null and void. It was for the House to deal with the Bill as it saw fit and proper.

Motion put and carried.

The House accordingly resolved itself into the said committee.

Mr. ALEXANDER MARTIN in the Chair.

Hon. Mr. SULLIVAN moved the following—

Resolved, That it is expedient to introduce a Bill to improve and consolidate the Laws relating to Bills of Sale.

Resolution agreed to.

Hon. Mr. SULLIVAN moved the following :

Resolved, That for the services respecting Bills of Sale the Prothonotary shall receive for the use of the Government, the following fees, namely :

For Filing each Instrument, including Affidavits, and entering the same in a Book, —— cents.

For Filing Assignment of each Instrument, including Affidavits, and for making all proper endorsements in connection therewith, —— cents.

For Filing Certificates of discharge of each Instrument, including Affidavits, and for making all proper Entries and Endorsements connected therewith, —— cents.

For searching each paper, —— cents.

For copies of any Document, with certificates prepared, filed under this Act, —— cents for every hundred words.

For comparing any Document, purporting to be a copy of Document filed, —— cent per hundred words ; and for certifying same to be a copy, —— cents.

He did not propose to make any change in the fees, agreed upon last year, as recorded in the Journal for 1884.

Resolution with blanks agreed to.

Hon. Mr. SULLIVAN moved that the first three blanks be filled up with the word "fifty," the fourth with the word "sixteen," the fifth with the word "ten," the sixth with the word "one," and the seventh with the word "fifty," and said that there was a good deal of exception taken last Session to these changes. He had no wish to steal a march on the House with this Bill. He desired that it should have the fullest consideration. It certainly affects the very poorest class of people in the country, as the rich man can always protect himself. When a man has been seized upon, and his Stock taken, no matter how many seizures have been made, he should be placed in no worse position as to costs, than at first.

Hon. Mr. MACDONALD said that the fees in this Bill had been kept pretty high. In the Office at Georgetown, the Bills of Sale were kept in an office, without any Safe, and if a fire took place, they might be all burned up. Provision should be made for a Safe.

Hon. Mr. PROWSE thought no harm would be done if those Bills of Sale were all burned up, as they were frequently a means of fraud by placing goods beyond the reach of the creditor. Every debtor has a right to give to all his creditors an equal right to his money or his goods. By means of the Bill of Sale, the rights of several creditors are often given away to one man. Imprisonment for debt having been abolished, a dishonest man now frequently puts his goods and chattels out of the reach of all but one of his creditors, from whom he receives all the accommodation he requires.

Hon. Mr. SULLIVAN said that the argument of the honorable member for Murray Harbor was in favor of doing away with Bills of Sale altogether. He (Mr. S.) saw no reason why a man should not give a Bill of Sale upon his goods and chattels instead of a mortgage upon his farm. He may have no Real Estate, and may have goods and chattels, upon which he desires to give a Bill of Sale. It would be hard to deprive people of this privilege. Why should not the owner of a thousand dollars worth of goods have the same privilege as he who has power to give a mortgage on a farm worth

that amount? The rights of all parties should be protected as much as possible.

Motion put and carried.

On motion Mr. Speaker resumed the Chair; and the Chairman reported the resolutions agreed to.

Resolved, That a Committee be appointed to prepare and bring in a Bill pursuant to the said resolutions.

Ordered, That honorables Sullivan, Ferguson and Mr. Blake do compose the said Committee.

Hon. Mr. SULLIAAN, from the last preceding Committee appointed, presented to the House a Bill, as prepared by the Committee, to be intituled "An Act respecting Bills of Sale," and the same was received and read the first time.

Ordered, That the said Bill be read the second time to-morrow.

Hon. Mr. CAMPBELL, a member of Her Majesty's Executive Council presented to the House,—

Statement — Expenditure on Charlottetown and Southport Ferry, including wharves, steamers, &c., from 1st February, 1869 to 31st December, 1884.

Received and read.

Ordered, That said Returns do lie on the Table.

Hon. Mr. SULLIVAN said that a few days ago he placed a notice on the Order Book setting forth that, at an early day, the House would be asked to consider the question of Winter Communication between this Island and the mainland of Canada, and the manner in which it is being carried out by the Dominion Government. He now proposed to submit that question to the consideration of the House. When the documents relating to this matter were presented to the House, and a motion made that they do lie on the table, the honorable member for Tignish suggested that this day should be fixed for the discussion of the question. As the Government had shown no disposition to shirk or delay the consideration of this very important subject, it was not thought necessary to adopt that suggestion. The resolution which he (Mr. S.) now proposed to submit to the House for its consideration, is precisely ths same as that which he read on that occasion, and of which due notice had been given on the Order Book. The honorable Leader of the Opposition was not in his place; but he had intimated to that honorable gentleman before he left town that this discussion would commence this evening, that no advantage would be taken of his absence, that it would probably be prolonged until the time mentioned by him for his return, and that it was the desire of the Government that he should be one of the members of the Committee to prepare the Address. The resolution he would now move, is as follows:

Resolved, That an humble Address be forwarded to Her Majesty the Queen, representing the failure of the Dominion Government to carry out that part of the Terms of Confederation which requires the Government of Canada to establish and maintain efficient steam service for the conveyance of mails and passengers between the Island and the mainland of the Dominion, winter and summer, thus placing the Island in continuous communication with the Intercolonial Railway, and the Railway system of the Dominion, and praying that Her Majesty may be pleased to cause such action to be taken as shall remedy the grievance complained of, and shall compensate Prince Edward Island for the non-fulfilment of the aforesaid Terms, and that the Legislative Council be requested to join in such Address.

He supposed that he need not inform the House that this question is, so far as this Province is concerned, one of the highest importance. It is also of moment to the Dominion Government and to Her Majesty the Queen, who was the third party to the Terms of Confederation. These Terms were agreed upon by the House of Commons and Senate of Canada, and by both branches of our Provincial Legislature; and the compact was entered into by the consent of the Imperial Government and sanctioned by Her Majesty the Queen as one of the parties thereto. Her Majesty is therefore the party whose province and high prerogative it is to see that justice be done to both parties who entered into Confederation. We, in this Province maintain that we have done everything on our part to carry out the terms of Union. We have given to the Dominion Government all the power and authority it was possible to give them, so far as imposing and levying taxes upon our people are concerned, and so far as all matters affecting them as a Government are concerned. But we complain that on the part of the Dominion Government, they have not kept faith with us, and have not carried out their portion of the compact entered into at Confederation, viz.: "to provide efficient Steam service for the conveyance of mails and passengers between this Island and the mainland, of the Dominion Winter and Summer thus placing the Island in continuous communication with the Intercolonial Railway and the railway system of the Dominion." He need hardly say to those who are members of this Legislature, and acquainted with the circumstances of our people, and their facilities for trade, commerce, and navigation, that the offer of the Dominion Government to provide continuous steam communication for us during the year round, was a great cause of our willingness to enter into Confederation, and that our people are very much disappointed that the compact has not been kept by the General Government as it should have been. We all know how the Winter Service has been performed. The late Dominion Government, equally with the present one, and the

present as well as its predecessor, had failed to carry out the Terms of Union, so far as this Province was concerned. The question now arises whether the people of this Island are to remain silent and quiet and to allow this solemn obligation to pass year after year unfulfilled and unconsummated. Our people are required to pay their taxes to the General Government, and have therefore a right to expect that the Terms of Confederation be fulfilled, or that the Dominion Government confess that they are unable or unwilling to fulfil them. We should have a fair understanding on this question. The Government and Legislature of this Province have again and again demanded from the Government of Canada that the terms of union be carried out and it is a duty they owe to themselves, to the Province, and to those who come after them that they should do this. So far as the present Government are concerned, they have done everything in their power to have those terms observed. It was well known that this Island was not very willing to enter Confederation, for many years, but at length consented to do so on certain conditions, among which was the one that efficient and continuous steam service for the conveyance of mails and passengers between this Island and the mainland be maintained winter and summer. The Legislature had, on two different occasions, in the Session of 1881 and again last Session, addressed the Dominion Government in reference to this matter, calling their attention to the fact that the terms of Confederation had not been fulfilled, and asking for compensation for the loss sustained by this Province on account of that non-fulfilment. There is now nothing more that we can do to have that solemn compact fulfilled, than to approach our most gracious Sovereign, and to ask her to see that justice be done to her subjects in this Island in reference to this matter, and that the Dominion Government be required to carry out the terms of Confederation. If any honorable member of the House would propose any other method of dealing with the question, be did, not hesitate to say that if it commended itself to their judgment, the Government would be willing to adopt it; but, at present, they saw no other course open to them than the one now proposed, viz.: to approach Her Majesty the Queen, and ask for the redress of our grievances. This was the course proposed by the Legislature, last Session, in its Address to His Excellency the Governor General in reference to this matter. The Dominion Government were then informed that that was the last appeal to them, and that if a favorable answer were not accorded without delay "the Legislature desire that the Government of the Province invoke the interference of Her Majesty the Queen by laying a statement of the grievances complained of at the foot of the Throne." That memorial was acknowledged in o of the papers now on the t of the House. Since then, the tion of the House and of

the Dominion Government has been called to the fact that the terms of union with respect to this matter have not been fulfilled, by the occurrence of a very distressing accident a couple of months ago, to the couriers and passengers who undertook the perilous passage of the Straits between the Capes in open boats. The Local Government again brought the matter to the notice of the Dominion Government, representing the duty imposed upon them by the Legislature to take this step. The Reply was that the matter would receive "due consideration." He was as strong a party man as any honorable member of the House; but he felt that that phrase had been used so frequently in reference to memorials from this Province that we could hardly accept it as a satisfactory answer. The Dominion Government may have something in view with respect to this matter, or they may not. Under such circumstances, it becomes our duty to present our grievance before the highest court in the land. Now, it is very well known to the people of this Island, that although the Dominion Government have made some provision for the carriage of mails and passengers to Cape Traverse from this City, they have merely continued the old system in vogue before Confederation, of carrying the mails across the Straits in open boats during the season when the navigation was interrupted by ice. It may appear strange and singular that no provision whatever has been made by them for the conveyance of passengers across the straits during Winter, at any time since Confederation. Such, however, is the fact, although they are bound to carry passengers as well as mails. They are bound to give us, under Confederation, continuous Steam communication, in order to place this Island in connection with the Intercolonial Railway and the railway system of Canada. It may be said that their duty is to carry the mails only, and not to carry passengers. That is not in accordance with the terms of union; and to show that it is not, the Dominion Government have constructed a line of Railway from the main line to Cape Traverse. As they are bound to place us in connection with the Intercolonial Railway, they should also have supplied Railway connection on the other side of the Straits. Every person in the Dominion, and in the Empire, is, to a certain extent, interested in our having railway connection from the other side of the Straits with the railway system of the Dominion, and we have as much right to such facilities there as on this side. Every person knows, however, that when a crossing is made to the other side of the Straits, from this Island, passengers and mails have to be conveyed forty miles in old open sleighs over very rough roads to reach the Intercolonial Railway. Even if the Dominion give us the means of crossing the straits in Winter, the terms of Confederation would not be fulfilled. They must provide railway connection with the railways of the Dominion, as soon as the other shore is reached, in winter, as well as in summer. Until they supply the connecting link on the other side, they have not fulfilled the terms in that respect. It must be very clear to every person on the Island and outside of it, that this has not been done, and that they have failed to provide us with that accommodation which they undertook to provide. It may be said that an ample opportunity has not been afforded them to give this Province the communication which they undertook to furnish. Well, twelve years may be considered a sufficiently long period for the Dominion Government, having at their command experts and engineers, to pronounce upon the best method of navigating the Straits and to enable them to make reasonable effort to show that they were really in earnest in endeavoring to fulfil the terms of Confederation. This Province is now in no better position than when we entered Confederation; and it becomes every member of the Legislature to require the fulfilment of those terms, without any further delay. This would not only benefit the people of this Island, but those of the Dominion as well. Our trade relations with the other Provinces are now very great, and it would be for their interests as well as ours to have sufficient and proper steam communication between this Island and the Intercolonial railway. Every province in the Dominion has a direct and pecuniary interest in the fulfilment of the terms of union with this Island, and in the

Dominion Government's carrying out its obligations, in good faith, to all ot them. Unless this be done, the people of this country can never have faith in Confederation. This question presses itself upon us with very great force, but he would not take up time in any farther remarks. He was almost tired bringing this matter before the House. The people of this Province are strongly in favor of an appeal to the highest Court in in the British Empire to secure their rights under Confederation, and unless the terms of union be carried out, the people of this Province will be greatly disatisfied. (Applause.)

Mr. SINCLAIR agreed with his honor the Leader of the Government that the question now under consideration is one of the most important that has come before the House during the present Session. The people expect Parliament to take as strong action with respect to it, as it is possible to take. In his opinion, the resolution did not go far enough. We should state in that resolution that unless the Dominion Government are prepared to do us justice, and to fulfil the terms of union, those terms should be cancelled altogether. If this question were submitted to a Court for Arbitration, our safest course would be to demand the fulfilment of the terms of union, or that the union be annulled. When this Province was forced to take refuge in Confederation, our Financial affairs were in such a condition that we had no other alternative. When we accepted the terms of union, we were given to understand that the Dominion Tariff would not be increased to the extent it has been increased. Our financial condition at that time was such that if we had remained out of Confederation, we would have to remit to England, annually, the sum of $160,000 in gold, to meet the interest on the Railway Debentures. Under these circumstances, we were forced to do that which we were very unwilling to do,—to accept Confederation on the best terms we could obtain; and the offer of efficient and continuous steam communication for mails and passengers during winter was a strong inducement to accept the terms offered. According to the figures submitted by the honorable member for Kensington, if our Tariff out of Confederation had been as high as at present, our Revenue would have been sufficient to meet the interest on the cost of the Railway as well as all our other expenditures, and to leave a surplus. If this statement is correct, we have been losers instead of gainers by accepting the terms of Confederation, apart from the fact that those terms have never been fulfilled so far as winter communication is concerned. On account of our isolated position, the Dominion received this Province into Confederation with a nominal debt of fifty dollars per head. They also promised to give us continuous steam communication with the mainland, winter and summer, for the conveyance of mails and passengers; but they have utterly failed to provide that accommodation. The means of conveyance in open boats during the winter season is altogether insufficient, and unsafe for either mails or passengers. As a result of this, business communications often remain at the Capes for a week or ten days before being conveyed across the straits. This causes great loss and inconvenience to our business men, the amount of which can hardly be estimated. It is not the Island alone which suffers for want of efficient steam communication with the mainland; the other portions of the Dominion also suffer for want of communication with this Island. It is true that neither the late nor the present Dominion Government have treated us as they should have done, but he considered that the latter have given us a slap in the face, in the treatment we have lately received. After so many years experience, they must see that in attempting the crossing of the Straits in winter, life is not safe. During the present Session of the Dominion Parliament in reply to a question by Honorable Senator Haythorne, as to whether or not it was the intention of the Government to place another vessel on the Georgetown-Pictou route, as a consort of the *Northern Light*, Sir Alexander Campbell submitted the following memoranda from the Department of Marine :

"It is not the intention of the Government to place another steamer on the route as consort at present, but they have the steamer *Lansdowne* in reserve, which vessel is fitted for ice service, and in case of any accident to the *Northern Light* would be available for the service.

"Capt. Finlayson reports that he will try to cut the *Northern Light* out of Georgetown in the beginning of March, and if she can then make trips without incurring undue risks to life and property every effort will be made to run the vessel regularly the remainder of the season.

With reference to the service at the Capes, Sir Alexander's words were :

"The Government have determined to take it out of the hands of the contractors and make it a governmental service, The memorandum which I have from the Department states that it is also proposed to transfer the winter boat service between the Capes Traverse and Tormentine from the Post Office Department to the Marine Department, and it will, after this winter, manage this service, and a steamer will probably be placed there to assist passengers and mails to cross between the board ice. An officer of the Marine Department will be directed to make observations as to what will be required to render the crossing at the Capes efficient. Now, I think if that is done that the service so far as it is possible under the physical conditions that exist, will be made as efficient as it can be made under those circumstances. In the first place while the boat can run, the

Northern Light, that seems to be a good fair boat for the service, and if not, the *Northern Light* some other boat will do the duty. I think my honorable friend, under the circumstances I have mentioned, will find that there is some excuse for the non–completion of the boathouse before now. I hope my honorable friend will find in that some assurance on the part of the Government that we are disposed to do all in our power to carry out what we admit to be the pledge that was given to Prince Edward Island, and so far from there being any disposition on our part to do as the honorable gentleman from Halifax seemed to think some one of us had done to treat it in a light spirit, we desire to treat it as we ought to treat it, with a sense of our duty to the country, and as we ought to treat it—as a very serious and important service to be executed to the best of our ability, and with such appliances as we can put there in order to carry out the spirit of the terms upon which Prince Edward Island joined her fortune to ours." This information he (Mr. S.) had obtained from one of our Island representatives. Now, if it is not the intention of the Dominion Government to place a second steamer on the Georgetown–Pictou route, it is impossible for them to perform that service as it should be performed. We know that the *Northern Light* has not been able to do as well as a large and more substantial boat would have done. Under these circumstances, it was their duty to have placed a boat of the latter description there.

He was sorry to hear the honorable member for Murray Harbor acknowledge that we shall never have continuous steam communication with the mainland by means of navigation. Also a member of the Dominion Senate declared that " you might as well attempt to run a steamer through the Rocky Mountains as through those Straits at times in winter." Such statements coming from our own men are damaging to our interests. Until the very best effort has been made to navigate the Straits in Winter, we cannot tell what may be done. It was not at one time supposed that such efficient service as the *Northern Light* has rendered could be performed by any steam vessel. But he believed that a much stronger and larger boat with more powerful engines would have done far better. There is no reason why the Dominion Government should not expend $100,000 in providing suitable boats for that service, instead of parsimoniously dealing with us, as stated by the Archbishop of Halifax, "like an old huxter woman would have done." Was this the way to carry out the stipulations they entered into at the time we entered into Confederation ? The fact is, we have been treated in a very dishonorable and dishonest manner; and he felt when he read the Reply of the Minister of Marine to Mr. Haythorne's question in the Senate, " that it was not the intention of the Dominion Government to place a second steamboat on the route," there was no great hope of their intention of carrying out the terms of union. When we look at the instructions given to the captain of the *Northern Light* with respect to the running of the vessel, "That any damage done to her would be at his risk," and the fact that all the answer we have received to the Memorial of both Houses of the Legislature, last Session, is that the matter will receive "due consideration," we have little to hope for or expect from them. Nothing, therefore, remains for us, but to lay our case at the foot of the Throne, and to endeavor to secure justice through that source. Every man in the House and in the country will acknowledge that unless the terms of Confederation are carried out to the letter they should be cancelled altogether. This is the strongest pressure we can bring to bear in pressing for our rights with respect to this question. We ask for no favors at the hands of the Dominion Government. We ask simply that the compact entered into at Confederation be fulfilled, or that it be cancelled. There is no doubt they will be just as strongly opposed to this as they were with reference to Nova Scotia, and that they will either fulfil the terms of union or recompense us for the non-fulfilment of those terms, if they cannot accomplish what they undertook to perform. Taking this view of the matter, the resolution was not as strong as he would like it to be. In his opinion the Local Government had also been neglectful in the performance of their duty in connection with this matter. When the sad accident on the Straits occurred, in Janu

ary last, they should at once have made a proper representation of our position and of the manner in which we have been treated. There is an idea throughout Ontario and elsewhere that this Province was paid in full for its Railway, which is contrary to the fact. Much ignorance also prevailed with reference to the difficulties experienced in the passage across the Straits, and few people in the Upper Provinces had any idea of them. He therefore though it was the duty of the Government at that time, when there was an excellent opportunity to make an impression, to send a Delegation to Ottawa for the purpose of presenting our claims, and insisting upon our rights in as strong and forcible a manner as possible. The Government may send as many papers there as they wish, but these will not secure the object sought, unless accompanied with something stronger. The Leader of the British Columbia Government succeeded by pressing their claim in person in England. Mr. Mackenzie, the Premier, was forced to go and defend his side of the case, and declared that the resources of the Dominion would not warrant the construction of the Pacific Railway within the time specified in the treaty. British Columbia said: "Well do as much as you can," and she gained her point. The same argument would apply to this Province. The Dominion Government should construct two large and powerful steamers for the winter navigation of the Straits and shew that they were doing all in their power to fulfil the terms. The present boat is a m re experiment, yet wonders have been done by it. He himself had been aboard that vessel when she split large pans of ice for several chains ahead of her. A large and po re ful boat would, no doubt, have done much more. The *Northern Light* is now icebound in Georgetown, while the Gulf is comparatively free of ice. If there were another boat, she could have made regular trips for some weeks past. The Expenditure of $100,000 annually on the part f the Dominion Government should not stand in the way of the fulfilment of the terms of union. As matters now stand, the Dominion Government are trifling with our interests, and we are losing heavily. He would advise demanding through the Imperial Government, either compensation, or separation from the Dominion. If Canada refuses to fulfil the compact entered into by her at Confederation, let it be abrogated. A private bargain would be settled in that way, and why should not this one be dealt with in a similar manner? The means of conveyance across the straits is unworthy of the name. It provides no accomodation whatever for a lady or an aged person to cross to the mainland, or to come to the Island from the other side. If we have no accommodation for passengers across the straits in winter, we should have it supplied at once. The Dominion Government were given full power to tax this Province to any extent they pleased, and they have taken the fullest advantage of it. It is our duty, therefore, to press for the fulfilment of their part of the compact, and he would like to see the resolution state that the terms of union must be either fulfilled or cancelled. This was his view of the matter, and he thought it the only safe one to take. If we had charge of our own tariff and our own finances, in ten years, we would be far better off than under the Dominion, with a very limited subsidy. As matters now stand, we shall be compelled either to run into debt or to levy taxes which our people will be very unwilling to endure. If the Dominion Government will not at once fulfil the terms of union, he for one, would be prepared to ask for the abrogation of Confederation.

Hon. Mr. PROWSE seconded the resolution, and said that he could not add much to what had already been stated. His honor the Leader of the Government had put the case before the House in a particularly lucid manner. He (Mr. P.) also, agreed to a considerable extent with the honorable member for Strathalbyn, but that honorable gentleman made some statements with which he could by no means agree. This question has been agitated for some years, and he was glad to see that it is now occupying the attention of the public men and the people of this Province more than ever before. It appeared to be misunderstood by many people in the Dominion, outside of this Province, who do not appear to realize that our grievance is caused by the non-fulfilment by the Dominion Government of the compact entered into with us at Confederation. As a Province, we have no right to ask the General Government to place on the winter route to the mainland, one steamer, or fifty steamers. In fact, it is against our interests to say that the terms of union can be carried out by steamers at all. If we say that we must have ten steamers, and they all afterwards proved unsatisfactory, the Dominion Government could reply: "We have given you all that you asked for, and have fulfilled our part of the contract." We know that some of the gentlemen who became the strongest opponents of Confederation in this Province, were opposed to it mainly on the ground that we as a people, could not start in the race on the same footing as the other Provinces were started. But the Dominion Government said that they would place this Province on the same footing as the other Provinces by giving us continuous steam communication with the mainland winter and summer. It appeared that the question of winter communication was, to those gentlemen, at that time, but a very small matter. They were going to have steam communication between England and Quebec all the year round. It will be observed that "navigation" was not even mentioned in the terms of union. The communication was to be by "efficient steam service." For this reason he (Mr. P.) did not think the term "navigation" should be used by us in connection with this ques-

tion. It appears that when the terms of union were drawn up and signed, the Dominion Government had not decided upon the mode by which steam communication was to be kept up between this Island and the mainland, winter and summer. The words of the terms in reference to this matter are as follows:

"Efficient steam service for the conveyance of mails and passengers to be established and maintained between the Island and the mainland of the Dominion, winter and summer, thus placing the Island in continuous communication with the Intercolonial Railway, and the Railway system of the Dominion." This steam service was to be for the "mails and passengers," and was to place this "Island in continuous communication with the Intercolonial Railway and the railway system of the Dominion." This means that we were to have the same communication with the other Provinces as those Provinces were to have between themselves. We should therefore hold the Dominion Government to the literal fulfilment of the terms of union, and the less we have to say with respect to steamers and iceboats and the terminus on this Island, the better. Some people may believe that the terms of union may be fulfilled by means of navigation, but if we admit that principle, and agree to accept it, we would be bound, after the expenditure by the Dominion Government of large sums of money in endeavoring to carry it out, to accept the result, whether satisfactory or not. If we admit that the terms may be fulfilled by navigation, it would be unfair after a heavy expenditure on their part to turn round and ask them to adopt some other plan. He wished to make a remark or two respecting the "larger and stronger boats" proposed by the honorable member for Strathalbyn for the Georgetown–Pictou route. It is reported that there is now an ice barrier fourteen feet in thickness across the entrance of Georgetown Harbor. Now, is it possible that any steamer could break through such ice and make such trips as would fulfil the terms of union? The fact is, we need never expect continuous steam communication with the mainland in winter by steamers. He would now read the instructions given the captain of the *Northern Light*, by the Minister of Marine and Fisheries, last year, showing that the latter had a much greater regard for the safety of the boat than for the fulfilment of the terms of union in providing "efficient steam service for the conveyance of mails and passengers between the Island and the mainland of the Dominion, winter and summer." Those instructions were such as no ship-owner would have given to a captain in command of his vessel. Copies of them were presented to the Senate of Canada by Sir Alexander Campbell on the 24th February, 1885, and are to be seen in the Printed Debates of that Body for the Session of 1885. They are as follows:

OTTAWA, Jan. 12, 1884.

SIR,—Referring to my letter of the 14th December, 1882, I have again to instruct you to use your own judgment as to whether the *Northern Light* should run, and you are to incur no risk, where by the safety of the vessel may be endangered by being caught in the ice. No risk also is to be incurred for the purpose of carrying over any particular passenger or passengers, and the Department expects that you will use your judgment in all matters affecting the running of the boat, and will hold you responsible for her safety.

I am Sir,
Your most obedient servant,
(Signed.)   WILLIAM SMITH,
Deputy Minister of Marine.

Capt. A. Finlayson,
Northern Light,
Pictou, N. S.

The gentleman who gave these instructions to the captain of the *Northern Light* could never have seen a vessel. No honorable member of the House would give such instructions to a captain in charge of his vessel. If any captain received such instructions, he would fasten his vessel to the nearest wharf and leave her there. But the captain of the *Northern Light* was to run no risk with that vessel—not even that of an ordinary summer day—although all vessels are obliged to run some risk upon the water. If anything happened to the *Northern Light*, the people of this Province would demand another boat. It appeared, therefore, that the work performed by that vessel was to be taken as a fulfilment of the terms of union ! In reply to a telegram from some person, the following telegram was sent to the captain of the *Northern Light* in January, 1883, viz:

OTTAWA, Jan. 16, 1883.

Captain Finlayson,

Steamer *Northern Light*,

Georgetown, Prince Edward Island.

Telegram received urging Department order you run; responsibility is with you; expect you to run no undue risks.

(Signed.) A. W. McLELLAN.

Two days later, on receipt of a telegram from Capt. Finlayson, asking for instructions the following was sent him.

OTTAWA, Jan. 18, 1883.

Captain Finlayson,

Steamer *Northern Light*,

Georgetown, Prince Edward Island.

With knowledge of ice, you must be Judge, and held responsible for safety of boat. Incur no undue risks.

(Signed) WM. SMITH.

It seems that a pretty strong pressure was brought to bear upon the captain of the *Northern Light* to continue his trips, that he then telegraphed to the Department of Marine, and was told not to run her, but if he did run her he would be held responsible.

The last Telegram was as follows:

OTTAWA, Jan. 10, 1885.

Captain A. Finlayson,

Steamship *Northern Light*,

(Care Messrs. Noonan & Davies,)

Pictou.

Advisable make daily round trips when practicable, having regard safety vessel.

(Signed) WM. SMITH.

These were probably the instructions which the captain had been receiving from the beginning. He (Mr. Prowse) could not, however, agree with the honorable member for Strathalbyn when that gentleman stated that in this Address we should insist on the fulfilment of the terms of union or the dissolution of our union with the Dominion. The two parties to the contract may be compared to two men Smith & Jones entering into partnership. While Smith is fulfilling every condition of the partnership, Jones is living on the fat of the land, doing nothing. If Jones worked as hard as Smith does, there would be ample profits for both, but he has not. It would be unfair to say that they should withdraw from the partnership on equal terms for they have not equally contributed to the capital. If we should be forced to withdraw from Confede-. ration, there would have to be a tremenduous bill of costs and expenses handed back to us, as the Dominion Government have not fulfilled their part of the contract. When the terms of union were offered this Province by the Dominion, the latter admitted that continuous steam communication with the mainland summer and winter was an absolute necessity to us. Reciprocity with the United States was also to have been obtained, if possible. But what has taken place since then? The National Policy has been introduced, and has forced all the Provinces of the Dominion to trade with each other, instead of with foreign countries. He believed that there is now ten times as much trading between the various Provinces, as in 1873; when we entered Confederation   Such being the case, how much greater the necessity for carrying out the terms of union respecting winter communication with the mainland, than when the union was consummated? It appeared to him that our want of unanimity and earnestness with respect to to this question, is the great barrier to our success in securing our rights. When British Columbia was admitted into the Dominion, it was on condition that a certain great work was to be completed within a given time. That work was the construction of the Canada Pacific Railway which was to be commenced within two years from the date of union. British Columbia with a white population of only 11,000 at that time, insisted upon the literal fulfilment of the terms of union. The Mackenzie Government declared that the terms could not be fulfilled; but that did not satisfy British Columbia containing only about one-tenth of our present population. They united themselves in a Society called the "Terms of Union Preservation League," and stood as one man in demanding the fulfilment of the terms. Mr. Mackenzie wanted to get the people of that Province committed to the acceptance of something less than the fulfilment of those terms, and sent an Agent to induce them to modify their claim, and to report to him if there was any probability that an Election would result in a return of Representatives in favor

of a modification. But the people stood firm and united in favor of the fulfilment of the terms of union, and made an Appeal to Her Majesty the Queen. The result of that Appeal was that the Dominion Government were informed that the terms of union must be fulfilled; and they were forced to construct the Canada Pacific Railway at a cost of $100,-000,000. With this example before us, it is our duty to prosecute our case in a decided and united manner, and not to cease doing so, until the terms of union with the Dominion are fulfilled. The Dominion Government may say to the Imperial Government that it is impossible to fulfil the terms of union to the letter, and may try to force us to be satisfied with something less. But we should not be satisfied with anything less than the literal fulfilment of those terms. He (Mr. P.) therefore hoped that the Address to Her Majesty the Queen will be such as will commend itself to this honorable House, as well as to the other Branch of the Legislature.

Mr. PERRY said that it was not his intention to oppose the resolution. The loss accruing to us, owing to the non-fulfilment of the terms of union by the Dominion Government has been very much felt by our people. Notwithstanding all the efforts of our Representatives in the Dominion and Local Parliaments to secure justice to this Province respecting this matter, almost nothing has been done in that direction. In his opinion, however, the Local Government have not done exactly what was expected of them by the people in reference to this question. From February 1884 to February 1885, no correspondence took place between the Local and Dominion Governments with respect to the fulfilment of the terms of union. This was not what the country had a right to expect after the Joint Address of both Houses to His Excellency the Governor General, last Session. Immediate action was asked for in that Address. We asked that immediate steps be taken to fulfil the terms of union. But the House has nothing before it to show that the Local Government have followed up that demand, or that action will be taken by the Dominion in reference to the matter. In his opinion, this resolution did not go far enough. It should make provision that the Address to Her Majesty the Queen be presented to her by a delegation from the Government of this Province. His honorable friend the Leader of the Government, had been on dele gations to Ottawa, and he (Mr. P.) was proud to say the honorable gentleman had been successful. While his honor confined his applications to the Dominion Government on the Piers Question to Minutes of Council, Resolutions and Joint Addresses, he was unsuccessful; but when he went in person and made his claim, he secured his object, even exceeding his own expectations. The country had a right to expect that a delegation should be sent to Her Majesty with this Address, and that an answer be obtained to it. If this course is not pursued, we shall not probably hear the result of our application to the Imperial Government for a long time to come. Under such circumstances, our people will continue to suffer from the non-fulfilment of the terms of Confederation until more active steps are taken to secure our rights from the Government of the Dominion. If the Government are in earnest in dealing with this question, they will not consider a few hundred dollars expended on a delegation to wait upon the Imperial Government, for the purpose of enforcing our claims, thrown away. We are certainly entitled to full compensation for the loss we have sustained owing to the non-fulfilment of the terms of union, and he thought our claim under that head should be made a separate case. There are two separate and distinct cases to be laid before the Imperial Government. He therefore hoped to see the resolution amended, and that provision be made for the appointment of the delegation which he had suggested. As the hour was now late and the time for adjournment had arrived, he moved that the debate be adjourned.

Motion put and carried.

House adjourned until to-morrow forenoon, at ten o'clock.

I. O.

WEDNESDAY, March 25.

Mr. Speaker in the Chair.

BILLS OF SALE.

The order of the day for the second reading of the Bill intituled "An Act respecting Bills of Sale" having been read the Bill was accordingly read the second time.

Hon. Mr. SULLIVAN said that all the leading provisions of this Bill had been explained to the House when the resolution, upon which the Bill was founded, had been submitted. The Bill was similar to the one that had been passed by the House last year, the only difference being in respect to the clauses that had been disagreed to last Session.

On motion the House resolved itself into a committee of the whole.

Mr. JOHN MACLEAN in the Chair.

The first clause having been read.

Mr. BLAKE asked for an explanation of this part of the Bill.

Hon. Mr. SULLIVAN explained that the clause only referred to actual mortgages or conveyances of chattels, which were usually called "Bills of Sale."

Clause agreed to with the blank.

Hon. Mr. SULLIVAN said the blank in this clause referred to the time in which mortgages of this kind should be filed. Last year ten days was considered ample time, and he would move that the blank be filled with the word "ten."

Mr. A. MARTIN said that while the time might be long enough in the City, it might be entirely too short a period in the country to allow persons having mortgages of this kind, to get them placed on record. Persons who take Bills of Sale will get them registered as soon as possible but circumstances might sometimes prevent them from getting this done for ten days after the mortgage was executed. He did not think any harm would arise if the time was extended to twenty days instead of ten days. The time before the mortgage was registered did not make a great deal of difference, as the Bill of Sale would be of no effect until it was placed on record. He did not think it would at all times be possible for parties in the country to get the documents registered within so short a time as ten days. He would move in amendment that the blank be filled with the word "twenty" instead of the word "ten."

Hon. Mr. MACDONALD said he would second the motion of the honorable junior member for Belfast. It was often difficult to get the witnesses to documents of this nature, to make the necessary affidavits in order to have them registered, and it would be better to give the person taking the Bill of Sale, an opportunity of having this part done without inconvenience.

Hon. Mr. SULLIVAN said the time suggested by honorable members was too long. The Island is not very large and the whole public doing business are interested in this matter, as it is most desirable that when mortgages of this kind are given, they should be immediately placed on record. Innocent persons may make purchases of goods that have been mortgaged in this way and may suffer loss on account of doing so. Some trouble might be occasioned on account of the difficulty of getting witnesses to prove to the grantors execution of the mortgage; but as an acknowledgement by the grantor does equally as well as proof by the witness, the difficulty anticipated by the honorable member from Georgetown would not arise. The time had been extended last year from five days unto ten days, and he considered that was ample time to enable parties holding these documents to place them on record.

Hon. Mr. MACLEOD thought any reasonable time would be acceptable to the public. In reference to the purchase of goods that have been mortgaged in this way, if the mortgage was not registered before the articles were purchased, it would not bind them. The principal objection to extending the time for registering these documents, is that it allows persons to hold unregistered assignments for a longer time, whereby an opportunity may be afforded the fraudulent of obtaining goods that would not be given them if the Bill of Sale was registered.

Mr. D. C. MARTIN said it did not make any difference what time was allowed parties to register these documents, for Bills of Sale did not bind as against a third party, until they were registered.

Amendment carried.

Clause as amended agreed to.

On motion Mr. Speaker resumed the Chair. Progress was reported and leave given the Committee to sit again.

House adjourned for one hour.

G. F. O.

AFTERNOON SESSION.

Mr. Speaker in the Chair.

On motion of Honorable Mr. Sullivan, the House resumed the Debate on the resolution relating to winter communication with the mainland of the Dominion.

Hon. Mr. SULLIVAN said the debate on the resolution was adjourned on the motion of the honorable member for Tignish (Mr. Perry,) and that honorable gentleman had a right to resume it, but as he was absent, perhaps some other member of Opposition would take his place for the present. He hoped that before the conclusion of the Debate, the honorable gentleman would be found in his place.

Mr. FARQUHARSON said in the absence of the honorable member for Tignish, he would make a few remarks on the question before the House. We have a strong and unquestionable claim, upon the Dominion Government for the fulfilment of the terms of union, as well as for compensation for the loss we have sustained on account of the non-fulfilment of those terms, during the past twelve years. That loss had been estimated by the Government last Session, at five millions of dollars. Whatever the amount of our loss really is, it is very large indeed, and should be made good to us. If we cannot obtain something from the Dominion Government in this way, we shall very soon have to resort to direct taxation. This Province entered Confederation on certain conditions or Terms, to which there were three parties, viz.: the Local and Dominion Governments and the Imperial Government, — the latter being a consenting party. From what we know of the dignity and honor of Her Majesty's Government, we have reason to conclude that they will not permit any injustice to any of their colonies. One of the conditions of our union with the Dominion was, that we were to have continuous steam communication with the mainland of the Dominion, winter and summer, and we have just cause for complaint that this condition has never been fulfilled. We are contributing as much, per capita, as

any Province in the Dominion to the general Revenue, and have, therefore, a right to be placed on the same footing, so far as inter-communication is concerned, as the other provinces are. Previous to Confederation, we were in a better position, financially, than any of the Lower Provinces. We were able to pay our debts and to meet all necessary expenditures. Our people were very lightly taxed, and the average duties on goods imported were only 12½ per cent. Under these circumstances, the Government of the Dominion made overtures to us, offering us, among other advantages, continuous steam communication with the mainland winter and summer. By reference to the *Parliamentary Reporter* for 1881, page 244, it will be found that during the discussion of the same question, at that time, he had quoted some figures, and stated that for the year ending 31st January, 1873, previous to Confederation, our total imports were $1,605,241.05, and that the duty paid into the Treasury amounted to $262,577.14. It was then supposed that, under Confederation, $250,000 should meet all our expenditures. Our average duties at that time were $16.36 per cent, while under the present Tariff they are $27.89 per cent. Now, he contended that the difference between these figures represents our loss under Confederation. During the remarks alluded to, he made the following statement with respect to the loss suffered by this Island in the year 1879 : "The Customs duties paid at P. E. Island from June, 1874 to 1879 inclusive, amounted to

	$1,534,286.92
Inland Revenue (6 years)	290,050.03
	$1,824,336.95
Duties each year	304,055.75
Receipts from Post Office, 1879	44,000.00
Bill Stamps	1,526.12
	$349,571.87

This makes our annual payment to the Dominion Treasury $349,-571.87 per year, while we received from that source the sum of $299,-458.44 per year, showing a loss to this Province of $50,117.53, to which must be added indirect duties paid by consumers in P. E. Island to Canadian manufacturers, (imports being for six years), $78,550.06, making a total annual loss to us, of $128,667.59 under Confederation. These figures are not as high as those submitted by the honorable member for Kensington, during the present Session, but it must be remembered that they make no allowance for an increase of our Imports, since Confederation, although those imports have certainly increased very largely indeed. Even making no allowance for any increase, the figures he had just quoted show a total annual loss to this Province, under the Dominion of $128,667.-59. In preparing those figures in 1881, he went into the full Trade returns of the Dominion, and he was now satisfied that he was under, instead of over the mark. The resolution now under consideration was, he supposed, as strong as the Government could make it, under the circumstances. The

Dominion Government have lately promised to erect boat houses at the Capes, and to take the ice boat service into their own hands. They may, therefore, say that the Legislature of the Province is premature in forwarding the proposed Memorial to Her Majesty the Queen with respect to this matter. But all that they have done to fulfil the terms of union to this date has not been of much account. He had expected that they would have made an effort to provide a second boat to assist the *Northern Light* but they have not done so. Some honorable members have gone so far as to say that it would be utterly impossible for the Dominion Government to fulfil the terms of union by means of navigation. Now, this was going too far. Gentlemen who understood the situation much better than he (Mr. F.) did, had no doubt respecting the possibility of navigating the Straits during the whole of the winter season. Only one route has been tried by steamboat. Honorable members on the Government side of the House say *Northern Light* is not large enough, or powerful enough, for the service required. If so, what might we not expect from a suitable boat? In his opinion Souris would be a better winter port than Georgetown. When all the different routes have been tested by a strong substantial and powerful boat, we shall be in a better position to judge as to what route should be chosen. But this will require an experience of some years, and he would never give up the hope that the Straits could be navigated during the whole winter, until a thorough test by suitable boats had been made. We should insist on the fulfilment of the terms of union, and full compensation for the loss already sustained on account of their nonfulfilment, up to the present time. We must act as one man and insist upon having our rights. On one occasion, the Legislature of British Columbia passed a resolution similar to the one now before this House, and, also, making provision that it be conveyed to Her Majesty by a delegate, to be appointed for that purpose. Mr. De Cosmos, the Premier, was, himself appointed the Delegate. A reference to the matter was contained in the Speech of the Lieutenant Governor of that Province at the opening of the following Session (Mr. Farquharson here read the quotation alluded to). Now, he (Mr. F.) thought the result of the action of British Columbia was sufficient to encourage us in our present action, with respect to the question now under consideration. If the Government do their duty in connection with this Address to Her Majesty the Queen, they will follow it up with other documents giving all necessary information with reference to the matter of winter communication. He hoped that no admissions will be made that the navigation of the Straits in winter is impossible. One thing is certain, and that is, whether we send a delegation to England or not, every argument made use of in this House in connection with

this question will be produced in Downing Street, and will have to be met. The Dominion Government will say that they promised to fulfil the terms of union, but that certain members of this Legislature admitted that it would be impossible for them to do so. By making admissions of that kind, honorable members give away our case. Although the Dominion Government have had in years past, millions of a surplus they never attempted to improve the means of crossing at the Capes, and the result has been that several persons have been maimed for life. In his opinion, these persons have good claims upon the Dominion Government for compensation. All passengers by the ice boats could only cross the Straits by making an arrangement with the couriers, as the latter were not bound to convey them across. In many cases, the men who work the ice boats are inexperienced and unqualified for the business, being picked up for the first time. He had crossed the Straits several times at the Capes, and knew this to be a fact. The measure now about to be taken in reference to this question is in the interest of life and property. We have a right to have a certain amount of freight conveyed across the Straits in winter. It should be an outlet for our exports in the fall, and an inlet for spring goods. The Government should not rest satisfied with sending the proposed memorial to Her Majesty the Queen, but should press our claims in the best possible and most reasonable way, until they secure our rights in reference to this very important matter.

H'n. Mr. FERGUSON said that the question under consideration was one of very great importance to this Province; and no matter had ever come before the Legislature in which our people were more interested. Yet it did not call for much discussion, as it is very easy to convince this honorable House and the country that we, as a people, have been very badly treated in the matter of winter communication with the mainland. The question has been so much discussed of late that there is not that incentive to speaking on it, that formerly existed. But if the House were to come to a silent conclusion upon the matter it might be regarded as if we were not really in earnest. Taking this view of the question, honorable gentlemen around the Board should freely express their opinions, and as few discordant notes should be sounded as possible. There should not be much difference of opinion between the Government and Opposition on the matter, and all party discussion should, as far as possible be avoided. He was very sorry that some honorable member of the Opposition, in the absence of his Leader, did not rise and second the motion of the honorable Leader of the Government. He had expected that the honorable member for Strathalbyn, while upon his feet, would have done so. He was not altogether satisfied with that honorable member's remarks. The honorable gentleman complained

that the Government had not made the resolution as strong as they should have done, and that they had not coupled with it a threat that if the terms of Confederation were not immediately fulfilled, we would demand separation from the Dominion. Now, he (Mr. F.) could not agree to that proposal, for he thought that the unity and harmony of the Dominion should not be interfered with on account of differences on such questions as this. It would be wrong to threaten on every occasion of unfair dealing, a separation from the Dominion. In fact he was of opinion that such a threat would rather injure our cause, than otherwise. The British Government are naturally proud of their colonies, especially those which now compose the Dominion of Canada, in their uniting and building a great highway from ocean to ocean, binding their people together and making them one The Mother Country has taken a very great interest in this Confederation from its inception; and if, in our appeal to the Imperial Government for the fulfilment of the terms of union, we couple with it a threat of severing the connection with the Dominion, it would show that we are but slightly attached to the union. The honorable member for Tignish, who, he hoped, would soon be able to resume his place in the House, found fault with the Government for not having, at an earlier date, proposed an appeal to the Queen in reference to this question. He thought the honorable member for Strathalbyn would not agree with that honorable gentleman on that point. It was not advisable to precipitate an appeal to Her Majesty without having made every possible effort to secure from the Dominion Government the fulfilment of the terms of Confederation. When an Appeal is made, it can be shown that the Government of this Province have, for a long time, borne patiently with the neglect of the Dominion Government to fulfil those terms. Our claim will be all the stronger on account of our having made every possible endeavor to secure justice from the Dominion before making the appeal to the Imperial Government. Both the honorable member for Strathalbyn and the honorable member for Tignish were formerly members of the Dominion House of Commons, but he had yet to learn that either of them had ever raised his voice with effect, on this question, during the whole five years of their term. It was certainly their duty to have raised the question, and they cannot now, therefore, complain of slowness on the part of the Local Government in dealing with it. He (Mr. F.) was glad to observe that a different tone is beginning to prevail in the speeches of honorable members of the Opposition in regard to this matter of Winter Communication, and he hoped that, in the interests of the people generally, there was an end to the small and contemptible course formerly pursued. The honorable member for Murray Harbor, above every man in this Province, had ever been prominent in insisting as a member of the Government, in every possible way, that it was the duty of the Government and people of this province to demand the fulfilment of the Terms of Confederation; but an attempt was made by the Opposition Press to hold him up as an object for contempt, because he sounded the key note to the people of this Island on this question. He (Mr. F.) hoped that in future we shall have less of this, and that all classes and parties will concur in pressing this question to a settlement. While this Government are in power, and take their stand in demanding justice for this Province, they should receive the moral support of the people in the settlement of this great question. He could not agree with the honorable member for Strathalbyn as to the causes which led this Province to enter Confederation. He could not see the advantage which would arise from the introduction of that matter into the present discussion. If he understood the honorable gentleman aright, the Province was in his opinion compelled to take that step through financial embarrassment in connection with the construction of our railway; and that it was impossible for us to have stood the strain of the remission of $160,—000 per year to London to pay the interest on the cost of that Road. He could not agree with that statement. The contractors for the construction of the railway agreed to take Provincial Debentures in payment for the work, and if our Local Banks had not speculated in those Debentures, and involved themselves in difficulty, in connection therewith, we would have been in a first rate position financially. Although he (Mr. F.) did not go as far as did the honorable member for Kensington, as to the amount of difference between our payments to, and receipts from the Dominion Treasury, at the present time, he believed that our Tariff out of Confederation would not have been required to be raised as high as at present to provide for our meeting the interest on the railway debentures. The true cause of the financial difficulties which existed previous to Confederation, was that the Banks undertook to deal with the Railway Debentures. Becoming involved they brought their influence to bear upon the Government in favor of union with Canada, and Confederation was the result. If this Province contributes to the funds of the Dominion Treasury anything like the sum stated by the honorable member for Kensington the other day, it would be very well able to bear the burden of $160,000 per year for the payment of the interest on the Railway Debentures, and would have been quite able to meet all its financial obligations out of Confederation. At any rate, he did not think we were financially compelled to join the Dominion or that we were in such a position that had not the Dominion came to our rescue we could not have held our head above water. In his opinion, no contention could be more injurious to this Province than that of the honorable gentleman in reference to this matter. The circulation of such statements was calculated to lead gentlemen now in the Dominion Parliament, but who were not in public life in 1873, to come to the conclusion that the Province would have been overwhelmed in financial difficulties had not the Dominion come to our aid. Had the Local Government, at that time pursued its own course, and made a further increase in the Tariff, we could very easily have met all our financial obligations. There were other great questions which had a powerful influence upon the minds of our public men at that time in favor of Confederation. When Confederation was agreed upon by the four earlier Provinces, several great works were in contemplation, among which was the Intercolonial Railway, improvement of the Canals, the purchase of the Hudson Bay Territory and the construction of the Pacific Railway. As one who was in favor of Confederation from the beginning, he was almost entirely influenced by the conviction that such great undertakings as those alluded to, could not be carried out by the separate Provinces. He had observed the discusssions going on for many years with regard to the construction of the Intercolonial Railway. Every possible effort was made on the part of the larger provinces to some agreement as to what part of the expense of construction each province should bear, but every attempt to do so failed. This being the case, he looked upon the construction of that great work, and others which were necessary for the future prosperity of the country, as being a strong reason for the union of all the Provinces. With respect to this Province and its means of winter communication with the Mainland, he felt that we not only lacked the means, but the support and influence necessary to give us continuous steam communication. In our isolated position, out of Confederation, we could not secure the co-operation of the sister Provinces necessary to accomplish this. These were powerful reasons amongst others which induced him to give his adhesion to Confederation. Although he was still a believer in Confederation, and although his hopes with regard to that great measure had been carried out, in some respects, he had to confess that with regard to this question of winter communication with the Mainland, he never dreamed that this Province would be left for twelve long years, during a period of two or three months of each winter, with no better facilities for the conveyance of mails and passengers across the straits than was afforded forty or fifty years ago. Now, it is well known that previous to our acceptance of the Terms of Union, the Local Government of this Province were approached a second, and even a third time by the Dominion without success, owing, in no small measure, to the fact that in the terms offered us no guarantee was given that continuous and efficient steam communication with the Mainland,

winter and summer, would be maintained, and it was not until that accommodation, which we now find in the terms. was provided for, that the people of this Province consented to Confederation. That provision was contained in words as full and explicit as the English language could make it, as follows :

" Efficient Steam Service for the conveyance of mails and passengers to be established and maintained between the Island and the Dominion, winter and summer, thus placing the Island in continuous communication with the Intercolonial Railway, and the Railway system of the Dominion."

He (Mr. F.) thought every honorable gentlemen, in the House would agree with him that it would be impossible to select words to make a bargain more binding than those just quoted. In the first place, the "communication" was to be by "Steam," and it was to be "efficient" and "continuous" between the Island, "the Intercolonial Railway, and the Railway system of the Dominion." Now, the earlier offers of terms of union to this Province did not embrace that condition, and it was only after repeated offers were rejected that the proposition with respect to "continuous steam communication" was made and accepted, showing clearly that it was one of the chief inducements to our acceptance of the Terms of Confederation. The commercial advantage of this communication to the Dominion, as a whole, was not the leading consideration, nor was it the main consideration which led to the construction by Canada of the Intercolonial and Canada Pacific Railways. In a report of a speech at a Conference on the Confederation scheme, at Halifax, in the year 1864, he found that Sir John Macdonald stated most emphatically to the people of the Lower Provinces that, "We are ready to come at once into most intimate connection with you. This cannot be fully procured I admit by political union simply. I don't hesitate to say that, with regard to the Intercolonial Railway, it is understood by the people of Canada that it can only be built as a means of political union of the colonies. It cannot be denied that the Railway, as a commercial enterprize, could be of comparatively little commercial advantage to the people of Canada."

From the speeches of other gentlemen on that occasion, he found that they placed great stress on the fact that the Road would bind all the different Provinces together, and render indissoluble the bonds of union. He would now quote from the speech of a gentleman in the Dominion Parliament, made last year, on the Pacific Railway resolutions, — a gentleman who had not been previously a member of that Parliament, and who, on that account, probably extended his remarks on that question further than other gentlemen had done. Those remarks were as follows:

" What is it, then, that, in this day and on this continent, can tend to bring us, draw us, and hold us together in bonds of national unity, with a oneness of aim and a oneness of interest? I think I will speak within the knowledge of all when I say that there is only one thing to do it, that is, a continuous, a speedy, and an uninterrupted bond of communication between all parts of the country, making every distinct member and section of this country easy of access to every other member and section of the country. That is the element that is to bind us together. Our merchants are to know each other from British Columbia to Cape Breton; our people are to become acquainted with each other from the Provinces by the sea to the Provinces in the far North West, as soon as and wherever they may be formed; we are to draw together as the members of one family; Ontario is to cease sitting down here by the broad lakes—thinking that she is sufficient to herself, and careing nothing for those who are about her, especially in the smaller Provinces away by the sea; the smaller Provinces down by the sea are to forget their prejudices against these upper Provinces, and are to become better acquainted with them in interest and in social relations; the Province of Quebec is to come and join hands with the people of the other Provinces, and we of the other Provinces are to become better acquainted with our *confrères* of the Province of Quebec, and, learning to know them better, are to learn to like them better. So, in all ways, whatever can take place to bind together the trade interest, and social interest, all the interests of the different parts of this great Confederation, is the thing which and will draw us together, keep us together, make us a living and progressive unity, in a national or country point of view. Now, one step farther, What is the kind of communication which we can have which shall join these Provinces together? Can we have a water communication which would be sufficient? No, Sir, that is impossible. Outside of the difficulty of having a water communication at any season of the year, for more than one half the width of this continent of ours there is another half of the year when the ice king lays his hand upon that form of communication, and makes it impossible to us. The only form of communication which is adequate, which is continuous, which is uninterrupted and uniform is that communication which comes from the construction and opening and completion of a trans-continental line of railway, which shall gather, Sir, in one hand the outlying Provinces of the far east, and in the other the outlying Provinces of the far west, and shall unite in bonds of intercourse and trade and social communication all the different parts of this country with every other part. I earnestly and honestly believe that the confederation of the four Provinces is not complete, that the confederation and joining together of every part of this Dominion is not complete, that it will not be held to be complete, until the iron bands of a railway trans-continental and Canadian, shall join every part of this great Dominion together in the bonds of commercial and of social intercourse. Therefore, I was in favor of Confederation because it gave us a country, I was in favor of this expansion to the bounds we now have, because it gave us a great and illimitable country, I am in favor, and cannot but be in favor, of the speedy and quick and certain construction of that which is essentially necessary to make us a united, and so a permanent, a successful, and a progressive people."

Now, these are the sentiments of a leading gentleman in the Parliament of Canada, on the construction of the Pacific Railway from a Dominion point of view. He alluded to Professor Foster. The sentiment has found its response in the hearts of the people of this country, that the various sections of the Dominion, must be bound together by uninterrupted steam communication, otherwise the union will be only on paper. Looking at the great importance attached to the union of the older provinces, and of the newer ones, also; and to the construction of the Pacific Railway through the entire country, uniting all the Provinces, we have a right to ask why continuous steam communication with the mainland of the Dominion should not be granted to us in order that we may be treated in the same way as our sister Provinces have been treated? He was sorry that statements had been made in the Dominion Parliament respecting this Province, which were incorrect, and which have had a very injurious effect upon our claims. In the year 1880, the Leader of the Opposition in the House of Commons made some very elaborate calculations with respect to all the Provinces, showing the amount which each had contributed to the Revenue of the Dominion and to what extent each had been a burden and an expense to the General Government. The result of these calculations went to show that Ontario was a kind of milch cow to the other Provinces, and that all of them, but herself, were drains upon the Dominion Treasury; in short, that she was keeping up the whole family. Honorable E. Blake, to whom he referred spoke on that occasion as follows; "Now, Sir, assigning to each Province the Revenue derived from it, as shown by the Public Accounts, and charging each Province with its local service as are by the Public Accounts distinguished and assigned to the separate Provinces, the results are as follows; * * * For Prince Edward Island the Receipts were $1,496,000, the Expenditure $2,264,000, and the Deficit $1,027,000." Now, that statement, even if it were true, should not prevent the Dominion from fulfilling the compact made with this Province at Confederation; but it would be a very strong reason why members of the Dominion Parliamen should be very unwilling indeed to vote for additional expenditures for this Island. But Mr. Blake's calculation was not true. It was based altogether on false promises. It does not show where the duty on the goods consumed here was paid. Mr. Blake gave credit for that duty to the Province where the port of entry was situated. It is well known that the larger and older Provinces import directly from other countries, and supply the merchants of the smaller Provinces. But this fact was left wholly out of sight, and he could not, therefore, acquit Mr. Blake of great indifference to truth in making so erroneous a statement as that, and giving it currency, knowing it to be incorrect. Yet it remains without correction or retraction

so far as that gentleman is concerned. He (Mr. Ferguson) felt justified in charging Mr. Blake with a wilful misrepresentation in this matter, because in making a similar calculation for Ontario, he made liberal allowance for duties on goods entered in Montreal but consumed in Ontario. He (Mr. F.) had heard it stated that the Representatives from this Island, in the House of Commons, were to blame for not answering Mr. Blake's statement. This is not just, for in the session of 1882, Mr. Hackett, member for Prince County, called attention to Mr. Blake's speech, as follows:

"I remember that in 1880, the honorable Leader of the Opposition stated that Prince Edward Island had extracted up to that time some thing like $1,027,000 more out of the Dominion Exchequer than she had paid into it. In the last session, I think the Honorable Finance Minister also stated that we had largely overdrawn. I think that is very unfair. If that is the only reason why our Public Works are not attended to, it is a poor one indeed. It is a fact that the imports of dutiable goods into Prince Edward Island have fallen off considerably within the last few years. In 1876, the total imports of dutiable goods into Prince Edward Island amounted to $1,590,981, and for the year ending 30th June, 1881, they amounted to $907,825, or a falling off of $683,156. Now, although the trade and navigation returns show a falling off of imports direct to the Province, still it is a well-known fact that the people use as many dutiable goods as heretofore, although the goods have not been imported direct from foreign countries. They are purchased at other ports, of the Dominion. The goods that are imported into the ports of Halifax, St. John, Montreal, and Toronto are bought by the Prince Edward Island traders. The duty is paid at the port of entry and credited to the Province in which it is entered, and as a matter of course, the people of Prince Edward Island thus get no credit for the amount of Revenue those goods pay."

That he (Mr. F.) thought a sufficient answer to Mr. Blake; but an incorrect statement, once made, by a gentleman occupying so high a position, receives a wide circulation, and it is impossible to controvert it in every quarter. That gentleman's figures have been accepted almost over the whole Dominion as being correct, and have damaged our interests as a Province. Unfortunately, those calculations have gone on and on, and have been read again and again on the floor of the House of Commons, as a gentleman of Mr. Blake's standing is taken as an authority in such matters. A false impression has, therefore, gone abroad, and the correction has not reached those most influenced by it. He had listened to the speech of the Honorable member for Kensington with respect to this matter, showing a very different state of things from that stated by Mr. Blake, and correcting the misstatements of the latter. It is a very difficult matter to arrive at exact figures in dealing with this question, the productiveness of a Tariff being so much affected by a variety of circumstances. If we were out of Confederation to-morrow, no one pretends that we would import so largely from the other Provinces as we now do. Our trade would be directed into other channels, and it would be utterly impossible to estimate how much we would, under those altered circumstances, pay in the way of duties compared with what we do at the present time. Some of the Provinces of the Dominion are larger contributors, per head, to the general weal and prosperity than others are. Owing to our isolated position, we cannot become manufacturers to any great extent, and must purchase a large portion of the goods we consume from the other Provinces. The larger Provinces are, therefore, receiving the larger portion of the profits of trade. British Columbia imported nearly all her goods direct from foreign countries, and therefore received full credit in the returns for all the duties actually paid. She did not enjoy any considerable trade with the Dominion, owing to the want of communication by Railway, and therefore showed a large amount of duties paid in proportion to population. It was matter for very great regret that those erroneous calculations by Mr. Blake had ever been made, as they placed this Province in a false position before the people of the whole Dominion. Then, again, the Toronto *Mail* newspaper saw fit to admit to its columns articles grossly erroneous, stating that the cost of the Prince Edward Island Railway had been paid by the Dominion, instead of by this Province. This same error seems to run through the minds of nearly all the public men of the

Dominion, and to obtain to a very great extent. It showed a great want of the spirit of fair-play when the *Mail* refused to admit to its columns the reply of Dr. Jenkins to the article alluded to; particularly as that reply was very moderate in its tone. As a Province, we have suffered many disadvantages through misrepresentation in various quarters. When this question of winter communication came to be dealt with, it was not expected that the Dominion would be able to grapple with the difficulty and overcome it all at once. Under the McKenzie Government, the old steamer *Albert* was fitted up and placed on the Georgetown and Pictou route; but she was altogether unfit for the service and miserably failed as all knew she would fail. Later on, the *Northern Light* was placed by that Government on the route. This boat did considerable service at the commencement and close of the winter season, and has proved a good experiment in solving the difficulty, but the disadvantages in connection with her have been almost as great as the advantages. The loss and disappointment have been almost equal to the benefit received from her. That she was not wisely designed for the service required of her, has been amply proved. It was discovered on the very last trip she made, that her stern is very much better adapted for breaking through the ice than her stem is; and she made her way through eighteen miles of ice stern foremost. This shows that the Dominion Government have been dealing in a most hap-hazard way with this important matter, and that they have not provided a boat properly designed for the service. Although the *Northern Light* has become less sea-worthy than she was, no other boat has been placed on the route. The Minister of Marine and Fisheries promised during the last session of the Dominion Parliament that another boat would be built to relieve her, but it turned out that the new one was intended to relieve the Light Houses, and no other boat was brought to the assistance of the *Northern Light*. Turning to the Capes Route, what do we find? When we entered Confederation, the mail service was conducted in the same old-fashioned manner as it had been thirty or forty years previously, and to-day, twelve years later, it is still being carried out in the same old way! The small, open boats now used there are still being dragged along over the ice and paddled through the open spaces of water as they were half a century ago! The Dominion Government have never seen it to be their duty, in the interests of this Province, to contract for the means of conveying a single passenger across the straits! As a matter of fact, every passenger who, for the past twelve years, has crossed from this Island to the mainland, has done so at his own risk; and his conveyance has been a mere matter of grace on the part of the mail couriers. Although the Dominion Government were bound by the Terms of Confederation to provide "efficient steam service for the conveyance of mails and passengers," "winter and summer," no contract at all has been entered into for the conveyance of passengers. They may say that the winter navigation of the straits is a difficult thing to accomplish, and that we must be reasonable. Will they say that it was impossible to have suitable boats manned by a sufficient number of men to take across the straits safely all persons who presented themselves for the passage? Will they say that there are insurmountable difficulties in the way of their doing this? No. It would have cost a little more money than at present, but that is all. What was clearly possible of accomplishment has not been carried out. The public returns show that since the *Northern Light* was on the Georgetown–Pictou route, she was laid up on an average 64 days in each winter. During no year was provision made for the conveyance of passengers by the ice-boats when the *Northern Light* ceased running. Passengers by the Capes route were called upon to pay for their passage, and work their passage into the bargain. From Cape Tormentine to the Intercolonial railway, a Branch line could be very easily and cheaply constructed, but, for about forty miles, there is no means of reaching the Intercolonial except by sleighs dragged over snow banks, or roads and fields half bare. Yet, according to the Terms of Union, the Dominion was bound to provide for us steam connection on the other side of the Straits, with the Intercolonial railway. Will the Domin-

ion Government say that it is impossible for them to provide for this Province continuous steam communication, in winter from the Intercolonial railway to Cape Tormentine? There are men in the present Dominion Government who assisted in making the Terms of Union, who knew as much about the winter navigation of the Straits as we did, and they will not say that it is impossible to carry out more efficiently the terms in this respect. They will not say that for twelve years it was im— possible to construct a Branch line of Railway from Cape Tormentine to the Intercolonial. Three years have passed since a grant was made for the construction of the Cape Traverse Branch Line, and yet it was only the other day that this short road was opened for traffic. Not a shovelful of earth has been thrown up by the Dominion to connect Cape Tormentine with the Intercolonial railway, by a Branch line. He did not think they could offer any material excuse for not pro— viding suitable means for the conveyance across the Straits of passengers as well as mails, in the winter season. All this shows that they have made no serious effort to fulfil their obligations to this Province. It is, also, matter for regret that when the money was voted for the Cape Traverse Branch an opinion appeared to prevail among the public men of Canada that the Province was receiving more than its due share of the public money. The fact, that such a feeling was entertained by some of the leading members of

Parliament caused no small annoyance to the people of this Province. Among the men referred to, was the Honorable Mr. Mackenzie, the Leader of the late Dominion Government, On pages 1437-8 of the Dominion *Hansard* for 1882, may be found the following in reference to the Cape Traverse Branch:

"Mr. ANGLIN. This is a small piece of line forming a portion of a through line which we are bound by our treaty with the Island to finish if possible."

Mr MACKENZIE —"I think we have done very well by the Island, and we have carried out the terms of union to the utmost possible extent."

It is a matter for surprise that a leading man like Mr. Mackenzie, who, for a long time was First Minister of the country should have allowed himself to make such a statement. Mr. Anglin, had been stating in the course of his speech that there was great reason to doubt whether the Local Legislature of New Brunswick would grant a sufficient subsidy for the construction of the Cape Tormentine Branch, that $3,000 per mile was insufficient for the purpose, and that there should be some prospect of its receiving some assistance from the Dominion Government. Mr. Mackenzie said that the Government should give no grants in aid of the construction of Branch lines of that kind. Yet that line would not only be a Branch road for the counties of Westmoreland and Northumberland, but would form part of a line to connect the Intercolonial with Cape Tormentine, in accordance with the terms of union with this Province. It was certainly the duty of the Dominion Government to have built that line and to have operated it, and not to have left it to any company to do so. The Road should have been located in such a way as to make the best and shortest connection with the Intercolonial Railway. When Sir Charles Tupper stated that this road should be in the hands of the Government, Mr. McKenzie made remarks in opposition thereto. It is gratifying to find that the leading Journals in the Dominion are taking a much broader view of this question than formerly. Among the utterances of leading men on the matter, after the Capes disaster, that of His Grace Archbishop O'Brien, of Halifax, was particularly worthy of note; and he thought we ought to feel thankful to that gentlemen for his timely and vigorous letter to the press with reference to it. The following is a quotation:—

"I now deliberately assert that there are no words too strong to condemn the inhuman weakness of the authorities, or their ignorant flippancy in the Commons regarding that service. I am not writing this in a party spirit; the Liberals were the same when in power; both parties are equally culpable in that regard. *

*   *   *   *

The question of winter communication interests all the Maritime Provinces. It was the hope of improvement, in this regard, that gave the strongest impetus to confederation on the Island. The Dominion agreed to keep up "continuous steam communication with the mainland." True, the *Northern Light* has done some good; but no attempt has been made to improve on her—a thing which could easily be done. At the Capes, where the mails must cross for, at least, two or three months every winter, no attempt at improvement has been made. Things are as they were thirty years ago. The most fertile Province in the Dominion is less cared for than the Hudson Bay Territory in the wilds of the North-west. Captain Irving, who has grown gray in ice-boat service, made an offer a few years ago to provide, at a very small cost, what his experience has suggested as useful. The post office authorities offered him three hundred dollars—he had asked, I think, five or six. Is not this outrageous? This contemptible haggling, unworthy of a huckster woman, was solemnly indulged in by ministers, for I suppose it must have gone before the ministers of the crown, and mails and passengers were left to cross as of yore."

These expressions, coming as they do, from so influential a man, have had a weighty effect upon public opinion. The Montreal *Herald* had, also, important editorial articles upon this subject, from which he would quote the following :—

"It is evident that, if faith is to be kept with the people of Prince Edward Island, some better and safer means must be found of keeping up communication between the province and the continent during the winter time. It must be remembered that the Government of the Dominion is under precisely the same obligation to have that communication regular and constant as it is to build a railroad to British Columbia ; and we all know how much it has done to fulfil its treaty obligations with the Pacific Province. The amount of money required to do all that can be done, short of cutting a tunnel under the Strait (which is seriously advocated by some Islanders) will take but a comparatively small sum of money."

In another article the *Herald* goes on to say,—

"It is no wonder that the people of Prince Edward Island complain that faith has not been kept with them by the Dominion in the matter of mail communication. Up to last night there was no mail from the Island-Province for eight days. For one whole week the only communication between the Island and the rest of the world was by a Telegraph cable. This is certainly not keeping up constant communication for mails and passengers by steamer between the Island and the Mainland, as the Dominion is bound by treaty to do. The inefficiency of the service is certainly a disgrace to the Government. The obstacles which nature has placed between the Island and the continent in the winter time are certainly great, but these are far from insurmountable, and it must be confessed that very little indeed is being done by the Government to overcome them. The mails are carried by private contract. The contractors get the merest pittance for risking their lives and encountering great hardships in carrying out in a very imperfect manner the treaty obligations of the Dominion. It must be remembered that the passage is not often made in less than five hours of hard, continuous toil, and it sometimes takes eight or ten hours—and all this for twelve dollars. The Dominion Government should have taken charge of the business long ago.

They should not have suffered a service which they are bound in common honesty to make efficient, to be carried on in the miserable and miserly way described. . . . . . When it is considered that the faith of the people of Canada is pledged to keep up mail communication between Prince Edward Island and the mainland in winter as well as in summer, it might be supposed that the Government would, without hesitation or delay, take every practicable means and spare no reasonable expense to carry out its treaty obligations. That it has not done so, the evidence adduced in this article is sufficient proof. No one will contend that the means of conveying the mails and passengers across the Strait, described by Captain Irving, are sufficient. And everyone connected with the Island knows that its inhabitants every winter suffer hardship, loss and inconvenience for the want of that efficient communication with the mainland which the Dominion is bound to furnish."

Such articles in the *Montreal Herald*, and the letter of the Archbishop will have more effect upon the public men of the Dominion than all the speeches members of the Legislature could make for an indefinite length of time. Such writings are weighed very carefully all over the country, while remarks made in this House are apt to be attributed to Local feeling. In contrast, and very unfortunate contrast to the sentiments of the *Montreal Herald* on this subject, are the editorials of the *Patriot* newspaper, the organ of the Local Opposition. During the term of the Mackenzie Administration, its friends in this Island were so faithful to that gentleman that none of them would admit that any fault could be found with him.

Mr. FARQUHARSON—The Honorable member lays all the blame on the Mackenzie party.

Mr. FERGUSON thought he could claim for himself that he was quite as willing to censure the present Dominion Government when they deserved it, as to point out the shorcomings of their predecessors. He had read extracts particulary bearing upon the manner in which our winter communication with the mainland is being carried on at the present time, and had shown the utter neglect of the Government to provide for the conveyance of passengers and to construct a Branch line of railway from Cape Tormentine to the Intercolonial railway. He would, also, add, that some two years ago, the Dominion Government voted a sum of money for harbor improvements at Cape Tormentine, but that up to the present moment, not a single dollar of it has been expended. Although a supporter of the present Dominion Government, he had not spared them in the present discussion, when their actions deserved censure. Although he congratulated some members of the Opposition on their moderation in the present debate, he could not congratulate their organ the *Patriot* newspaper on the manner in which it had dealt with this important question. That paper professed to be a patriotic journal, edited by a patriot of the purest water, and he would contrast its article of this evening and which was handed to him since taking his feet with those of the organ of the Canada Pacific Railway Syndicate, already quoted. The *Patriot* said :

THE APPEAL.

"Messrs. Sullivan & Co., are again at it. Now it is an appeal to Her Majesty the Queen, on the subject of the Island's neglected rights and claims, especially in the matter of winter communication with the mainland. The whole thing, on their part, has the appearance of political clap-trap. In our opinion, their purpose is to lead the minds of the people away from the Island's affairs generally, and their stewardship in particular. It is another instance, on a small scale, of the methods resorted to by governments of large countries in Europe to lead the minds of people away from local or home interests by means of a foreign complication or war. Russia, with Nihilism eating out her vitals, and the lives of the reigning family and the throne ever in jeopardy, marches an army to far-off Afghanistan, threatening British prestige and interests, all for the purpose of enlisting the attention of the people with the prospects of a war with Britain. Our Tories are following the same idea or plan of turning our people's attention from their empty treasury.

An appeal across the water against Sir John who was lately there, and given the toga and red breeches, and who came back with the big letters. G. C. B., chalked between his shoulders, does not look very promising. The main hope the Island has to secure its rights is to batter and bang and hammer away at the wall of indifference raised so high by the present Dominion Government. Per-

sistency, unaccompanied by partizan toadyism, will finally accomplish the desired end. Sullivan & Co., may test the efficacy of an appeal to the Queen, but as our winter communication has very little bearing on Imperial questions, we do not anticipate any very decided action thereon by the Home Government. British Columbia is of great importance to England on the Pacific coast for her navy, and it was essential for the welfare of the Empire that said Province should be connected with Canada East by a railway. Hence the interference in her case. With the Island it is somewhat different, and we are afraid she will have to paddle her own canoe."

Here the action of the present Local Government, and of the majority of the people's Representatives in this House, is compared with the action of Russia in marching an army into Asia for the purpose of drawing off the attention of her people from difficulties at home. The article, states that the Government are making a raid on the Treasury at Ottawa, when they send a Delegation there to obtain for this Province its lawful rights While the Government is striving to serve the interests of the people of this Province, this organ of the Opposition endeavors to weaken their claim, to show that they had no case, and that it was only a scheme to divert the attention of the people of this Island from an empty Treasury at home ! Yet this paper is edited by a gentleman who, at one time, held a seat in the Dominion Cabinet at Ottawa. To carry out the *Patriot's* idea, the Grit Party in this Province must be the Nihilists at home. Its object seems to be to do anything at all which would weaken the Government, no matter how the province may suffer. Never mind, says he, going to England to secure our rights; batter away at the Government. Notwithstanding the mild nature of the observations made during the present discussion by the Honorable member for West River, that paper is determined that this question of our rights with respect to the fulfillment by the Dominion, of the terms of union, shall be marred and weakened as much as possible, and that every means must be resorted to, to thwart the intentions of the Government and Legislature. According to this article, Her Majesty the Queen has no right to say that the terms of Confederation shall be carried out, as "it has very little bearing on Imperial questions." It is really too bad that this course should be pursued by the Organ of the Opposition. But it is evident that the influence of those who control it is not as great as they desire, and that they cannot do all the mischief they wish to do. Notwithstanding all the opposition of the organ, alluded to, he felt persuaded that the Government will be able to secure justice for this Province in respect to the matter now under consideration. They were hampered to the same extent on the Piers question by the same organ, which took great pains in pointing out that there was not a single *wharf* in the Dominion of Canada that had been taken over and kept in repair by the General Government. It endeavoured to show that the latter might "maintain *piers*, but not to maintain *wharves;* that certain piers on the St. Lawrence should be maintained by them because the tide there always ran in one direction, but that they should not be expected to take over and repair our piers. While the matter of the piers was still pending, and the Dominion Engineers were examining and reporting upon them, the organ of the Opposition Party was busy quoting Dictionaries to show that wharves and piers were altogether different things, and that because the tide always flowed in one direction in the St. Lawrence —and the current rapid—the piers on that river were the only ones which the Dominion Government should maintain. The following quotations is from the *Patriot* of 15th March, 1883 :

"In the above list of works (harbors and piers enumerated in the Report of the Public Works Department for 1876-7) we cannot discover that Prince Edward Island has failed to receive the same justice as the adjoining Provinces. There is not a sylable in the report about wharves. But perhaps the Deputy Minister of Public Works, as the *Examiner* asserts about Mr. Laird, did not understand the meaning of the word "Pier." He appears to apply that word and the "Breakwater" indiscriminately. Mr. Laird has, therefore, good company in the ignorance with which he is charged by the *Examiner*. The authors of the two first dictionaries to which we referred appears to be in the same deplorable darkness. The Globe Dictionary, published by Collins, of Glasgow, Scotland, gives the following concluding definition of the word "Pier,"—"A mass of stone work projecting into the sea for breaking the force of the waves; a wharf or landing place." Here the idea ot a breakwater is the leading of breakwater is the leading one sought to be conveyed. Worcester, an American author, defines the word "Pier" thus:—A mole or jetty carried out into the sea to break the force of the waves; to form a harbor or landing place, etc." The meaning of wharf or landing place in connection with the term is quite a secondary one according to both the authors quoted, and we think any of them will compare favorably as guides in lexicography with the self-sufficient, but not very wise or learned writer for the *Examiner.*

With respect to securing compensation from the Dominion for our expenditure on piers, since Confederation, the same organ, on April 3rd, 1883, goes on to say :

"We are sure the manly, independent, spirited Yeomanry of this Island would sooner pay Assessment twice over than submit to such humiliation. If we have any valid claim against the Dominion Government, let it be presented in a respectful and dignified manner ; but do not permit the Government of the Island to demean its people in the eyes of the world by adopting the acts of the scheming beggar who creeps into your kitchen, and partly by a wail of poverty, and partly by *colored* statements of services rendered perhaps to your grandfather, and partly by threats, seeks to gain the needful."

"Blue ruin and desolation" is the cry of the Grit organ at all times and on all occasions while the present Local Government are in power. To obtain our just dues from the Dominion Government is put down as "scheming beggary." There is good reason for believing that there were men at Ottawa who opposed every movement of the Government on the piers question. There were also men among the Grit party at home who did all that lay in their power to prevent our securing better terms before entering Confederation. The probability is that the Province would have received a much larger indemnity for its piers, were it not for the *Patriot's* articles in reference to it. All the actions of the Government were misrepresented, and they were declared to have "trumped up" colored statements in order to obtain money to which the Province was not entitled. From the remarks of the honorable member for West River on the question now under consideration, he had expected that the Government, in dealing with it would have received the cordial support of the Opposition, although he did not expect they would find the slightest fault with anything the Mackenzie Government had done. But from the article now contained in their organ, it is evident that such is not the course they intend to pursue. "Those whom the Gods intend to destroy, they first drive mad." The Opposition have shown their want of political tact in dealing with this question. Instead of dealing with it from a broad and liberal stand point, they take the opposite course. If the Government had the cordial support of all outside and inside the House, they could not fail to secure the fulfilment of the terms of union. But they now feel that they will succeed without any support from the Opposition, and that all the credit of that success will be theirs.

I. O.

WEDNESDAY, March 25.

Mr. D. C. MARTIN said he only wished to say a few words on this question as it was a matter upon which all inhabitants of the Province should be unanimous. The question, however, was to important for honorable members to allow it to pass with merely a silent vote, for it was a question that had been discussed both in the Dominion Parliament and the Provincial Legislature, and was of vital importance to the welfare of this Island. He was very happy to observe the manner in which this debate had commenced, and to find that both parties were willing to make this a provincial and not a party matter; but he was sorry to hear one of the most prominent speakers on the Government side violate that rule this evening, by making an unprovoked attack upon the Opposition party. The honorable member seemed to be actuated by the command given by Admiral Nelson to his Captains at the battle of the Nile "If you cannot see my signals, or cannot make them out, attack the enemy's ships." And so it is with the honorable member for East River, after advising honorable members

to abstain from dragging partizanship into this debate, he turns round and abuses the editor of the *Patriot*, Mr Blake and the Opposition party in general. We should not approach the consideration of this matter in that way. This Province is asking the Dominion to carry out the terms of confederation and although Mr. McKenzie or any other honorable gentleman said that the Dominion had carried out our terms, yet so long as we said they have not done so, it will make very little difference to the success or failure of our demands. As one member of the House, he (Mr. D. C. Martin) was willing to support this measure, but as a matter of fact it could not be denied, that Sir John's Government had not done as much for this province, in this respect, as McKenzie's did when they were in power. Since the McKenzie Government gave us the *Northern Light* what had been done to improve this service? It was disgusting to think that the Dominion Government had allowed the Capes Routes to be put up at auction and sold to the lowest bidder, and that their doing so had prevented any improvement being made in that service. It is a most arduous service this crossing at the Capes and should have been taken, in charge by the Dominion Government years ago It is not however, for the people of this province to say how the conditions of the terms of union should be carried out, all we ought to do is to urge on the Dominion the fulfilment of terms. In looking over the Minute of Council that had been sent by the Local Government, he noticed that it is there shown how very remiss the Dominion Government had been in answering the Joint Addresses that had been sent by the Legislature of this Province in the years 1881 and 1883, and that a very just remonstrance was included in it against the short and formal replies to these documents that had been forwarded to the Government of this Province. No honorable members could have anything to say against the Government urging our claims on the Dominion Government. How the Dominion Government should carry out this part of the contract is not for us to say but we must insist that the terms are fulfilled. The honorable Commissioner of Crown Lands had no right to say that the Opposition are trying to throw cold water on the efforts of the Government to obtain a settlement of this matter. He (Mr. D. C. Martin) as one member of the Opposition was willing to help the Government. The Opposition had done what they could to further this object and had made no objections to the passing of the several joint addresses that had been forwarded by the Legislature. It is unfair to say the Opposition were against pressing our claims in this matter, and he hoped the present appeal would be successful. The honorable Commissioner of Crown Lands said "that those whom the Gods wish to destroy, they first drive mad." Judging from his (Mr. F.'s) speech the dissolution of

that honorable member is not far distant.

Mr. BLAKE said he deemed it the duty of every honorable member to speak on this question, as it is one of the most important that ever came before this honorable House. He (Mr. B.) had listened to the speech of the honorable Provincial Secretary with attention and had experienced great pleasure in doing so. After listening to so able a speech he was afraid that anything he could say on the question would fall flat on the ears of honorable members. Without repeating much of what had already been brought to their notice, no honorable member can hope to interest the House. It is no credit to either of the Dominion Governments that we have been so badly used in this matter, that we have to resort to Her Majesty the Queen to get the rights guaranteed us at Confederation. When the bargain was entered into, a solemn compact was made between Prince Edward Island and the Dominion of Canada. It is well known that Prince Edward Island had carried out her part of the agreement and it is most unjust that the Dominion had not carried out their part also. When our case is laid at the foot of the throne there is no doubt but we will get the justice that has been so long denied us. It is very little to the credit of the general government that for twelve long years they have neglected to carry out this part of of a bargain that was so solemnly made. The promise contained in this part of the terms of Confederation, helped many, who were opposed to our entering the Dominion, to change their views. Looking at our isolated position during many months of the year, many were opposed to entering the Union. They maintained we were not in a position to obtain the same advantages as the other provinces. When, however, the benefits that would accrue from the fulfillment of this part of the terms, when the better position we would be in to trade with other parts of the world was pointed out, it was then considered advisable for us to become an integral part of the Dominion. He, (Mr. B) greatly regretted that the present Dominion Government had not endeavored to carry out the terms of Confederation more effectually than they had, for he had been a strong supporter of that party, and always considered they would do this Province justice in this matter. On this question, however, he had changed his mind, for whatever shortcomings the Government had in this matter, there is no excuse for the present Government, as they are the parties who made those terms, and who never objected to this section of the bargain when they were inducing this Province to enter the Union. They, consequently, had no excuse for not carrying out this part of the agreement. Since the *Northern Light* was put on, no efforts have been made to improve our winter communication, and although the *Northern Light* has lessened the time we are debarred from communication with the out-

side world, yet it was well-known that long periods occur, when no passages can be made by this boat. It was the duty of the General Government to have improved the Capes route and to have made it as efficient as possible. The dangers of the Capes route were known, and had been brought prominently to the notice of not only this Province, but of the whole Dominion, and this season they had nearly cost the lives of many people of this Province. It is said there will be no changes without a revolution, and perhaps this accident may be useful in place of a revolution, as it had called the attention of the Press and the public to this matter. The Dominion Government have intimated that they intend taking this matter of crossing at the Capes into their own hands, and it is to be hoped that they may yet improve this service so as to make it at least partially successful. The Local Government had been faithfully performing their duty, although the Opposition had charged them with slumbering over the matter. It is true they have not been able to induce the Dominion Government to carry out the terms of Confederation as efficiently as we require, but it is well-known that the Address forwarded last year, intimated that that was the last time the fulfillment of our compact would be asked from the General Government, and that compensation was expected for the term of years that had elapsed. It was also distinctly stated that the next Address would be sent to Her Majesty as one of the high contracting parties at the time of Confederation. It may be said that it is impossible to carry out the terms of Union. Whether that be so or not, the Dominion Government promised to give this Province continuous and efficient steam communication, winter and summer, and it is not our duty to tell them how their bargain shall be carried out. When Her Majesty saw that we have such good reasons for complaining, when the facts are laid before the Throne, and the dangers to which her loyal subjects are so often exposed are brought to her notice, there is no doubt but that feeling of justice that actuates her councils, will no longer require us to submit to such great disadvantages. The honorable senr. member for Belfast said that it was no difference what remarks had been made by leading men of the Opposition on this question, but in his (Mr. B.'s) opinion, the position which they occupy and have occupied, tends to give great force to what they say. The honorable Mr. McKenzie, who occupied the honorable position of Leader of the Dominion Government a few years ago, and who is generally regarded as a man of truth, said that the Dominion had carried out the terms of Union with Prince Edward Island very well. No doubt the honorable gentlemen, was satisfied that what he stated was correct, but we know that our terms are not carried out anything like as well as they should be. It is most important that gentlemen occupying his position should be rightly informed on matters of this kind, as such utterances will have a great effect in prejudicing our case when it is presented to Her Majesty. The remarks of Mr. Mackenzie may be quoted against the interests of this Province, and will, together with the honorable Mr. Blake's statement that we had received over $1,000,000 over what we had paid into the Dominion Treasury, have a great effect against our interests in this matter. Unfortunately the same opinion is entertained by many of the members of the Dominion Legislature from Ontario and he (Mr. B.) had heard some of them express exactly, the same opinions. They say "what do you Islanders want? You are wanting more all the time, what right have you to consider Ontario the milch cow of the Dominion." This shows that these people think we get more than we deserve and it is most unfortunate that these views should be entertained and expressed by so many leading men of the Dominion. It was an unfortunate day when we entered Confederation. He (Mr. B.) had always been opposed to it, and it was only on account of certain circumstances that occurred in 1873 which made it necessary for us to join in with the Dominion, that we had consented to do so. We were led to believe by those who advocated this measure, that we would be all right after we entered the Union, but it seemed as if there were many things yet to be desired. The honorable member for Springton asked what would the alternative be if we did not get the bargain carried out? Would it be separation? That was an open question and one on which great difference of opinion existed. Such a thing may happen that we may be asked to take our choice. It may be said that it is impossible to carry out the Terms of Union and the Dominion may give us back our freedom. He believed we would be better out of Confederation. It will be said that it will be impossible to carry on our Government and the expenses of our Railway without direct taxation, but he (Mr. B.) believed we can manage our own affairs with the taxation at present imposed by the Dominion. If our railway was managed in the interest of the Province there would be less loss in working it than there is at present. Although the railway was built to further the interests of Prince Edward Island, and although paid for by the people of this province, it is not run in our interests, for the tariff adopted by the authorities is the same as that charged on the other railways of the Dominion. If cheap fares and rates were adopted our people would be induced to use the road more often than they do and in this way it would pay much better than it does now. It is an open question and if we were relieved from Confederation it no doubt would be considered. We find there is something of the same spirit in the Legislature of Nova Scotia now sitting at Halifax for a Resolution has been brought in asking for separation from the Dominion. We know there is a

great deal of satisfaction in the Dominion. While we have a fine country and the elements of a great nation, there is very little union between the several parts of it, for nearly every province is asking for better terms. If Confederation continues means must be adopted to satisfy the Provinces, for it is no use for a country to be confederated without union. It was a great undertaking to attempt to join so many provinces, with so many different interests, into one Confederation. The Confederation has all the natural elements of a great nation and it may be from want of public spirit that so many say they want separation. The Dominion Government should see the want of union between the province or they lack the foresight that the rulers of so great a country should possess. He (Mr. B.) hoped before these questions are settled that the Dominion will take a proper view of their obligations and carry out our compact as effectually as they did that with British Columbia. When the people of British Columbia applied to the Throne for fulfilment of their terms of union they soon got them, and although the honorable Commissioner of Crown Lands had quoted from the "Patriot" where it said that British Columbia was of more importance than this province, yet if it was right for British Columbia to have their terms of Confederation carried out, then surely ours should also be attended to. He hoped the action of the Government would be coincided in by both branches of the Legislature as there was nothing like being united on a question, of this kind that was for the interest of this province. While he (Mr. B.) believed in party government he considered that a strong opposition kept the Government from committing many unworthy actions, but this question should be above all party and should only be judged from a provincial stand point. In former days party feeling had often been carried too far, and our present position was in a great measure owing to it. It was sincerely to be hoped that the days of such feelings had gone by for ever. He would not further occupy the time of the House as anything further would only be a repitition of what had already been said on this matter, excepting to express the hope that this most important question will be carried to a successful termination.

Mr. RICHARDS said at the late hour which this debate had reached, anything but short speeches would be out of place. It was, however, the duty of honorable members to express their views of questions of importance, such as the one under consideration. For the last few months there had been considerable agitation on this matter, an agitation which has extended from one end of the Province to the other. The speakers in this House yesterday had divested their addresses of any party tendencies, and he was surprised at the honorable Commisssoner of Crown Lands taking

a different manner when disussing this matter. Last year the honorable member had compared a journey he had taken up west as going from Jerusalem to Jericho, but his speech this evening might more properly be called by such a name, as he had travelled over a great deal of ground foreign to the question. This question should be kept free from party politics, as it was one on which both parties should agree. Both the present and former Dominion Government have been equally negligent in fulfilling this part of the terms of Confederation. Subsection 7 expressly provides for efficient steam communication for the conveyance of mails and passengers winter and summer, thus placing the Island in continuous communication with the mainland and the railway system of the Dominion. This compact had not been fulfilled. It was one of the inducements that had been held out to the people of this Province, who were known to be greatly opposed to confederation. After twelve years what has been done to carry out this part of the terms ? No doubt the "Northern Light" had been a success, and had demonstrated that a larger boat would have done a great deal more, but it is impossible to cross on the route where she is stationed in mid-winter. The same system of crossing at the capes is practiced as prevailed twenty-five years ago, and is well known to be most unsatisfactory. Many say a tunnel is the only way which our communication can be kept up continuously.   The honorable senior member for Murray Harbor gets credit for having originated this idea and it is to be hoped that he (Mr. P.) will live to see the day his pet scheme will be carried out.

Hon. Mr. PROWSE said he did not think the Tunnel was impossible and was glad to see the honorable member becoming a convert to the same views.

Mr. RICHARDS said the honorable member and the Government should bring this question of building a tunnel to the notice of the Dominion Government. If it is practicable, no time should be lost in having the matter tested. During January, February and March in each year it is almost impossible to cross the straits by navigation and if a tunnel is practicable, he (Mr. R.) did not see why it had not been brought to the notice of the Dominion Government long ago. The honorable member for Kensington said in his speech on the Address in reply to His Honor the Lieutenant Governor, that he believed a tunnel could be constructed, and when two honorable members, one of them a member of the Local Government and the other a supporter, believe in the feasibility of this project, they should bring it to the notice of the Dominion Government. The Address we are now considering is, under the circumstances, the best movement the Legislature can take in this matter. Last session, by the Address then passed, we told the Dominion Government that it was the last time an appeal would be

made to them respecting this question, and we have now nothing left to do, but appeal to Her Majesty. There is no doubt but this Address will be carried unanimously and he (Mr. R.) hoped that it might be the means whereby a better system of keeping up communication during the winter months would be inaugurated.

Hon. Mr. MACLEOD said he did not intend saying a great deal on this question, as it had been so fully discussed, not only this session, but during the previous sessions when Addresses had been passed requesting the Dominion Government to carry out the terms of Confederation. In these Addresses we have put forward our very best arguments, and since the Dominion Government had not replied to our just complaint, the only recourse we now had, was to appeal to Her Majesty the Queen. We are just as important as was the Province of British Columbia, when Her Majesty interfered and said that the compact made with that province must be fulfilled. The terms made with British Columbia provided that a Railway over thousands of miles should be constructed, and notwithstanding the great expense, it is well known that this work is now nearly completed. We have no right to think the British Government is unjust, and will only act to protect the rights of a province when it is for British interests to do so. Is this the character we should give Britain in her relations to her colonies? This question of winter communication was one of the great causes why this province entered Confederation, as we were then promised steam communication winter and summer. It was this promise that influenced the people of this Island, as much as anything else, to throw in their lot with the Dominion. It is true the proprietary claims and the desire of the tenants to have these claims settled was an inducement to many of our people, and also the burden of our railway debt was feared by many others, but the expense of building the Railway and buying the Lands could have been met if sufficient tariff had been imposed. If a tariff, as high as the one at present imposed by the Dominion had been adopted, sufficient revenue would have accrued, not only to have paid for our Railway and Lands but to have carried on winter communication much more effectually than has been the case during the past twelve years. The Dominion Government were most anxious that this Island should join the Union and promised us this efficient steam communication winter and summer. He (Mr. McL) had lately been reading the speech of Sir George Cartier, delivered at the Conference held here in 1864, and it was a good illustration of the blandishments that had been thrown out to induce us to enter the union. He (Mr. McL.) would read part of the speech, which is as follows :

"When I think of the nationality which can be formed if we can but bring the Provinces under one Federal Government, it seems to me I see before me—and I am now speaking by a sort of metaphor—a great British American nation, with the fair Provinces of New Brunswick and Nova Scotia as the arms of the national body to embrace the trade of the Atlantic. None could make so fair a head as Prince Edward Island. This national body will then want a trunk, and we in Canada having the "Grand Trunk," can afford to be the trunk to the nation. The two Canadas will stretch with their toes far out to the west, and bring as much as possible of the western territory into the Confederation."

We see in this that he calls us the "fair province" of Prince Edward Island, and advocated that our communication should be more efficient than it was. Some honorable members had referred to the fact that Mr. Blake had submitted figures to the Dominion Parliament showing that this Island was a drain on the Dominion Treasury, but he (Mr. McL.) did not think that affected the question. Whether we are a drain or not we have been promised certoin services, one of which is continuous communication, winter and summer. As the Dominion is a party to the compact, and as we have surrendered our revenues, they must carry out the terms they agreed to. It is not under discussion whether we take more from the Dominion Treasury than we pay into it. The only answer we have received to the Joint Addresses that had been sent in 1881, 1883 and 1884 was "that the matter was under consideration." They have made no excuse for not fulfilling their agreement. Some say it is impossible to carry out the terms, but the Dominion Government has not informed this province that it is impossible for them to do so. Whether the compact can be carried out or not it is not for us to say, but one thing is certain they have not made any great experiments to see if it can. They have only placed the *Northern Light* at one place and only one route has been experimented on. Some say that a route from West Cape to New Brunswick is practicable. Others that from Cape Bear to Nova Scotia is the proper place, but no experiments have been made to ascertain if this service can be performed more satisfactory than it is at present. Supposing they say the ice is a complete barrier and that the service is impossible excepting by the ice boats at the Capes, then they should improve that system, for no doubt it could be greatly improved, and proper provision for the conveyance of passengers should be provided. The Dominion Government have a right to compensate this Province for not carrying out the compact they entered into. At the time this compact was made, it was well known that the Straits of Northumberland was filled with ice during the winter months, and that the service of carrying the mails in open boats had been carried on for twenty years previously. They knew the hardship of this service and yet they promised to overcome it and carry on the service continuously. If they cannot carry out this service as efficiently as they promised,

they should improve it as much as possible and recompense the province for the non fulfillment of the Terms. If they find they cannot carry out the Terms made, they should either r lease us from our bargain or pay us compensation for the damages we have received on account of their failure to do so. The Dominion Government had a right to treat us fairly respecting this matter, but both parties had been equally guilty in this respect. The McKenzie Government had made the experiment of the *Northern Light* and the present Government are making expenditures for Railways and Boat Houses at the Capes; but, notwithstanding, it is nearly twelve years since we entered Confederation, no provision has been made for the conveyance of passengers at the Capes. Some honorable members have said that the sufferers by the late accident had a legal claim against the Dominion Government but as no contract had been entered into with the Couriers for the conveyance of passengers, they cannot hold the Dominion Government liable for the injuries they had received. Passengers are only taken by the Couriers as a favor and it is not as servants of the Dominion that they take them. This question has been debated in both branches of the legislature and every part of it has been well explained and he would not further detain the House, excepting to hope that this Address will be supported unanimously by the legislature.

Mr. YEO said he would make a

few remarks. He had been very much pleased at the manner in which this question had been approached by honorable members on both sides of the House, excepting the honorable Commissioner of Crown Lands. That gentleman in opening his speech had given very good advice, and he (Mr. Yeo) was very sorry that the honorable member did not follow it himself. The honorable gentleman had said, that as few discordant notes as possible, should be sounded in discussing this question. If he (Mr. F.) wished to make a point against the Opposition some other opportunity might have been taken to do so, and he might have left this matter to be discussed on its merits. Other honorable members who had spoken, adopted a much better method of discussing this question, for it was a fact that could not be disputed, that neither Government had attempted to do justice in this matter, for twelve years had elapsed without any improvement in our winter communication. It is true the MacKenzie Government had made an experiment by building the *Northern Light*, which had been, as an experiment, fairly successful No one steamer, however, can keep up continuous communication and he doubted very much if it can ever be accomplished in that way. How the terms should be carried out lies with the Dominion Government, and as we had carried out our part of the bargain they should do the same. It is well known that up to this time they had not done so, and

although we are a small province they had a right to carry out the Terms of Union. We have been very particular in this matter, for, with the exception of what the *Northern Light* has accomplished, we are no better off in this respect than before we entered Confederation. It cannot be denied that great difficulties exist in carrying out this part of the Terms, but they existed when we entered the union, and were well known at the time the compact was made. If these difficulties had happened since the agreement was entered into, there would be some excuse for the failure of the Dominion to carry out this part of the Terms. For his own part, as one member of the House, and for the Opposition he would promise to give the Government every support in carrying out this demand for the fulfillment of the Terms. In a matter of this kind they stand as the representatives of the people and it is the unanimous wish of the whole province that the Legislature should endeavor by every possible means to have this compact carried out. In this matter we have the interests of the Province to look to and should not care whether the Dominion Government would be embarrassed by our doing so. We ought to give the Government every support in this matter as the sooner it is brought to a conclusion, the better for the people. If the terms can't be fulfilled then the sooner we know it, the better it will be for us. This part of the Terms of Union was one of the principal inducements we had for entering the Union and nothing has been done towards carrying it out, excepting that two boats now cross where only one used to. No attention had been paid to that part of the Terms in which the transport of passengers is promised. The couriers at the risk of their lives convey the mails across the straits, and any passengers who venture the passage had to place a strap over their shoulders and get across the best way they can. To show how little the Dominion Government realize their duties in this matter, he (Mr. Yeo) need only refer to the instructions that had been given the Captain of the *Northern Light*. No ships owner ever gave such instructions to their captains and we cannot blame the Captain of the *Northern Light* for running "no risks" when his orders were that he was not to do so. He believed the people of this Province would support them in this matter and he had every faith in the British Government who would see that our rights are respected and justice meted out to us. He could say a good deal on this question, but as the matter has already been fully discussed, he would not further detain the House, only to say that he would give the resolution his hearty support.

Hon. Mr. LEFURGY said the question of winter communication was of great importance not only to the people of this province but to those who do business with us. He was sorry it was necessary to bring such a resolution before the House, as it impeached the Dominion Government for failing,

during twelve years, to carry out the solemn compact they had made. He looked at this matter in two different ways both of which caused him sincere regret. First that the General Government had failed to carry out one of the principal clauses that induced us to go into confederation, and secondly, that it will weaken the tie between the Provinces. If such strong inducements had not been held out to us before we entered Confederation, we would not have joined our fate with the Dominion, and it is hard to judge whether it would have been better if we had not done so. However we made a solemn contract with the Dominion Government and we now want them to fulfill it to the letter. We are not going to tell the General Government that we want them to put on two steamers here or to build more accommodation there, but we ask them to fulfill the contract and give us that continuous Steam Communication, Winter and Summer, with the Mainland that the Terms of Union guaranteed this province. The men who made this compact should know what they were agreeing to do. The Straits of Northumberland were then just as difficult to cross during the winter season as they are now and our delegates were not to blame if they got the Government of the Dominion to agree to this part of the Terms. Although the wording of this part of the Terms is so strong, neither party in the Dominion had done their duty in respect to carrying out this matter, and leading men on each side are equally to blame. The honorable Commisioner of Crown Lands when addressing the house to-night had referred to the speech of Mr. Foster in the Dominion Parliament, who had referred to the Canada Pacific Railway as the great national highway of the Dominion. The Dominion Government had bound us as one for-tieth of the Dominion to pay our share of $80,000,000.00 that this highway will cost, we can readily understand that it is not on account of the 40,000 people who live in British Columbia, that this great expense had been incurred, but because this Railroad will be a highway for the traffic of our Country. Although Prince Edward Island is said by the *Patriot* to be of not so much im-portance as British Columbia, it does not follow that our contract should be ignored. When our Government made a bargain with the General Government, because we are not very numerous, is no reason why the contract should be unfulfilled. It is, however, not the 100,000 people who at present live in this Province that should be considered, but the 300,000 or 400,000 people who may live here in the futue. This matter will be of benefit to our children's children and the question should be settled without delay, for the Dominion had been receiving all our revenue since we went into Confederation. When we went into Confederation the crossing at the Capes was pretty much as it is to day. He (Mr. L.) had crossed fourteen or fifteen years ago, also four or five years ago and again this year, and there was no difference in the ac-commodation provided other than the first time he had made this journey. The service is in the hands of private individuals and no improvement will be made while it remains so. He believed both the late and present Domin-ion Governments have been asked for improvements to carry out this service but when we send them a minute of Council respecting this matter, all they said was that the matter was under consideration. The McKenzie Government under-took to build a steamer for this service but a great deal of discus-sion has arisen whether she is any good at all. He (Mr. L.) never condemned the *Northern Light.* He had crossed in her two or three times, and notwithstanding she had not been built for that service or properly built for the serv ce she was calculated for—being too much of a wedge shape—she has done good service in demonstrating that the Straits can be navigated to a certain extent. Although we may have a reasonably satisfactory service during the summer and first part of the winter, it cannot be denied that a considerable time elapses every winter during which no trips are made, and we have good reason to find fault with the Government for not attempting to carry out this service more effect-ually. The Boat is kept lying up for three months at a time during the winter and it was a queer way for the Government to show their anxiety to fulfill their contract, when they wrote to the Captain of the *Northern Light* "not to run any risks." This has shown us that the Dominion Government are not as anxious to fulfill the terms of union as they should be, and it is a good reason why we should go to the foot of the Throne to ask redress. In reference to our finances, and what has been said respecting our revenue, both before and since we entered Confederation it was pretty hard to arrive at a decision, whether it was better for us to be in or out of Confederation. Things had changed a great deal since we joined the Dominion, and it is hard to say whether we would not have done as well, if we had remained a separate province. If, as had been estimated by an honorable member a short time ago, our revenue that goes to the Dominion Government amounts to $800,000 per annum and if we only get $400,000 a year in return, we have made a bad bargain. Considering that the Dominion had completely failed to carry out the terms of Union, with respect to winter communication, it was time we carried our complaint to some other place to see if we cannot get justice. If the Dominion Government say it is impossible to give us winter communication, we should get indemnity for the loss we sustain by not having it. They cannot say they made this bargain without knowing the difficulties that had to be overcome, or that they had no intention of fulfilling this part of it. If, by sending Engineers to survey the Straits, they show that a tunnel cannot be built, then if we do not get the $5,000,000 that we have claimed, we will get reasonable compensation for our loss. If we had continuous communication such as is promised us in the Terms of Union, $5,000,000 could not buy it from us and in fact hardly any sum would persuade us to give up so great a boon. The Tunnel is not an impossibility and it is for the Dominion Government to show that it cannot be built. When a private individual cannot carry out any bargain he enters into he must pay an indemnity, and there is no reason why a Government should not do the same. We must go to the Throne if we cannot get redress from the Dominion and see if we cannot get more satisfaction from that source than we have been able to obtain from the Federal Government. He did not think the people should lose sight of this question and he was much pleased to see the Opposition Party in this House come forward and support the movement that had been commenced by the Local Government to obtain our just rights. He had understood the honorable member for Bedford to say that he is converted to the idea that a tunnel is practicable and that several other honorable members had also the same views. Whether the Terms are carried out by a tunnel or by navigation it is for the Dominion Government to say. They have not done so in either way, and in consequence we have brought up this resolution. As our sentiments have been often recorded, respecting this question, it is unnecessrry to say much at the present time. He (Mr. L.) however hoped and trusted that this question would not be lost sight of, but will be followed until a satisfactory answer is obtained. Not only this House but the people and press of the province should be united in this matter, as not only our own people, but all who trade with us are effected by our want of winter communication; and no sum of money can express our annual loss on this account. When we look at the accident on the straits last winter, which if it had turned out a little differently, might have occasioned a loss to the province not easily remedied; it should make us all determined to leave no stone unturned, until some better means of winter communication was provided.

Mr. A. MARTIN said he did not consider honorable members should allow this resolution to pass without expressing the views they held on this most important question. Although he did not wish to trespass on the time of the House, he would not be doing his duty if he allowed this subject to pass without any discussion. He was very glad to see party feeling eliminated in this debate, whatever may be the case outside of the House. The honorable Leader of Government had approached the matter in a very courteous manner and has given every opportunity to honorable members to freely express their views on this most important question. He (Mr. M.) had always thought that the Local Government should be very careful not to be cajoled by any improvements at the Capes, such as building Boat Houses or even putting on additional steamers, into

acknowledging that we had a fulfillment of the Terms of Union. He was glad however to find from the expressions of honorable members during this debate that they appeared to think that nothing had been done worthy of being called a fulfillment of the Terms guaranteed this Province. During the first conference that had been held to discuss Terms of Confederation, when it was found that Prince Edward Island could not connect with the Intercolonial Railway—a railway that was to connect the other Provinces of the Dominion together so as to form one country—the Island would not consent to enter the Union, and it was not until years afterwards—until this great objection was promised to be removed—that the people of this province agreed to enter the Union. From speeches delivered at the first conference it can be easily seen that it was the intention of the promoters of the Union to bind all the Provinces together, and the fact that this Island would not participate in the advantages of the connection was a great reason why we opposed the Union. He intended to have read some extracts from the speeches that had been made at that time, in reference to this matter, but as it was so late he would not trespass on the time of the House. He thought the Dominion Government had treated them contemptuously in reference to this matter; and they should, as a province, resent such treatment. When we joined the Dominion we were told we would be treated as the "pet of the family" and would receive more than justice, instead of which we have been treated with studied neglect. It does not become the Dominion Government to do so, and we must adopt the recourse that the Terms of Confederation gave us. We have every right to expect that justice will be accorded us when we appeal to Great Britan and he felt assured, our just claims would be satisfactorily granted. He (Mr. M.) was very glad they had brought in no party feelings into this discussion for although the Press might wish to make this a party question, it was not in the interest of the province that it should be made one. It was highly creditable to honorable members that they had not taken a similar view, but had considered the matter from a provincial stand point.

Mr. HOOPER said he was glad to see so much unanimity on both sides of the House. Each speaker had adopted the rule of looking at this question from a provincial, rather than a party stand point. Only one honorable member, the Commisioner of Crown Lands, had diverged from this rule and his action had only more strongly brought out the better conduct of other honorable members. In his (Mr. H.) opinion the time had arrived when we should know if the Dominion Government intended to carry out the Terms of Confederation. If they cannot carry out the terms they promised us, the compact is broken, and the sooner we know it the better. He was talking to one of the original 94 who had been in favor of Confederation and that gentleman had

admitted that it would be better for the Island if we were free from the Union. The only thing we can do is to express our opinion that the Dominion should carry our the Terms of Union or give us our freedom.

Mr. BEER said he would not make any extended remarks at the late hour to which this debate had reached. The Resolution before the House is a very important one and should receive the unanimous support of this House and the residents of the province. Although some honorable members on the Government side of the House had spoken against allowing party feelings being introduced into this question, all of them had not done so. When his honorable colleague said that he hoped no discordant notes would be sounded on this occasion and that it would not be made a party question, he (Mr. B.) thought the honorable gentleman would have followed the same course himself; but no sooner had the honorable gentleman said so, than he (Mr. F.) rushed into the question of the piers and wharves and endeavoured to make some political capital against his opponents. If it was his idea that this question of winter communication should be discussed on its merits, why did he throw a firebrand of this nature into the discussion and attempt to get party feelings aroused? He said the Opposition not only had opposed the Government in the matter of the piers and wharves, but that they were also against this question. This honorable gentleman was the only member of the House who attempted to get up party feeling on this matter and the course he (Mr. F.) had adopted should be severely censured. The honorable Leader of the Government stated that the Government had done every thing they cou'd do to press this matter on the Dominion Government. but he(Mr. B.) could not allow that statement to pass unchallenged, as we expected the Government would have done a great deal more than they had. He (Mr. B.) contended that they have not done all they should have done. It is in the recollection of honorable members that this House passed a strong resolution last session, the last paragraph of which read as follows :—

"The Legislature trust that this most important matter, which they now for the last time bring under the notice of the General Government, may immediately engage their attention, and that a favorable answer will be accorded without delay, otherwise the Legislature desire that the Government of the province invoke the interference of Her Majesty the Queen by laying a statement of the greivances complained of at the foot of the Throne."

Here the Legislature informed the Dominion Government that unless a favorable answer was given this province, that we would appeal to Her Majesty the Queen. By this resolution the Local Government were instructed what they should do, in case a satisfactory answer was not received from the Dominion Government. Have they done

as they were instructed? No; twelve months had passed and the Local Government have not, raised their little finger in this matter except by a minute of council again asking the Dominion Government to grant what this $H_{o}us_{e}$ said should not again be asked. They had not followed the instructions this House had given them, for we told them, that if a satisfactory answer was not returned to the joint address of both branches of the Legislature, that they should appeal to the Queen. They had gone alltogether beyond their instructions and deserve the censure of the House. The honorable Leader of the Government said there was not much difference between the MacKenzie and the present Dominion Government in respect to this question, but it should not be forgotten that the MacKenzie Government had made an honest effort to carry out the Terms of Union by building the *Northern Light,* whilst the present Government had given us nothing.

Hon. Mr. Prowse said the present Government had rebuilt her.

Mr. Beer, — The present Government had sent the captain of this steamer instructions not to "run any risks" showing that they could not have rebuilt her in a proper manner. They had been told by the honorable senior member for Summerside, that, if it was an impossibility to carry out the Terms, we should get an iudemnity. It was a question of great doubt, if it can be shown that it is an impossibility to carry out the Terms, whether we can hold the Dominion Government liable for damages. He (Mr. B.) agreed with the honorable member for Murray Harbour (Mr. Prowse) who had said that it was not an impossibility and beleived we should insist on the Terms being literally carried out. The present Dominion Government had not carried out the bargain entered into with this province, or shown any disposition to do so, in fact we were being insultingly treated by the present Government. He (Mr. B.) could see no other manner of procedure than the mode that was now adopted, and on that account would support it. Our damages, on account of this part of the Terms not being carried out, were very great, and the amount claimed in the resolution passed last session was not to large to compensate us for the loss we have sustained. If we get the Terms carried out, as they should be, and get compensation for the time that has passed, we will be in a better position than we have been since we entered the Union. He trusted this address will receive the consideration that the justice of our case deserved and that our Terms will be carried out to their fullest extent.

Honorable Mr. ARSENAULT said as this was one of the most important questions that would come before the House this session, he would ask permission to make a few remarks. It was well known to honorable members that we have often applied to the Dominion Government for redress of our grievances in respect to winter communication. As they had not replied to our applications in a satisfactory manner, it is now our duty to make application to higher quarters and he hoped our appeal would be more successful this time. On this occasion the honorable Commisioner of Crown Lands had been blamed by some honorable members for taking a party view of this question. He (Mr. A.) noticed that the honorable member had in the long and eloquent speech he had delivered this evening blamed both parties in the Dominion Parliment for their inaction in this matter. What called forth a little party feeling in the honorable member's speech was the stand a newspaper that is called 'The Gospel of the opposition" had taken in this matter, ridiculing the address to the Queen. If the Opposition in this House are not making a party question of it, their friends, outside of the House, wish to do so and no blame should be attached to the honorable Commisioner of Crown Lands for exposing the unpatriotic conduct of these men. After we have waited eleven or twelve years, it is high time for the Dominion Government to do something towards carrying out the Terms of Union as efficiently as we have been promised. This question has been discussed for the last four or five years at almost every session of the Legislature and our views have been ably and strongly brought to the notice of the Dominion Government; and anything he (Mr. A.) could now say would not put the matter in any more favorable light thin it had beea.

Hon. Mr. PROWSE asked for leave of the House to make an explanation and said he was glad to learn that so many honorable members were becoming converted to a belief in the possibility of a tunnel being built between this Island and the Mainland. He had been much gratified at the letter of his Lordship the Archbishop of Halifax, who had carried the idea even further than he (Mr. P.) had ever intended. He congratulated the opposition and the House upon the action they had taken in this matter and he was much pleased to think that this resolution will be passed unanimously. He, however felt very indignant that the *Patriot* should have been allowed through its columns to give such unpatriotic ideas to the House and the country; and he felt sure they all repudiated the sentiments that came at so inopportune a time.

Mr. BENTLEY said he had expressed his views on this question a few nights ago when the Address in answer to the Speech was under consideration. He beleived the Government were taking the right steps in this matter, as it was the most important question that had come before this assembly for some time. Both sides had approved of the action of the Local Government in this matter although some honorable members, especially the honorable member for Southport, had found fault with the delay that had occurred. Some delay, however was necessary in order to

bring the matter to a proper point. It would not have looked well to rush to the Throne, without first exhausting all possible means of obtaining satisfaction from the Government of the Dominion. He (Mr. B.) would ask the honorable member for Southport why the late Government did not take up this matter and urge the settlement of this question as energetically as he now tells us should be done by the present Government when any blame of this kind is charged against the present administration he (Mr. BEER) should not forget that his own friends are equally guilty of not attending to this most important subject. Another thing should not be forgotten. The Government could not obtain an Address of both branches of the Legislature to forward to Her Majesty, until the meeting of the Legislature took place, and he was much pleased to see that the Government had brought up this question before any other important business had been introduced. He (Mr. Bentley) had no intention of making extended remarks at this stage of the Debate, but he would like to correct a statement he made the other evening in reference to the statement of Honorable Mr. Blake in the Dominion Parliment. He (Mr. Bentley) said that Mr. Blake's statement respecting expenditure and receipts by Provinces had not been replied to, but he was glad to know that the statement had been replied to by the honorable member for Prince County: (Mr. Hackett). He was surprised to find a man of Mr. Blake's information making such an abuse of figures, even if they were contained in the official reports. There was no doubt but the honorable member knew the circumstances of the case as well as any honorable member on the floor of this House, as well even as the honorable member for Sou'hport, and yet he (Mr. Blake) had tried to injure the interests of this Province. The fact that an allowance was made for the Province of Ontario, showed that he (Mr. Blake) throughly knew what he was talking about; for if he had not, he would have made the same allowance for the province of Quebec, which he knew he did not. In view of the statements of Mr. Blake and Mr McKenzie, if their statements are to be believed, we will get justice from the present Government, sooner than we will from the Party with whom these gentlemen are allied. Our Terms specify efficient steam communication, winter and summer, and no person can say that our terms have been carried out. Our claim is quite clear and when we go to the British Parliment, no doubt our case will be attended to. The statement he (Mr. B.) had formerly made was important, in that it showed that we were paying more to the Dominion Government than we receive from them. If the statement of Mr. Blake had been true we would occupy a very different position from what we now do. Some honorable members say we should ask for separation from the Union, but he (Mr. B.) did not thiuk it would be advisable to do so. He did not bring this matter up for the purpose of making political capital against his opponents, but he thought they should be more patriotic than to suggest such a course. If we were cut off from the Dominion we could hardly expect to remain unmolested, and, in consequence we might be the cause of trouble to Her Majesty's Government. We should exhaust every lawful means before asking for separation from the Dominion and should not take any action towards such a course until every means had been tried in vain, to obtain what in justice we should have.

Mr. JOHN McLEAN said he did not intend making a long speech as it was now late or rather early in the morning. He was pleased to find honorable members of the Government willing to take an independent stand on this question. They had censured not only the late Dominion Government, but also the present one as well. The Opposition had also acted fairly well in this matter although they have not gone so far in censuring the late Dominion Government as honorable members on this side of the House. Neither Governments had given the satisfaction we might have expected from our Terms of Union and which we have a right to claim as our lawful due. Some honorable members had gone so far as to say that if our claims were not fulfilled, that we should be released from our compact and from the Union. He did not know if it was good policy to ask to be released from the Dominion. Our best policy and strongest point, is to be determined to ask for the fulfillment of the Terms that we received upon entering Confederation. It is not judicious to say we want to be released. It is better to maintain that as we have fulfilled our part of the Terms and are prepared to do so in the future, as well as in the past; so the Dominion should carry out what they engaged to do. Many people in the Country thought the present Government were not sincere in this matter, but the Minute of Council they passed this winter and forwarded to the Dominion Government and the present action of the Government showed that they are most anxious to have this matter satisfactorily settled. He thought the Government deserve credit for the manner in which they had approached the Dominion Government on this subject. Their action in this has corresponded with how they acted in reference to the pier money. We know they did not take the amount the Dominion Ministry wished them to accept as payment in full, but insisted on having a further amount placed to our credit on this account, and we know that they put the matter so strongly and in such a light that the Federal Government saw we were only looking for what we were justly entitled to and what was our lawful right. In the same way this question of the fulfillment of the Terms of Union has been approached. He (Mr. J. McL) was much impressed with the remark of the honorable senior member for Charlottetown that no answer had been received from the Dominion Government to the last Minute of Council that had been sent. It showed that the Federal Government were considering the matter in a different way than formerly; as to other communications only formal acknowledgements had been received. It would not be good policy to send an Address to the Home Government before all means had been exhausted of getting our rights from the Dominion Government. As this had been done he heartily approved of the resolution. We have waited as patiently as any people could be asked to do and it was now right and proper that we should appeal to the Throne as a final remedy.

Motion put and carried.

Hon. Mr. SULLIVAN moved that a committee be appointed to join a committee of the Legislative Council to prepare an humble Address to Her Majesty the Queen, in accordance with the resolution just passed.

Motion put and carried.

The following Committe was appointed,—Hon. Messrs. Sullivan, Ferguson, Prowse, Arsenault, Messrs. Yeo, Sinclair.

Hon. Mr. SULLIVAN moved that a message embodying the action of the House be sent to the Legislative Council.

Motion put and carried.

The House having continued to sit until after 12 o'clock (midnight) adjourned until to-day, 26th inst., at 10 o'clock forenoon.

G. F. O,

THURSDAY, March 26th,

Mr Speaker in the Chair,

A Petition from the City Council of Charlottetown was presented to the House by Honorable Mr. McLeod, and the same was received and read, praying that an act be passed to amend the several Acts incorporating the City of Charlottetown.

Ordered, That said Petition be referred to a Special Committee to report thereon by Bill or otherwise.

Ordered, That Messrs, McLeod, Beer and Blake do compose said Commitee.

Hon. Mr. McLeod from the last preceding Committee appointed, presented to the House a Bill as prepared by the Committee, to be intituled: "An Act in further amendment of An Act to Incorporate the City of Charlottetown," and the same was received and read the first time, and was ordered to be read the second time to-morrow.

A Petition of J. O. Reddin, Stewart Burns, and others, was presented to the House by Hon. Mr. McLeod, and the same was received and read, praying that an Act be passed to Incorporate the Baptist Churches of P. E Island.

Ordered, That said Petition be referred to a special Committee to report thereon by Bill or otherwise.

Ordered, That Honorables, McLeod, Lefurgy, and Mr. John McLean do compose said Committee.

Hon. Mr. McLeod from the last preceding Committe appointed, presented to the House a Bill as prepared by the Committee to be intituled "An Act to secure the benefits of Incorporation to Baptist Churches of Prince Edward Island," and the same was received and read the first time, and was ordered to be referred to the Special Committee on Private Bills to examine the same and report thereon.

A Petition of Alexander Laird, R. H. McDonald, and others was presented to the House by Hon. Mr. Lefurgey, and the same was received and read, praying for "An Act to Incorporate the Mutual Agricultural Fire Insurance Company,"

Ordered, That said Petition be referred to a special Committee to report thereon by Bill or otherwise.

Ordered, That Hon. Mr. Lefurgey Mr. Bentley, and Hon. Mr. Arsenault do compose said Committee.

Hon. Mr. LEFURGEY from the last preceding Committee appointed, presented to the House a Bill as prepared by the Committee to be intituled: "An Act to Incorporate the Prince Edward Island

Agricultural Mutual Fire Insurance Company," and the same was received and read the first time.

Ordered, That the said Bill be referred to the Special Committee on Private Bills, to examine the same and report thereon.

A message from the Legislative Council by Mr. Ball their Clerk, stating that a Committee had been appointed to join a Committee of the House of Assembly to prepare an humble Address to Her Majesty the Qeen on the non-fulfillment of the Terms of Confederation with respect to winter Communication with the Mainland by the Dominion Government, and praying Her Majesty to remedy the grievance complained of.

On motion of Hon. Mr. Sullivan, seconded by Hon. Mr. Ferguson,

Resolved, That a Supply be granted to Her Majesty.

"An Act to enable the Minister and Trustees of the Free Church Congregation in the City of Charlottetown to sell certain lands," was read the second time and committed to a Committee of the whole House. The House accordingly resolved itself into the said Committee.

Mr. BENTLEY in the Chair.

Hon. Mr. McLeod said that this Bill was intended to confirm a title to certain lands in Charlottetown. The wrong Corporate name was used in the deed. The Church Trustees, having no longer any use for the building and lands, sold them to J. D. McLeod, who now finds that in consequence of the use of the wrong corporate name of the Free Church, the title was questionable. A cautious purchaser would not purchase the property without having the matter rectified. The Bill involved no other principle.

The Bill was then read, clause by clause, and agreed to without any debate.

On motion, Mr. Speaker resumed the Chair, and the Chairman reported the Bill agreed to, without any amendment.

Ordered, That the Bill be engrossed, and that it be read the third time to morrow.

House adjourned until to-morrow forenoon at ten o'clock.

I. O.

FRIDAY, 27th March.

Mr. Speaker in the Chair.

REGISTRATION.

Hon. Mr. SULLIVAN introduced a Bill intituled "An Act to amend an Act further to amend the Act regulating the registering of deeds and instruments relating to lands and to repeal the laws heretofore in force for that purpose".

The bill was read the first time, and it was, on motion, ordered that it be read the second time to-morrow.

REPORTS.

Hon. Mr. CAMPBELL, a member of Her Majesty's Executive Council, presented to the House by Command of His Honor the Lieutenant Governor:

Report of the Commissioner of Public Works for the year 1884.

Ordered, That the said Report be referred to Committee on Public Accounts.

Hon. Mr. FERGUSON, a member of Her Majesty's Executive Council, presented to the House by command of His Honor the Lieutenant Governor:

Reports of the Commissioners of the Provincial Exhibition and of the Commissioners of the Government Stock Farm, 1884.

Ordered, That the said Reports do lie on the Table of the House.

Hon. Mr. McLEOD, a member of Her Majesty's Executive Council, presented to the House by command of His Honor the Lieutenant Governor:

Report of the Commissioners and medical officer of the Poor House for the year 1884.

Ordered, That the said Report do lie on the Table of the House.

House adjourned for one hour.

G. F. O.

AFTERNOON SESSION.

Mr. SPEAKER in the Chair.

The Hon. Mr. Sullivan from the Committee appointed to join a Committee of the Legislative Council to prepare an humble Address to Her Majesty the Queen, representing the failure of the Dominion Government to carry out that part of the Terms of Confederation which requires the Government of Canada to establish and maintain efficient steam service for the conveyance of mails and passengers between this Island and the mainland of the Dominion, winter and summer, thus placing the Island in continuous communication with the Intercolonial Railway, and the railway system of the Dominion, and praying that Her Majesty may be pleased to cause such action to be taken as shall remedy the grievance complained of, and shall compensate Prince Edward Island for the non-fulfilment of the aforesaid Terms,—presented to the House the Draft of an Address as prepared by the Committee, which Address being again read at the Clerk's table was agreed to by the House.

Hon. Mr. SULLIVAN moved that the Address be engrossed.

Mr. PERRY said that when the resolution relating to this question was before the House, he made a few remarks in connection with it, but was too ill to say all that he intended on that occasion. He would, therefore, take the present opportunity of making some further observations. So far as the Address itself, was concerned, he was very well pleased with it, and he hoped it would have the desired effect, and secure to this Province the fulfilment of the terms of union. It was but right that we should not specify the ways and means of carrying on continuous steam communication with the mainland in winter. Her Majesty should be allowed to ascertain for herself the obstacles that present themselves to the navigation of the Straits during that season. Both sides of the House seemed to be agreed with respect to this very important question, and in the action that should be taken in reference to it. He thought the Government should appoint a commission or delegation to lay this memorial at the foot of the Throne; and hoped that the papers and documents relating to this question would not be locked up in the desks of members of the Government for a whole year before being forwarded to the proper quarter. He was sorry to say that from April, 1884, to February 1885, nothing was done by the Government to press our claims and secure our rights in connection with this matter of winter communication. The word "we" should not be used so frequently in the Address,—the word "Legislature" should have been used instead. But he supposed that it would, nevertheless, be understood in England, as they make similar mistakes there. No benefit can arise from throwing blame upon any particular Government of the Dominion for the

non-fulfilment of the terms of union. Suffice it to say, that our whole population of 108,000 demands the fulfilment of those terms to the letter, or that said terms be dissolved altogether. He hoped no time would be lost in having our rights attended to, and in doing us justice; and that before another winter is upon us, our demands will be satisfied. He felt unable, owing to the effects of his recent illness, to do this subject anything like justice, but he was glad to hear that it had been well ventilated by honorable members on both sides of the House. The Opposition, in particular, had handled it in a proper spirit, and free from party bias. He hoped the Address would have the desired effect.

Hon. Mr. SULLIVAN was glad to see that the illness of the honorable member for Tignish had only resulted in the renewal of his mental vigor. He (Mr. S.) had already stated his views on this very important question at length, without party feeling or bias of any kind. This was a matter which should be discussed altogether apart from party politics, and he was sorry that the honorable member alluded to, had allowed his politics to influence him in speaking with reference to it. The Opposition had been blaming the Government for being tardy in pressing the fulfilment of the terms of Confederation upon the Dominion Government during the recess. This accusation was groundless. The Joint Address of both Houses, which was passed, last session, was duly forwarded to Ottawa, stating that unless the General Government took the necessary action with reference to this matter, it would become necessary to memorialize Her Majesty the Queen, in order to have our grievance redressed. To that Address, an answer was duly received, which is now on the table of the House, stating that the subject would receive due consideration. As honorable members were aware, through the press, the Prime Minister was absent from Canada about three months after the prorogation of Parliament, in May last, and it was late in the Autumn when he returned. Common courtesy was sufficient to dictate to the local Government that before taking the present action the Dominion Government should have the fullest opportunity to consider the matter, and that there might be no undue haste on our part. The Government therefore believed they were acting in the interests of this province in giving the Dominion Government full and ample time to consider this important question, and that a memorial to Her Majesty the Queen would have all the more force from their having done so. the Legislature is only a Committee of the people of this Province' and it was thought advisable that when this matter is presented to Her Majesty it should be done with all the force the two Branches composing it could command; and that through it our people should speak as with one voice, claiming the fulfillment of the terms of union. It was not because the Government wished to shirk their responsibility in connection with this question that they had delayed until now in taking further action; but because they wished to bring it to a successful issue. He had no need to inform the Opposition that this is a question requiring the fullest consideration, and that in dealing with it the Government should be fortified with everything that could give their action strength and force. Unless the Imperial Government be approached in a proper manner, and without undue haste, we cannot expect a satisfactory result to our application. We must be able to show that we have given the Dominion Government the fullest opportunity to consider the whole question. Unless we can show that the Dominion Government have been memorialized with respect to our claims, and that no satisfactory answer has been received, it is clear that our action in appealing to the Imperial Government would reveal undue haste on our part. When the Dominion Government stated that the matter was under consideration common sense would dictate that a fair and reasonable time should be given them for that purpose. The time has been short enough up to the present date; but the Government think that action should have been taken on the matter ere this. As to the use of the word "we" in the memorial to Her Majesty, he (Mr. S.) took exception to the objection of the honorable member for Tignish with respect to it. The Address is a joint one, and hense the use of the word "we". It has emanated from both Houses of the Legisla- ture, and the Lieutenant Governor. He did not wish to take up the time of the House with further remarks. He had merely risen to say that the Government were far from shirking their duty with reference to this question, and that he believed the Address would commend itself to every honorable member of the House and also to the mind of every reasonable man in the country.

Motion put and carried unanimously.

Hon. Mr SULLIVAN moved the following:

Resolved, That a Committee be appointed to join a Committee of the Legislative Council to prepare an address to His Honor the Lieutenant Governor, requesting that His Honor will be pleased to forward to His Excellency the Governor General for transmission to Her Majesty the Queen, the humble Address of both Houses on the failure of the Dominion Government to carry out that part of the Terms of Confederation which requires the Government of Canada to establish and maintain efficient steam service for the conveyance of mails and passengers between the Island and the Main- land of the Dominion Winter and Summer, thus placing the Island in continuous communication with the Intercolonial Railway and the railway system of the Dominion, and praying that Her Majesty may be pleased to cause such action to

be taken as shall remedy the grievance complained of, and shall compensate Prince Edward Island' for the non-fulfilment of the said Terms.

Mr. YEO seconded the resolution, and asked whether it was the intention of the Government to send a Delegation to England to present the Address to Her Majesty and to enforce our claims to the fulfilment of the Terms of Confed- eration, for he was of opinion that a Delegation appointed by the House would have far greater weight than one appointed by the Government.

Hon. Mr. SULLIVAN said that the matter had not yet arrived at that stage. It is a question whether or not the Opposition should be represented in such a Delegation as had been spoken of by the honorable gentleman who had just sat down. The Govern- hent had not yet decided as to what cource they would pursue with respect to this matter. It would be for them to consider whether or not the expense in con- nection with the sending of such a Delegation should be incurred. He would like an expression of opinion from the Legislature in reference to this matter. If a Delegation was to be appointed, it should be done in accordance with the expressed wish of the Legislrture. This is not a party question, but one which affects the interests of the whole Province. Both Parties should be united in all action taken with respect to it. He would be glad to hear the opinion, or to receive a suggestion from the honorable Leader of the Opposition, as to the advisability, or otherwise, of appointing a Delegation to represent our interests in England in connection with this Address to Her Majesty. It would be satisfactory to the Government to know whether it was the desire of the Legislature to have such a Delegation appointed. It was to be inferred that the Honorable Leader of the Opposition approved of the appointment of a Delegation in order that the case of this Province might be adequately laid before the Imperial Government, or he would not have alluded to it in the manner he had. The Government, however, had not considered the matter at all, up to the present time, and had not therefore come to any decision in reference to it.

Mr. Farquharson thought the honorable Leader of the Government appeared very desirous to hear an expression of opinion from the Opposition with reference to the propriety of sending a Delegation to England to lay our claims as forcibly as possible before the Imperial Government with respect to the non-fulfilment of the terms of union by the Dominion Government. But the Government, no-doubt intend to do as they please in the matter, irrespective of the Opposition. No doubt, some of the members of the Government would like a trip across the Atlantic in connection with this matter. Looking at the indebtedness of the Province at present, it did not appear to be in keeping with the interests of the country to incur such an expense. A Dominion Election was talked of, and even if a Delegation from the Government were sent to England, it was a question if it would do anything to handicap Sir John McDonald. Although he (Mr. F.) had been reported as having expressed himself in favor of a Delegation, it was a mistake, as he had never done so. He hoped the Government would not waste a whole twelve months before forwarding the Address to Her Majesty. He thought the remarks of the honorable Commisioner of Crown Lands on this question wholly uncalled for, as they were calculated to injure our case. We should not magnify the difficulty of navigating the Straits in the Winter. This is a matter with which the Dominion Government have to deal. Let us not attempt to make our case worse than it really is. Political questions should not be dragged into this discussion.

Hon. Mr. FERGUSON was sorry to hear that his remarks on this question did not give satisfaction to some honorable gentlemen on the other side of the House. The main object of those honorable members seemed to be to hit at the present Government of the Dominion, but if any one happned to intimate that the MacKenzie Government did not do everything right, they were sorely offended indeed. The main offence which he (Mr. Ferguson) committed seemed to be that he quoted from a speech made by honorable Mr. Blake which was unfavorable to our claims as a Province. Well Mr. Blake's speeches were not made in a corner; they have been read everywhere. His (Mr. F.'s) object was to show that some of Mr. Blake's statements with reference to this Province were wrong, and his conclusions with respect to the sum we contribute to the Dominion Revenue, unfair and fallacious. He also showed that Mr. MacKenzie's statement that the Dominion had done very well for the Island was a most ridiculous one. If his (Mr. F's.) remarks, in reply should ever happen to meet the eyes of those gentlemen, they will admit their correctness.

Mr. J. R. McLEAN said that it was very unfair for the honorable Leader of the Government to construe from the remarks of the honorable Leader of the Opposition that the latter desired the appointment of a Delegation to press our claims before the Imperial Government in connection with this question. If such a Delegation was to be sent, both sides of the House should be represented in it; but if we cannot afford to incur the expense in connection therewith it would be injudicious to appoint Delegates. In his opinion, our present financial position was such that we could not afford to lavish an expenditure in connection with such a Delegation.

Hon. Mr. Sullivan said that with permission of Mr. Speaker and of the honorable Leader of the Opposition, he would make a few observations. The latter honorable gentleman was either in favor of a Delegation or he was opposed to it, and should, therefore, explain his position with reference to the matter. He would ask the honorable gentleman to state whether he was in favor of, or opposed to a Delegation. He would expect the honorable gentleman to assist the Government in securing for this Province every dollar due it from the Dominion as compensation for the loss incurred by the nonfulfilment of the terms of union. The honorable member should therefore, answer the question asked.

Mr. SINCLAIR thought the question asked by the honorable Leader of the Opposition a most reasonable one, but the reply had not been, by any means, a courteous one. So far as his (Mr. S's) own personal opinion went, he thought a Delegation would be more effectual than any papers would be; but he spoke for himself alone. But such a Delegation should represent the Legislature, and not the Executive Council. British Columbia sent a Delegate to look after her interests in England, and she was very successful. If the Leader of the Government had said: "We have not yet had the matter under consideration, but before the House rises we will state what we will do," his course would have been a straightforward and consistent one. A strange thing about all Conservative Governments was that they thought themselves above Parliament, and that they could act independently of it. The present Government had expended a considerable sum of money without a vote of Parliament, and the question of the Leader of the Opposition with respect to a Delegation was a suitable and proper one to ask. The Opposition had no power to move in reference to a Delegation, and they had no desire to do so.

Hon. Mr. SULLIVAN said that it was not the intention of the Government to send this Address to Her Majesty the Queen by a Delegation, but they would do so through the proper channel.

Resolution put and carried unanimously.

Ordered, That the same Committee who prepared the Address to Her Majesty the Queen, be a Committee, on the part of this House, to prepare the said Address to His Honor the Lieutenant Governor.

Ordered, That the said Resolution be communicated by message to the Legislative Council.

Ordered, That the Honorable Mr. Sullivan do carry the said message to the Council.

Hon. Mr. FERGUSON said that he wished to correct a report of the remarks he had made, as published in the *Patriot* newspaper in answer to a question asked by the honorable member for Strathalbyn, respecting Interest paid the Banks, and also the Interest received from them, by the Government. In the answer he gave, he stated most emphatically that in the early part

of the year 1884, 7½ per cent. was charged by some of the Banks, but later on 6 per cent., only, was charged; and that 4 per cent was allowed on deposits

Mr. BEER had not heard 7½ per cent. mentioned by the Honorable Commissioner of Crown Lands on the occasion referred to; but 6 per cent. was stated to be the Interest paid.

Hon. Mr. FERGUSON was quite sure that the statement he made in answer to the question was the same as he had just made. He had stated that during the earlier part of the past year, 7½ per cent. was charged the Government by some of the Banks.

Mr. D. C. MARTIN thought the *Patriot's* report was not far wrong. He had heard nothing said about 7½ per cent. having been paid.

Mr. SINCLAIR was, from the first, impressed with the fact that in proportion to the debt, the amount of interest charged was too large. The House had a right to know when the Government commenced to pay six per cent on balances against them.

Hon. Mr. FERGUSON said that in one of the Banks, the rate charged for the whole year was only six per cent. In former years, the rate paid all the Banks was 7½ per cent.

Hon. Mr. SULLIVAN said that the Government paid a lower rate of interest than that paid by the

Davies Government. The latter paid eight per cent. on overdrafts and received four per cent. on deposits.

House adjourned for one hour.

I. O.

FRIDAY, March 27.

EVENING SESSION.

Telephone Company.

The Order of the Day being read for the second reading of the Bill to be intituled "An Act to Incorporate the Telephone Company of Prince Edward Island."

Hon. Mr. SULLIVAN moved that the House do now go into the order of the day, and said: This Bill was for the purpose of incorporating certain persons in Prince Edward Island into a Company under the name of the Telephone Company of Prince Edward Island, and to give them the privilege of erecting wires for conveying messages by Telephone. The business of conveying messages in that way was new in this Province, but from the experience of those who have had the advantage of using this way of transacting business, he thought it desirable to extend the facilities the Telephone affords to different sections of the Province. The Telephone had been found to work satisfactorily in the city of Charlottetown, and was, no doubt, a great public convenience. The persons who have applied for this Act of Incorporation intend to form a company to carry on the business of conveying messages by telephone with a capital of $25,000, in 1,000 shares of $25.00 each, so that the interests of the company may be distributed among a large number of persons. The Company also pray for the privilege of erecting posts along the highways and over streams in the country, and along the streets of incorporated towns or cities. The lines of wire to be attached to such posts are not to be less than 18 feet from the surface of the ground in order that they shall not interfere with the public travelling the roads. The other provisions of the Bill are to enable the Company to carry on their business in a suitable and proper manner, to enable them to dispose of their stock, and for other purposes usually required by corporations of this kind. There is one provision in the Bill that it will be proper for the House to seriously consider, viz., the one by which the Company seek the exclusive privilege, for a certain number of years, of carrying on this business. They ask that no other Company shall be allowed to compete with them in this business for a term of ten years, and it will be for the House to decide whether this privilege should be accorded them. They also wish to be exempted from taxation either in Charlottetown or throughout the Province during this term. Happily there is no taxation throughout the Province, but no doubt they think that a change of Government may take place, although, judging from present appearances, that misfortune for the Province is still far distant, and they wish to guard against it. This request will be for the House to dispose of. They desire that not only real estate, but also stock and personal property shall be exempt. It was not likely that the Company would acquire much real estate, but if they do a profitable business, the city may think it desirable to impose taxation on the stock of the Company. There is at present a Bill before this Legislature which has been read the first time, that deals with the question of taxation for civic purposes, but if this part of the Bill passes it will exempt the Company from any such taxation. It is, however, a matter entirely for the Legislature to determine. He thought the Bill as a whole would commend itself to the wisdom of the House, although some sections of it may require amendment. It was desirable that such a mode of communication should be established, so that persons residing in Georgetown, Summerside and other places may have this easy mode of communicating with one another.

Motion put and carried. The House accordingly went into Committee.

Mr. HOLLAND in the Chair.

The first and second clauses were read and agreed to. On the third clause being read:

Hon. Mr. SULLIVAN said this clause is a little objectionable. It was the duty of the Legislature to protect the country as well as the towns. If this clause is passed, as it is at present, in any place outside the city, the Company can place their wires as near the surface as they like. In the country, people often have to haul bulky articles, like hay and straw, and if there is no provision made for having these wires placed at a proper distance above the surface of the ground, people may be liable for damages for interfering with the Company's lines. Another thing should also be remedied, viz., the clause says that in towns they may have one line of posts, but for any more must ask the consent of the officers of the town or city, and that these posts shall be erected under the supervision of the officer in charge of the streets of such town or city. It is desirable, not only in Charlottetown or other towns, but also in the country that these posts should not be a nuisance. That the Company shall not put them up in front of a man's windows or where they will interfere with the comfort of the inhabitants. They should be erected under the supervision of the officers who look after the streets in the towns and in the country under the Road Supervisors. These posts must be put where they will not be an inconvenience to the public. As some times it is necessary to widen our roads, and where these posts are erected, may become the centre of the road after it is widened, the company should move the posts when directed to do so by the officer in charge of the roads and streets, and the road officers should have full power to make any change respecting the posts or wires that is necessary for the public convenience. As many streams are crossed by bridges which constitute part of the highway, and as this Company will have the right to erect posts along such bridges, provision should be made, that in case any repairs are to be made to any bridge or causeway, that it shall be in the power of the person having charge of said work to have these posts removed while said work was being performed or for such time as the road officers should determine. The persons promoting the Bill have embodied in it what they would wish to obtain, but it is for this Legislature to guard the interests of the Province; so that no undue advantage may be obtained by either corporations or individuals. He would move in amendment that the whole clause after the words Prince Edward Island be struck out and the following be inserted:

"Provided the said Company shall not interfere with the public right of travelling on or using such highways, streets, bridges, water courses or rivers, or with the repairing, rebuilding, reconstructing, renewing, widening, enlarging or improving the same; and provided that the Company shall not at any place within the limits of this Province affix any wire less than eighteen feet above the surface of any highway, street, river or place; and the Company shall not carry more than one line of poles along any street or place within the limits of any City, Town or Incorporated village,

without the consent of the municipal Council having jurisdiction over the streets of such city, town or village; and provided also that the location of wires and posts shall be subject at all times to the approval of the Supervisor or Chief Inspector of Roads in the District through which the same may pass, and in case of cities, towns or incorporated villages shall be subject at all times to the approval of the city or town surveyor or other officer having supervision of the streets or ways thereof."

He (Mr. S.) thought this amendment would meet the wants that he had referred to. It placed the Company under the supervision of the officers in charge of the streets and roads. If the city finds its officers playing into the hands of the Company, it will be an easy matter to remove them. It was better that the officers in charge of the roads should have the directing of where these lines shall be placed.

Mr. BEER said he would like to see this Company get every encouragement, but he did not think it right to give them exclusive rights. In the city, the Council should have authority to regulate all matters affecting the streets, and the Legislature should not over ride this right by giving this Company the privilege of erecting posts on their streets. The consent of the City should first be obtained before privileges of this kind are granted. The Company are asking for power to affix wires to the poles they erect in the city and it has been found that these wires are very inconvenient, especially in case of a fire. He believed the wires of the company might be carried underground as well as overhead on posts, and the municipal Government should be consulted before this question was decided. He agreed with the amendment excepting that part that allowed the company to erect posts in the city without the consent of the City Council.

Hon. Mr. SULLIVAN said the Act would be no good without the company can get their wires outside of Charlottetown and if this question is undecided, the city Council may throw obstacles in the way. If a provision in accordance with the views of the honorable member for Southport is put in this act, it will defeat the bill. A majority of the City Council might oppose the formation of this company or impose such conditions that it would be impossible for the company to proceed with the undertaking, and the country districts of the province will be deprived of the facilities the formation of the company will afford them. The company had first asked for the privilege of erecting two lines in the city, but he (Mr. S.) suggested as a compromise that the Legislature should allow them the privilege of erecting one line. It would be the duty of the supervisor to see that no damage was caused the streets by the erection of these posts. The posts of the telegraph company have been erected along our streets and highways and have done no harm and it is only right that this company should be protected and allowed to erect their posts in the same way. He was afraid if the amendment suggested by the honorable member was adopted that it would make the bill inoperative. The City Council can authorize its officers to see that the posts and wires are placed properly so as to cause little or no inconvenience. The company cannot get the consent of the City until it becomes organized and this cannot be done until a certain amount of stock is sold. It can easily be seen that the stock can not be sold without the privilege this bill contained were granted.

Mr. SINCLAIR said he approved of the amendment that had been submitted. These wires should not be less than 18 feet from the surface at any place. The road officers should have power to remove these wires at any time it was necessary to do so, or to change the route they followed, but care should be taken not to damage the line or to cause serious loss to the Company.

Mr. FARQUHARSON said he agreed with the Honorable Leader of the Government that we should encourage this Company. If this matter was left to the City Council sometimes they might be in favor of the Company and sometimes against it, as the Council are not always to be relied on. He did not think there was any serious objection to giving the Company this privilege. In large cities where thousands of these wires are placed, no great trouble has been experienced from their erection, and it was not likely they would cause any trouble in this city.

Mr. BLAKE said he agreed with the honorable member for West River, excepting what he had said about the City Council, as they were as reliable a body of men as could be found in any city. He believed this Bill will afford great convenience to many persons not only in the city but in the country as well, and he wished to see it passed. The height at which the wires will be placed, viz., eighteen feet, will be found sufficiently high to cause no inconvenience. If the suggestion of His Honor the Mayor was carried out it would stop the Bill. Whilst the present City Council might do nothing against the interests of this Company, a future one might act differently, and no men would risk their money in an enterprize that might be so easily damaged.

Mr. BEER said he would be very sorry to jeopardize the success of the Bill. There was a Telephone Company in operation in the city already and he did not know whether this company was intended to interfere with the one already established. He felt anxious that the wires of these companies should be laid under ground, but as the honorable junior member for the city was satisfied with the Bill, he would be also.

Hon. Mr. PROWSE said the question before the Committee affected the country more than the city. The city had good accommodation in this way already. The Telegraph Company had a monopoly on this Island and instead of extending their wires, are curtailing their operations. The Telegraph Company had closed their office at Montague Bridge, and great inconvenience has been caused the residents of that section of the Province. He (Mr. P.) hoped this Telephone Company would be successful and that they would extend their lines to all parts of the Province. If they do the Telegraph Company will get their eyes opened and will be forced to do more for the accommodation of the people than they have done in the past. The wires of such companies are extended by thousands in other cities and have not been found to be detrimental. The city of Charlottetown is not very large, and the streets in it are much wider than those of many other cities. Owing to the smaller population of this city, we cannot suppose that so many wires will be erected as in larger places. If the City Council had power and would compel this Company to put their wires under ground, it would stop the formation of this Company. It is considered essential to civilization that the freest manner of communication should be established, either by telegraph or telephone. While he was opposed to granting monopolies, and while thinking that a monopoly of five years was long enough to enable this Company to become properly started, he would not oppose granting them a term of ten years, if refusing to do so would jeopardize the Company's formation.

Clause as amended agreed to.

On the next clause being read:

Hon. Mr. SULLIVAN said this clause meant that this Company might amalgamate with any other Company, or that they may buy out or lease any other Company's lines, or may sell their lines to another Company. He did not think there was anything objectionable in this provision.

Clause agreed to.

On motion, Mr. Speaker resumed the Chair, the Chairman reported that some progress had been made and asked leave to sit again.

A message from the Legislative Council was received, intimating that a Committee had been appointed to join a Committee of the House of Assembly to prepare an humble Address to Her Majesty the Queen, respecting the failure of the Dominion Government to carry out that portion of the Terms of Union which guaranteed this Province efficient steam service for the conveyance of mails and passengers between the Island and the mainland of the Dominion, winter and summer, thus placing the Island in continuous communication with the Intercolonial Railway, and the railway system of the Dominion. Also, that the Legislative Council had passed "An An to amend An Act to incorporate the Charlottetown Woolen Company," and "An Act to incorporate the Charlottetown Mutual Fire Insurance Company."

Winter Communication.

Hon. Mr. SULLIVAN, from the Special Committee appointed to prepare a draft Address respecting the failure of the Dominion Government to establish and maintain efficient steam service with the mainland, submitted the Address as prepared by the committee, and moved that the same be received and read.

Motion put and carried.

The Address was received and read, and is as follows:

To the Queen's Most Excellent Majesty:

MOST GRACIOUS SOVEREIGN,—We, your Majesty's most dutiful and loyal subjects, the Legislative Council and House of Assembly of Prince Edward Island in General Assembly convened humbly approach Your Majesty and represent, that:

1. Prince Edward Island entered the Confederation of the Dominion of Canada upon 1st July, 1873, on certain terms and conditions set forth in the order of Your Majesty in Council, dated 26th June, 1873, and of which terms the following is one: "The Dominion Government shall assume and defray all the charges for the following service, viz.:—Efficient Steam Service for the conveyance of mails and passengers, to be established and maintained between the Island and

the Mainland of the Dominion, winter and summer, thus placing the Island in continuous communication with the Intercolonial Railway and the railway system of the Dominion."

2. During no winter season since the time of the said Union has the service provided by the Dominion Government been efficient, or the communication with the Mainland continuous.

3. The Dominion Government having shown no sufficient disposition to fulfil their obligation towards the Island in this matter, we are reluctantly compelled to approach Your Majesty, as one of the parties to the articles of Confederation, and pray Your Majesty's intervention to obtain for us that justice to which as a Province of Canada we are entitled by the Terms of Union.

4. Prince Edward Island is separated from the mainland Provinces of Canada by the Strait of Northumberland, and during the winter season which generally begins about the first December and lasts until the end of April, the harbors and rivers are frozen, while the passage of the Strait is impeded, though at no time wholly prevented by floating ice. Previous to the Union the only connection with the mainland during winter was by means of ordinary boats, dragged across the drifting ice, and propelled by oars through the stretches of open water between Cape Traverse on the Island, and Cape Tormentine in New Brunswick—a distance of nine miles.

5. During the first winter after Confederation (1873-4) no attempt was made by the Dominion Government to provide such steam service. During the two subsequent years (1874-5, 1875-6) an old wooden steamboat which had for years been engaged in ordinary navigation, but without a single qualification to fit her for the winter navigation of the Strait, was placed upon the route between Georgetown, one of the Island ports, and Pictou, in the Province of Nova Scotia; and, as was to be expected, she utterly failed in the service required of her. At the commencement of the winter 1876-7 a new steamer called the *Northern Light* was placed upon this route. This steamer was not constructed for the service, but was designed for another purpose, and therefore her work can be regarded only in the light of an experiment.

6. The service performed by the *Northern Light* has been most unsatisfactory, her trips being irregular and the accommodations she has afforded has been neither continuous nor efficient. According to the official returns for the last four years, there has been an average in each winter of sixty-four days, during which she has been entirely laid up. Nor does this furnish any idea of the irregularity of her trips before she entirely ceased running in each of these years, but only of the continued period when she was laid up and inoperative. At times she

has been ice-bound for periods ranging from ten to twenty-four days, to the imminent danger of passengers and mails. Upon one occasion, four years ago, some of the passengers—among them women and children—were forced after remaining on board several days, to leave her and walk a distance of many miles to the shore, when night overtaking them, they received injuries from cold and exposure, which resulted ultimately in the death of one of the party.

7. During the time when the *Northern Light* is laid up, the people of the Island are obliged to resort to the old method of crossing between the Capes (Traverse and Tormentine) already described, a route attend with much hardships and great danger. In the month of January last a party of twenty-two persons were detained on the ice for two days and one night in an attempt to make the passage, when they suffered most severely from cold and exposure—the majority of them being badly frozen—and several have since suffered amputation of their limbs as a result of the injuries then received.

8. One of the principal inducements held out to the people of this Island to enter the Confederation, was the promise contained in that clause of the Terms of Union quoted at the opening of this memorial, and they naturally expected that a union with the Dominion would bring them uninterrupted communication at all seasons of the year with the rest of Canada and of the world. They believed that they would thereafter enjoy equal facilities for intercourse with the other Provinces as those Provinces enjoyed between themselves, and that thenceforth they would participate in the many benefits and advantages accruing from the Intercolonial Railway and other public works upon the Mainland from which they had previously been debarred for a great portion of the year. Cut off, as they had always been for nearly five months of the twelve from all communication with the Mainland, except by a most uncertain and dangerous route, the promise of continuous communication with the Intercolonial Railway and the railway system of the Dominion was, indeed a strong incentive to them to surrender their self-government and unite with Canada.

9. The inconvenience and loss which they have suffered in consequence of the failure of the Dominion Government to provide them with the efficient communication promised, are incalculable, while the disappointment to their reasonable expectations has not tended to enhance in their estimation, the value of a connection with the Dominion, but on the contrary, has awakened a feeling of discontent which though a matter of regret, is not unnatural under the circumstances. Were it only the transport of freight and merchandise that was stopped during the winter, they would have good reason to complain of being precluded from the benefits of the Intercolonial and other railways which their more

fortunate neighbors on the Mainland enjoy; but their chief grievance is that, in direct violation of the solemn compact upon which they entered the Confederation, and to which Your Majesty was graciously pleased to be a party, the Dominion Government have not provided that efficient or continuous means whereby mails and passengers can be transported to and from the Mainland.

10. The people of this Province, we submit, have just ground of complaint at the inaction of the Dominion Government, and at the extraordinary apathy which has been shown in regard to the interests of this Island, in the matter of communication with the Mainland. Nine winters have passed since the *Northern Light* was first placed on the route, and, notwithstanding the fact that her inefficiency for the service was apparent from the outset, no other steps have been taken to fulfil the Terms of Union. From the time the *Northern Light* ceases running until she again resumes her trips, a period averaging as already mentioned, sixty-four days each year the Post Office Department transmits the mails by the route between Capes Traverse and Tormentine, and during this period in each year, the Dominion Government have, at no time since Confederation, made any provision whatever, for the transport of passengers, who are forced to make such arrangements as best they can for crossing to and from the Mainland. This unaccountable neglect on the part of the Government of Canada is the most direct

violation of the Terms of Union which we are called upon to represent to Your Majesty. Moreover the Dominion Government have established no communication between the Intercolonial Railway and Cape Tormentine, so that travellers are compelled in passing between these points, to drive in open sleighs a distance of forty miles, in the coldest and most stormy portion of the year. Between Cape Traverse and the line of the P. E. Island Railway, a distance of about twelve miles, railway connection has been opened and that but partially only this winter, although provided for by Parliament three years ago.

11. The derangement of business consequent upon the irregularity of the mail service, when for many days at times no communication is had with the rest of Canada, exercises a most prejudicial effect upon the interest of the Island. The hardships of travelling, which only the strong and robust are able to endure, and the dangers attendant upon the present mode which have been most painfully exemplified this winter, are other disadvantages from which the people of this Province suffer most acutely.

12. The feeling that they are being unjustly treated is not without strong foundation. In order to fulfil the Terms of Union with British Columbia, a province of less than 15,000 of a population, exclusive of Indians and Chinese, Canada has contracted for the construction of nearly three thousand miles of railway at a cost of more than

eighty millions of dollars. This gigantic undertaking is being pushed forward at a rate unparalleled in the world's history, and a vast expenditure is being made, and still more is contemplated, in acquiring and subsidizing other railroads and in forging the links to bind the scattered Provinces from the Atlantic to the Pacific; yet the fulfilment of the Terms of Union with this Island, by providing the means of communication over a Strait only nine miles wide is postponed from year to year, without any thought, it would seem, that thereby a sacred obligation is being violated, and an immense injury being done to a large body of people.

13. This grievance of which we here complain has been repeatedly brought to the notice of the General Government, while, session after session, the representatives of the Island in the Dominion Parliament have called attention to the non-fulfilment by Canada of her pledged faith with this Island. In 1881 we addressed the Governor-General-in-Council upon the subject, and prayed for the adoption of measures to remedy the state of affairs complained of as well as for compensation for the loss sustained on account of the non-fulfilment of the Terms of Union. This address was duly acknowledged, but no practical results followed, and upon the notice of the Dominion Government being again directed thereto, assurances were returned in both of the years 1882 and 1883, that the question was under their consideration. Again last year we

addressed His Excellency in Council with a like petition and claiming five millions of dollars for the loss sustained to that time on account of the non-fulfilment of the said Terms, and we also informed the Dominion Government that we then approached them for the last time, and that unless a favorable answer was accorded without delay Your Majesty's interference would be invoked. Beyond a simple acknowledgment of this Address no attention has been paid to it. Again on the 20th February last, the Executive Council of this Island called the attention of the Dominion Government to the various steps which had been taken by the Island to obtain a settlement of the question, and reminded them of the decision at which we had arrived last year to appeal to Your Majesty, and that no alternative was left except to carry that determination into effect. To this minute the same unsatisfactory answer was received, which has been invariably given. Copies of the correspondence referred to will be transmitted to Your Majesty herewith.

14. In this the 12th year of their connection with the Dominion, instead of enjoying that efficient and continuous steam communication with the Mainland which was guaranteed them, the people of P. E. Island are for a very considerable portion of the year dependant upon the mode which their fathers initiated upwards of sixty years ago, before steam power was ever applied for purposes of locomotion. During these 12 years, they have

patiently awaited the fulfilment by the General Government of the Terms of Union in this particular, until we are reluctantly constrained to say that the Dominion Government have evinced a marked indifference not only for the welfare of this Island, but for the sanctity of their own obligation as well.

15. Satisfied that this state of things cannot longer continue without a breach of that harmony which is so indispensable between the Provinces of the Confederation, and feeling that the Island is being treated unjustly, and its prosperity seriously retarded, we appeal to Your Majesty and humbly pray, that you will take the premises into your most gracious consideration, and require that justice be done by the Government of Canada to you Majesty's loyal subjects of this Province, by the immediate establishment and maintenance of efficient steam service for the conveyance of mails and passengers between this Island and the mainland of the Dominion, both winter and summer, so as to place the Island in continuous communication with the Intercolonial Railway and the railway system of the Dominion; and further, that Your Majesty will be pleased to require that the Government of Canada compensate this Island for the loss which has resulted to its inhabitants, by reason of the non-fulfilment of the Terms of Confederation, in the particulars complained of herein.

Ordered, That the Address be engrossed.

Ordered, That the same Committee be appointed a Committee to wait on His Honor the Lieutenant Governor to request him to forward the said Address to His Excellency the Governor General for transmission to Her Majesty the Queen in accordance with the wish of this branch of the Legislature.

On motion the House resolved itself into a Committee of the whole to further consider the Bill intituled "An Act to Incorporate the Telephone Company of Prince Edward Island."

Mr. HOLLAND in the Chair.

On motion or Hon. Mr. Sullivan, the blanks in the clause read were filled with the words "twenty" and "two," when the clause was agreed to.

Another clause being read:

Hon. Mr. SULLIVAN said this clause referred to the monopoly desired by the Company.

Mr. BEER said he would oppose this clause, as he believed in free trade in ventures of this kind, as well as in general business. This Company would not go into this business without expecting to make money out of it, and it was not desirable to give them a monopoly of the telephone business, especially as another Company had already the business in the city.

Mr. D. C. MARTIN said this clause would interfere with the Company that was already doing business.

As the present Company had enterprize enough to start the telephone business in the Island they should be protected.

Hon. Mr. PROWSE said he thought it would be proper to give this Company the right to extend the facilities their business afforded to the country districts. The expense of establishing communication of this kind in Charlottetown was nothing to what would be required to extend it to the country. He was against monopolies being granted, but was willing to encourage the formation of this Company, by giving them a monopoly for five years for all places outside of the city. It would not be fair for the Legislature to step in after these persons had spent their money in starting this business, and by incorporating similar Companies, deprive these persons of any benefit their enterprise might procure. He would give this Company the exclusive right for five years of extending their wires outside of the city limits.

Hon. Mr. SULLIVAN said it would not be fair to give this Company the monopoly of the Telephone business of the Province. It was a question whether it would be fair to confine the Company in existence already, to the city, as they might wish to extend their business to other parts of the Island.

Mr. FARQUHARSON said the present Company had not applied for an Act of Incorporation by which they could extend their lines to the country, and they had given no intimation that they had any intention of doing so.

Mr. A. MARTIN said this question was of more interest to the country than it was to the city. The Telegraph Company are not giving the encouragement they should to country districts, of which the case of Montague Bridge was an instance of how little respect this Company had for the convenience of the public. The present Company are not asking for anything more than any Company would require who start a new enterprize of this nature. He did not think the Legislature should put any obstacles in the way of the passage of this Bill as the only objectionable clause in it has been amended. The Company at present doing Telephone business have not asked for an Act of Incorporation and without it they can not extend their lines outside the limits of the city of Charlottetown. As this Company may be the means of affording increased accommodation to the Belfast district he would like to see this Bill passed. He hoped if the Company went into operation that they would extend their wires to Belfast and Montague.

Mr. MATHESON said he disagreed with the honorable member for Belfast. We do not know but this Company may buy out the Company at present doing business and may charge exorbitant rates, both in town and country. If both Companies have an opportunity of doing business, rates will be lower and the people of the Province will reap the benefit.

Hon. Mr. FERGUSON said the Bell Telephone Company, a branch of which was established in the City of Charlottetown, was acting under a charter from the Dominion Parliament, and it was a matter of doubt whether the passing of this Bill would prevent them extending their lines outside the city. The object of establishing companies of this nature is a good one, provided the Company goes to work in good faith. If they do so, they should be encouraged. The object of this Company is to connect Charlottetown with the towns and villages of the Island, and it will afford a great deal of accommodation to all classes of the people. He did not know whether this Company will establish an Exchange Office at Summerside, but if they do not, this Bill will prevent the Bell Telephone Company doing so which will be a matter for regret.

Hon. Mr. LEFURGY said he understood the present Telephone Company intended to establish an office in Summerside this spring, and if this Bill is passed it may prevent them doing so, and cause a hardship to that town. We want to be careful in passing Bills of this kind. Telegraph and Telephone communication are part of civilization, and if this Bill will extend their operation, he would support it, but perhaps this Bill may interfere with the other Company, and we may have to pay higher than we would if it did not pass. He was opposed to monopolies of all kinds, but as this Company will hardly operate all over the Island, as the distance between the offices will be so long, he thought they should get five years monopoly. He did not know whether they were bound to go on if they got this Bill. If they don't go on with the Company, it will prevent other companies forming to carry on this work.

Hon. Mr. SULLIVAN said this clause only applies after the Company commence operations. It would, however, be just as well to consider the matter a little further.

On motion Mr. Speaker resumed the Chair, the Chairman reported progress and asked leave to sit again.

On motion of Honorable Mr Sullivan, seconded by Honorable Mr. Ferguson,—

Resolved, That a supply be granted to Her Majesty.

House adjourned until to-morrow forenoon, at ten o'clock.

G. F. O.

SATURDAY, March 28.

Mr. SPEAKER in the Chair.

Registration of Deeds.

The Order of the Day being read for the second reading of the Bill to be intituled "An Act to amend An Act further to amend the Act regulating the Registry of Deeds and Instruments relating to the titles of lands, and to repeal the laws heretofore passed for that purpose." Said Bill was accordingly read the second time.

Hon. Mr. SULLIVAN moved that the House do now go into the Order of the Day, and said this Bill was not intended to repeal any of the laws respecting the registering of Deeds, as honorable members might suppose from hearing the title read, but it was simply an amendment to the Act passed in 1881. The Act to which this is an amendment authorizes that when a deed is executed abroad, the witness may go before the Mayor of a city, a Consul or Consular Agent, a Commissioner duly appointed for taking acknowledgments to deeds, or a Notary Public, and make an affidavit to the due execution of the deed; and either of these officers may make a certificate that the witness has proved before them the said fact, which certificate would entitle the possessor to have the deed recorded in the Registry Office in this Island. The old form of the Act authorized the witness to go before a Justice of the Peace, who would then get a Notary Public to certify that he was really a Justice of the Peace and competent to act. A good many deeds have been executed under the old form, but owing to the change in our law, the Registrar cannot admit them for registration. Some of the parties to these deeds are dead and it is considered advisable to so amend the Act that these deeds may be admitted to registra-

tion. This amendment provides that when the witness goes before a Notary Public and proves to the execution of the deed that the Registrar may accept the same as sufficient proof.

Motion carried.

House resolved itself into a Committee of the whole House.

Mr. JOHN MCLEAN in the Chair.

Mr. JAMES R. MCLEAN said as formerly it was necessary for a witness to appear before a Justice of the Peace. If a witness died before proving to the execution of the deed will it do to prove to the hand-writing of the witness in order to get the deed registered ?

Hon. Mr. SULLIVAN said there was a provision in the law to that effect.

On motion, Mr. Speaker resumed the Chair, and the Chairman reported the Bill agreed to without amendment.

Ordered, That the Bill be engrossed.

Ordered, That the Bill be read the third time on Monday next.

An Act to amend the Act respecting the Garnishment of Debts.

The Order of the Day being read for the second reading of the Bill to be intituled, "An Act to amend the Act respecting the Garnishment of Debts." Said Bill was accordingly read the second time.

Hon. Mr. SULLIVAN moved that the House do now go into the Order of the Day, and said this Bill was not very long as it only contained a few provisions respecting the Garnishment of Debts. This law is now necessary as there is no imprisonment for debt or bankruptcy law in the Province. There should be sufficient means provided to enable creditors to garnishee their debts. This Bill simply makes some provisions that are not in the Acts relating to this matter, already on our statutes. One of its provisions is to apply the Act for the Garnishment of Debts to insurance policies. If a person has insurance on his property and a fire occurs, this Act will enable the creditor to attach the money in the hands of the Insurance Company. This provision should have been in the original Bill as it is a most necessary one. This is the principal provision in this Bill; the others are only machinery for carrying it out. It is provided in this Bill that all sums, liquidated or not liquidated, in the hands of the Insurance Company, can be garnisheed, as well as sums that have been adjusted before the attachment is issued. He thought this Bill was advisable as justice has failed in cases of this kind for want of a similar law.

On motion the House went into Committee of the whole House.

Mr. HOOPER in the Chair.

Mr. FARQUHARSON said he thought the honorable senior member for the City should give some explanation of the Bill that had formerly been passed. It is said that the old Bill is very expensive and cumbersome, and did not apply to many cases that arise.

Hon. Mr. SULLIVAN said this was a very ingenious way for the honorable member to get legal advice for nothing. No doubt the honorable senior member for the City would have much pleasure in explaining the law to the honorable member for West River if that gentleman would call at his office. Of course lawyers could not be expected to work without pay, and the honorable member for West River would require to provide the usual fee before getting the information he was so anxious to obtain.

Hon. Mr. McLEOD said this was a very desirable amendment, as it would lessen the costs of garnisheeing. The costs of garnisheeing are often more than the debt, and this amendment provides that several amounts may be garnisheed by the one operation. It also provides that unliquidated amounts can be garnisheed. If a party suffers loss by fire, you cannot take out an attachment to garnishee until the amount is liquidated. This Bill will greatly simplify the working of the present Act.

On motion of Honorable Mr. Sullivan an amendment was added to the Bill.

On motion Mr. Speaker resumed the Chair, and the Chairman reported the Bill agreed to with an amendment.

Ordered, That the Bill be engrossed.

Ordered, That the Bill be read the third time on Monday next.

On motion of Honorable Mr. McLeod, the Bill intituled "An Act to enable the Minister and Trustees of the Free Church congregation in the City of Charlottetown to sell certain lands," was read the third time and passed.

A petition of John Caven, R. E. Gaul, J. G. Eckstadt and others, of Charlottetown, was presented to the House by Mr. Blake, and the same was received and read, setting forth that the petitioners were desirous of being incorporated as the Charlottetown Conference of the Saint Vincent de Paul Society, and praying that an Act be passed to incorporate the said Company.

Ordered, That the said petition be referred to a special Committee, to examine the same and report thereon by Bill or otherwise.

Ordered, That Mr. Blake, Hon. Mr. McLeod and Mr. Beer do compose the said Committee.

Mr. BLAKE, from the last preceding Committee appointed, presented to the House a Bill as prepared by the Committee, to be intituled "An Act to incorporate the Charlottetown Conference of the Saint Vincent de Paul Society," and the same was received and read the first time.

Ordered, That the said Bill be referred to the Special Committee appointed to report on every private Bill, to examine the same and report thereon.

House adjourned until Monday forenoon, at ten o'clock.

G. F. O.

————

MONDAY, March 30.

Mr. SPEAKER in the Chair.

"An Act to amend An Act to regulate the Registry of Deeds and Instruments relating to the title to land, and to repeal the Laws heretofore passed for that purpose" was read the third time and passed.

An Act to further amend an Act respecting the garnishment of Debts was, also, read the third time and passed.

House adjourned for one hour.

I. O.

————

EVENING SESSION.

Mr. SPEAKER in the Chair.

Hon. Mr. MACDONALD, from the special Committee on private Bills, and to whom was referred the Bill to be intituled "An Act to

Incorporate the Prince Edward Island Agricultural Mutual Fire Insurance Company," reported the Bill to be of a private nature and liable to fees; and recommended that thirty Dollars be charged.

Ordered, That the report be adopted, and that the Bill be read a second time to-morrow.

Hon Mr MACDONALD from the Special Committee on Private Bills, and to whom was referred the Bill to be entitled: "An Act to Incorporate the Charlottetown Conference of Saint Vincent De Paul Society", reported the Bill of a private nature and liable to fees; and recommended that ten Dollars be charged. He said some parties had waited upon him, and stated that as their Society was of a charitable nature, the Bill might well be exempted from fees. If the House had no objection, this proposal might be acceded to.

Mr. BLAKE said that the Bill was a very short one, and as it relates to a charitable society, he would move that the report be referred back to the Committee for amendment, by striking out that part of it recommending that a fee be charged.

Mr. BEER said that as one member of the Committee on Private Bills, he had no objection to the motion made by the honorable junior member for the City, as the institution was, he believed, a charitable one. There was a Rule that no Private Bill should be allowed to pass without payment of fees, but he had no objection to the proposal to exempt this one.

Hon. Mr. CAMPBELL said that it was decided last Session, that no Private Bill should pass without the payment of a fee. He thought that decision should be adhered to in the present, and all other cases.

Hon. Mr. SULLIVAN agreed with the honorable Commissioner of Public Works with respect to this matter. This society is a charitable one, but no more so than were the Hospitals which had lately been incorporated. If there was any objection to exempting the Bill from the payment of fees, he would, himself, pay them.

Mr. PERRY said that, last Session, the House had altered the Report of the Committee on Private Bills in one well-known case; and he did not see why it could not do so in the present instance. Exacting a fee in this case was taking money from the poor—robbing Peter to pay Paul.

Mr. J. R. McLEAN asked whether it was right for the House to charge a fee for passing a Bill of this kind? He was surprised at the statements made by the honorable Commissioner of Public Works with reference to it. That portion of the Report recommending that a fee be charged should certainly be struck out.

Hon. Mr. SULLIVAN announced that he had paid the fee.

The Report was then adopted,

and it was ordered that the Bill be read a second time to-morrow.

Hon. Mr. MACDONALD, from the Private Bill Committee, to whom was referred the Bill to be intituled "An Act securing to the Baptist Churches in Prince Edward Island the benefits of Incorporation," reported that the Bill was of a private nature and liable to fees; and recommended that Ten Dollars be charged.

On motion, the Report was adopted, and it was ordered that the Bill be read the second time to-morrow.

On motion of Honorable Mr. Sullivan, the House resolved itself into a Committee of the whole, to take into further consideration the Bill to be intituled "An Act to Incorporate the Telephone Company of Prince Edward Island."

Mr. HOLLAND in the Chair.

A clause having been read.—

Hon. Mr. SULLIVAN said that this clause would give the Company a monopoly for a certain term of years, or until their business was firmly established. He thought five years would be quite long enough. It would not be right to interfere with the Company now doing business in Charlottetown, and therefore this Bill would not interfere with the City. It would be easy to extend the period at the expiration of the five years. As telephone communication over the whole Island would afford great facilities to business men, he thought a Company making provision for it should be encouraged to the extent now proposed. He moved that the clause, with the blank, be agreed to.

Motion put and carried.

Mr. SINCLAIR said that monopolies always work injuriously. The advantage is always in favor of the Company and against the public. It may be well, however, to give a Company a short one of three years, to encourage them in their enterprise. The existing Company, it is said, wish to extend their business to Summerside, and he thought they should be encouraged to do so. The House should be very cautious in reference to such matters as this. He would move that the blank be filled up with the word "three."

Mr. FARQUHARSON thought a monopoly of five years short enough for the work required to be done. We cannot now get along very well without telephonic communication.

Hon. Mr. MCLEOD did not think it was the intention of the present City Company to do business outside of Charlottetown. Their wires pass over the houses of the citizens, and any one of the latter might at any time sue them for trespass. He thought the new Company would do business at a much lower rate. The charge, per annum, by the present Company is $30.00, which is very high. The new Company intend to erect wires all over the Island. Business between Charlottetown and Summerside will be greatly facilitated by the telephone, as a five minutes conversation will be sufficient to do many kinds of business. Five years will be a sufficiently short monopoly, as it will require two years to put the lines in order for work.

Mr. J. R. McLEAN did not believe in monopolies of any kind; but as telephonic communication would benefit the whole Island, a short period might be allowed for the establishment of the business. If too short a period is fixed, the Company might not consider it sufficient for the purpose intended. A term of five years was, he thought, short enough.

Mr. SINCLAIR said that if there is room on this Island for another Company to commence operations, it was clear that there should be no monopoly. The public interests should be safely guarded. We should have telephonic communication with the mainland, as telegraphic communication with it is very expensive. The Company which first erects wires over the Island will certainly have the advantage over all competitors. As it would take, perhaps, two years to set up the wires, he would not object to the term being fixed at five years.

Mr. BLAKE was not generally in favor of monopolies, but as telephonic communication would be an immense advantage to the country, he would be willing to extend it for a period of five years to this Company. Looking at the time

required to place the wires in position, the proposed period would be sufficiently short for the purpose intended.

Mr. MATHESON said that there was no guarantee that this Company would extend its wires all over the Island, to the towns and villages, such as Souris, Alberton, Summerside, etc. We should have such a guarantee before granting the monopoly now asked for.

On motion, the blank in the clause was filled with the word "five."

Next paragraph was then read, providing for an exemption from all taxes for a term of years, of the Telephone Company.

Hon. Mr. SULLIVAN said that this clause would exempt all the property of the Company, whether real or personal, from municipal, provincial and school taxes. He did not approve of making such exemptions, but as telephonic communication would vastly benefit the country, he thought it might be granted in the present case. Nobody will suffer because this Company is not taxed for a period of five years.

Mr. BLAKE had no objection to the principle of exempting from taxation for five years, this Company, but this was a matter which should be left for the City to deal with, as its powers were already very much limited. A Bill was now before the House, asking that certain classes of property may be taxed by the city, and he thought the city only should regulate this matter of exempting this Company.

Mr. J. R. McLean: — Have matters come to such a pass that this House must surrender to the city its right of taxing or exempting all corporations doing business in country districts, towns and villages, the head-quarters of which are in Charlottetown? The House has certainly the power to deal with the question of exempting this Company from taxation. He would support the clause.

Hon. Mr. Lefurgey thought the city had a perfect right to tax or to exempt from taxation telephonic lines extending from it to the various parts of the country.

Hon. Mr. Sullivan agreed with the honorable member for East Point (Mr. J. R. McL.) that the Legislature alone had a right to deal with this question. Telephonic communication is a new business in this Province, and he felt quite sure this Company would not enter into it unless its members see their way clear to make it a profitable one. Charlottetown and Summerside corporations, before this Bill is passed, would have the right to tax the offices which this Company may establish within their limits, but they would have no right to tax any other property belonging to it. Important as those towns are, and anxious as the House is to legislate for their benefit, the members of the Legislature have a duty to perform irrespective of any municipal corporation, and should

deal with this question as a Provincial one, for the benefit of the whole Island.

Mr. Beer did not agree with the Honorable Leader of the Government, or with the honorable member for Souris, with respect to this question. He did not think it right for the Legislature to take from Charlottetown and Summerside the privileges which had already been conceded them. It had already given the city the right to exempt from taxation any new enterprise. The Charlottetown Boot and Shoe Factory and the Woolen Factory had been exempted from taxation for a term of years; and there was no reason why the Telephone Company, under this Bill, would not be granted equal priviliges, if it applied for them. After conferring upon the city the right to exempt new industries from taxation, the Legislature should not step in and take from it that right, as was now proposed.

Hon. Mr. Prowse said that if this Bill referred to Charlottetown alone, the matter would be entirely different, but it did not do so. Under this measure, telephonic communication is to be extended over the whole Island, and therefore the question is a provincial, and not a civic one. Would it be fair to the towns and villages in the different parts of the Island to entrust the question of exempting this Company from taxes to the City of Charlottetown? By so doing the Bill might never come into operation at all. A former

City Council refused to have water introduced into the City, and it is possible that the present one might not exempt this Company from taxation. He did not wish to give the city an opportunity of deciding whether or not the country shall have telephonic communication.

Mr. J. R. McLEAN said the Company would never know when they were secure against civic taxation, if this matter were left to the city for its action thereon. He wished to see the question of exemption from taxation decided upon by the House.

Hon. Mr. FARQUHARSON said that under the new City Bill, the personal property of this Company would be liable to taxation. He did not think this question should be relegated to the City Council, as it is a very changeable body, and there is no guarantee that the Company would be exempted from taxation for a period of five years. The House should decide the question.

Hon. Mr. McLEOD had no doubt that if the City Council were asked to grant the proposed exemption from taxation for five years, they would willingly do so. Telephonic communication with the various parts of the Island would be of more value to the citizens than to the people of any other section of the country, and they would therefore be more interested in having it established than the latter. The wires passing from post to post have never been taxed by the city. As the provision for exempting

this Company from taxation, was in the Bill, it would, perhaps, be as well to allow it to pass. No citizen would object to the clause.

Mr. D. C. MARTIN said that if this clause is allowed to pass, the City Bill will have to be amended, as the latter proposes to tax all corporations.

Hon. Mr. FERGUSON said that as to amending the City Bill, there would, no doubt, be a good deal of that done when it comes up. When the present Bill came before the House, he was of opinion there should be no exemption from taxation; but when he considered that this telephonic communication is for all parts of the Island he thought it would be very wrong to place it in the hands of the City Council the power of taxing this Company, as such a course might prevent country districts from receiving the advantage sought for. He thought his honorable colleague would have spoken out in behalf of the country districts instead of the town. He felt it his duty to support the clause.

Hon. Mr. CAMPBELL said that this Bill did not effect the City alone, it affects the whole Island. The city already has telephonic communication, but the country districts have not. The City Council should not have power to deprive those districts of a privilege which the city itself enjoys. As a Company like this should have all possible encouragement in establishing the required communication, the House should exempt it from taxation for a period of at least five years.

Mr. BEER felt as much bound to protect the interests of his constituents as did his honorable colleague, and if he saw that giving the City Council control of the matter of taxing this Company would operate against their interes, he would object to it. But he was not of that opinion. The city had never been slow in exempting from taxation any new industry, and he believed it would be willing to do so in regard to this Compamy.

Mr. BLAKE said that the City was ever ready to afford all possible encouragement to new industries by exempting them from taxation. Judging from the spirit of some remarks which had fallen from some honorable members during this debate, he was afraid the City Bill would not be satisfactorily handled. The city should be more liberally dealt with than in the past. It had not received justice.

Mr. JOHN McLEAN said that this was a Bill in which all sections of the Island were interested. Charlottetown had its own industries, in which it had a particular interest; but this measure concerned the country. If this matter of exempting from taxation this Company were handed over to the City Council, it might result in the defeat of the object sought to be attained. He agreed with the honorable member for Campbellton, that there should be some provision making in compulsory for the Company to establish telephonic communication between all parts of the Island.

Mr. SINCLAIR said that if he were a representative of the city, he would consider this Bill interfered with its present rights. The city has the privilege of making the proposed exemption from taxation, and yet the Legislature is now stepping in and preventing it from exercising that power. Why give to the city such a privilege, if it is not to be permitted to exercise it? It should be left to the city to decide whether it was willing to lose a portion of the revenue which it had a right to receive.

Mr. BENTLEY said that the passing of this clause would not deprive the city of any existing right or of any tax now received by it. But it would prevent the city from taxing this new industry. No company would undertake to provide telephonic communication, unless they could make it pay. If this Company were taxed by the City Council, it would be compelled to charge higher rates for its messages, and thus the burden would bear upon country districts. The Legislature had the sole right to regulate this matter.

Mr. ALEX. MARTIN, thought this question had been pretty well discussed, and that the clause should pass as it at present stood. No loss would accrue to the City by the proposed exemption.

Hon. Mr. LEFURGEY,—What is

the use in Summerside and Charlottetown asking the Legislature to pass laws to enable them to regulate and levy their taxes, if their privileges are to be ignored in the manner now proposed ? The city has a right to levy certain taxes, and if this clause is passed, it will, to a certain extent, be deprived of that right.

Hon. Mr. PROWSE said that he wished to give this Company the assurance that it will be exempt from taxation for five years, because he desired to see telephonic communication established between all the towns and villages on the Island, and that it be supplied at lowest rates. Montague Bridge once had telegraphic Communication, but it was withdrawn, and he now hoped to see telephonic communication established between that place and Charlottetown. In fact, if sufficient encouragement be given this Company, the telephone may drive out the telegraph system altogether, and we may secure much cheaper communication with the mainland than we at present possess. We are paying more dearly for our telegraphic communication with the mainland than are the people of the other provinces with any other part of the Dominion. He believed this measure would be fruitless without the provision contained in this clause, and therefore was bound to support it. It would not in the slightest degree interfere with the privileges now enjoyed by the City Corporation, and would be an assurance to the Company that they will be exempt from taxation without any further application to the City Council.

Hon. Mr. McLEOD said that probably the reason this Company asked for the provision in the Bill was that they had some doubt as to the power of the City Council to exempt them from taxation. What is meant by the word "industry ?" It always means some mechanical work, or some manufacturing operation, and it is doubtful if the term applies to telephonic communication. In addition to this, it must be remembered that this business will not be confined to Charlottetown, but will be extended over the Island. It is not strictly an industry such as a cloth or shoe factory carries on, and he did not think it would come under the exemptions of the City Act. Telephonic communication is of great value to Charlottetown in case of fire, causing a vast saving of time. Looking at this fact, he felt sure the city would not complain of this exemption from taxation. Aside from this, however, the operations of this Company do not come within the list of "new industries;" the City Law will not apply to them, and the City Council, of course, could not exempt them from taxation. He would support the clause as it now stood.

I. O.

Mr. GORDON said if the Bill before the Committee only related to Charlottetown and Summerside he would be inclined to support the views of the honorable member for the City, but this Bill will affect the whole Island, and for that reason he would support it as it is. The industry, if it can be called such, of conveying intelligence by means of the Telephone is only in its infancy, and before five years such new inventions may be discovered as will supercede the invention that is now to be introduced. He did not think it would be judicious to extend the term too long, for if we do we may be shut out from the advantages to be derived from the inventive genius of the age.

On motion, the clause with blank was agreed to.

On motion the blank was filled with the word "five."

Clause was then read and agreed to.

On motion of Honorable Mr. Sullivan the following clause was added to the Bill:

"Nothing in this Act contained shall be held, or construed to apply to, or affect any Telephone Company, person or persons, or body corporate now doing telephone business in this Province."

On motion, Mr. Speaker resumed the Chair, and the Chairman reported the Bill agreed to with certain amendments.

Ordered, That the Bill be engrossed.

Ordered, That the Bill be read the third time to-morrow.

Mr. D. C. MARTIN, in accordance with notice on the Order Book, asked the Commissioner of Crown Lands to lay on the table of the House a statement showing in what townships are contained the unsold lands mentioned in his official report for the year 1884, submitted to the House, and the number of such acres in each township; also the number of acres in each township held by squatters; the estates deficient of the quantity of land which they were represented to contain, and to what extent the said estates respectively have been found deficient.

Hon. Mr. FERGUSON said he would be prepared to give an answer to morrow.

Mr. BEER asked the Commissioner of Crown and Public Lands, what action, if any, had been taken towards the purchase of the estate of Mrs. Smith, on Lots 24 and 33, and other proprietors, and also whether it is the intention of the Government to purchase those estates at an early day.

Hon. Mr. FERGUSON said: "In reply to the question just asked by my honorable colleague. I have to say, that on the 15th December, 1881, the Honorable Leader of the Government addressed a communication to Mrs. Smith, requesting her to state in writing the lowest price at which she would sell her land to the Government, to which Mrs. Smith replied on the 20th of January, 1882, offering to sell her estate consisting of 4,112½ acres, for the sum of $28,875. A close examination of the estate in regard to quality of land, rate of rent, etc., showed that this price was unreasonably high, probably nearly, if not altogother, double as much as a capital sum representing the rental, and three times as much as the tenants on the estate would be willing to pay for their holdings. Under these circumstances the Government saw no advantage likely to arise from continuing a correspondence with Mrs Smith. The Government have had no correspondence with any other proprietor. The Government is willing to purchase the Smith estate and other lands which are fairly of the character of proprietory estates, should they be offered at reasonable prices."

Mr. BEER said he supposed this reply covered both questions.

Hon. Mr. FERGUSON,—Yes.

Mr. FARQUHARSON repeated his question respecting returns asked for by him some days ago.

Hon. Mr. CAMPBELL said the returns asked for would be laid on the table of the House to-morrow morning.

Mr. FARQUHARSON also asked the Commissioner of Public Works to lay upon the table of the House a statement giving the names of all parties supplying coal to the public buildings of this Province; as to how the contracts were let, the quantity supplied to each building, and the price per ton paid to each party, for the year 1884.

Hon. Mr. CAMPBELL said the return asked for was being prepared and would be ready to-morrow.

Mr. PERRY asked the Commissioner of Crown and Public Lands to lay on the table a statement showing in what case, if any, has the purchase price of Government land been reduced within the last three years, from the original value set upon the same by the department. Also a statement showing the number and names of landholders in the different townships who have not agreed to purchase the lands of the Government; also what rents have been received, in each, from such holdings since 1876. Mr. Perry also asked the Commissioner of Public Lands to lay on the table a statement, showing the amount received in the Land Office for each of the months of January, February and March, 1885.

Hon. Mr. FERGUSON said the information asked for will be laid on the table of the House at an early date.

Mr. MATHESON, in accordance with notice placed in the Order Book, asked the Commissioner of Crown and Public Lands to lay on the table of this House a statement showing the names of the holders of land upon which no payment has been made within the last ten years, and quantity of land held by every such person.

Hon. Mr. FERGUSON said the information asked for will be laid on the table of the House at an early date.

Mr. BEER asked the Honorable Commissioner of Public Works whether it is the intention of the Government to cause to be opened this spring a public road leading from the Brackley Point Road, Lot.33, to the Royalty Junction of the P. E. I. Railway.

Hon. Mr. CAMPBELL said the matter was under consideration of the Government, but he was not in a position to give a positive answer just now.

Mr. BEER said he had asked this question two years ago and had received the same answer.

Mr. BEER asked the Honorable Commissioner of Public Works whether it is the intention of the Government to cause to be opened this spring a public road leading from Southport to Clifton, Lot 48

Hon. Mr. CAMPBELL said this road will be opened this spring. A portion of it is already opened, and remainder would be as soon as some difficulties with the holders of some land had been arranged.

Mr. BEER said he did not think there was any difficulties with the holders of the land through which this road passed. The trouble he

understood was on a part of the road further away than the part he had referred to.

Mr. BEER then asked whether it is the intention of the Government to cause a suitable house, or waiting room, to be erected on the Prince Street Ferry Wharf, for the accommodation of the passengers crossing on the Southport ferry.

Hon. Mr. CAMPBELL said he was not in a position to answer this question.

Mr. BEER further asked the Commissioner of Public Works to lay on the table of the House a return showing in detail the expenditure by the Government from the 1st day of January, 1884, to December 31st, 1884, on the following Government works, viz.:
Government House,
Provincial Building,
Prince of Wales College,
Normal School,
Poor House,
Hospital for the Insane,
Queen Square fence,
Stock Farm,
Southport Ferry,
Steamers *Elfin* and *Southport*,
together with the names of all persons employed on said works, and the different amounts paid to each person, both for work and material, and also what amounts have been expended on any of said works from December 31st, 1884, to March 27th, 1885.

Hon. Mr. CAMPBELL said he would like to know what the honorable member meant by expenditure on Southport Ferry. As honorable members know there was a yearly contract for this service, he did not see what further information was wanted. The expenditure on the steamers and on the docks will be laid on the table of the House to-morrow. The other returns asked for are being prepared, and will be brought down as soon as possible.

Mr. BEER said, last year, reports of this kind were delayed until the end of the session, and honorable members were prevented from getting the information they had a right to get. He hoped that more help would be employed, so these returns will be placed on the table of the House at an early day.

Hon. Mr. CAMPBELL said there was only one set of Books in his department, and the Secretary was working at them as hard as he could. The Opposition are asking for so many returns that it took a great deal of time to get them ready. The honorable member, however, will be disappointed, as these statements will soon be ready, and they will not afford him the gratification he anticipated.

On motion of Honorable Mr. Lefurgey, it was ordered that the Bill intituled "An Act to incorporate the Prince Edward Island Mutual Fire Insurance Company," be read the second time to-morrow.

On motion of Honorable Mr. McLeod, it was ordered that the

Bill intituled "An Act securing to the Baptist Churches of Prince Edward Island the benefits of incorporation," be read the second time to-morrow.

House adjourned until to-morrow forenoon at ten o'clock.

G. F. O.

TUESDAY, March 31.

Mr. SPEKER in the Chair.

MR. BENTLEY offered to present a petition from Hugh Walker, Benjamin Webster, George Ives, and others, tenants on a portion of Lot 28, asking to become the owners of their farms under equal privileges with others who are now freeholders; and said that he thought the Government should grant the prayer of the petition, and purchase from the proprietors the small estate of which the farms of the petitioners form a part. It is the policy of the Government to convert, if possible, all the leaseholders into freeholders; and there yet remains a balance of of $50,000 or $60,000 of $800,000 granted this Province by the Dominion Government for that purpose. He was glad to hear from the hon. Commissioner of Crown Lands that the Government are prepared to purchase at reasonable rates, all the remaining small estates, for he (Mr. B,) believed some of those proprietors are willing to sell at a fair valuation, when compared with what has been paid for some other lots. He moved that the petition be received and read.

Mr. SINCLAIR:—The hon mem-ber for Kensington knows very well, and the Government also know that the House cannot receive this petition, as, if granted, it would involve the expenditure of money from the public treasury The rules of the House forbid its reception.

Mr. HOLLAND seconded the motion of the hon. member for Kensington, his hon. colleague, and said he regretted that some of the tenants on Lot 28 should be compelled the third time to ask the Government to purchase the estate on which they reside. They have been very badly used indeed. In fact all the tenants on the small estates have been ill used by the various Governments of this Province, which have refused to relieve them from a state of bondage. Tenants on an estate of 499 acres are excluded from the benefits of the Land Purchase Act, while those on one containing 500 acres are benefited by it. Why should such a dis tinction be made? All tenants should be granted equal privileges with respect to the purchase of the freehold of their farms. He believed that there are 20,000 acres in the various small estates not affected by the provisions of the Land Purchase Act. A very slight amendment to that Act would give the Government all the power necessary to enable the tenants on those estates to become freeholders. If this were made the small proprietors would be willing to sell their estates to the Government at reasonable prices.

On Lot 28 there are about 2000 acres held in this way. The ten-ants are crying loudly for action on the part of the Government with respect to this matter, and people generally have great sym-pathy for them If this question is not soon taken up, it will be serious for the Government.

Mr. J. R McLEAN said that if the mover and seconder of this motion had spent one fourth of the time now taken up in reference to this matter, in reasoning with the Government with respect to it, something might have been gain-ed; but he could not understand their present action. It seemed to him perfectly ridiculous that the business of the country should be delayed in this way.

Hon. Mr. SULLIVAN saw no im-propriety in the course pursued by the two honorable members who had brought this matter before the House. Of course it would be for the Speaker to decide as to whether or not the petition should be received, but there was no reason why those honorable gentle-men could not make the motion they had made. There is nothing to prevent an honorable member from seeking to present a petition. If the petition is not received by the House, as he presumed it would not, it could be referred to the Executive Council, where it would be carefully considered. It is certainly very desirable that all the tenants on this Island should become freeholders.

Mr. BEER thought it a pity that the honorable member for Kensington did not present his petition to the Executive Council, and that he did not bring the matter to the attention of the Government when the honorable member for Rustico brought a similar case to their notice. There are several small estates which he desired very much to see purchased by the Government, among which was the Smith estate on Lot 33. He had been hoping that when his honorable colleague became Commissioner of Crown Lands he would have taken steps to have that estate purchased; but he was sorry to hear that since 1881 or 1882 no correspondence with the proprietor had been carried on with reference to its purchase. The small estates should certainly be purchased by the Government, as well as the large ones. We have the money for the purpose, and there is no reason why it should not bo used in assisting tenants to become freeholders. He hoped the Government would take the necessary action to secure so desirable a result.

Hon. Mr. FERGUSON was glad that his honorable colleague had expressed himself in favor of the purchase by the Government of the remaining small estates, for at one time the honorable gentleman advised the tenants on those estates to purchase their own freeholds. This was when the honorable gentleman held a seat in the Executive.

Mr. FARQUHARSON said that in his district there were several parties complaining very much of the want of action on the part of the Government with respect to the purchase of the small estates there. He thought the Government should compromise the matter with those proprietors, for their tenants were under great disadvantages. In North Wiltshire there are two of those estates, and others in Rustico. The Government will be remiss in their duty if they do not take action in reference to this matter. The tenants have a right to be placed in a position to become freeholders.

Mr. SPEAKER declined to receive a motion for the reception of the petition, stating as his reason that the prayer thereof conflicts with the 25th Rule of the House relative to the initiation of money votes.

Hon. Mr. CAMPBELL, a member of Her Majesty's Executive Council, presented to the House, by command of His Honor the Lieutenant Governor, the Returns of Expenditure for the year 1884, of thirty-four Road Supervisors in Queen's, Prince, and King's Counties.

Also Estimates of said Supervisors for the year 1885.

Ordered, That said Returns and Estimates do lie on the table.

Ordered, That the first standing Order of the House relative to Private Bills, be suspended to enable a member to present a petition.

A petition of Daniel Davies, John Ings, Horace Haszard, Simon

W. Crabbe, and others, was presented to the House by Mr. Blake, and the same was received and read, praying that an Act be passed to incorporate "The Charlottetown Waterworks Company."

Ordered, That said petition be referred to a special Committee, to report thereon by Bill or otherwise.

Ordered, That Mr. Blake, Honorable Mr. McLeod and Honorable Mr. Campbell do compose said Committee.

Mr. BLAKE, from the last preceding Committee appointed, presented to the House a Bill as prepared by the Committee, to be intituled : "An Act to Incorporate the Charlottetown Waterworks Company," and the same was received and read the first time, and referred to the Committee on Private Bills, to examine the same and report thereon.

A petition of the City of Charlottetown was presented to the House by Mr. Blake, and the same was received and read, praying for the passage of "An Act Incorporating a Company with full power to introduce water into this City."

Ordered, That the petition do lie on the table.

Ordered, That the first standing order of this House relative to Private Bills be suspended, to enable a member to present a petition.

A petition of Reuben Tuplin, D.

Darrach, and others, inhabitants of the village of Kensington, was presented to the House by Mr. Bentley, and the same was received and read, praying that an Act be passed to amend "An Act relating to Accidents by Fire in Kensington, Prince County, and for the removal of nuisances from the streets thereof."

Mr. BENTLEY said that during the past year a number of amendments to the Act now in force were found to be necessary. In order that the law might be made clearer and more easily understood, it is thought better to pass a new Act.

Ordered, That the petition be referred to the House in Committee of the whole, to-morrow.

Hon. Mr. CAMPBELL, a member of Her Majesty's Executive Council, presented to the House.

Statement showing amounts paid for works without tender, etc., by Public Works Department, 1884.

Contracts entered into from January 1st, 1885, to 24th March, 1885.

Memorandum.—Coal purchased for the Public Buildings, 1884.

Ordered, That said papers do lie on the table.

The Order of the Day being read for the second reading of the Bill to be intituled, "An Act to incorporate the Charlottetown Conference of Saint Vincent de Paul Society."

Said Bill was accordingly read the second time and committed to a Committee of the whole House. The House accordingly resolved itself into the said Committee.

Mr. JOHN MCLEAN in the Chair.

The Bill, having been read, clause by clause, was agreed to, without debate.

On motion, Mr. Speaker resumed the Chair, and the Chairman reported the Bill agreed to.

Ordered, That the Bill be engrossed, and that it be read the third time to-morrow.

"An Act to Incorporate the P. E. Island Agricultural Mutual Fire Insurance Company," was, on motion, read a second time, and committed to a Committee of the whole House. The House accordingly resolved itself into the said Committee.

Mr. JOHN MCLEAN in the Chair.

The first clause having been read,—

Mr. J. R. MCLEAN said the House should have some explanation in reference to the principle of this Bill. It had a very comprehensive name, and may aim at having preference over the Insurance Companies already established in this Province.

Hon. Mr. MCDONALD said that the Private Bill Committee did not take exception to the name of this Bill, nor would they have objected to the name of the Bill introduced last Session for Incorporating the "Island Publishing Company" if the word "Patriot" had been used instead of the word "Island."

Hon. Mr. SULLIVAN thought the Clerk should have been asked to read over the whole of this Bill before the House went into Committee upon it, in order that all might understand it. It is a very important Bill, and, if passed, the consequence to those who are incorporated by it may be found to be more serious than they imagine. Not only are the members of the Company to be incorporated, but their Heirs, Administrators and Assigns also. He had never seen such a provision in a Bill of this kind. He thought it a very objectionable one.

Hon. Mr. LEFURGEY did not see this Bill until day before yesterday. Mr. Bell, of this Island, who has been a lawyer in the Province of Ontario, framed it; and he (Mr. L.) presumed that gentleman advised the insertion therein of all the provisions it contains. Having been drafted by a professional man, the Bill should be considered regular.

Mr. J. R. MCLEAN said that Mr. Bell may be a very clever man; but a number of these Institutions had sprung up in Ontario, of late, and had run down as rapidly as they rose. It is singular that the heirs, administrators and assigns should be held responsible for the acts of men who undertook such things as are provided for in this Bill, which is a very extraordinary one.

Mr. BENTLEY thought the principle of the Bill a good one. He was present at the meeting of the Agricultural Society, at which it was stated, and the feeling was a general one, that this Institution would be a great benefit to farmers who would avail themselves of its advantages. He did not think any honorable member had any good cause to take exception to any part of it. No doubt the honorable member for East Point had some self-interest in opposing such a measure as this; but the good sense of the House would appreciate it, and deal with it on its merits. It is particularly intended for the benefit of the agricultural classes of the Province. Its name was, he thought, a very proper and significant one. He believed that it was calculated to promote the object for which it was framed.

Mr. ALEX. MARTIN thought the formation and incorporation of such Companies as this should be encouraged, as large sums are now annually paid to Insurance Companies whose head-quarters are not in this Province, and the money leaves the Island. We should encourage home Institutions. He would support the Bill.

Hon. Mr. PROWSE thought the principle of the Bill a good one, and he hoped it would prove a success. As far as he could at present understand it, he would support it.

Mr. BENTLEY said that some of the members of the Company belonged to Queen's County, but the greater number belonged to Prince.

Hon. Mr. McLEOD said it was a very unusual course to pursue to include the executors, administrators and assigns, as well as the original members of the Company, in a measure of this kind. The Bill should be read over very carefully, before being passed clause by clause, in order that its provisions may be seen and understood. It would be impossible to say whether the first clause was a proper one, until this was done.

On motion, the Chairman of the Committee then read the whole Bill, after which, Mr. Speaker resumed the Chair, progress was reported, and leave obtained to sit again.

House adjourned for one hour.

I. O.

Mr. SPEAKER in the Chair.

Hon. Mr. SULLIVAN, a member of Her Majesty's Executive Council, delivered to Mr. Speaker a message from His Honor the Lieutenant Governor, and the said message was read—all the members of the House being uncovered—and is as follows :

"A. A. MACDONALD, Lieutenant Governor.

The Lieutenant Governor transmits to the House of Assembly the accompanying copies of Despatches and Minutes of Council, having reference to the refund by the Government of Canada of moneys expended by the Government of Prince Edward Island on certain piers therein referred to.

.Government House,
        23rd March, 1885."

1. Copy of Despatch from Lieutenant Governor to Under Secretary of State, Ottawa, on the subject of wharves and piers, dated 5th May, 1884.

2. Copy of Despatch from Under Secretary of State, Ottawa, to Lieutenant Governor, dated 13th May, 1884, on same subject.

3. Copy of Despatch from Secretary of State, Ottawa, to Lieutenant Governor, dated 4th June, 1884, respecting claim for maintenance of piers.

4. Copy of Despatch from Lieutenant Governor to Secretary of State, Ottawa, dated 3rd December, 1884, referring to Minutes of Executive Council of this Province of same date, respecting claim for refund of moneys expended by them on certain piers, and deputing the Honorable the Attorney General to proceed to Ottawa to confer with the General Government on the subject.

5. Copy of Despatch from Under Secretary of State, Ottawa, to

Lieutenont Governor, dated 9th December,- 1884, on same subject.

6. Copy of Despatch from Under Secretary of State, Ottawa, to Lieutenant Governor, dated 23rd December, 1884, respecting refund by the Dominion Government of moneys expended by the Government of this Province on certain piers.

7. Copies of Extracts of Minutes of Executive Council of this Province, on same subject, dated 3rd December, 1884.

Ordered, That the said Despatches and Papers do lie on the table.

On motion of Honorable Mr. Sullivan, seconded by Honorable Mr. Ferguson, the Order of the Day was read for the House in Committee of the whole on the consideration of the Supply to be granted to Her Majesty.

Budget Speech.

Hon. Mr. SULLIVAN moved that the House do now go into the Order of the Day, and said that in doing so he desired to make some observations upon the financial state of the Province. For some time past it had been busily represented in the Opposition press that the Island was hopelessly in debt, to an amount variously estimated from $60,000 to $120,000. It was very possible that some honorable members were surprised, when the report of the Provincial Auditor was placed in their hands, to find that there was actually a balance o the credit of the Province upon he transactions of the past year of early $1,000. The total receipts ad been $280,271.23, and the exenditure $279,545.35, leaving a alance in favor of the Province of 725.88. It was true that, at the lose of the two previous years, here had been a small deficit. The present Government had been striving since their accession to power in 1879, to pay of the obligations incurred by the present Leader of the Opposition and his colleagues in the previous administration.

The Opposition had charged the Government with preparing Estimates which were incorrect and unreliable, and which had never been adhered to; in short, that the Government had been expending the public moneys just as they thought proper, without any regard to their Estimates. Such was not the case. But he (Mr. S.) could remember very well when some of the honorable gentlemen opposite were members of a government with whom it was a very easy matter to make Estimates. In fact, that Government estimated a "sum sufficient" for almost every large item. They had a "sum sufficient" for Education, a "sum sufficient" for Legislation, a "sum sufficient" for Printing and Stationery, etc., etc. And when, in 1872, the honorable member for Southport was Finance Minister, there was a "sum sufficient" for the payment of the interest on the public debt, and heaven only knew how much the public debt was at that time. The honorable gentleman himself did not know, for

otherwise he would have been able to estimate the amount of interest on it. Further on, in the Estimates for 1872, there was West Point Light House, a "sum sufficient," expenses of Investigating Engineers brought here from the United States to condemn the Railway, a "sum sufficient!" Location of branch lines, a "sum sufficient." For almost every alternate item, a sum sufficient. Under such circumstances, it was impossible for the Government of that day to exceed their Estimates, as they were given a *carte blanche*. They could spend whatever they required, and yet come down to the House and say that they had not exceeded their Estimates! That was the way in which the public business was managed in those days! He had been told that the Estimates of last year were very incorrect, and that according to the Public Accounts, the Government had exceeded them, and had thus deceived the House and the country; but when moving the House into Committee of Supply, last Session, he had said: "It is, of course, impossible to tell what may happen during the year, but the Government have no reason to doubt that payments expected by them will be made before its close. Should their expectations be verified, there will be a considerable surplus. If the worst happen, the receipts will be only $18,000 short of the amount required. But he would predict that the worst would not happen, and that the Province would be in a good position financially at the end of the year." Now, that statement had been verified by the facts. He had said that if nothing unexpected happened, the Estimates would probably be found sufficient to carry on the public business of the year. But it was well known that many unforseen and unexpected things had occurred during the past year. The months of June and July were remarkably wet, the Commissioner of Public Works has been obliged to duplicate the expenditure upon most of the roads and culverts which had been seriously damaged by freshets, and therefore the vote was insufficient to meet other required expenditures. This caused a largely increased expenditure in his department. Many of our farmers, especially in Prince County, knew, to their cost, that so wet was the season, that they lost a large portion of their crops; that the first seed sown was destroyed, and a second sowing had to be put in. Owing to the same cause, the Government found it necessary to expend on the roads and bridges a much larger sum than they had estimated. The extra expenditure on bridges amounted to $8,690.60, and on roads $8,122.97, or about $17,000 in all. The repairs to the steamers on the Southport ferry cost $4,034.59 above the amount estimated. The maintenance of the Hospital for the Insane—another matter beyond the control of the Government—cost $1,084.25 more than was anticipated. Every one knew that this expenditure was regulated by the number of inmates; and that number, last year, unfortunately for this Province, was larger than ever before, and, he hoped,

larger than ever would be there again. The number of applications for admission had been much greater than during any former year, there having been in one week, no fewer than eighteen. As this caused an increased expenditure in connection with that Institution, the estimate was exceeded to the extent already stated. There was, also, an additional expense on the Provincial Building. During the continued wet weather, the water had come through the roof, and it was found necessary to have it thoroughly repaired, in order that the interior should suffer no damage. That expenditure amounted to $1,222.54. There was another item of expenditure over which the Government had no control, viz., Education. That branch of the Public Service costs, to-day, a very large sum of money. The Honorable Leader of the Opposition had been instrumental in placing on the Statute Book of this Province a very expensive School Act, under the operation of which, last year, more than one hundred and five thousand dollars had been expended, being an increase over the previous year of over $4,000. As honorable members were already aware, the expenditure under that head was largely influenced by the supplements voted in the country districts, and therefore if the estimate was exceeded to the extent of four or five thousand dollars no one could find fault. No Government could possibly estimate, to a certainty, the exact amount required for Education. The bonus to teachers helped also to swell that amount. These uncontrollable expenditures amounted, in all, to about $28,000, over the amount estimated. On the other hand, one source of revenue, viz., Public Lands.. did. not yield as large a sum as in the previous year. The cause of the falling off in the receipts from that department was the wet weather, which had more particularly affected Prince and King's counties, and as there was a short crop, the people were less able to pay their instalments. The receipts were $6 000 less than had been expected from that source. If to this were added the $28,000 of expenditure over estimates already referred to, we had a total of $34,000. He had stated last session that if the full amount of the pier money were not received from Ottawa there would be a deficit on the year's operation of $18,000. This sum, added to the $34,000, gave a total of $52,000, which showed the correctness of the statement he then made. The Government had been told that no reliance could be placed on their estimates, because the result of the year's operations was not precisely what they anticipated. He would ask, was there ever a Government that came out, at the end of any financial year, just as they expected? He thought not. He would like the honorable member for Strathalbyn to compare the estimates of the years 1877 and 1878 with the expenditures for these years. The present Government were declared by the Opposition press to be bunglers, and destitute of all ability to manage the finances of the Province, because their expenditures,

in a few instances, had exceeded their estimates, owing to causes over which they had no control. When the Leader of the Opposition and his friends were in power, they brought down Estimates for a "sum sufficient" for all the principal departments of the public service. He had before him the Estimates for 1877 when Mr. Davies led the Government, and also the speech made by that gentleman, on the motion to go into Committee of Supply. Mr. Davies' Estimate of Expenditure for that year was $282,792, but the actual expenditure was no less than $331,632. showing an Expenditure over the Estimate of $48,840. Yet there were no untoward circumstances to cause this; no storms, no wet season—no reason whatever for exceeding the amount voted. People whose reading was limited to the only Opposition newspaper of to day would no doubt be surprised to hear that the Davies Government exceeded their Estimates in 1877 to the extent of over $48,000. Where was the patriotism of the *Patriot* in those days? Was Mr. Davies denounced through the Province as a bungling financier? No! The *Patriot* patted him on the back, and nothing too good could be said about him, and the honorable member for West River. He would now glance at the figures for the year 1878, when the Government still held the reins of power. How did the Expenditure for that year compare with the Estimates? Matters were becoming worse as time passed. During that year Mr. Davies made a speech on the motion to go into Committee of Supply, in which, prob·bly for the purpose of diverting attention from his mismanag· ment of the finances, he violently attacked his opponents. He then estimated the revenue for 1878 to be $323,189, and the expenditure, $322,766.94 ; but honorable members would be surprised to learn that the expenditure reached the sum of $334,133.29, to which must be added the amount carried forward to the next year's accounts, viz., $60 071.95, making a total of $394,205.24 of actual expenditure. The error in the estimates for that year was, therefore, $71,438.30. The actual receipts were $312,- 684.34, instead of $323,189, as Mr. Davies had estimated, and the deficit $31,520 90. The present Government had met the public requirements during the past year with an expenditure of $287,045.35, and had a surplus on the year's operations of $725.88 ; but Mr. Davies had expended, in 1878, no less than $394,205.24, and had a deficit of $81,520.90 ! Had it not been for the legacy transmitted to him by his predecessors, Mr. Davies would have had a much larger balance against the Province at that time. But this was not all. There was then a very prominent gentleman at the head of the department of Public Works, who was very anxious to keep up the best possible appearance in the working of that department, and to make everything look well, on the outside at least. Towards the close of 1878 this official found it necessary to ask people who had performed work and completed

contracts for the department, not to present their accounts for pay. ment until after the close of the year. The road supervisors were also asked not to forward their returns until the new year came in, in order that the expenditure for 1878 might appear as small as possible in the Public Accounts. In addition to this a suspense account was opened for that department, and after the 1st January, 1879' the items contained therein were entered in the ordinary books, and charged as transactions of the new year. In this way no less than the sum of $60.071.95 was carried forward from 1878 to 1879, as was proved by the accounts for the latter year. The total expenditure for 1878 was therefore $394,205.24, or $71,- 438.30 beyond the sum estimated by Mr. Davies. Compare this amount with the sum by which the present Government exceeded their estimates, viz., about $30,000 and the latter was found to be much less than the half ; yet the late Government came down to the House with smiling faces, and perfectly satisfied at what they had done. Why were not these facts given to the world by the organ of the Opposition ? The worst feature of the expenditure of the Davies Government, just alluded to, was that their expenditure was altogether a controllable one, except in the matter of Education. During the year 1878 they paid only three-quarters' salaries to the teachers, having carried forward the remaining quarter to 1879 ; yet the Opposition accused the present Government with deceiving the country, because they did not provide for the payment of five quarters' salaries for the teachers. Every schoolboy knew that there were only four qur'ers in the year, and that such a course was altogether unnecessary. But the Opposition maintained that a year under the present Government should have five quarters, and that when they were in office it sh uld have only three! It was clear that when they charged the present Government with having committed errors in any respect, they themselves were more than four times as guilty, without any excuse at all, such as the present Government had.

He would now call the attention of the House to a few facts, by way of contrasting the course pursued by the present Government with that pursued by their opponents on the other side of the House. In the year 1876 he was a member of a Government of which the Honorable Leader of the Opposition was also a member, and which introduced and carried through the Legislature an Act relating to the Civil Service, which was intended to place the finances of the Province upon a new basis, and on a different footing from what they had previously been. The incoming Government had therefore an opportunity of carrying out that system in its integrity. Instead, however, of confining themselves to the expenditures authorized by that measure, they increased them to an extent wholly unwarrantable. Compare the expenditure on Education, under the

present Government, with that of their predecessors. During the past year the present Government expended thereon, no less a sum than $105,185.09. Now, there was no Province in this Dominion, and no country in the world, which expended so much money for Education, in proportion to its means, as did this Island. He believed that the School Act was doing good service in the country districts, and hoped that it was doing as well in Charlottetown. In the year 1873 the Davies Government expended upon Education only $65,550.13, against $10,185.09 in 1884, showing a difference in favor of the present Government of $39,634.96, or in round numbers $40.000. The Government had been charged with extravagance by their opponents, and with respect to this matter they had to plead guilty to the extent just stated But this large expenditure was for Education, and it was their duty to make it, as it was in the interests of the country. A reference to the Report on the Public Accounts for 1878 would disclose that the administration of justice, during that year, under Mr. Davies, cost $30,304.74. Now, the expenditure last year under that head was only $19,422.62, showing a saving of nearly $11,000 in that item alone. Then, again, take the salaries of the public officials and compare those of 1878 with those of 1884. As honorable members were already aware, the first step taken by the present Government on coming into power was to reduce the salaries as well as the number of the officials, one individual, in some cases, being called upon to do the work previously done by two or three persons. In this way a saving of no less than $11,138 31 was effected, the expenditure for salaries in 1878 having been $45,165,67, while that of the past year was $34,-027.36. The saving of expenditure in the departments alluded to showed only a part of what the Government had done in that direction; but it afforded good evidence of what had been accom plished. The amount of unpaid accounts carried forward at the close of the past year was only $7,500, while the amount carried at the close of 1878 by the Davies Government was $60,071.95. It would thus be seen that the comparison was greatly in favor of the present Government, and against their opponents   The real expenditure of 1878 was seen to be $394,205,24, and that of 1884 $287,045.35. showing that the present Government had met the public requirements last year, with an expenditure of $107,159.89 less than that of the late Government. He would defy the Opposition to successfully contradict this statement. To the latter sum must be added the sum expended on Education over and beyond that of the Davies Government in 1878, viz., $39,634.96, and we had a total of $146,794.85. If the present Government had not been required to expend more for Education in 1884 than was expended in 1878, that would have been the annual amount of the saving to the country effected by them. The Honorable Leader of the Opposi-

tion could not controvert this statement. To these figures he would direct the attention of the House, and of the country. This might appear a small matter to the Opposition, and to their press, which endeavored to stigmatize the Government as beggars, while endeavoring to secure the just rights of the Province from the Dominion Government; but it was not so to the people of this country. The delegates who had been sent to Ottawa to press our claims and secure our rights, by the Opposition press styled the 'three jolly beggars," because they had endeavored to do their duty to this Province in the matter of the piers. That press, he did not hesitate to say, was a disgrace to this Province. It denounced and belittled the delegation, and almost went so far as to say that the Prouince was not entitled to the money claimed as compensation for its piers. It also declared that the word "piers" had quite a different meaning from that which the Government were endeavoring to attach to it, and exerted its utmost strength to prevent this Island receiving one dollar of the money. But the Government were, notwithstanding all this, enabled to press our claims properly, and with sufficient dignity and self-respect to secure a settlement of the matter. He did not think this Province had any reason to be ashamed to go to the Dominion Government, and to demand payment of the amount which they owed us. It was the duty of those who represented this Island at the time Confederation took place, to see that the line between Dominion and Provincial works was properly drawn, and the General Government performed the service that properly belonged to them; yet some of those gentlemen had made this matter a secondary consideration. Instead of levying taxation upon the people of this Province at an enormous rate, as their predecessors had done, the present Government had been collecting the debts due us from the Dominion Government. They first collected the amount due for the support of penitentiary criminals. Before that claim was made we had been paying for the maintenance of those criminals. That duty should long before have been relegated to the Dominion Government, but those who ought to have attended to the matter neglected to do so. The present Government pressed our claims in reference to it, and received in all, on account of those claims, about $22,000. They then took up the matter of the piers, and received on account of them the sum of $53,222.19, beside the amount of tolls, viz., $6,096.88, received as wharfage, for which we were willing to give them credit, but which in their generosity they did not ask us to deduct from the sum due us. We had, therefore, received on account of the piers in all, $59,319.07. We should also receive a further amount of $24,-240, to which reference was made in the papers on the table of the House, on account of other piers which had been taken over by the Dominion Government. Beside that, a further amount was allowed the Local Government for tolls,

amounting to $1,908.90; so that, altogether, we should receive from the Dominion as compensation for our piers, the sum of $85.467.97. That was the sum secured by the delegates during their mission to Ottawa in connection with the piers' question. In addition to the compensation received for the piers, all those works were handed over to the General Government, to be sustained and kept in repair by them for all time to come. For that purpose the sum of $12,000 was placed in the Dominion Estimates for last year, and $8,000 for the present year. By adding these amounts to the sum secured on account of piers, we had a total of upwards of $105,000 up to the close of the current year. Before that time, a settlement would have been made, and this Province relieved for all time of the obligation of maintaining and repairing its piers, which was more, under its straightened circumstances, than it was able to do in a satisfactory manner. He noticed, in one of the newspapers, a statement to the effect that the Public Accounts were eminently satisfactory so far as they went, but they did not go far enough. Any person could see that there was a surplus on the transactions of last year, and that the public indebtedness of the two previous years had been reduced by that amount. It was also clear that the total indebtedness was very much less than it was a year ago. But we were asked, through the press, what the Province could show in assets against that sum? He thought it a pity that from the time we entered Confederation a capital account had been opened, in order that the public might be made aware what our assets were, and the total amount of them. He could easily show that those assets were worth nearly two millions of dollars. Among them were all the public buildings owned by this Province, such as the Provincial Building and Government House, the Court Houses in the towns and country districts, the two Asylum Buildings, the College and Normal School Buildings and property, the Stock Farm and Buildings, the ferry steamers, the bridges and culverts; and all the other public works. The unsold public lands and the sums due the Land Office should also be included. The value of these assets was enormous, and compared with them, our little indebtedness was scarcely worthy of mention. This ought to be sufficient to show that our finances were in a sound and healthy condition. But the assets mentioned did not comprise all. How did we stand with the Dominion? We had a balance to our credit there, on ordinary account, of $975,872.90, and on land account, of $52,023.29, making a total of $1,027,896.19. We could, therefore, draw from that source to-morrow a sum which would pay off at once our little two–penny–half–penny indebtedness. But as we received interest on the money to our credit at Ottawa, we preferred not to withdraw from capital, knowing that we could easily square our account at home without doing so.

The estimates for the present year were on the table of the House, and as he stated last year,

unless something unforeseen occurred to require a much larger expenditure than was at present expected, the amount would be sufficient to meet all the requirements of the country. The Commissioner of Public Works had prepared his estimate of expenditure with great care, and that gentleman informed him (Mr. S.) that no further amount would be required so far as he could tell at the present time. He would now show how the Government proposed to meet the expenditure of the present year. The total expenditure was estimated at $252,556.22. To meet that amount we should have the Dominion subsidy, $173,537.20; and from Public Lands, $50,000. Owing to circumstances already alluded to, the sum received from the Land Office, last year, was lower than was anticipated, but it was to be hoped that Providence would favor our farmers this year to a higher degree, and that better crops would crown their labors. Should such be the case, those receipts would probably reach the amount expected. The fees from the Provincial Secretary's Office were set down at $1000, and from the Prothonotary's Office at $1,500. From the Office of Registrar of Deeds the sum of $5,500 was expected. The revenue from that source had largely increased, and up to the present date, was far beyond that of last year. The receipts from the County Courts were falling off, and were estimated for this year at $2,000. The abolition of imprisonment for debt was one of the chief causes of that decline. From the Hospital for the

Insane, the receipts would probably be about $1,500. From Prince of Wales College, Private Bills, Peddlers' Licenses, Fines and Penalties, Rent of Warren Farm and Vendors' Licenses, further sums would be received making the total receipts $236,727.31. We were, also, entitled to receive from the Dominion Government, on account of Piers, the sum of $24,240' which, added to the ordinary receipts made a total revenue of $260,967.-31. That was to say the estimated revenue for the year was $260,967,-31, and the expenditure $252,556.-22, leaving a surplus of $8,411.09. If things turned out as the Government, expected, these figures would represent the receipts and expenditure of the year. The actual figures might, however, vary a little from the sums stated, for every honorable member and every sensible man in the country knew that it was impossible to state precisely what the exact revenue and expenditure would be. If the receipts for the present year reached the sum anticipated, and the expenditure now estimated were not exceeded, the indebtedness would be still further reduced at the close of the year to the extent of the expected surplus, leaving a balance of only forty-four thousand dollars against the Province. During the year 1878 the Davies Government levied no less than $48,000 in direct taxation ; they also received from Public Lands $54,000 and from capital account at Ottawa $37,000, and yet, when they went out of power, they left an indebtedness of $81,520,90 ! With this fact staring them in the face, the present Oppo-

sition were proclaiming far and near that the Government had mismanaged the public finances ! They had been enquiring about the interest which the Government were paying in the Banks, although they should be ashamed to ask such a question. The honorable member for Strathalbyn should remember the year 1872, when the Government, in which that honorable gentleman held a seat, hawked the railway bonds about the Lower Provinces for sale. That was the state of affairs at that time, when not a Bank on the Island would trust that Government. Although their own political friends were directors of some of those Banks, the latter had no faith in them; and would not lend them a dollar ! They were then compelled to go to New Brunswick, where they obtained a loan at one per cent. per month, on the personal promissory note of their Provincial Secretary ! When the late Government were in power they paid no less than eighteen per cent. for money to meet their expenditures, for the cost of collecting moneys under the Assessment Act was afterwards found to amount to that rate. When the present Government had a balance against them at any of the Banks, as they sometimes had, they paid only six per cent. interest on it, but they had just as frequently a large sum to their credit, and received on it four per cent. interest. He contended that this Province was in a very prosperous state, notwithstanding the short harvests of the past year in some sections of the country. As proof of this, our farmers had large sums to their credit in the Savings Banks. In the year 1878, before the present Government came into power, the amount on deposit was $371,074.35, but honorable members would be amazed to learn that on the 30th June, 1884, the amount was no less than $1,412.26, being an increase of $1,041,620.61 in six years! This showed that our farmers were in a prosperous state, and that the policy of the Government was conducive to their best interests. If the Government now expended as lavishly as did their predecessors in 1878, some of our farmers would to-day be spending $30 per year in direct taxes, while the greater number would be paying at least $10 per year. But the country had been saved all that by the economy of the present Government. With respect to the balance of $44,000 already alluded to, he had to say that the Government had some other claims against the Dominion Government, among them one of considerable importance, on which the House had already expressed an opinion, and in connection with which we had demanded compensation. He alluded to the question of winter communication with the mainland. If we had a good claim for five millions of dollars, surely we should be enabled to pay off our little indebtedness of forty-four thousand when that claim was satisfied. He had no doubt whatever that the Imperial Government would have justice meted out to this Province in connection with this matter, and that the Government would, before long, be in a position to come down to the House and state that they had been suc-

cessful in dealing with it, as they had been in reference to the piers question. He laid these estimates before the House in the fullest confidence that the record for the year would be in accordance therewith. When the late Government were in power, they were denounced at public meetings held all over the Province from East Point to North Cape. During the term of the present Government, not a meeting had been held for the purpose of condemning any of their actions. It was true that some people thought it would be better to levy an assessment upon the country, and to raise a larger revenue, but the Government thought otherwise. If the people asked that a direct tax be levied upon them, no Government would be so ungracious as to refuse so reasonable a request, and perhaps the Legislature would accommodate them. As they had not been taxed, they had the money in their pockets. He had to thank the House for listening so attentively to the observations he had made. He felt it his duty in justice to himself, and to the great Liberal-Conservative party of this Province, to place upon record the transactions of the Government so far as the Public Finances were concerned. This was the principal matter with which the Government had to deal, and one which should be of very great interest to the people of this Island. He believed that the Government had carried out in good faith to the best of their ability, the high and important trust imposed in them, and that they had husbanded the resources of the country in every possible manner consistent with the public interests. Feeling that the Government had discharged their duty faithfully, he submitted these statements to the House and to the country, satisfied that the people, when they had had time to consider them would be convinced that the affairs of the Province were to-day managed as well, if not better, than ever before in its history. (Great applause.)

I. O.

Mr. YEO said before the question was put he would like to make a few remarks. He, however, had no intention of following the Honorable Leader of the Government's long rambling speech. He (Mr. Y.) had often listened to that honorable member making statements wide off the mark, but he (Mr. Y.) did not think he had ever heard so many wide and reckless statements as they had listened to this evening. The honorable member commenced by stating that the Opposition press said that the finances of the Province were in a helpless state of debt, estimated at from $60,000 to $120,000. If the Opposition press made such a statement, he (Mr. Y.) did not consider it was far astray. The honorable member then went on to show that the expenditure of the year 1884 was less by the sum of $725.88 than the receipts. Although the honorable member wished to make it appear that there was a surplus of this small amount on last years transactions, he had afterwards to admit that there was a considerable debt hanging over the Province.

He (Mr. Y.) thought it could easily be shown that our debt is now pretty large. The Public Accounts show that at the end of 1884, the debt of the Province amounted to $53,931.70. In order to show even this balance we have as assets the old Duty Bonds which, some time ago, the Honorable Leader of the Government said were worthless. The amount of these Bonds is $5,849.14. If this amount is added to the debt of the Province it will show a balance against us, at the end of last year, of $59,881.11. He (Mr. Y.) also noticed that an amount which was deposited in the Bank of Prince Edward Island, on which there would be considerable loss, was also called an asset. This loss should be added to our indebtedness. His honorable friend had tried to show that they had paid four quarter's salary to Teachers within the year. While this might be quite correct, and while he (Mr. Y.) had no intention of following the lengthened argument that had been used to support this assertion, nevertheless the fact could not be denied, that about $25,000 was due the Teachers of this Province at the end of the year, which sum is not taken into account in making up the balance sheet. When we add these amounts together, we find that there is a debt on this Province of over $84,780.00, besides outstanding debts unpaid at the end of the year; a return of which has been asked for, but not brought down. Using the same argument that the Honorable Leader of the Government used respecting the transactions of the year 1878, we find that close on to $85,000 will be required to pay our indebtedness at the end of last year, without reckoning the loss on the amount deposited in the old Bank. His honorable friend had referred to the large amount that is being spent for Education, but notwithstanding all he (Mr. S.) had said on this subject, the fact remains that if they had paid the quarter's salary of the School Teachers that was due on the 31st of December, they would have been as much in debt as ever Mr. Davies had been while he was Leader of the Government. That the quarter's salary due the Teachers of this Island on the 31st December, 1884, was not paid last year, and must be added to our indebtedness at the end of year, is a fact that cannot be contradicted. His honorable friend had gone over the old story of comparing the expenditure of the present Government with that of the Davies Government. Honorable members had no objections to listen to this old story, although it is getting very tiresome, but a comparison of this kind did not explain why the present Government had so greatly exceeded their expenditure. He (Mr. Y.) found fault with the Government that their expenditure had so greatly exceeded the amount voted by this honorable House last year. If the Davies Government had exceeded their estimated expenditure, that was no justification for the present Government. The two cases should not be compared together. The present Government had no extra expenditure that could not be calculated, excepting that for Education. When the Davies Govern-

ment were in power they had the Asylum and other large public works under construction, and it was impossible to calculate the amount that would be required during the year. The present Government had no extraordinary expenditure of this kind, and great fault should be found with the Honorable Leader of the Government for his erroneous estimates of last session. This year, he (Mr. Y.) believed that the estimates submitted to the House are just as incorrect as they were last year. Last year the amount calculated for roads was $15,500, and we find that $23,622.97 was expended! He would ask any honorable member of the House whether less was required for the roads this year than last year? Judging by his own district he (Mr. Y.) believed that a much larger amount would be required this year. The Honorable Commissioner of Public Lands knew that many people in Prince County had purchased land from the Government, who had no roads to get to their farms. The people of this Province must be the most contented in the world or there would have been a rebellion here long ago. In the face of having spent $23,600.00 last year, the Government have the audacity to say that this year they can carry on the road service efficiently with only $15,500.00 He (Mr. Y.) felt sure honorable members would see that this was a very incorrect estimate, and that the Government were only trying to deceive this House and the people of the country. In the same way the amount estimated last year for Bridges was

$22,000.00 and yet we find that $30,690.60 was required to keep these important works in repair. As large, if not a larger amount, than was expended last year will again be required, for it is known that large contracts have already been contracted for as much almost as in the estimates, and it is to be supposed that the small balance of this amount that still remains, will be sufficient to supply the needs of the Province until next year? Last year it was estimated that $1,200.00 would pay the out-lay on Ferry steamers. The Oppo sition said the amount was entirely too small and it could be now seen that nearly $5,000.00 had been required It was only de-ceiving the country to put such small amounts in the estimates and it was not treating parliament right. It is the duty of the Gov-ernment to ask the House for a sufficient sum to carry on the legi-timate expenditure of the Province. In 1877 and 1878 His honor the Leader of the Government held the same views that he (Mr. Y) now advocated and had attacked the policy of the Davies Govern-ment, in a strong speech because they spent more money than they had asked for. He (Mr. Yeo) would be corroborated by the hon-orable members for Murray Har-bor and Summerside, who were members of that Government and are conversant with what took place at the time and can give full explanations of what had been said. The honorable Leader of the Government also made refer-ence to the great reductions the present Government had made in

the expenditures, particularly in the Civil Service and printing. It was well known, however, that the present party had stolen the policy of the Davies Government in this respect. Many of these reforms were inaugurated by the Davies Government and these men now reap the benefit of them. If any honor is due on acount of these re-forms, their predecessors should get the benefit of it, for if they had not been introduced before the present Government came into power, we would not have them yet. The honorable gentleman had also re-ferred to the mission of himself and his fellow Delegates to Ottawa, about which we know so little. He (Mr. Y.) did not think they had conducted this matter in a proper way. If the province had a claim against the General Gov-ernment, it should be presented in a proper manner and followed up in a dignified way and the amount should not be paid us on account of the 'urgency of the case' as had been the case in the present in-stance. This money is being doled out to us by instalments, notwith-standing the fact that it had been decided by the highest Court in Canada that the Provincial Gov-ernment had a just claim and that it was our right. The Govern-ment should have demanded this money as our right, and not have gone to the Dominion Govern-ment asking for a 'payment on account.' If our finances had been in a proper state, the Government would have been in a position to assert our claim in a dignified manner. The $53,222 that was voted by the Dominion Parliament was to be payment in full of this claim, but we are now told that we will get $24,240 more, while he was very glad to see the Island getting her just debts paid he would like to get it as a right and not as a favor, and he maintained that the Government had not acted in a dignified manner with respect to this matter. The honorable Leader of the Government had stated, that the telegram that he (Mr. S.) had sent from Ottawa in reference to the Pier money, was correct. While he (Mr. Y.) was glad to hear such was the case, he did not understand why it was that although our claim was $139,000, that we were only to receive $78,000 on account of it.

Hon. Mr. SULLIVAN said the telegram he sent mentioned no sum.

Mr. YEO said that did not materially affect the subject he was discussing. The telegram did not say that $139,000 would be paid; but he said that the amount of our claim would be paid. A newspaper of this city, known to be inspired by a member of the Government, had a leading article on this matter and said the Government would receive this amount of $139,000, and he thought it should be explained why so much smaller an amount has been accepted? The honorable gentleman had gone on to say that $6000 additional had been received on account of these Piers, but all he (Mr. Y.) could understand was that the Dominion Government had paid last year $53,222.19 and will pay $24,240.00 this year, making in all $77,462.19

as payment in full. The honorable gentleman also said that the Dominion Government taking these wharves or piers, would be a great relief to the Province as that Government will have to provide for their maintenance in the future. Although the Dominion Government had placed some amounts in their estimates last year and this year for this service, yet many of our important shipping places have not the accommodation they require. He (Mr. Y.) knew of one wharf in his own District that would require a large amount expended on it to make it fit for shipping, and yet no provision has been made for it One would fancy when listening to the honorable Leader of the Government that he had not drawn any large amount from our capital at Ottawa, and yet it is well known that over $120,000 has been drawn from that source while the present party have been in power. He (Mr. S.) had endeavored to show up that the province had valuable assets such as the Colonial Building, Government House, and other public buildings, which every school boy knows are not available as assets. And yet he wants the country to believe that these assets are owing to the economical management of the present administration, whereas we all know that we had all these buildings before this Government came into power. The estimates amount to $252,556.22. It is apparent that this sum will meet the requirements of the country and that there must be an over expenditure on our Public Works this year, greater en than it was in 1884. When e come to that part of the hon- rable gentleman's speech in which e are asked to consider the re- ceipts coming into the Govern- ent, we find the honorable Leader f the Government taking an ntirely different course. He ow estimates receiving greater mounts than he will receive. he Public Lands, for instance. re estimated to produce $50,000 his year which every one knows is nore revenue than can be ex- ected from that source and other ources of revenue are magnified n the same way. Even if they do eceive this amount and even if the ther amounts prove to be correct, notwithstanding the Pier money they expect this year, he (Mr. Y.) believed that at the end of 1885, we would be at least $20,000 more in debt than we were at the end of last year. Our expenditure will not be less than $280,000 and that is $20 000 more than even the Government themselves expect to receive. If this amount is added to the $74 000 we owed at the end of last year, not saying anything about the old duty Bonds and the loss on the deposit in the Bank of Prince Edward Island, it will prove that the finances of the Province are in a bad state. The honorable gentleman boasted of carrying on the Government with- out taxation, but it was well known that for years they were glad to receive from the Assess- ment Act, the amount necessary to balance their accounts. He (Mr. S.) said they had been paying off the debt left them by their prede- cessors while the Assessment Act

was in force, notwithstanding the fact that the Public Accounts show, that in the second or third year after they came into power they had a surplus at the end of the year. They had been paying off no debts lately, but had been running the country deeply into debt. The honorable gentleman had a very ingenious way of allu- ding to our finances. Although at the end of the past year nearly $57,000 was due the Banks, he (Mr. S.) told us that sometimes the Government received interest from their deposits in the Banks. When honorable members on this side of the House tried to find out what interest was being paid, they did not get very satisfactory answers ; but from the amount that is charged for interest in the Public Accounts of last year, it is evident that they must have been deeply in debt during the greater part of the time. The interest paid shows that $75,000.00 had been due for the whole year, for the interest paid amounted to $4,500.00. The honorable gentleman did not, in his estimates of revenue, tell us where he expected to get the $45,- 000 that even he admitted we would be in debt, but said that he supposed we would be entitled to receive a greater sum than this as compensation for winter com- munication. He (Mr. Y.) feared that the necessities of the Govern- ment would drive them to accept less on this account from the Do- minion Government than they should take. The "urgency of their case" will cause them to say that they will take something "on account." The Legislature had

passed a strong Address to Her
Majesty and he (Mr. Y.) hoped the
Government would not allow party
exigencies to induce them to compromise the interests of the Province. Although we may be poor,
we are proud and much as we dis-
like taxation, the people of this
Province would submit to it rather
than submit to injustice. He
asked the Government not to allow
the urgency of *their* case to induce
them to accept one dollar less than
our lawful right. No meetings, it
is true, have been held condemning the present Government.
What is the reason? Because
the conduct of the present Opposition is very different from that
of the Government when they
were on this side of the House.
Some honorable members of
the then Opposition went from
"Jerusalem to Jericho," denouncing
the late Government and it was no
wonder that some meetings had
been held and some excitement
created.

Hon. Mr. CAMPBELL said the
Opposition of that day had a
great deal of truth in the charges
they brought against the Government, not like the present Opposition who have not one charge to
bring up, that is worthy of consideration.

Mr. YEO said the present party
obtained the Government under
false pretences. The honorable
Leader of the Government said at
Summerside, he would not be a
member of a Government which
imposed taxes on the people. When
the people were told that the Gov

ernment could be carried on without taxation it is no wonder they
became dissatisfied and gave the
present party their support. Now,
however, the people are again dissatisfied as they find that the Government have not carried out the
promises they made and there is a
strong reaction all through the
country; and when the election
comes off the Government will
then be found to be as dilapidated
as the Bridges and Public Works
of the Province are now.

Mr. FARQUHARSON (Hear, Hear.)

Mr. Perry said that he did not
expect that honorable members of
the Government would ask the
House to go into Committee on
this important question without
giving better information about
the finances of the Province than
honorable members had yet received. As the hour was late it
would be better for the Government to move that the debate be
now adjourned. After spending
three weeks doing nothing, not
meeting each day at ten, eleven,
twelve or even at one o'clock, they
now want to rush the business
through in one evening.

Hon Mr. CAMPBELL said the
honorable member had been away
to Rustico, when he (Mr. P.) should
have been attending to his duties
in the House.

Mr. PERRY said yes, he had been
out there looking at the bad roads.
He (Mr. P.) intended to move the
adjournment of the debate and see
if honorable members will risk

ieir lives by staying here at this unseasonable hour. It was unreasonable to insist on putting the ouse in Committee after only vo speeches had been deliverd on iis most important subject. If iey expect the debate on the udget will only last one night iey will be disappointed. Peraps this is the reason that the espatches so lately placed on the able of the House, had been kept ack. It showed that the Government wished to keep something from the House, when these papers have been kept in the Clerk's room, or somewhere else, since the 24th of December last until a few minutes before going into Supply. Of course the honorable members of the Government knew all that was in these despatches, but the Opposition had no opportunity of knowing what was in them and he believed it was his duty to sound the alarm, and let the Government know that the House was not to be treated in this manner. As no doubt it would be necessary for him (Mr. P.) to refer to these despatches, he would ask the honorable Finance Minister if there are any other despatches besides the ones that have been laid before the House?

Hon. Mr. SULLIVAN said when the honorable member asked his question in a proper way, he will get a satisfactory answer.

Mr. PERRY said he had just got the answer he expected. It was not a very civil way to reply to a question of this kind; but he supposed that there were no fur-

ther despatches. If there are no more despatches to be laid before us, we do not know if the honorable gentleman who is Premier of the Province, went to Ottawa, during the recess We are not told that he ever got there, not even told if he sent a despatch to Sir John as he had on a former occasion, saying "I am here." Hon. members had a right to know if any further correspondence had taken place between the Government and the Dominion Cabinet on these important matters! They had not received all the information they should have in order to carefully consider questions of such great importance, and he (Mr. Perry) was very much afraid that even some of the papers they had heard read this evening were only garbled despatches. It was unreasonable to ask the House at this late hour to debate this important subject and he would move that the debate be now ad, journed.

Hon. Mr. SULLIVAN said : if the honorable member was tired, there would be no objection of having the debate adjourned; but in his opinion the honorable member for Tignish, might speak now, just as well as to-morrow morning. The Government, however, would not press the matter.

Motion put and carried.

House adjourned until to-morrow forenoon, at ten o'clock.

G. F. O.

WEDNESDAY, April 1.

Mr. SPEAKER in the Chair.

Mr. D. McKAY asked the honorable Commisioner of Public Works, whether the Government had received a Petition asking that a Pier be built at West River Bridge to enable the Steamer Southport to call at said point; and what the Government intend doing in the matter ?

Hon. Mr. CAMPBELL said the Petition had been received from certain inhabitants of Lots 30 and 65 praying that a Dock would be built at this point. At present persons going to town, had to cross the river at the Bridge and in consequence had to go a considerable distance out of their way. The Government are repairing Shaws Wharf at present in order that better accomodation may be afforded the people of this section. He (Mr. ·C.) thought that the petition would be granted.

Mr. BEER said he was glad to hear the Honorable Commissioner of Public Works say that he intended repairing this wharf. He (Mr. B) would also call the attention of the honorable gentleman to the wharves on the East River, which are used as ferry wharves by the steamer that goes to Mount Stewart.

Hon. Mr. CAMPBELL said the wharves referred to by the honorable member were different from this one, and were not ferry wharves.

Mr. PERRY in accordance with notice on the Order Book asked the Honorable Commissioner of Public Works, what action the Government intended taking with respect to the petition of certain inhabitants of Little Tignish, Lower Kildare, Lot 2, etc., asking a grant of money towards finishing bridge across Little Tignish Pond, Lot 2. In explanation he (Mr. P.) might say that the people of that locality had commenced building this bridge, which will shorten the distance to Brookwater. He (Mr. P.) observed that the Road Supervisor had placed a sum in his estimates for this purpose, and he would like to know if the Government intended to grant the help that this most necessary work should receive.

Hon. Mr. CAMPBELL said the petition referred to by the honorable member had been received by his department. This bridge had been commenced near where there is another bridge already built. It had been commenced without consulting the Government, and from the nature of the work that is done already, he did not consider the Government would be justified in expending any more on it.

Mr. PERRY said : The honorable gentleman said that the people had commenced this Bridge without consulting him and he supposed that was a grievous offence. It was not true, however, for he (Mr. P.) had written to the honorable gentleman over two years ago, asking him to have this Bridge built. He said the work was not well done nor worthy of having public money expended on it. If such is the case, how is it that Mc-Carthy the Road Supervisor had sent in a strong recommendation in favor of a sum being granted for this work? If that recommendation is any good, an amount should be granted.

Hon. Mr. CAMPBELL said this is not the Bridge that McCarthy had recommended. It is at little Tignish, whereas this one is at Tignish Pond.

Mr. PERRY said the Petitition asking for this money is accompanied by a certificate from Mc-Carthy, and if he (Mr. C.) knew anything about his department he would know that he (Mr. P's.) statements were correct.

Mr. PERRY in accordance with notice in the Order Book asked the Com. of Public Works, what action he intends taking with respect to the Petition of certain inhabitants of Montrose, Western Road, &c., praying that the centre line Road from the Western Road towards Huntley may be widened, so that it may be passable for the travelling public. He said that this road was commenced a good many years ago. It is generally called the Seven Mile Road. The road is a very narrow one as persons on each side of the road claim the land, one party saying his line was here and another saying his line was there and the space between these lines is so narrow that it is impossible to make the road wide enough to allow two carriages to pass one another. Some years ago an Act was passed giving the honorable Commissioner of Public Works power to open all roads a width of forty feet. As this road is used by many persons, it is a hardship to have it so narrow and he (Mr. P.) wanted to know if any means will be adopted to have it widened.

Hon. Mr. CAMPBELL said his attention had been called to this matter two years ago. It is true the Seven Mile Road is an old road and it is so narrow that no two carriages can pass one another on it. He (Mr. C.) had visited it last year and found that one man there claimed ninety chains along the line of this road, and said that the road that was opened came off his land. He (Mr. C.) had been trying to compromise the matter between the persons who own the land on each side of the road, but if it is not soon settled, he would have to force the full width of the road from these persons. This will cause some cases of hardship, notably that of Cole and Campbell, but if these men had slept on their rights it was not his fault. He was afraid he would have no alternative, but force the road.

On motion of Mr. Blake the Bill intituled "An Act to incorporate the Charlottetown Conference of the St. Vincent de Paul Society" was read a third time and passed.

On motion of honorable Mr. Sullivan the debate on the grant of a Supply to Her Majesty was resumed.

Mr. PERRY said, when he last had the pleasure of addressing this honorable House on this question it was nearly twelve o'clock, p. m., and he should feel thankful to the House, especially the Government side of it, for consenting to adjourn this debate at his request. When the adjournment took place he (Mr. P.) was maintaining that as a large portion of the revenue of the Province was to be derived from Ottowa, from the Dominion Government, that the despatches concerning these matters should have been laid before the House earlier in the Session, and that this House should not have been kept in the dark concerning them until about one minute and a half before the honorable Leader of the Government made his Speech on the resolution to grant a Supply to Her Majesty. The Dominion Government had refunded monies that had been expended by this Province in former years, and as this was obtained through negotiations between the Local and Federal Governments during recess; it was the duty of the Government to have laid all papers and despatches received in connection with this matter, before the House at the earliest possible time after the Session had commenced. How can the Opposition pass an opinion on this large portion of our receipts, when they do not know how they were obtained ? What he (Mr. P.) complained of was that the Opposition had not been fairly treated and had not been put on the same footing as honorable members on the other side of the House. The honorable Leader of the Gov-

ernment had never gone so far back in order to find matter to put in his Budget Speech as he did on this occasion. He (Mr. S.) had travelled back to 1878, 1877, 1876 and even to 1875. He (Mr. S.) might have gone a little further back, to 1874, when he was Solicitor General and held a seat in the Government in order to make a comparison; instead of comparing Mr. Davies' expenditure with what is now spent. Did he (Mr. S.) not know that the honorable members friends the honorable member's for Summerside, Murray Harbor and Georgetown were also members of the Davies Government and were equally responsible for any wrong doing that had then taken place ? When a person travelled too far back in history, it often became unpleasant and the honorable gentleman should spare his colleagues. Like a schoolboy repeating his lesson the Speeches of the honorable member are all alike, for he praises his own government; by finding fault with all governments that had preceded it. If we believe the honorable gentleman, his government is the only right one we ever had. In his Budget Speech last year, he (Mr. S.) said that $249,379.94 was all the money required for the Public Services of the Province. He (Mr. P.) had reminded the honorable member last Session that it was impossible to carry on the business of the province with that amount; but had been told that this was a good government, an immaculate Government, that was good friends with both Sir John and the elements. Let us see how far the honorable Finance Minister's calculations have proved correct. This year the honorable gentleman told us last Summer, especially in the western part of Prince County that it rained every day,—that the brooks overflowed, and the crops were destroyed on this account, the payments to the Land Office were much smaller than he expected. We find some honorable members on the Government side of the House saying that the crops were good last year and we have been told that things were never so prosperous. It is hard for poor members of the Opposition to know what to believe. My honorable friend tried to show last year oats, straw, parsnips, &c., were abundant.

Hon. Mr. FERGUSON said: Does the honorable member quote from the Speech delivered at the opening of the Session?

Mr. PERRY said the Address in answer to the Speech said that the oat crop was abundant and before he sat down he would read from it, to satisfy the honorable Commissioner of Crown Lands. It seemed that the few remarks he (Mr. P.) had been making had touched honorable members of the Government to the quick, especially the honorable Commissioner of Crown Lands who was getting very uneasy. Perhaps he was uneasy before, as it is rumored that the Government intend making an alteration in the Land Office, that they intend to have only one department for Public Lands and Registration of Deeds, and that the honorable member will lose his salary.

Hon. Mr. SULLIVAN said he did not wish to interrupt the honorable member, but he really wished his honorable friend would read the paragraph about the abundant crop of oats, straw and turnips that he says is in the Address.

Hon. Mr. FERGUSON said he must remind the honorable member that the Speech said the Harvest last year was not so abundant as in former years.

Mr. PERRY said the honorable Leader of the Government could read the paragraph himself when he (Mr. P.) was done. The honorable gentleman made sad mistakes last year. He was to have a large revenue enough to pay all demands, but what was the result? After looking at the estimates made last Session and comparing them with what was actually received, we find that over $10,000 of a mistake was made by the honorable gentleman. Last year, the Land Office was put down for $52,000 and we find that only $46,033.74 was received. In the Provincial Secretary's Office where $3,000 was expected only $994.70 was received. In the Prothonotary's Office, which the honorable Leader of the Government should be well acquainted with, and about which he should know, as he has constant access to it, he (Mr. S.) said last year, we would receive $2,000 in fees, whereas we find that only $1,657.13 was obtained. He (Mr. S.) said these fees were increasing in amount; but they were actually decreasing, for the receipts in former years had been much greater than they now are. The Registry Office was expected to produce $5,000, but only $4,306.80 was received; and so on through all the estimates that were laid before us last year, we find that a great shrinkage had taken place. By adding up the sums that are short in the several departments, we find that he (Mr. S.) had received $10,049 less than the honorable member estimated. Out of the portion of the Revenue that amounted to less than $100,000 the Finance Minister went astray over $10,000! Last year the Opposition had warned the Government that $249,000 was not sufficient to carry on the business of the country, and we now find that they exceeded their estimates by $30,000. The Government had actually expended $30,000 more than this honorable House granted them last Session. Have they asked for a vote for this amount? No! If they had spent $250,000 over the amount granted them, they would not ask this House for a special vote for the amount they had so expended. He (Mr. P.) was astonished at the arbitrary way the Government treat this honorable House. The Opposition are not so much surprised at this conduct, and it is the way the present Government always act. Last year, his honorable friend said the Roads and Bridges of the Province were in a good state of repair and that they wanted very little repairs during the ensuing year. The honorable members for West River and St. Peters had told the Government that the Roads and Bridgers were not in good repair, that a horse had got his leg broken in one of the rotten bridges in a country district; but they were met with a flat denial from honorable members of the Government. We now find that over $30,000 had been expended on Bridges during the past season, notwithstanding the fact that this House only granted $23,000 for this service. Things had turned out just as the Opposition expected. If much attention had been bestowed on the Bridges of the Province during former years, if they were in the good state of repair that the Government said they were, why was $10,000 spent on them over what the House had been asked to grant? He (Mr. P.) did not see much use in the Legislature voting any sum for supplies, if the Government will spend one hundred per cent more than the peoples representatives gave them power to do. When on this part of the subject he was reminded of what had been done in the first precinct of the first district of Prince County. Last year he (Mr. P.) had put $20 in the road scales of that district for a certain road, and he found that not one dollar of it had been expended where it was intended. Not one amount that had been placed in the road scales of his district had been expended where it was voted for. These road scales are no good, they only deceive honorable members, who often find to their great dissatisfaction that not one dollar was expended where it should be. Will the Honorable Commissioner of Public Works give me $20 this year for my district, over what it otherwise receive in the ordinary way? While speaking about the bridges of the Province, it reminded him that although the Honorable Leader of the Government tried to excuse the over expenditure on this account, no serious storms had occurred last year, that no bridges had been carried away by freshets. We find the Government condemning good bridges and building new ones, such as the one at St. Peter's Bay, in order to create popularity for some of its members. The old bridge at St. Peter's was a good one and although great political prayers were made, that the tide would rise and carry away this old bridge, no tide came and consequently the old bridge had to be condemned by the Government. We find that the new bridge is being built from land on one side of the Bay that is owned by some one, to land on the other side that is owned by a political supporter of the party, and the contract is being performed by another supporter of the party, notwithstanding the fact that the old bridge was good and only wanted a little repair to make it serviceable for years. Although the approaches of the old bridge were in excellent order, and only required the expenditure of a few hundred dollars to make it passable, yet the Government condemned this bridge and are building one that will cost $3,500, besides extras, of which, no doubt, there will be a good many. In the face of the financial state of the Province, notwithstanding that prominent men of the Government are every year going to Ottawa and begging for a "small payment on account," this is the way the

Government are throwing money away! How would they have met these expenditures if the Dominion Government had not come to their rescue and given them $24,000, notwithstanding the fact that the amount voted last year was to be "payment in full." The Honorable Leader of the Government said they had to pay the debt left by the Davies Government. How was that debt paid? Was it not paid by taxing the people for three years after this Government came into power? The debt was not left by the Davies Government, but it was left by the Government which had for Solicitor General the Leader of the present Government. The honorable members for Murray Harbor, Summerside and Georgetown passed the Assessment Act and now they repudiate their own Act. The present Government made so much use of the political horse that rode Mr. Davies out of power that the last year. the Assessment Act was imposed, they had $14,000 of a surplus after paying all the debt that was against the Province. Notwithstanding the fact that they have paid out $120,000 of capital that has been received from Ottawa, and that they have spent about the same amount through the statute labor that has to be performed by the people, these honorable gentlemen have run the Province in debt $75,000 or $80,000. And they now have the political effrontery and audacity to say that they have carried on the business of the Province without taxation. The people are taxed much worse by the way they have allowed the

Province to run into debt, than they would be if the Assessment Act had been continued. The Honorable Commissioner of Crown Lands was bothered the other day to answer an enquiry respecting the rate of interest the Government was paying, and it is no wonder he was! What authority had the Government for paying over $9,000 in interest? The people of the country are willing to pay as they go, and do not want the Province to go in debt. They say we can pay our taxes, and if we cannot have a carriage costing $120, we will buy one for $75, and pay our taxes. What was the cry at the last election? We will carry on the Government without taxation for ten or fifteen years. They did not tell the people that they were going to spend hundreds of thousands of dollars of their capital, and the people were deceived. The Honorable Leader of the Government said the country was satisfied, that no meetings had been held condemning the Government. If the people are satisfied it is not hard to please them, but he (Mr. P.) had great doubts about the correctness of that statement. The reason no meetings had been held was because the gentlemen representing the Opposition Party were more modest than honorable members of the Government were when they were in Opposition. Although the Opposition know that the people are dissatisfied, we do not go around sowing the seed of political discord among them. It is quite easy to call meetings and pass motions condemning the Government; but by doing so a great deal of discord would be inaugurated and men's minds would be taken from their legitimate business.

Hon. Mr. FERGUSON—What did the Tignish Debating Society say in their resolutions?

Mr. PERRY said he saw Tignish before ever the honorable Commisioner of Crown Lands put his foot there and he knew the sentiments of the people of that place too well to mind what a few people who call themselves "we, the people of Tignish," might say. His honorable friend knew the resolution passed by that Society was not correct, and if he (Mr. F.) will father it as he ought to do, he (Mr. P.) would show him where the mistake was made.

Hon. Mr. FERGUSON said he never saw the resolution containing the protest against the honorable member until it was published in the press.

Mr. PERRY said the Honorable Minister of Finance made sad mistakes last year. He (Mr. P.) had already shown where over $10,000 more revenue had been expected than was actually received and that $30,000 excess of expenditure had been made without leave of this honorable House, so that last year the mistakes of the Government actually amounted to $40,000. When the Honorable Finance Minister stands up to make his Budget Speech his statements should be correct. The Honorable Commissioner of Crown Lands had not done justice when he did not lay on the table of this House the return that he (Mr. P.) had asked for, of receipts in the Land Office for the months of January, Febuary and March, 1885. He (Mr. P.) could not speak with the same advantage as he could if these returns had been laid before the House, and the honorable member, no doubt, will, when he follows me, endeavor to make some political capital on this account. He (Mr. P.) wanted these returns to show that the receipts in the Land Office this year, are falling off. The receipts in January, February and March, 1884, were less than those of these months in 1883, and, no doubt, those of 1885 have decreased in the same ratio. In order that the honorable member will not have an opportunity to say that the member for Tignish did not know what he was talking about, he (Mr. P.) would now move that the debate be adjourned.

Hon. Mr. FERGUSON said it was not yet one o'clock, the honorable member had better go on and finish his speech. Honorable members were so interested that no doubt they would be willing to wait until two o'clock itself, so that the honorable member might conclude his address.

Hon. Mr. SULLIVAN, said it was trespassing to much on the indulgence of the House to ask them to adjourn before the usual time.

Mr. PERRY said his address would probably take several hours to get through with as he had several departments of the Public Service to criticize, such as the Land Office, the Public Works and others; and it would take some time for him to finish discussing the many serious charges he had to bring against these departments.

Hon. Mr. SULLIVAN said as the honorable member, no doubt, had exhausted the supply of matter at his command, he would require some time to get a new supply. He (Mr. S.) hoped, however, that the honorable member will not ask honorable members to listen to the same assertions over again.

House adjourned for one hour.

G. F. O.

AFTERNOON SESSION.

Hon. Mr. FERGUSON presented the statement of receipts at the Land Office for the months of January February and March 1885, asked for by the honorable member for Tignish; which was recived and read.

Ordered, That the said Statement do lie on the table of the House.

On motion of bonorable Mr. Sullivan the debate on the grant of a Supply to Her Majesty was resumed.

Mr. PERRY said when he was addressing this honorable House before recess, he was endeavoring to show that the honorable Leader of the Government had not been correct in either his estimates of Expenditure or revenue for last year. He (Mr. P.) had shown that the estimate of revenue, that last Session had been submitted by the honorable gentleman, was astray $10,049, and that the estimate of Expenditures was astray $30,000. The honorable gentleman had stated last night that storms had carried away the Bridges and damaged the roads, and that the Government had a greater expenditure for these services on that account. The fact was that the ordinary expenditure incurred for these services was increasing from year to year If the future is to be judged by the past, these honorable gentlemen will be as much astray in their estimates this year as they were last year. If we look at the Journals of this House we find that the over expenditure is constantly increasing. In 1883 there was $20,000 and in 1884, $30,000 more expended, than was estimated when the Legislature was in Session and more than this honorable House was asked to grant. In 1885 they have asked for no more than they did in 1883, which every honorable member knew would be insufficient to maintain our Public Works this year. How are they going to obtain even the small amount they have asked this honorable House to vote? The receipts in the Land Office are falling off. This year in the months of January, February and March the amount received at that office was $2 000 less than they were last year during a similar period. Supposing that the elements are no

kinder this year than they were last year, and that the crops are destroyed, as they say was the case last year. How will they obtain $50,000 this year from that office? The honorable Leader of the Government told us that the farmers up west did not pay as much last year as they did in 1883, because the rain had overflowed their land and injured their crops. The honorable member for Rustico, in his speech on the Address the other day, said that: "The wheat crop was, however, a very good one. A large quantity of flour is generally imported into this Province, but last year's crop of wheat was sufficient for home consumption." As the wheat crop is said to be so excellent, we should not require to import one barrel of flour, but every honorable member knew that thousands of barrels of flour were imported last Fall. The honorable member goes on to say. "The oat crop is not so much depended on as in former years, but that of last year was in excess of the crop of 1883" He (Mr. P.) had stated that this statement was in the Address in reply to the Speech, but he found that it was in the Speech of the honorable member for Rustico. As the honorable member had not contradicted this report no doubt it was what he (Mr. McK.) said at the time. This proves that the honorable Finance Minister was astray when he said the bad harvest was the reason why the receipts in the Land Office exhibited so great a falling off. The honorable gentleman said last year: "The total expenditure for the year ill be $249,379.94. The Government believe that amount will e sufficient to maintain all the ranches of the Public Service dvantageously to the Province." e also went on to say "A bridge ay be carried away by a freshet, r a storm may occur, causing damage to the public works of the country ; but should nothing unforeseen happen, he thought, the sum estimated would cover all necessary expenditures for the present year." He (Mr. P.) was not aware of one Bridge that had been carried away by a freshet or by a storm and he challenged the Government to show one bridge that was carried away. Notwithstanding these are the words the honorable gentleman used last year and notwithstanding that no unusual expense was incurred, at the end of the year we find that over $30 000 had been expended in excess of the amount asked for. What faith can be placed in his Estimates this year after such errors had been shown in his calculations during the preceding year! The honorable gentleman asks this House to believe that he will receive $50,000 from the Land Office, notwithstanding the fact that only $46,000 was received last year and that the receipts for the three months that have elapsed this year, show a falling off of $2000.00! He (Mr. P) would like to hear the honorable Commissioner of Crown Lands explain how this was to be accomplished. The estimate for education is $3,000 or $4,000 less for the year 1885, than was actually expended in 1884, and

yet no explanations have been given, how this saving is to be effected. Is the Government prepared to make changes in the Education system of the Provin e? Must the Prince of Wales College go, and are they going to do away with it ? Perhaps that is the reason they are going to spend less for Education this year than in 1884. It looks very suspicious to see the organ, that the Government had been feeding for years, the organ that was the principal spoke in the carriage in which they rode into power, every week abusing this institution and telling its readers that the usefulness of the Prince of Wales College had gone. When the *Presbyterian* newspaper is allowed to go broadcast through the country casting violent aspersions on the Principal of this Institution, it looked as if the Government were going to make a change in that school. If Mr. Anderson is guilty of the serious charges that are made against him by this organ of the Government, if he is guilty, it is time that the Principal of the Prince of Wales College should go. It would be a disgrace to the country to allow such an institution to exist. He (Mr. P.) was not prepared to endorse what that newspaper said about this matter ; but the Government should be responsible for what their organ published on a subject of this kind. The Board of Education, which is largely composed of honorable members of the Government, should make inquiries respecting this grave charge that is made against one of their principal officers, and let us know if there are any grave errors in Mr. Anderson's report. The honorable junior member for Georgetown, no doubt, could inform this honorable House if the charge is correct. This newspaper is said to be inspired by the honorable Commissioner of Public Works and it is said in a late issue as follows : " We have just received this production. After the criticism and exposure of Professor Anderson's miserable English, last year, people thought that if the ability to compose one sentence correctly is in him, he would do his very best, after months of study and preparation, and write that sentence in his report for this year. But alas for the Principal of the Prince of Wales College and Provincial Normal School ! What an example to students and teachers and what an honor to the Education of P. E. Island in the eyes of the outside world." There is the opinion of this Government paper respecting a gentleman placed at the head of one of our principal departments, and yet these honorable gentlemen say nothing to defend their officer! If they cannot defend Mr. Anderson they should dismiss him. This newspaper goes on to say : "To give him all justice we quote his report, sentence after sentence in small type, not omitting a single word : —"The most noteworthy incidents of the Academical year 1884, was the Biennial Examination for scholarships. Here is either pomposity from the little man, or the want of being scholarly precise. Taking all the learned world, the matter "most noteworthy" during 1884 was the biennial examination held by him. How strange it was not introduced

by an awful convulsion of all nature, and closed with a total eclipse of the luminary of day ! But he evidently does not understand the meaning of words. He refers to it, as an "incident" which happens accidentally or by chance, while this biennial examination of his, took place by appointment made two years previously." Now, he (Mr. P.) contended that if these remarks are correct, it is time Mr. Anderson should go, if they are not correct, it was a slander that the government should not allow the *Presbyterian* to publish. He (Mr. P.) intended reading all this article to the House, but it was too long. The whole of the report of Professor Anderson is criticised in this way, and the article winds up by saying : "Here there are gross inacurracies by the score—grammatical blunders in every sentence— so far as we have proceeded we have quoted not two paragraphs. Surely in the Professor's own words we may declare that this production of the great man's " does not indicate such an understanding of the principles of grammar as ought reasonably to be expected of candidates 16 or 17 years of age."—as little or no improvement has been made by him on his report of last year. Alas ! we cannot say with him that " a little more practice in composition would produce results gratifying to the teacher and of good advantage to us, more in our next." This paper is read in Nova Scotia, New Brunswick, Quebec, Ontario, Manitoba and the North-west, and he (Mr. P.) hoped it was not the cause of the rebellion that had broken out there. When the Executive overnment have allowed a man ccupying so responsible a position o be so severely criticised, and ave not even tried to defend him, showed that something suspicious as contemplated by the present overnment. The present Administration have made many promises that they had not carried out, such as the abolition of the Legislative Council and doing without taxation. It is well known that they have not made an honest effort to abolish the Legislative Council, If they had, that body would now be among the things of the past. Although, for the last two or three years, no direct taxation had been collected, yet it was well-known that our resources were being squandered and that taxation, when it did come, would be much heavier than it would have been, if the Assessment Act had been continued. He (Mr. P.) had a few words to say about the Land Office. This Office yielded $46.033.74 last year. All the information that is given honorable members about the transactions of this most important department is contained in this little pamphlet of about 9 pages, and if this report gave an account of all the doings of the officials in that office, they have not been worked very hard. The number of Deeeds issued last year was only 508. Where five or six clerks are employed, more work than this might be expected. We all know that the Province had to pay these men, and they should be able to give more value for the money that they receive. The surveyors can give them the description of the lands that are sold in a few minutes and a smart man could fill up twenty-five or thirty of these Deeds in a day. It is time that this department was amalgamated with the office of Registry of Deeds. When we find that the head of this Department can go around canvassing the whole of Queen's County, as he (Mr. F.) did at the last partial election for the Dominion House of Commons, when we are told that he was away from his office twenty-five days during last summer, it showed plainly that there was not enough work in this Department for so many officials. We know that the Honorable Commissioner of Crown Lands is hardly ever in his office. One day he is at Belfast and another day at Rustico, attending political meetings. And then, not satisfied with going to political meetings, he must go lecturing in Tignish, Summerside and other places. The next thing we hear is that the honorable member is attending school meetings here and there through the Province. He (Mr. P.) would like to know how many days the honorable gentleman had been away from his office ? If he has been away seventy-five days, he (Mr. F.) should multiply that number by $5, and put that much money back into the Treasury. Travelling through the country is not the way the head of the Department can look after the business of that office. He (Mr. P.) believed that the head of this Department should not be on the floor of this honorable House. He believed this office gave that gentleman too much power on the eve of an election. He (Mr. P.) did not charge the gentleman at present holding this position with doing more than another person placed in the same situation might do, for men will use the weapons put into their hands; but the head of this Department should not be in this honorable House. The Land Office and the Office for Registry of Deeds should be amalgamated, and if the Government will bring in a measure to accomplish this object he (Mr. P.) would vote for it. If the Superintendent of Education had a seat at the Council Board, it would be nothing unreasonable, and the Government should make this change. In Ontario, with only five or six members of Council, the Minister of Education is one of the number. Nearly one half our revenue is expended for education, and yet if any honorable member wished for information respecting this Department, he had to go down stairs in order to obtain it. If we had a Minister of Education, no doubt, he would have taken Mr. Anderson's part, and would have been here to give any explanation that was required by honorable members, respecting these serious charges that are made against this gentleman. Although he (Mr. P.) was not so apt at making figures as his honorable friend the Commissioner of Crown Lands, he had been putting a few figures together in reference to the expense of the Land Office, under the present system. Judging by the expenses of this office, under its present management, for the past six years, this office will cost $120,000 of the people's money before it is finally closed. Now, the people have got to make up their minds that while the present Government are in power—and they say that they will be in power for the next twenty years—that $120.000 will have to be paid out of our revenues on account of the Honorable Commissioner of Crown Lande and his assistants. He (Mr. P.) thought it would be much better to make a present of this large sum of money to the poor people who cannot pay for their Lands, and not be harrassing them with precepts, as the present management were doing. He (Mr. P.) would read what the Commissioner, in his report for the year 1884, says about precepts,— "The total number of precepts issued against purchasers in default since 1880 is 194, of this number 58 farms have been paid for in full. In 86 cases the land having been purchased by the Commissioner, has been resold on the receipt of not less than 20 per cent. of the Government claims, and on as short terms as it was found practicable to insist upon. Fifty holdings sold under precept remain in the hands of the Department." Does that show that the people are able to purchase their farms when 50 of them had not been able to pay even 20 per cent. of the amount due on them. The Government had allowed interest and compound interest to accumulate for years, and when the poor man, who had commenced in the woods with only his axe and his hoe, began to make a living for himself and his family, the Honorable Commissioner of Crown Lands pounces down upon him and takes from him the plot of land upon which the best of his days had been spent. In the

anual that was published last
ear by the authority of the Pro-
incial Government, great en-
)uragement was given to English
rmers to come here and settle,
ıd perhaps the Government hope
this way to get the farms sold
at they have now on their hands.
: the Land Office was amalgamated
ith the Office of the Registrar of
f Deeds one head would be enough
or the two offices and a consider-
ble saving would thus be effected.
f so much money had to be lost by
eeping this office open it would
e better to give the amount to the
oor men who are buying their
arms, and allow them to pay the
iterest on the balance they would
;ill owe to the Attorney General.
y doing this we would each year
receive the natural revenue of the
:ountry, and the Land Office would
be closed in two years. If it is
:ontinued in the same manner as it
s at present, twenty years will not
;ee it closed. The present Government will not close it as they know
it as a good political engine, and, if
for no other reason, he (Mr. P.)
would like to see this office closed.
The honorable Leader of the Gov-
:rnment said the Province had $4,-
)00,000 or $5,000,000 of assets. He
Mr. S.) should also have counted
;he Black Bog of Squirrel Creek
ıbout which we read in the Manual
)ublished last year under the
ıuthority of the Government. No
)ne will doubt the accuracy of this
)ook, and, no doubt, it took a long
while to compile it, for it contained
ı lot of information not generally
known. This book said that

"Lennox Island had 20,200 tons of Peat, valued at $4 per ton, making a total of — $ 80,800

Squirrel Creek, 500,000 tons, at $4, — 2,000,000

Black Bank, 1,777,248 tons, at $4, — 7,108,992

$9,189,792."

Here was an asset worth talking
about, and it was a wonder that
the honorable gentleman had not
included this in his list of our
assets. The book that contained
this statement cost the Province
$600 or $700, and was published
by authority. While the cost of
this book was excessive, if the information it contained was reliable
or likely to advance the interests
of the Province, not so much fault
would be found with the Government on account of it; but it was
a shame to send such a misstate-
ment of facts abroad. This book
said there was one County Court
in each County. Every page of it
contained just such silly errors, and
yet the country had to pay for it.
The Honorable Finance Minister
had gone on to show, while deliver-
ing his Budget Speech, that the
revenue for the present year would
amount to $260,967.31, and said
that if they received all he expected
that there would be a surplus at
the end of the year of $8,000,
*provided he did not exceed his
estimated expenditure.* If we judge
the future by the past, the honorable member will expend a great
deal more than he estimated.
Nothing occurred last year to
authorize the expenditure of any

extraordinary amounts. Last year they increased their expenditure by $10,000 over what it was the year before, and this year the expenditure will exceed that of last year by over $40,000. Instead of having a surplus of $8,000, he (Mr. S.) will have a deficit of $32,000. What cheek the honorable gentleman had to ask this House for only $252,000, when he knows very well that he will expend $285,000 or $290,000 before the year expired. It was a god send that the the Government received the $24,000 from the Dominion Government this winter. If they had not received it, there would have been a General Election and the Opposition would have had to unravel the tangled skein that the Finances of this Province are getting into. It amused him (Mr. P.) to hear the correspondence respecting the Piers read by the clerk of the House. He did not hear one word about the time when the Attorney General was in Ottawa. We do not know whether he (Mr. S.) was there at all or not, excepting that $400 has been paid out of the funds of this Province for his expenses. One of the reasons why he (Mr. P.) was anxious to have a delegation sent to England with the Address to Her Majesty was, because the Government failed to get any satisfactory answer when no delegates were sent to press their claims. He was afraid that if the Government do not act better in the future than they did in the past, that they will fail in their object of getting compensation for non-fulfillment of the Terms of Confederation. It

was amusing to notice that the General Government, when carrying out the directions of the House of Commons said, that it was on account of the "urgency of the case" that the money for Piers had been paid last year. Sir John knew that the Local Administration could not carry on the Government any longer unless he helped them and on account of the "urgency of the case" he gave way and did not compel the Government to sign "a receipt in full." The honorable Leader of the Government said honorable members of the Opposition would be surprised to learn that there was a surplus of nearly $1,000 on last year's transactions. It would have been a remarkable thing, if the Government had had a surplus on the ordinary revenue and expenditure of the year, but when it is remembered that last year $53,222.19 was received from Ottawa, that they will not receive this year, it was not so much of a surprise to this side of the House. If they had paid the ordinary expenditure of the year out of the ordinary revenue then the Opposition would have been surprised, for it is well known that $280,000 cannot be paid with $240,000. There is no doubt but the Government have a debt of $100,000 and he (Mr. P.) believed the people will call them sharply to account for it. The honorable Leader of the Government last year had told them that his estimates were the most correct ever submitted to this House, but he (Mr. P.) thought he had clearly shown that such was not the case. The honorable member had made any allusions to other expenditure f the year 1877, but it was only aying a poor compliment to the onorable member for Summeride who was a member of the overnment during that year. If lose items are not put through ke chain lightning when the ouse went into Committee on them, the several sums will receive that attention from the Opposition that they deserve.

Hon. Mr. McLeod said he would promise not to detain the House very long with the remarks he intended to make. It seemed extraordinary that the honorable member for Tignish, who had so long been a member of the Legislature and had also sat for a number of years in the House of Commons at Ottawa, should be so lax respecting the rules of Parliament. The honorable member said that the sum of $53,222.19 had been voted by the Dominion Parliament last Session, and that the Dominion Government had no other duty than to pay the amount to this Province. He (Mr. P.) said there was no "urgency in the case," and tried to ridicule the matter because these words were used. The honorable gentleman ought to know that when a sum was voted and not expended during the year that it could not be paid without again being put in the estimates. The Dominion Government not having adhered to the terms of the former vote,—that this amount should be payment in full, had to pay this amount in a special way. Parliament has given power to the Government to pay certain amounts

in case of urgency, and it is on this account that the despatches containing the notice that this sum would be paid, are expressed in this way. The money had been voted as "payment in full," and it could not be paid unless the Local Government gave a receipt to that effect. The honorable member had twitted the Government about the bogs up west that are alluded to in the Manual published by the Government. Did not the honorable member know that these bogs were private property, and consequently could not be reckoned as assets owned by the Province. The honorable member had also discovered that this book said there is only one County Court in each County. Was not the honorable member aware of the fact that although there are several circuits of each Court in each County, that there is only one County Court in Prince, King's and Queen's Counties. The honorable member said it was improper to make such statements as they brought discredit on the Province. Did the honorable member not know that although we have only one Supreme Court for the Island, that yet there are several circuits of that court? The honorable member had more knowledge than he pretended. He (Mr. P.) pretended ignorance in order to find fault with his opponents. He said the name of the Honorable Leader of the Government was not mentioned in the despatches from Ottawa referring to the piers money, and that it was very doubtful if the Honorable Leader of the Government had been in that city, although $400 had been charged in the Public Accounts last year as the expenses of his mission. Every honorable member knew that such was not the facts of the case, and that the honorable member for Tignish knew better than he pretended. The honorable member also said that the Honorable Commissioner of Crown Lands should not have a seat in this honorable House. If the honorable member for Tignish was Commissioner of Public Lands he (Mr.McL.) did not know that any damage would arise if the head of this department had not a seat in this House; but the present Commissioner is a most valuable member of the House if for no other purpose than to keep the honorable member for Tignish in his proper place. We know that in Ontario, the Province in which the friends of the honorable member were in power, that Ministers at the heads of Departments are in the Local Legislature and no harm had yet arisen in consequence thereof. There might be a change in the Government of this Province before the next 20 years had passed, and as we know that the honorable member for Tignish had advised the tenants holding Government land not to pay the Government, to let them do without it, if the honorable member should ever become head of this department and was not responsible to the House, dire results would follow. The honorable member also said that he was glad the Government had obtained the additional amount on account of piers, but it was very doubtful if the honorable member was much gratified at seeing the present administration obtaining this amount for the Province. The Government had obtained $78,000 in spite of the Opposition party, their press and their representative at Ottawa.

Mr. FARQUHARSON said the statement of the honorable member is not true.

Hon. Mr. McLEOD said the *Patriot* newspaper is said to be the mouth-piece of the Opposition party in this Island, and the honorable member for West River told this House last session that he was responsible for what was published in that newspaper. That paper ridiculed our claim for the maintenance of wharves and piers, and said our wharves were just like those on the mainland. They searched the dictionary to prove that wharves and piers were not identical. This course was followed until they saw that the question was a live one, and that the Government were so successful in the matter, that for very shame they had to say nothing more against our claim. That was the attitude of the *Patriot* when our claims were first presented, but what did Mr. Davies do when the delegation from this Province went to Ottawa? When the demand of the Local Government of this Province was before the Dominion Government, and under their consideration, an honorable member from New Brunswick placed a notice in the Order Book of the Dominion House of Commons, asking the Federal Government whether they were going to pay any money to New

Brunswick on account of piers. The Dominion Government, seeing this question on the Order Book, would naturally say, "We must be very careful in this matter as New Brunswick and the other Provinces will be putting in claims, if we grant Prince Edward Island this money." How did Mr. Louis H. Davies connect with this question asked by Mr. King, of New Brunswick? He asked the question for this honorable gentleman, and there can be no mistake in supposing that Mr. Davies instigated the question, especially when the fact is remembered that Mr. Davies has a seat very near Mr. King in the House, at Ottawa.

Mr. FARQUHARSON said the same thing had lately been done in this House, in reference to a Bill that had been introduced by the honorable member himself.

Hon. Mr. MACLEOD said, taking into consideration that this was a question of great importance to this Province, should Mr. Davies have asked this question even if it were to oblige another honorable gentleman? The Government of this Province, were at this time seeking payment of the amount that had been expended on Piers within this Island and Mr. Davies knew it. What object had Mr. King in seeking for money that the other Provinces never expected and do not now expect? There is no doubt about the matter, the question was placed on the Order Book at the instigation of Mr. Davies and in order to damage the interests of Prince Edward Island.

Mr. YEO asked what opposition was given by the Opposition Party to this claim?

Hon. Mr. MACLEOD said the question was spoken of both in this House and outside of it, the Opposition sneered at it and it was a worthless asset. There is no use in taking up the time of this honorable House by quoting the words used by the Opposition respecting this matter for every honorable member knew the attitude taken by the Opposition against this claim. We would never have received the $78,000 that is already voted on this account, if the Government had not taken the action they did. And we have received even more than that, for the repairs of these wharves will cost from $25,000 to $30,000 per annum, and this amount had been saved the Province for all time to come. By securing this claim, the Government have succeeded in adding as good as $600,000 to our Capital at Ottawa, for we know that at 5 per cent. that sum would be of no greater service to this Province than we have obtained by getting the wharves and Piers taken off our hands. This claim had originated with the Government. The question had not been even suggested by outsiders when a decision had been reached by honorable members of the Government in reference to this matter. Some honorable members of the Opposition said that it was the Holman-

Green case that suggested this matter to the present Government when that case was first tried, the question of who owned the shores was not raised and it was not until the case had gone to the Supreme Court at Ottawa that the question came up, as affecting that case. In 1881, a question had been asked by the honorable member for Bedeque, as follows:

"Mr. Holland asked the Commissioner of Public Works whether any cotract has been let upon the Cape Traverse Wharf, and if not what steps he intends taking towards reconstructing or improving the said wharf?

Hon. Mr. Campbell replied that no contract had been let, that the Government had come to the conclusion that the work was one that should be attended to by the Dominion authorities." By this we see that so long ago as 1881, the Government had decided that Wharves and Piers were under the jurisdiction of the Dominion Government and that the Local Government did not intend spending any money on them. The honorable Leader of the Opposition said that the Government had drawn $120,000 from our capital at Ottawa. Surely the honorable member was aware that these refunds were part of the sum placed to the credit of this Province at the time we entered Confederation, for the purpose of bringing Proprietor's Estates. It is true that the receipts at the Land Office had been spent as ordinary revenue; but all the Governments of the several Pro-

vinces of the Dominion use these receipts for the same purpose. It should also be remembered that the amount received from the Land office by the present Government was not nearly so large as what had been received and spent while the Opposition was in power. The honorable member also said that we have no Public Works of importance to build, that we did not have an expensive work like the Lunatic Asylum to construct. The fact was well known that the present Government had expended as much for building the Asylum, as the late Government, and that the maintenance of that institution costs a great deal more than it did when the late Government were in power The Opposition complain that the Goverment did not go in a dignified way to obtain payment of our claims from the Dominion. He (Mr. McL.) thought that we should prosecute claims of this kind in a vigorous manner and the result has shown that the method adopted by the Government was a proper one. The Government is also blamed for asking an amount on account. No blame should be laid against the Government for doing so, as it is most reasonable to suppose, that when a large question of this nature was under consideration, that the Dominion Government by consenting to pay something on account of it admitted the principle that they owed us for these expenditures. Having obtained a payment on account, the Dominion Government could not refuse to pay any further amount that this Province was entitled to.

he honorable Leader of the Opposition is very much afraid that the ecessities of the Government may iduce them to accept less than ney should on acccount of the onfulfilment of the terms of .iion with respect to winter com· iunication; but the honorable entleman need not be alarmed. 'he Government will act in the ime manner on this question as hey did on the Piers question. ome time ago the organ of the pposition told its readers that he Government had executéd a receipt in full " for all claims on ccount of expenditures on Piers nd Wharves. Instead of doing o, the Government not only have ·eceived $53,222 19 on this account, but will also receive $24,240 this year and have given no receipt in full. Yet we have other claims that we expect to get paid and the Government will give no receipt in full until they are adjusted. There is no fear of the Government accepting a less amount than the Province is entitled to in lieu of winter communication. The Government have shown that they can prosecute our claims successfully and the people of the Province give them credit for doing so. He (Mr. McL) knew of no dissatisfaction arising from the operation of the Road Act the present Government had placed on our Statutes. He heard of no meetings being called to condemn the Government. Although meetings had been called asking for Public Works required in the Province, yet no resolutions conlemning the Government had been passed at them. These facts are a good indication that the people are satisfied with the presnt Administration. The honorable member for Tignish had exhausted every conceivable subject in order to find a charge against the Government. He attacked the Prince of Wales College and said "it must go" but he (Mr. McL.) would leave that subject between the honorable member and the Editor of the *Presbyterian.* The Government had nothing to do with that newspaper, as it is wholly owned by the gentleman who conducts it, and they were not responsible for what was published in it. He (Mr. McL.) would not trespass any further on the time of the House as no charges of a serious nature had been brought against the Government by honorable members of the Opposition.

Motion carried.

Mr. JOHN MACLEAN in the Chair.

House in Committee of Supply.

Hon. Mr. SULLIVAN moved a resolution granting Salaries of Attorney and Advocate General, Clerk of the Crown, Prothonotary, Sheriff and expenditures for Jails, Court Houses, &c.

Mr. YEO asked why the amount for Court in Georgetown had been increased from $40 to $60. He also noticed that the Keeper of that building had his salary doubled. There may be good reasons for these changes but he (Mr. Y.) would like to know why? When any increase is made in these items the Committee had a right to know why it is done?

Hon. Mr. CAMPBELL said the increased amount was for painting the outside of the building.

Reaolution put and carried.

Hon. Mr. SULLIVAN, submitted the following resolution :—

Resolved, That the following sums be granted, and placed at the disposal of the Government, for the following services, viz.,—

Coroner's Inquests	$300

Resolution put and carried.

Hon. Mr. SULLIVAN submitted the following resolution :—

Resolved. That the following sums be granted, and placed at the disposal of the Government, for the following services, viz.,—

Mileage members Executive Council	$500
Printing and Stationery	100

Resolution put and carried.

Hon. Mr. SULLIVAN submitted the following resolution :—

Resolved, That the following sum be granted, and placed at the disposal of the Government, for the following services, viz.,—

Elections	$300

Resolution put and carried.

Hon. Mr. SULLIVAN submitted the following resolution :—

Resolved, That the following sums be granted, and placed at the disposal of the Government, for the following services,—

Salary of Chief Superintendent of Education	$1,200
Salary of Clerk to Superintendent of Education ·	800
Salaries of Inspectors of Schools	1,600
Salary of Principal of Prince of Wales College and Normal School	1,500
Salary of first Professor of Prince of Wales College and Normal School	1,100
Salary of second Professor of Prince of Wales College and Normal School	800
Salary of third Professor of Prince of Wales College and Normal School	700
Salary of District Teachers and Supplements	92,000
Bonus to Teachers	2,000
Scholarships, Prince of Wales College	480
Travelling expenses Chief Superintendent of Education	200
Printing and Stationery	500
Fuel, etc., Prince of Wales College and Normal School	600
Miscellaneous	100

Mr. FARQUHARSON said this was an important resolution, as nearly half the revenue is voted away in it. He did not know what policy the Government intended to adopt in reference to the Prince of Wales College. As this institution had been attacked by the leading newspaper that supports the Government, he thought the Government

st be in sympathy with that
ack, when they had not vindi-
ed the Principal. It was scan-
ous the way Professor Ander-
's name had been dragged into
it newspaper. It did not speak
ll for the Government when they
d not defended this gentleman
om such an attack. In his (Mr.
s.) opinion the Prince of Wales
ollege was costing the Province
o much money. It was a ques-
on whether it was wise to let the
venue run away in this manner.
our Professors are not required,
vo would be enough. The Gov-
nment should inaugurate the
olicy of reducing the cost of
ducation. There would be no
ifficulty in saving $25,000 a year
i this Department alone. Last
ession he (Mr. F.) had spoken about
he little need we had for an
Attorney General, costing $1,300 a
year, a salary altogether too much
or the work performed by that
official. If we must have an
Attorney General he (Mr. F.) would
also give him control of the Land
Office. With the sum that would
hus be saved we could employ a
ompetent engineer to look after
he Public Works that are going to
decay. The Commissioner of Crown
Lands has lost his chance to make
, long speech and he is crying over
t, but he will have more reason to
ry when he loses his office, which
e soon will. The supplement to
'eachers is a question that should
e taken up at an early day. Over
10,000 are spent in supplements
nd a saving will have to be effected
a some way or we will be sunk
rretrievable in debt. He (Mr. F.)
id not know that the bonus to

teachers was given to the proper
persons. School teachers who have
been teaching ten or fifteen years
are, in general, old fogys, and the
younger teachers who have been
employed two or three years are
better entitled to a bonus than
these teachers, who only continue
teaching because they are fit for
nothing else.

Mr. D. C. MARTIN said this was
a very important item. With
regard to the Prince of Wales
College, he (Mr. M.) considered it a
most useful institution, an institution that has done a great deal for
country boys. There may be some
force in the remarks of the honorable member for West River, that
there are two many professors in
the institution, but it should not
be forgotten that the Normal
School has been amalgamated with
the College. In old times there
was only one professor in the
Normal School, but one person
could not attend to the large number of persons who now attended
this school. He thought other
means might be taken to lessen the
expenditure. The schools of the
Province cost $105,000 last year,
and every one knows that is an
excessive sum to pay for education,
considering the amount of our
revenue. Do the Government intend to take away the supplements
to the teachers when they intend
reducing the cost of education this
year? There is considerable diversity of opinion respecting supplements being paid by the Government.

Hon. Mr. FERGUSON said he did

not think it necessary to reply to the honorable member for West River respecting what he (Mr. Farquharson) said about the Land Office. That honorable member, sometime ago, attacked the Prince of Wales College, and perhaps he has inspired the *Presbyterian*. In reference to taking away the supplements now paid school teachers by the Government, the honorable member surely knew that such a change could only be accomplished by a radical change in the Education Act. The present Government have been expending large sums for Education during the time they have been in power During the six years that the present administration had been in power $587,-501.41 had been expended for education. Contrast this sum with the amount paid for this service ($388,377.50) during the six years immediately preceding the time when the present administration assumed control of the Government and we find that the large sum of $199,123.85 has been expended during the latter period over what had been spent for this service by their predecessors.

Mr. YEO said he could not understand why the Government expected a decrease this year in the amount required for this service. He did not think it was proper to place smaller amounts in the estimates than would be required. He was surprised the Government had not attended to the recommendation of the Superintendent of Education, made two years ago, and again repeated in last year's report. It said as follows:

"I would again recommend that three Inspectors be appointed instead of two as at present. This addition to the staff would add materially to the efficiency of the schools. The matter of inspection, which is one of the most essential to the welfare of our school system, is that which is least liberally provided for under our present school laws. While the Province pays for education each year at the rate of $11.89 per pupil in daily attendance, it provides only one inspector for every 247 schools. The work is altogether greater than the most enthusiastic inspector can overtake."

The Superintendent of so important a Department should be competent to speak on all matters connected with our Education System, and his (Mr. Montgomery's) recommendation should make some impression on honorable members of the Government. He (Mr. Y.) would like to know if it is the intention of the Government to appoint an additional inspector ?

Hon. Mr. CAMPBELL said there was a considerable amount expended last year for repairs to the Prince of Wales College. Not near so large a sum will be required this year.

Mr. J. R. McLEAN said,—When an important resolution like the one before the Committee was under consideration, he (Mr. McL.) expected that the Government would give some information respecting the different services for which this money was paid. It would be a step in the right direction if the Government would increase the teacher's salaries and do away with the amounts paid as supplements. There is a great deal of dissatisfaction, especially in the poorer settlements, respecting the payment of supplements. Where a district is well off they can pay a large amount of supplement to a teacher, and the Government had to pay a like sum, and these districts are able to get the best teachers. In this way great injustice is done the poorer districts. There was a great difference of opinion respecting the Prince of Wales College, but he (Mr. McL) would not like to lower the standard of education, nor would he wish to compel persons who wished to educate their sons to send them out of the Province in order to receive the training they would require. The article published in the *Presbyterian* was of a most damaging nature, and the Government are doing an injustice by not stopping such attacks, or by not changing the Superintendent of that institution. He (Mr. McL.) for several years had made application to the Government, through a notice entered on the Order Book of this honorable House, for the amount paid for printing without tenders, and he could get no information. He was not in favor of having political Attorney Generals and Commissioners of Crown Lands such as the ones now filling these offices. When men are paid for doing the work of a department, it is not right for them to be half the time stumping the country. He knew parties from country districts who, desiring to get information at these offices, had found that the heads of these departments were away and could not be found. He was surprised at the Government putting less in the estimates for education this year than they had expended last year. We know the expenditure in connection with education is constantly increasing, and a sufficient amount should be voted by this House to meet all necesary expenditure. The Superintendent of Education is an excellent officer, and the Government should pay some attention to his recommendations. The education of teachers is a most important matter, as a good teacher soon made a marked difference in the school over which he had charge. Respecting the amount for bonuses he (Mr. McL.) believed that young men are the best teachers, and the fact that a person had been teaching seven, eight or ten years is no guarantee that the persons is more worthy or better qualified than one who had only been teaching three or four years.

Mr. SINCLAIR said this was a most important resolution, as it affected one of the most important questions this House had under its control. The honorable Commissioner of Public Works had told them that the money expended last year for repairs to the Prince of Wales College was more than would be required this year for a similar purpose. There was a good deal said about the Prince of Wales College, both in the press and in the country. When it is considered that our young men, who have been educated in this institution, take a position highly creditable to the Province, it showed that the Principal of this school had performed his duty efficiently. The Principal had the reputation of being a good teacher, but if he is teaching doctrines that are against the Christian religion and corrupting the minds of our young men, he should be dismissed. In looking over this resolution he (Mr. S.) found that there is $3,000 additional for salaries and supplements of teachers, and only a reduction of $1,100 in the amount voted for repairs. He (Mr. S.) would like to know how the Government expect to expend less this year for this service than they did last year? This should be the last year this Parliament should be asked to vote away nearly one half of the revenue for education. The Government should take hold of the question and make such changes in the Act as would lessen the expenditure. Although it was necessary that some changes should be made in our present school system, he (Mr. S.) would not go for the abolition of the supplements to teachers. If a Committee was appointed this session, they could procure a large amount of information before next year, and have a report ready to submit at the next meeting of the Legislature. The expenditure for education is constantly increasing, and the Government cannot allow it to increase much more. They should adopt some means of curtailing it. He (Mr. S.) questiond if these bonuses should be given the way they are. Some who have only taught one or two years do more than many who

have been teaching for ten years. We have only two inspectors for the Province, and there is no report from the one who had charge of the Western Section of the Island. No Government should pay men their salaries unless their work was performed in a satisfactory manner. The amounts paid these inspectors are fixed by statute, and it was not too much considering the work that had to be done; but the Government should change the mode of paying the salary, so that the report of the inspectors should be put in before their salaries were paid.

Mr. BEER said he would ask honorable members of the Government why no report had been received from the western section of the Island?

Hon. Mr. FERGUSON said he did not think there was an great necessity for discussing the matter. When the Government found that the Inspector for the Western division was not doing his work in a proper manner, they induced him to resign, and had appointed a competent man in his place, who is doing the work well.

Mr. BEER said honorable members had a right to know why no report had been received from the western section of this Province. Are we to be told that the Government had no power to make any one of their officers give in his report? Why was the officer paid his Salary, if his report was not put in? The Government had a right to see that these reports are ut in every year and that they ad been recreant of their duty in ot having the matter attended to.

Mr. SINCLAIR the Inspector of he western Section should not ave been paid his Salary until iis report was made out and placed n the hands of the Government Respecting the expenditure last ear for repairs to the Prince of Vales College he (Mr. S.) noticed hat the Superintendent of Education in his report said as follows :

" I have to repeat what I said on former occasions in regard to the accommodation provided for Normal and Collegiate work in the building now known as the Prince of Wales College. It is entirely inadequate for the purposes for which it is used And although it has undergone repairs annually at considerable cost, no material improvement is visible as the result of these repairs."

It is extraordinary that no visible effects can be seen from the expenditure of money on that building and that no good arises from it. It was time a different course was adopted with reference to these expenditures, when the officer who looked after his department said that although honorable members of the Government were expending money year after year on this building, that no improvement was effected.

Hon. Mr. CAMPBELL, — what the Superintendent of Education means by this report is that the class-rooms of the College had received no improvement. The re-

pairs put on the Prince of Wales College last year were chiefly for heating the building during the winter season, and for putting a new foundation under part of the building, not so much money will be required for repairs this year.

Mr. FARQUHARSON, — Returns had been asked for weeks ago that would have given this Committee the information that honorable members are anxious to obtain. The honorable Commissioner of Public Works gets up and recites what he has done during the recess, but honorable members should have this information laid on the table of the House. If this was done it would save the Government considerable cross-examination. Many other returns are asked for, but we cannot get any information respecting how these amounts were spent. Large sums of money had been spent on this building over $3,500 and he (Mr. F.) wanted to know what had been done with it.

Hon. Mr. CAMPBELL,—If honorable members ask unreasonable questions, they must expect that some of the answers will be delayed. The Secretary of the Public Works department is working at these returns and they will be placed on the table of the House as soon as possible.

Mr. J. R. MACLEAN said the Vouchers of the payments would be as satisfactory as a statement. Formerly nothing else but Vouchers were asked for and it was the proper way to conduct the business of the country. What good is a statement without the Vouchers to show that the money has been paid to proper persons. · In reference to this gentleman who had not submitted his report, it seems extraordinary that the Government had paid him his Salary until his work was fully performed. He (Mr.McL.) did not know but this $1,100 that was paid for repairs of the Prince of Wales College was a political engine to be used for Election purposes. Last summer, a great many men were employed working about the Square, before the Election came off and perhaps that is the reason the repairs to this Building cost so much.

Mr. BEER said,—Judging from the remarks of the honorable Commissioner of Public Works the information required by the honorable members will not be tabled before the House gets through supply. The Commissioner said the Secretary of his Department was working at these returns. If the Secretary cannot do this work expeditiously why not get another person to help him? Mr. Morrison had many other duties to attend to besides making up the returns asked for by honorable members and additional help should be employed, so that honorable members can intelligently discuss the advisability of making these expenditures. The Superintendent of Education, (Mr. Montgomery) had represented in his report that the duties of the Inspectors had greatly increased and suggested that an additional Inspector should be appointed, as

two Inspectors were unable to keep up the work. It was the duty of the Government to pay attention to this recommendation. The Superintendent knew that two Inspectors cannot go all through the Province and attend to all the Schools properly. Instead of helping the Education system, the present Government are trying to injure one of the most important parts of the system by not providing for efficient and thorough inspection of the Schools. He (Mr. B.) expected that the Government would have appointed an additional Inspector before this.

Mr. YEO said,—The Commissioner of Public Works tells us that less money will be required for expenditure on the Prince of Wales College this year; but as the Superintendent of Education in his last year's Report said there was no improvement visible from the repairs made last year, it showed that there was a necessity of expending as much this year as was spent last year. Another part of the Report said the cost of Education was likely to increase for many years to come, yet the amount asked for this year was $3,000 less than was expended last year. This House had a right to know how the cost of this service was to be curtailed. The Government had no right to pay officers who do not do their work. He (Mr. Y.) found by the Public Accounts last year that the Inspector for the western division was paid $733. Any person who did his work should be paid, but we have a right to know whether the work was done. He (Mr. Y) would like to know why the Government had paid the Inspector of the western Division without having first got his report? The returns asked for by honorable members should be laid on the table of the House, and if the Commissioner of Public Works can not have those from his department prepared in a few days, he (Mr.C.) should give them the vouchers He (Mr.Y.) thought the honorable gentleman would have been anxious to give this information in order to show that amounts had been expended properly. As the report of the Superintent of Education said that no visible improvement had resulted from the expenditure on the Prince of Wales College last year, he (Mr.Y.) would like to know why a smaller amount was asked for this year? It was only deceiving the country and the House to place such estimates before them.

Mr. SINCLAIR said,—In the past there has only been one Report every six months from the Inspector of Schools A better way would be to have a monthly Report to the Superintendent of Education who would then be in a position to know how the Education system of the Province is being carried on. At present we are just allowing the teachers to work in any way they please, as the Inspectors have so many Schools to examine that many Schools were not examined at all. Last year the Province paid an Inspector for the western division and we do not know if he exam-

inee any of the Schools, for we have no Report of what was done.

Hon. Mr. FERGUSON, — The course suggested by the honorable member for Springton, respecting Inspector's reports is the one that is now adopted. Inspectors in future have to report to the Superintendent once a month. The Inspectors of Schools, as well as other officers of the Government are paid their Salaries every month and honorable members can understand that it was impossible for the Government to compel the Inspector of the western division to put in his Report at the end of the year. His salary had been paid him every month, and as he had neglected his duties all the Government could do was to appoint a more competent person in his place.

Mr. HOOPER said there was no doubt, but the work of inspecting one half the Schools in the Province was greater than the most enthusiastic Inspector could overtake. The Government should appoint an additional Inspector. Something could be taken from the salary of the Principal of the Prince of Wales College, who had a larger salary than this Province could afford to pay.

On motion of Mr. Beer Mr. Speaker resumed the Chair, the Chairman reported that some progress had been made and asked leave to sit again.

House adjourned for one hour.

G. F. O.

EVENING SESSION.

Mr. SPEAKER in the Chair.

The first standing order of the House having been suspended, to enable a member to present a petition,—

A petition of John C. Clark, Walter Simpson, John Dickieson, and others, inhabitants of Bay View and vicinity, was presented to the House by Mr. Sinclair, and the same was received and read, praying that an Act be passed for the purpose of Incorporating a Company to build a Hall for general purposes at Cavendish.

Ordered, That said petition be referred to a Special Committee to report thereon by Bill or otherwise.

Ordered, That Messrs. Sinclair, D. C. Martin and McLaren, do compose said Committee.

Mr. SINCLAIR from the last preceding committee appointed, presented to the House a Bill as prepared by the Committee to be entitled : "An Act to Incorporate the Cavendish Hall Company," and the same was received and read the first time, and referred to the Committee on Private Bills to report thereon.

Mr. BEER,—According to previous notice given by him on the Order Book, asked the honorable Commissioner of Public Lands to lay on the table of the House a statement showing all payments made on account of the Public Service from 31st December, 1884, to 31st March, 1885, and also what amounts are due or owing to the several Departments of the Public Service to March 31st, 1885.

Hon. Mr. SULLIVAN said that the statement is being prepared and will be submitted to the House in due time.

"An Act to Incorporate the Telephone Company of Prince Edward Island," was read the third time and passed.

On motion, the House resolved itself into a Committee of the whole to take into consideration a Petition for "An Act to amend an Act relating to accidents by Fire in Kensington, Prince County, and for the removal of nuisances from the Streets."

Mr. ALEXANDER MARTIN in the Chair.

The Petition having been read.

Mr. BENTLEY said that when introducing the Petition for this amendment, he explained the object of the Bill. The old Act was unsatisfactory, and required so many amendments that an entirely new measure was thought necessary. He moved the following resolutions which were severally agreed to, viz :

Resolved, That it is expedient to introduce a Bill to repeal the Act 47th Victoria, chapter 16, intituled n Act relating to accidents by, in Kensington, Prince County, d for the removal of nuisances m the streets thereof," and to ke other provisions, in lieu ereof, and to enforce such proions by the imposition of fines d penalties.

Resolved, That the assesors ould have power to assess the habitants and owners of prop ty in the said place in a sum not ceeding on hundred dollars in y one year.

On motion, Mr. Speaker reumed the Chair, and the Chairan reported that the Committee ad gone into the consideration of e matter to them referred, and ad come to two resolutions theren, which resolutions were again ead at the Clerk's table and agreed o by the House.

Resolved, That a Committee be ppointed to prepare and bring in Bill pursuant to the resolutions.

Ordered, That Mr Bentley, honrable Mr. Campbell, and Honorble Mr. Gordon do compose the aid Committee.

Mr. BENTLEY, from the last preeding Committee, appointed, preented to the House a Bill as repared by them, to be intituled: An Act respecting the village of Kensington, Prince County," and he same was received, and read he first time, and was ordered to e read a second time to-morrow.

Mr. D. C. MARTIN,—According to previous notice given by him on the Order Book, asked the honorable Commissioner of Public Works to lay on the table of the House a detailed statement of the Expenditure by the Goverment on Acorn's Bridge, District No. 9 ; Bird Hill Bridge, Lot 49, District No.9; North Pinette Bridge, Pownal Road Bridge, Village Green Road District, No. 9 ; Georgetown Road District No. 9., in the year 1884.

Hon. Mr. CAMPBELL said that the information asked for by the honorable member was already on the table of the House, in the Supervisor's Returns, except in the case of Pinette Bridge, which will be laid on the table, if necessary. The work done by Supervisors' Sales, and was paid for in a lump sum.

The Order of the Day for the second reading of the Bill to be intituled : " An Act securing to Baptist Churches of Prince Edward Island, the benefits of Incorporation," the Bill was accordingly read the second time.

Hon. Mr. MACLEOD moved that the Bill be now committed to a Committee of the whole House, and said that it is a very short one enabling any Baptist Church to become Incorporated without passing a Special Act for that purpose.

Motion put and carried.

The House accordingly resolved itself into the said Committee.

Mr. MATHESON in the Chair.

After a short time spent in Committee without Debate, Mr. Speaker, on motion, resumed the Chair, and the Chairman reported the Bill agreed to, without any amendment.

Ordered, That the Bill be engrossed, and that it be read the third time to-morrow.

Hon. Mr. MACDONALD from the Committee on Private Bills, and to whom was referred the Bill to be intituled : " An Act to incorporate the Charlottetown Waterworks Company," reported that the Bill is of a private nature and liable to fees, and recommended that twenty dollars be charged.

Ordered, That the Report of the Committee be adopted, and that said Bill be read a second time to-morrow.

The Order of the Day being read for the second reading of the Bill to be intituled " An Act to Incorporate the Prince Edward Island Mutual Fire Insurance Company," the Bill was accordingly read the second time and committed to a committee of the whole House.

The House accordingly resolved itself into the said Committee.

Mr. BLAKE in the Chair.

Hon. Mr. LEFURGEY said that the Bill had been read through the Chairman of the Committee, and therefore the House was acquaint-ed with its contents. A few farmers want a Bill to protect themselves against accidents by fire, and have therefore originated this measure. If any objections are offered to its provisions, the latter will be explained.

Mr. J. R. MACLEAN.—There is no provision in the Bill to limit the obligations of the parties who insure under it. In case a party is insured, and the assessment not paid up, it will rest with the Directors to decide whether it shall be paid up or not.

Hon. Mr. PROWSE.—It is not expected that this Bill will be satisfactory to the Insurance Agents of other companies, as it will assist in reducing their Incomes. Our farmers are very intelligent and know their wants better than some who would instruct them in such matters as this. They should receive what they are asking for, providing it does not conflict with the public interests.

Mr. J. R. MACLEAN understood what would operate in the interests of our farmers as well as did the honorable member for Murray Harbor. This Bill contains some very objectionable features, to which he (Mr. McL.) had just alluded.

Hon. Mr. LEFURGEY,—The honorable member for East Point does not want the farmers to become their own Insurers against accidents by fire, as he has his own interests to serve in that business.

e (Mr. L.) presumed that the en asking for this Act of Inorporation know more about hat they want than did the honrable gentleman. It is a mutual ffair, and if they secure one anther against accidents by fire, he House could not object. He horght the object of the Bill a ery laudable one, and that it ould result in much good for he class for whom it was intended.

Mr. SINCLAIR thought that the men who applied for this Act of ncorporation should know their own business pretty well. Their object evidently is to protect themselves from the heavy charges of other companies, and he gave them credit for their action in reference to this matter. Our farmers are protecting themselves in various ways. They protect themselves from the merchants by importing their own seeds.

Mr. FARQUHARSON thought the promoters of the Bill had no more right to use the title: "Prince Edward Island," than had the "Island Publishing Company" to use theirs. The Government should not make fish of the one and flesh of the other.

Hon Mr. MACDONALD said that there was a great dissimilarity between the titles of the two Bills alluded to by the honorable member for West River. The word "Agricultural" in the title of the present Bill, makes all the difference. Had the promoters of the Bill made such a distinction in its title, they would have been treated in precisely the same way.

Hon. Mr. CAMPBELL was glad to see such a Bill as this come before the Legislature. Protection is now the order of the day; and it is becoming infectious. The Bill originated in a farmer's club; —the right place to propose such a measure. We have been fleeced long enough by foreign Insurance Companies doing business on this Island, and it is high time for our farmers to start a Mutual Insurance Company. If a fire takes place in Charlottetown, the rates are at once raised to extraordinary figures, on the excuse that the citizens do not introduce Waterworks. Even the Government have been fleeced under that plea, to the extent of hundreds of dollars This Bill is a step in the right direction, and he hoped the Company will become a strong, powerful, and prosperous one. He believed protection good for all classes, and that the National Policy was the true policy for this country. He hoped that our farmers will not rest until they import their farming implements at one half the rates they are at present paying for them.

The remaining clauses of the Bill were read and agreed to without debate.

On motion, Mr. Speaker, resumed the Chair, and the Chairman reported the Bill agreed to without any amendment.

Ordered, That the Bill be engrossed, and that it be read third time to-morrow.

House adjourned until to-morrow forenoon, at ten o'clock.

I. O.

THURSDAY, April 2.

Mr, SPEAKER in the Chair.

Mr. YEÓ, in accordance with notice placed on the Order Book, asked the Commissioner of Public Works if it is intended to open a new road from the O'Leary road towards the Brae, Lot 9, the said road having been recommended to be opened by this House in the session of 1883.

Hon. Mr. CAMPBELL said he had visited the locality referred to by the honorable member, and had found that this was a road that had been partly made several years ago ; but there was a bad swamp on the route originally selected. If a route a little different was selected, there would not be near so much expense in constructing this road. As he (Mr. C.) believed the road was required, if it was at all feasible it would be opened. He, however, was afraid that the old line was impossible, and that another route would have to be selected.

Mr. YEO said he was glad to learn that this road would be opened. The petitioners were not particular what route was selected, so long as the road was opened near where it had been originally laid off.

A Message was received from the Legislative Council.

Mr. YEO, in accordance with notice placed in the Order Book, asked the Commissioner of Public Works to lay on the table of the House the vouchers for all payments made by the Department of Public Works in connection with the Rocky Point wharf and slip.

Hon. Mr. CAMPBELL said the expenditure made in connection with this service had abready been tabled. The vouchers for these payments are in the office of the Public Works Department, under the charge of the Secretary of the Department, and it is not considered desirable to place these documents on the table of the House. Every information required in reference to this matter could be ascertained by applying to the Secretary of the Public Works Department.

Mr. YEO,—The statement laid on the table of the House is not in detail.

Hon. Mr. CAMPBELL, in reply, said it was customary when men are employed by the Public Works Department for the person who has charge of the work to make out a pay list each week. When the list is audited by the Provincial Auditor, a check is made out in the name of the person who had charge of the work, and in that way the statement laid before the House does not appear to be in detail, although it is actually as on the books of the department.

On motion of Honorable Mr. llivan the House resolved itself to Committee of the whole to nsider further of a supply being anted to Her Majesty.

Mr. JOHN McLEAN in the Chair.

The resolution providing for ducation being again read,—

Mr. J. R. McLEAN said the item f $600 for fuel, etc., for the Prince f Wales College seemed a very rge one. He (Mr. McL.) did not e why this amount was not emized. $600 seemed an extra- rdinary large amount for fuel, nless the etc. required a pretty arge sum, He (Mr. McL.) thought his was a peculiar way of putting lown items.

Hon. Mr. CAMPBELL said a good many different services were paid out of this amount. The Janitor of the College is paid out of it, besides paying for coal, washing out the class rooms-and some other odd jobs that always have to be attended to in connection with an institution of this kind. Last year these services cost $800, but it is considered that $600 will be suffi- cient to defray all the expenses that will be incurred this year. The item also includes $8 per month that is paid for putting on fires during the autumn and winter seasons.

Mr. FARQUHARSON said the Com- missioner of Public Works spent $1,800 last year for the services for which he only asked $800 when the estimates were presented to the House. We may vote $600 for these services this year and he (Mr. C.) will spend perhaps $2,000. The coal for this institution only cost $300 last year and it should not cost any more this year. The Commissioner of Public Works had no right to exceed the amounts voted by the House. If he has made his calculations correctly the amount asked for should be suffi- cient for the year. No doubt the House was satisfied that the money was properly spent, but they did not wish to give the honorable gentleman unlimited power to spend what money he wished. The Superintendent of Education says that the cost of education is increas- ing each year, and he (Mr. F.) would like to know how the Gov- ernment made their calculations for this service so much less this year than the amount expended last year. The Superintendent should know all about this Depart- ment, and he said that the expen- diture of it is increasing. He (Mr. F.) believed it would take $107,000 this year to defray the expenses of that department. The Government had no right to exceed the amount voted for any service. Last year the Commissioner of Public Work's expenditure had exceed the amount voted in almost every instance.

Mr. PERRY said it was very strange that the reports of the Superintendent of Education and of the Principal of the Prince of Wales College, both said that noth- ing had been done for the expendi- ture of the large amount of money that is charged by the Commis- sioner of Public Works as being expended on the Prince of Wales College. The report of the Principal of the Prince of Wales College said :—"Notwithstanding the increased difficulty of our entrance examination, the numbers in attendance at the institution are as high as ever. But we are constantly reminded of the inadequacy of the accommodation to the proper discharge of our duties. The fact that we have forty young ladies in attendance, and that we can make no special arrangement for their comfort and convenience, is in itself proof that the present building is far from being suited to our numbers and requirements ; whilst the practical training of the student-teachers is weakened by the want of a hall and other equipments, which are absolutely necessary in a properly conducted Normal School. I trust that the time is not distant when we shall be provided with a building suited in all respects to the duties which we are called upon to discharge." He (Mr. P.) did not believe the Government knew what was in this report or they would have asked this House for a grant to provide this accommodation that Professor Anderson says is so badly needed. The Chief Superintendent of Education in his report says :—" I have to repeat what I said on former occasions in regard to the accommodation provided for Normal and College work in the building now known as the Prince of Wales College. It is entirely inadequate for the purposes for which it is used. And although it has undergone repairs annually at considerable cost, no material improvement

is visible as the result of these repairs." Here the Chief Superintendent of Education, who is employed by the Government to look after this Department, says that the repairs are not seen, are not visible. He (Mr. P.) was sure that $1,800 was not used for coal. Was there anything done for this money ? Was there no new classroom, nor any of the improvements asked for by these gentlemen provided ? If these gentlemen are worthy of receiving their salaries, which amount to $3,000 a year, why do not the Government carry out the suggestions of the heads of this department ? Instead of asking for only $600 for the repairing of this building, why do they not ask for a sufficient sum to make the improvements that their officers tell us is so urgently required. The Government have no right to spend any more money than this house grants, but they should place enough in the estimates to carry on the business of the country in an efficient manner. He (Mr. P.) expected to see the Honorable Leader of the Government ask this honorable House to vote the $30,000 that they had expended over the estimates of last year. It is not constitutional, it is trampling on the rights of the people to spend money without the consent of this honorable House. This House might as well not meet at all as to have the Government spending $290,000 when only $252,000 are voted. He (Mr. P.) hoped that his words would be heard all over the Province, that this Government had no respect for the people's representatives. It would be far more onest if the Government asked or $3,000 for repairs to the Prince f Wales College when they intend o spend it, than to put down a sum hat will be exceeded five times ver. It is no use asking the Government any questions for they will give no information about anything.

Hon. Mr. Prowse said it was a pity the honorable member had not charge of these matters, for then everything would be all right, at least he (Mr. Perry) would think so.

Mr. Farquharson said he would like to hear from the honorable senior member from · Murray Harbor, who seemed afraid to speak for fear he will clash with the honorable Leader of the Government. He (Mr. F.) wanted to know if the honorable members of the Government are satisfied to have the Commissioner of Public Works spending $1,800 when only $800 was voted. The Honorable Leader of the Government, in 1878, said that vouchers should be produced for every expenditure. He (Mr. S.) does not think so now. Honorable members are sent here to look after the interests of their constituents. Are the Government going to sit like dumb dogs and give honorable members no information on these important matters? No! We know they will give no information unless it is forced from them. He (Mr. F.) had no doubt but Mr. Morrison was working hard at other duties connected with his office, but that was no reason why the information required by hon-

orable members was not forthcoming. He (Mr. F.) had sat in this House for four years when there were only four honorable members on this side of the House, when it was very hard to get any information from the Government; but now we have a majority of the wealth of the Province on our side and we must get the consideration we are entitled to. The honorable Commissioner of Crown Lands has just taken his place, and is looking very well satisfied, but he (Mr. Ferguson) will not feel comfortable when the question of voting his salary comes up.

Hon. Mr. Prowse wondered if the House would never be done hearing of the wealth of the honorable member for West River. He (Mr. Farquharson) should table a schedule of all his possessions, so honorable members would know once for all, what he was worth. The honorable member endorses all that is said by the Opposition about deducting $5 per day from the salary of the hon. Commissioner for Crown Lands for the seventy-five days they say that hon. gentleman was absent from his office. Did he (Mr. Farquharson) deduct anything from Mr. Davies' salary for the time he (Mr. D.) went to Halifax as Attorney for the Dominion Government? Any time the Honorable Commissioner of Crown Lands is away from his office is spent in the service of his country; and no better service is rendered by that honorable gentleman than in exposing the actions of the honorable member for West River when he was a member of the Government.

Mr. PERRY said every honorable member knew that $1,000 had been spent on the Prince of Wales College last year over what had been voted in Committee of the whole House, and no information had been given of what was done with it. What has been done with this money? He (Mr. P.) contended that the country, through their representatives, had a right to know about these expenditures. Honorable members of the Opposition are not treated properly. Has anything been done for this large amount of nearly $1,100 that had been expended without leave of this Legislature? A small sheet of paper would give us all the particulars of how this amount was spent. He (Mr. P.) believed that the Government had made good use of this money, but the people's representatives had a right to know how it was spent. This proves the necessity of having the "Superintendent of Education on the floor of the House. The Government have no policy in reference to Education. They are afraid to touch this question. If you talk to them privately, they will tell you that they are in favor of doing away with the supplements to Teachers; but in this House you will not hear one word about it. He (Mr. P.) did not think honorable members of the Government were pulling very well together on this question. They knew that the question of doing away with the supplements had been agitated for some time, but the members of the Govern-

ment do not say one word about it. He expected that when the Government were asked for information respecting their expenditures that the honorable member for Murray Harbor would have given it. It seemed, however, that they must be content to do without it.

Mr. J. R. McLEAN said the item for printing and stationery for this department amounted to $500. The printing and stationery for the County Courts only cost $250, and he (Mr. McL.) did not see why so great an amount was required for this department. It seems to be very difficult to get any information from the Government. The Commissioner of Public Works had given them some little information about the $1,100 of over expenditure on the Prince of Wales College, and said it was for heating apparatus and repairs to foundation, etc. This was also an important item, and he (Mr. McL.) hoped some honorable member of the Government would come forward to give them some information about it. Every information respecting these important items should be given, and he was surprised that the Government did not place all vouchers and statements asked for on the table of the House. The actions of honorable members of the Government to-day were discreditable. The Opposition are prepared to treat them courteously if they act in a proper manner. He (Mr. McL.) had great doubts whether the Government represented the majority of the electors, and they should not be too independent.

Mr. SINCLAIR said this discussion had given honorable members an opportunity to look over the items in this resolution, and he (Mr. S.) did not consider the time was lost that was taken up in discussing them. He found that last year $500 was voted for this service, viz., printing and stationery, and that $800 was spent. He also found that every department is put down for a less amount than it cost last year, and yet last year the printing and stationery for the education department cost $316 over what was estimated for this year. Again, the amount for bonuses to teachers is not increased, although it is very likely that there will be a good many more to receive them this year. Altogether education will cost over $103,580 this year, and he (Mr. S.) did not see what was the use of voting less than we knew would be required. He did not think it was an honest way. He would like an explanation about the over expenditure on printing and stationery last year.

Hon. Mr. SULLIVAN said he did not know why the honorable member for Springton should say it was dishonest, if some of the items voted by this Legislature should prove insufficient to efficiently maintain the public service. He (Mr. S.) would explain why printing and stationery cost more than was estimated at the last session. Last year it became necessary to strike off copies of the school teachers' returns, a work that is only performed every three or four years. Last year was the year that this work was required, and this service

cost an additional expense of $300 or $400. In reference to what had been said about the Prince of Wales College, he might say that while it is true that the report of the Principal of that institution said that no improvement had been made, yet it should not be forgotten that the building belongs to the Province, and it is necessary to expend sufficient on it to keep it from falling down. The over expenditure that the Opposition are so anxious about was made in the interest of the Province. It is true this expenditure had made no improvement in the scholastic arrangements of this institution; but these repairs were necessary, and a similar expenditure will not likely occur for the next ten or fifteen years.

Hon. Mr. CAMPBELL said when the estimates were prepared last year, he was not aware that the furnaces and internal arrangements for heating the Prince of Wales College had to be repaired so soon, and that was the reason why the sum necessary to perform this work had not been placed in the estimates submitted last session. There is not a day but Professor Anderson requires some work to be done for that building or its furniture. If any honorable member will go down to the Public Works Department he (Mr. C.) could show him broken parts of desks, slates, etc., that have constantly to be replaced. It is true there is no improvement in the class-rooms from last year's expenditure. The greater part of last year's expense was for repairing the boiler and the foundation of the building.

Mr. D. C. MARTIN said the vote of the House had been exceeded by $1,100 in this one item. When $1,849 is put on a small building like the College there should be some improvements to show for it. Although the honorable Commissioner of Public Works said that so many broken pieces of desks and slates can be seen in his office, every honorable member knew that this large amount would not be spent for repairs to desks and slates. The report of the Superintendent of Education should be considered, and we ought to know how that money was expended. Honorable members had a right to know whether or not the Commissioner of Public Works kept one or two men around his office with this money.

Mr. SINCLAIR said it was noticeable that the Honorable Leader of the Government stated that a considerable amount had been required last year that the Government were not aware of when the estimates were prepared, and that the honorable Commissioner of Public Works followed the same line of argument to excuse there over expenditure. It is only what might be expected by this House, that honorable members of the Government would have these matters investigated before calling Parliament together, so that we would know what was required. If these expenditures had been made on account of some unforeseen occurrence, it would be according to the rule of Parliament for the Government to make them, but if they had taken on themselves to spend money for other purposes,

without a vote of this House, it was unconstitutional.

Hon. Mr. SULLIVAN said he did not say that he (Mr. S.) was not aware that this expenditure was necessary. It was found after the estimates were prepared for last session that it would be necessary to print a further supply of the teachers reports and returns. The Superintendent of Education thought it would be better to have them printed, although not many of them were afterwards used, and the supply on hand had proved nearly sufficient. The number of these reports that will be wanted during the year is hard to estimate correctly, but the fact that very few were actually required, showed honorable members that the Government's estimates were prepared properly.

Mr. J. R. McLEAN said the honorable member took an ingenious way of getting out of this matter. About every two years this extra expenditure is required, and if the matter had been properly looked into before the estimates were made up, it would be known that another supply would be required before the end of the year. He (Mr. McL.) had several times asked for a detailed statement of the amount paid for printing done without tender, but he had not been able to obtain it.

Hon. Mr. SULLIVAN said if the honorable member took the proper course he would have no difficulty in obtaining information about any public money that was paid by the present Government. For the information of honorable members he (Mr. S.) might say that Messrs. Bremner Bros. had performed the printing of these returns.

Mr. FARQUHARSON said it was the late Government that had inaugurated the improvement in the system of obtaining the public printing by which the expense was greatly lessened. No one had been louder in approval of this course than the honorable member for Murray Harbor and other honorable members who now are on the Government side of the House. Although these gentlemen had approved of Mr. Davies' conduct in almost every particular, shortly afterwards they jumped "Jim Crow" and left him. And now we find that they are doing the same about letting the printing by tender. The honorable member for Murray Harbor should have an explanation of his views on the School system he worked so hard to build up. The Opposition had asked for information on many public expenditures, but had been told to go down to the Public Works Office and look for it themselves. The Government had no right to give works of this kind without tenders being called for. He would like to know if the *Herald* office got any share of this money. These reports would not cost $50 and yet the printing of them is the only thing the Government offers as an excuse for spending over $300 He (Mr. F.) believed the *Herald* had been subsidized to denounce the Opposition.

If the Government paid public money for corrupt purposes, it is time the country knew it. It is well known that the Public Works Department is used for corrupt purposes, and, no doubt, some of the money that is charged to the Prince of Wales College went in this way.

Hon. Mr. SULLIVAN said if honorable members asked for these accounts in a proper way, they will be found to be very much below what the same work cost when the Davies Government were in power, although the work is done by the same firm that did it then. Coombs and Bremner Bros , were the only printers who were in a position to do this work, and when tenders were asked from them of what they would do it for, Bremner Bros., offer was found to be at the lowest rate.

Mr. YEO said this seemed only to be a small matter as the bulk of the printing is let by tender. The honorable Leader of the Government took credit to the Government the other night, when making his Budget Speech, for the correctness of his estimates. This year we find they are asking $2,000 less for Education than was expended last year, notwithstanding the Superintendent of Educaion in his report said as follows : " The Government expenditure for Education shows a conssderable annual increase since the enactment of the present school laws. This increase is likely to continue at the same rate for years to come. The expenditure in the direction in which this increa e is shown is not directly under the control of the Board of Education, but is dependent upon conditions which the Department of Education cannot restrict " Every part of the Annual Report of Public Schools for 1884, said that the expenditure was increasing or should be increased and yet the Government say that the expenditure this year will be less than it was last year. There is no curtailment mentioned in this report and honorable members cannot see where the saving is to be effected. It is only deceiving the country to submit such estimates to the House. Do the Government propose reducing the expenditure on the Prince of Wales College, notwithstanding the Principal of that Institution in his report says as follows : " Notwithstanding the increased difficulty of our entrance examination, the numbers in attendance at the Institution are as high as ever. But we are constantly reminded of the inadequacy of the accomodation to the proper discharge of our duties.' The Report of the Superintendents of Education said that no improvement was visible from the expediture of over $1,800 last year and how can the Government expect to spend less on that building this year? The honorable Leader of the Government had given a short explanation of why the expense of Printing and Stationery would be less this year, but that is the only explanation honorable members have received of how the amount of this resolution will be reduced below what the expenditure was last year.

When Vouchers are refused, honorable members had a right to a verbal explanation, so that they can satisfactorily explain these matters to the people. It may be said that this money is being spent for improper purposes and unless honorable members receive every information about these expenditures, they will not be in a position to contradict such accusations.

Hon. Mr. FERGUSON, said explanations had been over and given over again to the Opposition respecting this resolution, but they are determined not to be satisfied. It has been pointed out to them that the repairs on the Prince of Wales College last year were put on the outside of the building and to the heating apparatus. The report of the Principal of that Institution referred to improved accommodation for classes, but the Government have not made up their minds to do what that gentleman wants. The other night the honorable Leader of the Opposition in his Speech on the Budget, did not blame the Government for increased expenditure in this Deprtment, as he (Mr. Y.) knew this expenditure was not controllable. The repairs to the foundation and heating apparatus of the building and the extra amount for printing will not be required this year, so the Government have every reason to believe that the expenditure in this Department will be considerably decreased. Nearly the whole amount of this resolution is fixed by Statute and there is nothing debateable in it. The question of

Education might have been discussed when Mr. Speaker was in the Chair, but it is only wasting the time of the House to continue discussing what so often has been fully and satisfactorily explained.

Mr. J. R. MacLean said although the explanations that had been given respecting these items, might be satisfactory to the honorable Commissioner of Crown Lands, yet he (Mr. McL.) would like to have an explanation of the reason why the estimate for Education, had, last year, been exceeded by $3,000. He did not see how they could keep down the expenditure this year, unless some of the money paid last year had been missapplied

Mr. FARQUHARSON wanted to know what the Government intend doing respecting the Inspector's of Schools. The Superintendent of Education, in his report, had recommended the appointment of an additional Inspector. This was a most important part of the report. His idea would be to have three Inspectors appointed and to amalgamate the office of the Secretary of the City Schools with that of the City Clerk, whereby a considerable saving would be effected, enough almost to pay an additional Inspector.

Hon. Mr. PROWSE wished to call the attention of honorable members to a part of the Annual School Report for 1884, which the Opposition had not quoted. It is as follows : " During the year covered by this Report, much activity has been manifested in educational matters throughout the Province. The teachers as a class labored zealously, and, in the great majority of cases, successfully during the past year. Schools have been set in operation which had been closed for several years, and many districts formerly indifferent have been aroused to the importance of the advantages placed within their reach. Altogether the past year has been the most satisfactory in its educational results since the introduction of the Free School system." He (Mr. P.) did not see any reason why the Opposition should cavil at the way the Government were conducting our educational matters. The Opposition had quoted nearly the whole of the Report of the Superintendert of Education but had omitted the summary, which contained the gist of the whole matter, and judging from what he had just read, should be satisfactory, not only to the Government and Opposition but to the whole Province. It is true the Superintendent of Education had suggested some improvements that could be made, notwithstanding this fact, the manner in which our public schools are conducted was highly creditable to the Board of Education and should be satisfactory to the whole Island.

Mr. D. C. MARTIN said, no doubt the present school system had been successful and was the best one that could be adopted, but many of the people are in favor of doing away with the supplements to the teachers. The amount paid a

s

supplements do not appear in the Public Accounts and he (Mr. M.) thought they should be entered there. If the school system is to be fostered, the Superintendent's opinion that three Inspectors are necessary, should be regarded. Three Inspectors are required to go all over this Province and give each school the necessary attention. We know that last year, the Inspector of the western division gave in no report, and honorable members from Prince County should insist that the report of what was done in that section should be presented to this House. Notwithstanding all that had been said by honorable members of the Government, the fact remained that the Principal of the Prince of Wales College said that no improvement had been made to that building by the expenditure of the large sum, that the Public Accounts show had been paid out on account of it.

Hon. Mr. GORDON said while he admitted that the Opposition had only done their duty by criticizing the actions of the Government, the question might be asked, who are the Government? It is well known that the Government are simply the men whom the House selects to carry on the business of the Province. If the Opposition are not satisfied with the conduct of the Government the proper course for the honorable Leader of the Opposition to pursue is for him to move a vote of want of confidence, and if the majority of the honorable members of this House think as he does, the Government

must resign. From the knowledge of the country that he (Mr. G) had, he would venture to predict that the present Government had a long lease of power. The people consider it almost a miracle that the Government have been able to conduct the business of the Province in the satisfactory manner that they are doing, without an Assessment Act. He (Mr. G.) had said before and would again repeat it that when it was necessary to impose an Assessment Act, he would support it ; but until it is necessary to do so, it would be improper to put taxation on the people. From what he had seen of the actions of the Government, he believed, the revenue of the Province was carefully and judiciously expended.

Mr. FARQUHARSON said if the honorable senior member. for Georgetown can justify the Government in voting $2,800 a year for the Georgetown ferry, when they are $69,000 in debt, up to the 31st December last, it is no wonder he (Mr. G.) now supports them. It cannot be contradicted that the Province is deeply in debt. The Opposition have not yet commenced to criticise the doings of the Government. We are going to investigate the Public Accounts in a thorough manner and let the people see how their money is wasted. It could not be expected that honorable members of the Opposition would approve of the actions of the members of the Government. The Government have run the country into debt and we condemn them for doing so. We say that this Government is an incompetent

e. We want to see unnecessary penses cut down. The Commis- ner of Crown Lands should be rned out of his office. The Land ffice shou d be under the manage ent of the Leader of the Govern- ent whereby a large saving could e effected.

Mr. J. R. MacLean said,—Not- ithstanding what had been said y the honorable member for eorgetown there was a great deal f dissatisfaction in the country, specially in Kings County. No oubt the honorable member had iven an outline of what the Gov- ernment intended doing when he (Mr. G.) said he would vote for the imposition of an Assessment Act. If the Assessment Act had been continued during the past three years and a small amount collected thereby, the refunds we have re- ceived from the Dominion Govern ment might have been capitalized, and we would have our finances in a much better condition than we now are, with a debt of $128,000 The Davies Government had a small debt of $40,000, but by im- posing a small assessment they had been able to go out of power leaving a surplus of $3,000.

Resolution put and carried.

On motion of the honorable Mr. Sullivan Mr. Speaker resumed the Chair, and the Chairman reported that some progress had been made and asked leave to sit again.

Mr. D. C. MARTIN asked the honorable Commissioner of Public Works to lay on the table of the House, statement of expenditures on certain Public Works in the Fourth District of Queen's County. He (Mr. M.) said he repeated this question because the statement submitted by the honorable Com- missioner of Public Works did not give a satisfactory answer to his question, nor did it contain the information he wanted.

Hon. Mr. CAMPBELL said that he had given the only answer that was in his power to give. In re- ference to the information de- sired by the honorable member, all he (Mr. C.) could say was that it was contained in the statement that had been laid on the table of the House. Any further informa- tion can be obtained by the honor- able member if he will overhaul 2,500 road orders that are filed in the office of the Public Works De- partment.

Mr. J. R. MacLean in pursu- ance of notice in the Order Book asked the Commissioner of Public Works if it is the intention of the Government to open up and com- plete a new line of Road from Big Pond to Kelly's Road during the present year. Also, if it is the in- tention of the Government to build a new Bridge at Big Pond, King's County this year.

Hon. Mr. CAMPBELL said it was the intention of the Government to build all necessary Bridges and other improvements that are re- quired in the Province.

Mr. J. R. MacLean in pursu- ance of notice in the Order Book asked the honorable the Commis-, sioner of Public Works, if it is the intention of the Government to open and complete the Tarentum Road in King's County, or any portion of said Road this year in accordance with the request of a certain petition of Lauchlin McDonald and others.

Hon. Mr. CAMPBELL said,— This question no doubt refers to the road leading from Tarentum to Harmony Station. He (Mr.C.) did not know that any more of this road will be opened. What has been opened will be completed.

Mr. J. R. McLEAN in pursuance of notice in the Order Book asked the honorable the Commissioner of Public Works if it is the intention of the Government to put in a culvert and build up the Road at or near O'Hanley's hollow, Souris Line Road, during the present Summer?

Hon. Mr. CAMPBELL said,—There were several bridges that required to be repaired and built in the East Point District. All necessary ones that have been asked for, have been included in the estimates.

Mr. J. R MACLEAN in pursuance of notice in the Order Book asked the honorable the Commissioner of Public Works if it is the intention of the Government to open and complete the new road contemplated between Bear River Line Road and New Zealand, (of which a survey has been made) during the ensuing summer.

Hon. Mr. CAMPBELL said he had been negotiating with the parties who own the Land through which this road will run, and he (Mr. C.) thought that satisfactory arrangements had been made with the parties.

Mr. D. C. MARTIN wanted to know if any other answer would be given to his question respecting expenditures on Acorn's Bridge, and other Public Works in the Fourth District of Queen's County.

Hon. Mr. CAMPBELL said the answer had already been given in the returns and vouchers that had been laid on the table of the House.

Mr. FARQUHARSON wished to know if the statement asked for, by the honorable member for Southport a week ago, would be laid on the table of the House this Session.

Hon Mr. CAMPBELL said the statement was nearly ready and would be laid before the house in a day or so.

On motion House adjourned for one hour.

G. F. O.

———

AFTERNOON SESSION.

Mr. SPEAKER in the Chair.

A message from His Honor the Lieutenant Government, by the Usher of the Black Rod, requesting the immediate attendance of the House at the Bar of the Council Chamber. The House accordingly went up to attend His Honor in the Council Chamber, when His Honor was pleased to give his assent to "An Act to amend 'An Act further to amend the Act to regulate the Registry of Deeds and Instruments relating to the title of land, and to repeal the laws heretofore passed for that purpose," and "An Act to Incorporate the Charlottetown Mutual Fire Insurance Company."

The House having returned,—

Hon. Mr. SULLIVAN, a member of Her Majesty's Executive Council, delivered to Mr. Speaker a message from His Honor the Lieutenant Governor, and said message was read by Mr. Speaker, all the members of the House being uncovered, requesting that the House at its adjournment to-day, adjourn until the 4th day of April, instant.

Resolved, That the House, at its rising to-day, adjourn until the 4th April, instant.

On motion of Hon. Mr. Sullivan, the House resolved itself into a Committee of the whole to consider further of a Supply to Her Majesty.

Mr. BLAKE in the Chair.

Hon. Mr. FERGUSON moved a resolution containing a grant of $1,000 for a General Exhibition and $600 each for King's and Prince County Exhibitions.

Mr. YEO said that this resolution contained only the usual vote for exhibitions. He would like to see it increased, as the prizes had hitherto been far too small for the proper encouragement of exhibitors. People, under those circumstances, do not think it worth the time and trouble to compete.

Hon. Mr. FERGUSON said that the Government were very careful that the vote for Exhibitions shall not be exceeded. There was a small over-expenditure last year of $391.79, but it was nearly met by the balance of $300 remaining on hand from 1883. Owing to the efforts of the Commissioners for the General Exibition in securing gate money, the prizes were largely supplemented. If there had been as good management in the Exhibition for Prince County as in that for King's, last autumn, the amount collected in gate money would have been considerably larger than it was.

Mr. BENTLEY did not complain of the amount expended on the General Exhibition, but the amount granted for the County Exhibitions was entirely too small. Exhibition day at Summerside, last autumn, was a very stormy one, and the attendance was therefore much smaller than it would otherwise have been. At least $1,000 should be granted for each of the County Exhibitions. The cattle and sheep did not appear to advantage on account of the storm; and many who would have brought their animals to the Exhibition, left them at home. Agriculture is a very important industry in this Province, and should receive all possible encouragement. To expend only $500 or $600 in Prizes was next to doing nothing at all. In fact, it would be almost as well to give no prizes at all, and to have a stock competition without them. A larger sum should be granted for this purpose to the two outlying counties. Queen's has many advantages not enjoyed by the other two counties. If stock is to be improved and our farmers encouraged in that direction, a larger sum should be granted. As to the over expenditure for the General Exhibition, last year, he would have asked that King's and Prince be granted a similar favor, were it not for the explanation of the honorable Commissioner of Crown Lands.

Mr. SINCLAIR agreed with the last speaker that the receipts from gate money at the County Exhibitions depended very much on the state of the weather at the time they were held. The Exhibitions should be encouraged to the fullest possible extent. If the General Exhibition were held in rotation in each of the counties, it might work well. If held once in three years in Prince County, he thought the attendance thereat would be nearly as large as in Charlottetown, as the facilities for the conveyance of persons and cattle are equal. Charlottetown is, at present, the only place where shelter is provided for stock, and therefore offers greater conveniences to exhibitors, but the other counties might be placed in the same position in that respect. The city is, however, more centrally situated, having a larger area of country around it.

Mr. RICHARDS agreed to a considerable extent with previous speakers with respect to this matter. There is not as much interest taken in the County Exhibitions as there was some years ago on account of the insufficiency of the prizes to induce competition. The grant now proposed is altogether too small for the purpose intended; but he did not think the country sufficiently advanced for one annual Exhibition for the whole Island. The other two counties have not had the same advantages as have been enjoyed by Queen's County, and it would be well to continue the county exhibitions. The time may come, however, when one General Exhibition will be found sufficient for the Province each year. Until then the vote for the county exhibitions should be increased to give sufficient encouragement to competitors.

Mr. J. R. McLEAN was very desirous to see a larger grant for the county exhibitions,—the sum proposed being much too small to produce such a competition as should take place. Summerside is in a much better position for an exhibition than Georgetown, being more centrally situated. Georgetown is difficult of excess, except by rail. He thought the Government were not acting judiciously in allowing the Stock Farm to go down. They appear willing to allow private parties control of the importation of stud horses, and hese parties charge such high rices for the services of those orses that the poorer class of armers cannot afford to pay them. he Government are very desirous ɔ make the Stock Farm self-ustaining; but they should not be ɔ penurious in a matter of that ind. All the other kinds of stock eed improvement, and importa-ions should be made for that urpose. If some improved stock were imported and sold in the distant portions of the other two counties, it would be productive of great benefit to the country, and he believed it would realize reasonable prices, particularly if well advertised. Farmers residing there have to convey stock purchased by them a long distance, and it is but fair they should be placed in as good a position as those of the more favored portions.

Mr. MATHESON agreed with the last speaker that every facility for the improvement of their stock should be afforded the farmers of the more distant portions of the country, as well as those residing in the neighborhood of the towns. A larger grant should be voted for the encouragement of the county exhibitions. He understood that a large quantity of stock was sold off the Stock Farm last autumn, and that some of it was diseased.

Hon. Mr. FERGUSON said that this was the first time he had ever heard a complaint that diseased stock had been sold from the Stock Farm. He need hardly say that the statement was altogether groundless.

Hon. Mr. PROWSE said that the story respecting diseased stock being sold from the Stock Farm was the first one of the kind he had ever heard. With respect to statements made that the grant to the county exhibitions should be increased, he had to say that he could not agree with them. The object of these exhibitions is not so much to enable people to make money out of them as to pay the expense in connection with their exhibit. If the latter is done under the present arrangement, the object sought is attained. In return, the prize list is advertised, and the exhibitors receive the benefit therefrom. This is of greater advantage to the people than the prizes themselves. He did not think it would be advisable to bring the people all the way from the distant parts of the Island to a General Exhibition. The general attraction is in the local exhibitions, where parties come into competition with their neighbors and those with whom they are acquainted. The competition in Queen's County is open to the whole Province. This is right. The first town in the Province should enjoy the advantage arising from the General Exhibition. The The prizes are small owing to the great variety of articles for which they are offered, but this is a matter for the Commissioners themselves to consider. They could easily reduce the number of prizes, and thus increase their value. If the weather proves unfavorable at the county exhibitions, the appearance of the stock is very much injured, but he did not know that the Government would be justified in providing sheds for it. The explanation given by the honorable Commissioner of Crown Lands with reference to the $391.22 of over expenditure last year was, he considered, satisfactory.

Mr. YEO thought the general complaint was that there was not a sufficient number of articles rewarded with prizes, and that the latter were entirely too small. It is very expensive for people to bring their stock long distances for competition, and those living near the towns have everything in their favor. If this grant to county exhibitions could be increased, it would be money well applied. Charlottetown exhibitions has a great advantage in the sale of a large number of tickets, thereby increasing its funds to $2,400 or $2,500. Owing to bad weather in Summerside at the last county exhibition, the attendance was small. If the grant had been $200 or $300 larger, it could have been well expended.

Mr. BENTLEY supposed the grant was now fixed, but it was a great mistake to make it less than $1,000. He felt certain that people would not have taken their stock to the Dominion Exhibitions at Halifax and St. John were it not for the amount of the prizes offered. A considerable amount had been carried off from those exhibitions by our people in that way. The larger the prizes the greater the inducement to the people to exhibit. Quite a number of gentlemen are annually appointed Commissioners for the management of the exhibitions, who take no interest whatever in them, although a great deal depends upon the Commissioners and officers. Care should be taken to appoint only such men as will take an interest in the matter. He had heard no complaints respecting the stock sold from the Stock Farm, at Summerside, and thought it brought very fair prices. It would be a great advantage to have a large quantity of thoroughbred cattle distributed through the other counties. Farmers are beginning to take a very deep interest in obtaining improved stock, and it should be provided and offered for sale if possible. They cannot import it for themselves, and therefore the Government should take the matter in hand. If our breeds of cattle could be improved as much as the breeds of horses have been the country would be vastly benefitted. Our horses are in great demand abroad, and it would soon be the same with respect to our cattle, if the proper course were pursued.

Hon. Mr. FERGUSON said that perhaps in nothing was greater improvement noticeable in this Province, than in our annual Provincial Exhibitions. These Exhibitions have now assumed very respectable dimensions, and the vast improvement made has been brought about at a very small cost to the Province. This was very much owing to the liberality of the Lieutenant Governors by whose consent arrangements were made whereby a portion of the Government farm was devoted to exhibition purposes. Upon this area, cattle, sheep, horse and cattle sheds have been erected, affording great convenience to exhibitions. Over $1,100 was collected last autumn owing to the fact that all the gate money was collected. Almost three days were devoted to the exhibition. Both buyers and sellers attend. The result is the Provincial exhibitors is fulfilling the object intended, to a greater extent than ever before, and it is improving every year. The exhibition will not be at all inferior, because only $1,000 is voted to meet expenses, as the buildings have all been provided, and that without any additional cost to the Province. At first blush it might be thought that it would be best to have but one exhibition, annually, for the Province, to be held in rotation in each county. But it must be remembered that the facilities for the exhibition in Charlottetown are not possessed by the other two counties, and that if held there it could not be so successful. If the same facilities were possessed by each county, it would be well to have but one good general exhibition, and by centralizing our efforts, larger prizes could be offered. For the present it does not appear that anything can be done but to continue the present method. He thought the Prince County Commissioners should centralize their efforts as their exhibits are somewhat scattered. At Georgetown, owing to a better arrangement, the exhibition was more satisfactory. More gate money was taken owing to the grounds being better enclosed.

Mr. PERRY was in favor of retaining the county exhibitions. People of remote districts do not receive any benefit from the Stock Farm, and cannot compete with those who reside in the vicinity of Charlottetown. No effort has been made to distribute the improved stock among farmers of those districts, as should have been the case. In fact, those farmers should be instructed in reference to the benefits to be derived from the improvement of their stock by persons competent to do so. The farmers of every school district should unite and form a club for the purchase of improved stock, and exhibitions might be held in various sections of the country at which they could compete for prizes. There might be three or four of such exhibitions held in Prince County each year. Under such a system every farmer would try to excel his neighbor in stock-raising. This would be productive of far more good than lectures on "Love of Country." The outlying districts have been cheated out of their rights to a share of the benefits of the stock raised on the Stock Farm.

Hon. Mr. FERGUSON said that the honorable member for Tignish had got up a little exhibition of his own, but he had done so entirely at his own expense. He (Mr. F.) had attended all the exhibitions, but never met the honorable member at one of them, which showed how much interest the latter had taken in them. With respect to the distribution of the stock from the Stock Farm, the honorable gentleman was altogether astray,

The small stock are not sold at the Queen's County Exhibition at all, but are drafted away to Tignish, Alberton, St. Peter's Bay, Cardigan, Montague, etc., and sold to the highest bidders in those localities. The larger animals have been distributed fairly between the counties and sold at the county fairs. This has been done so fairly that no person has any ground for complaint. He held in his hand a statement of the expenditure upon the Stock Frrm during the past twelve years. The farm has been managed, all along, by gentlemen who receive nothing whatever for their services. During the six years before the present Government came into power, viz., from 1873 to 1878, inclusive, the running expenses of the farm amounted to $16,328.95, while during the past six years, viz., from 1879 to 1884, inclusive, the total expense to the Province was only $1,832.54, making a difference in favor of the present Government of $14,496.41. The present Government sold stock from the farm, and so did their predecessors. It is but fair to say that as the farm was improved and the stock upon it increased, more animals were sold. There are no animals now on the farm, except one or two kept for the use of the employees, that are not pure breed. Instead of no benefit to the country resulting from the management of the stock farm, the very contrary has been the fact, as has been shown time and again.

Mr. SINCLAIR said that strangers visiting the Stock Farm are surprised that so few animals are kept there. He thought if there were but one exhibition held in the Province, each year, larger prizes could be given, and there would be more keen competition, as it would be more centralized than at present. If the other counties would provide proper grounds and sheds these exhibitions could easily be held in each in rotation. The people of the other countries do not generally come to the General Exhibition after having attended the local one. If only one exhibition were held each year people from all parts of the Province would attend it, larger prizes would be given, more and better stock would be exhibited, more could be seen, and it would be more attractive to strangers. Our county exhibitions are not improving very much, and people will, of course, lose interest in them to a certain extent. To bring out proper competition there should be larger prizes and more centralization.

Mr. J. R. McLEAN thought the horses now on the Stock Farm are not at all equal to those kept there some years ago. The Government have sold off most of it, in order to make it appear that the farm is self-sustaining. Instead of being behind other farms the Stock Farm should be well stocked with all the best breeds.

Resolution put and carried.

On motion, Mr. Speaker resumed the Chair, progress was reported, and leave obtained by the Committee to sit again.

Hon. Mr. FERGUSON, as a member of Her Majesty's Executive Council, presented to the House,—

Statement of Expenditure by the Government, from January 1st, 1885, to March 31st, 1885.

Ordered, That said statement do lie on the table.

"An Act securing to Baptist Churches of Prince Edward Island the benefits of Incorporation," was, on motion, read the third time and passed.

House adjourned for one hour.

I. O.

Hon. Mr. McDONALD as Chairman of the Private Bills Committee submitted a report to the effect that the Bill intituled "An Act to incorporate the Cavendish Hall Company" is of a private nature and liable to fees, and recommended that the sum of $12 be charged

Report adopted.

Ordered, That said Bill be read the second time to-morrow.

The Order of the Day for the second reading of the Bill intituled "An Act to incorporate the Charlottetown Waterworks Company" having been read, the said Bill was accordingly read the second time.

Mr. BLAKE moved that the Bill be now committed to a Committee of the whole House, and said perhaps it was necessary that he should make a few remarks explaining the provisions of this Bill. This Bill has been introduced by leave of the House in answer to a Petition from certain gentlemen in Charlottetown, who are desirous of forming a Company for the purpose of introducing a plentiful supply of water into the City. It was unnecessary to say a great deal on the necessity there is of such a supply being obtained. It is generally admitted that the time has arrived when such a supply should be accessible to the citizens of Charlottetown. Some time ago there was a great difference of opinion with respect to the necessity of obtaining a plentiful supply of water by means of waterworks, but that difference has been settled. It is now generally admitted that the time to make a movement in this matter had arrived. In former times great objections were taken to make this a city work as the cost of the works would entail heavy expenditure and axation on the citizens. Those objections will all be met by the formation of this Company. No citizen will be obliged to use water from the Waterworks Company if he does not wish to. He (Mr. B.) did not know of any City of the size and importance of Charlottetown without waterworks, and it was time this improvement was made. This Bill is almost a copy of the Bill introduced into this House last Session and upon which there had been considerable discussion. Last year the Waterworks Bill had passed this House, but had been thrown out by the honorable the

Legislative Council on account of a petition that had been presented by the then City Council against it. Since that time an election had taken place and a large majority of the citizens had decided in favor of the introduction of water by a Company into the City; and a Mayor and City Councillors who were in favor of this question had been elected. When the Mayor and five Councillors were elected who were in favor of the Waterworks it showed that the majority of the citizens were prepared to go into the matter and support the introduction of water if a Company was formed. This Bill contains the necessary provisions to enable such a Company to organize with a capital of $150,000 and that they can increase their capital to $200,000. Machinery for electing Directors and other officers of the Company, and provisions for entering land for the purpose of placing pipes and other machinery requisite for the conveyance of the water into the City are also contained in it. The company will also have power to flood land necessary to form their reservoir. The Bill also provides for the appointment of arbitrators to assess the damages caused by the Company's operations or that may be incurred by carrying on their business as a Waterworks Company. As the Bill, no doubt, will be fully discussed when in Committee he would not say any further just now.

Motion put and carried.

House in Committee.

Mr. Bentley in the Chair.

First and second clause read and agreed to.

Hon. Mr. McDonald said this Bill seemed to be going through Committee very quietly this year. Last year there was a great deal of discussion on it. He thought it would be better if the City Council had taken this matter into their own hands as in general companies consider their own interests first and this Company may become a burden on the City. In nearly all cases where companies had been established to supply water to a City, the citizens have had to buy out the Company. People can do without whiskey but they cannot do without water, and it is surprising the quantity that will be used when good facilities are afforded people for obtaining it. It would be better for the City and would cost the citizens less, to build these works as a municipal work. The City could obtain money at a cheaper rate than any private Company and there would not be the same waste of water when every citizen had an interest in the works. Waterworks are generally considered a very good security, and even supposing that 5 per cent. interest had to be paid, it would only cost $7,500 per annum for the amount of capital that is required to start this Company. In a few years the citizens will be regretting that they did not take this matter in their own hands.

Mr. FARQUHARSON said that companies, as a rule are obectionable in matters of this kind; but he first wanted to see what the Company are asking from the citizens. If they are going to bring water into the City it should be good water, not water with frogs and toads, as well as greater impurities in it. This Bill should have a restriction of this nature in it. He (Mr. F.) believed there was good water under their feet. plenty for all household purposes. But as it was impossible to get sufficient water in case of fire, from wells. he was in favor of it being brought into the City by waterworks, if only for fire purposes alone. The late election in the City had shown that the citizens were in favor of waterworks and he would not oppose it.

Mr. BLAKE said the waterworks question had been before the citizens of Charlottetown for a great many years. If the city had to wait until the City Council built the waterworks, it would be a long while without them. One reason why so many approve of the waterworks now, is because only those who use the water brought by the Company will. have to pay for it: and many persons who are now in favor of the introduction of water by means of a Company, would be totally against taxing the City to do so. If people are disposed to put their money into an undertaking of this kind, he (Mr. B.) did not see that any person had cause of complaint. It is a certain fact that the City wants water for fire purposes very badly, and he hoped

the water the Company will bring in will not be of such a kind as the honorable member for West River was so much afraid of. It would be against the interest of the Company to bring any but the purest water into the City.

Clause read agreed to.

Mr. FARQUHARSON asked if there was a clause in the Bill providing that the expenses of valuing land or other property taken for the use of the Company, should be borne by the Company. When an arbitration is held who paid the costs?

Hon. Mr. McLEOD said there was a clause in the Bill which refers to where land is owned by an Infant, Idiot or other persons who are not capable in law of contracting or making sales of land or other property. This clause provides that in such a case the matter shall be referred to the Court of Chancery, who are the guardians of such parties.

Mr. D. C. MARTIN said he did not think such matters should be lelft to the Court of Chancery as it would involve heavy costs, perhaps more than the value of the property, to have the matter decided.

Hon. Mr. MacLEOD said frequently such cases are referred to this Court, especially in the case of lunatics and the cost fall on the lunatic's eptate In this case the Court of Chancery will likely see that the interets of these minors or others, for whom they are guardians, will be protected. In cases where Guardians are already appointed by the Court, these persons will appear in the Court and defend the interests of those they represent, and the Court will decide who will pay the costs. If it was part of this Bill that the Company had always to pay the costs on every case settled by arbitration, it would be very unfair. Many cases might be settled without going to the Court at all.

Mr. D. C MARTIN said there would be hardship in cases where taking land for the use of this Company will compel the person owning it to go the Court of Chancery to have the amount adjusted, such as in cases of persons of unsound mind The expenses incurred in valuing land owned by persons of unsound mind should be borne by the Company in all cases.

Mr. FARQUHARSON said the costs should be paid by the Company as the person of unsound mind can not contract for its sale. In any case the cost of the arbitration should be paid by the Company for they come to my land and take it without any leave.

Hon. Mr. McLEOD,—The matter stands this way. If the Company wants the land of a minor they go to the guardian of that minor and make an offer of what they will pay. If the guardian does not accept this offer the matter then goes to the arbitrators. If the guardian is an unreasonable man

and will not accept the amount the Company are willing to pay, it is not fair to ask the Company to pay the expense that is incurred.

Mr. FARQUHARSON said at present an infant or minor cannot sell his land nor can a guardian make a contract to do so for him ; but this law takes away that safeguard. He (Mr. F.) wished to know what provision was made, in case a person was absent from the Island. The Company might take the property of a person who was absent from the Island and not pay a proper amount for it.

Mr. SINCLAIR did'nt know that a guardian should have the right to appeal. There should be no appeal from the Court of Chancery, were no doubt justice would be done to all parties. The case should be decided in that Court and the costs should be paid by the Company.

Hon. Mr. McLEOD said the only right that may be affected by this clause will be in cases where the Company have to lay their pipes under the ground of minors, and it was not likely that many such would occur. Similar cases had arisen in connection with the Railway but no trouble had come out of them, for the Judge had heard all the matters affecting these cases and had given a satisfactory decision.

Mr. D. C. MARTIN,—In passing Acts we should legislate on principle and should not place laws on our Statutes that might bear heavily on infants or persons of unsound mind. When land of such parties is required by this Company, they had to go to Court in order to get a title to it. This House should protect the interests of parties of this kind against a strong corporation like this Water Company will become.

Clause agreed to, another clause being read.

Mr. FARQUHARSON said this clause left no discretion with the Judge as to the amount of the fine that should be imposed on persons interfering with or damaging the works of the Company. He thought that it was rather hard, as cases might arise where the guilt would not be so great as in others. In fact this clause would defeat the object aimed at, as Judges would not impose so serious a penalty, unless for a serious offence. He moved that the clause be amended by striking out the words "the sum of" and inserting the words "not exceeding" before the words $100.

Clause as amended agreed to.

On motion Mr. Speaker resumed the Chair and the Chairman reported the Bill agreed to without any amendment.

Ordered, That the Bill be engrossed and read the third time on Saturday next.

G. F. O.

___

Mr. SPEAKER in the Chair.

The order of the day for the second reading of the Bill to be intituled : "An Act respecting the Village of Kensington, Prince County," having been read, said Bill was accordingly read the second time and committed to a Committee of the whole House. The House accordingly resolved itself into the said Committee.

Mr. BLAKE in the Chair.

A clause having been read.

Hon. Mr. McDONALD said that this clause was similar to a provision contained in the Act in force in Georgetown 40 or 50 years ago. The assessors went out of office every year, and the regulations made by one set of men could not be worked by their successors.

Mr. BENTLEY said that if there were a permanent Chairman of Assesors appointed by the Government, he would be master of the situation, so long as they chose to keep him in office. This scheme would not prove acceptable to the people of Kensington. This clause was the same as that in the old Bill and no objection was offered to it.

Hon Mr. PROWSE thought this Bill should have been printed, and placed in the hands of every person in Kensington as it asks for privileges and powers that will never be required by that village.

Mr. BENTLEY said that when the honorable member for Murray

Harbor brings in a Bill for a similar purpose from his District, he (Mr. B.) would return the compliment. The Bill is merely intended to enable the people of Kensington to protect themselves against accidents by fire and to enable them to remove nuisances and keep the place clean. The village has already had one serious fire, from which it had suffered severely. The further progress of that fire was prevented, but the people want to be placed in a better position to contend with fires. Fire Enginss and Buckets are needed, and they hope the Government will assist them, as in the case of the other towns. They have a plentiful supply of water in wells.

Mr. ALEX. MARTIN did not think this Bill should be rushed through the House so hastily. In his opinion, it was entirely too lengthy, and after all, it would probably prove to be unsatisfactory. It needed to be amended in some of its clauses.

Mr. FARQUHARSON thought the Bill a very proper one. It was merely the Act of last Session amended.

Mr. PERRY thought the people of Kensington had a right to regulate their own affairs, and to tax themselves as they thought proper.

On motion, Mr. Speaker resumed the Chair, and the Chairman reported the Bill agreed to, without any amendment.

Ordered, That the Bill be engrossed, and that it be read the third time on Saturday next.

Mr. PERRY according to previous notice given by him on the Order Book, asked the honorable Leader of the Government what action was intended to be taken on the Petition of certain inhabitants of Tignish for an additional County Court for that section of the Country.

Hon. Mr. SULLIVAN said that it is not the intention of the Government to establish any more County Courts in any part of the Island.

Mr. PERRY according to previous notice, asked the honorable Commissioner of Public Works whether it was the intention of the Government to open up a public road to the shore at Horse Head.

Hon. Mr. CAMPBELL said there was a petition asking for the opening up of the road, and another against it, presented in 1883. He had been there and had examined the place, and found that there is already a private right of way to the shore, which is a continuation of a road already partly opened.

Mr. PERRY explained that if the private road were shut up or closed it would operate against the best interests of the people as a large quantity of fish is brought up from the shore by that way.

Hon. Mr. CAMPBELL was informed that no person would be

stopped from using that private road; but that the owner did not want to have it open to horses and cattle running at large.

On motion, House adjourned until to-morrow forenoon, at ten o'clock.

I. O.

___

SATURDAY, April 4.

Mr. SPEAKER in the Chair.

Mr. HOOPER, in accordance with notice in the Order Book, asked the Honorable Commissioner of Public Works if the Government have received a petition from the inhabitants of Lot 38, concerning the Conroy Road, and what action the Government intends to take in the matter?

Hon. Mr. CAMPBELL said such a petition may be in his office, but he was not very sure until he had time to examine to see if it was there. It may possibly be in the hands of the Clerk of the Executive Council, as sometimes petitions are sent to him by mistake. After he had seen the petition he would be better able to tell what action the Government intended taking on it.

Hon. Mr. SULLIVAN, in pursuance of a notice placed in the Order Book, introduced a Bill to be intituled "An Act to define the operation of Judgment Liens."

The Bill was received and read the first time, and it was ordered that it be read the second time on Monday next.

House adjourned until Monday next at ten o'clock, forenoon.

G. F. O.

___

MONDAY, April 6.

Mr. SPEAKER in the Chair.

Hon. Mr. CAMPBELL presented a statement of the expenditure of the Public Works Department on Public Buildings during the year 1884; also a statement of the Public Works Department on the steamers *Elfin* and *Southport* in the year 1884.

Ordered, That the above papers do lie on the table of the House.

The Bill intituled " An Act to incorporate the Prince Edward Island Agricultural Mutual Fire Insurance Company " was read the third time and passed.

Cavendish Hall Company.

Tee order of the day for the second reading of the Bill intituled "An Act to incorporate the Cavendish Hall Company " having been read.

Mr. SINCLAIR moved that the Bill be now read the second time and committed to a Committee of the whole House, and said this was a Bill to incorporate a number of persons who were desirous of building a Hall at Cavendish, in Queen's County. Schoolhouses in the country are not very well fitted for holding public meetings in, and this Company intend providing a building in which public meetings of all kinds may be held.

Motion put and carried.

House in Committee of the whole.

Dr. McLaren in the Chair.

After spending a short time in Committee Mr. Speaker, on motion resumed the Chair, and the Chairman reported the Bill agreed to with an amendment.

Ordered, That the Bill be engrossed and that it be read the third time to-morrow.

Hon. Mr. Ferguson, a member of Her Majesty's Executive Council submitted a return of the names of all persons who have not paid any amounts towards the purchase money of their Lands, into the Land Office during the past ten years, the said return having been asked for by honorable member for Campbellton.

House adjourned for one hour.

G. F. O.

———

AFTERNOON SESSION.

Mr. SPEAKER in the Chair.

"An Act to Incorporate the Charlottetown Water Works Company" was read the third time and passed.

Supply.

On motion of Hon. Mr. Sullivan, the House resolved itself into a Committee of the whole, to consider further of a Supply to Her Majesty.

Mr. BLAKE in the Chair.

Hon. Mr. SULLIVAN moved that the following sums be granted and placed at the disposal of the Government, viz.:—

Medical Superintendent's Salary for Hospital for Insane $1,000
Maintenance   17,500

Mr. SINCLAIR wished to know why this grant was less than that of last year. It seemed to him that this and some other votes are lessened for the purpose of making the accounts balance. Such grants should not be reduced unless there is good ground for knowing that the expenses will be less than those of last year.

Hon. Mr. SULLIVAN said that the present vote for running expenses was actually larger than that of last year, as a portion of the latter was expended for necessary repairs. The repairs cost over $1,600. This year it is not contemplated to make any repairs, excepting the most ordinary ones, so that this grant will be actually larger than the amount expended last year for the maintenance of the institution. Some of the repairs alluded to were made on the windows, in making them secure so as to prevent the escape of the patients. Iron shutters were put on the windows. These were very expensive, but they were thought necessary for the safety of the inmates. Some time ago, one or two of the patients escaped and it was necessary to prevent a repetition of it. All the items of those repairs are contained in the Report of the Public Works Department, now on the table.

Mr. FARQUHARSON said that the expenditure on this institution is very large, but honorable members would vote for it with pleasure, as it is a necessary one, and for the benefit of an unfortunate class of our people. There should be more room for male patients. The rooms occupied by the Doctor should be utilized for the patients. It is just a question whether a Doctor should reside out there at all. The building is now very properly connected with the city by telephone, and a Doctor could be sent for at any time. He hoped the Government were prepared to express their opinion on this point. If more room is urgently required, as he believed it is, the Superintendent should reside elsewhere. No time should be lost in carrying this out. Many patients will be glad to pay the fees required for their maintenance, and to obtain admission to the Institution. The Superintendent might just as well as not reside in the City, be within call at all times, and thus cause a considerable saving of expense to the country.

Hon. Mr. FERGUSON called the attention of the House to the continued increase in the cost of maintenance of this Institution. Years ago, he stated that it would require about $20,000 per year to meet running expenses, and experience has proved that he was not far astray in his estimate. The following statement will show the expenditure for maintenance of the Asylum under the present and previous Governments. It will also show the increased cost of the new establishment compared with old one :—

PREVIOUS GOVERNMENTS.

In 1873 the sum of	$ 4,542.00
1874 "	7,462.82
1875 "	9,457.00
1876 "	11,791.14
1877 "	9,647.40
1878 "	10,189.26
A total of	$53,077.62

PRESENT GOVERNMENT.

In 1879 the sum of	$11,758.12
1880 "	15,030.96
1881 "	14,290.98
1882 "	18,508.67
1883 "	16,828.40
1884 "	19,034.25
A total of	$95,451.38

The proposed grant this year is $18,500. It will be seen that the expense of maintenance is creeping up to $20,000 per annum, and, in time, will probably exceed that sum. As compared with the six years expenditure under previous Governments the six years under the present Government have cost $42,373.76 over the amount spent by their predecessors.

Mr. BEER thought the grant now proposed for the maintenance of the Hospital for the Insane sufficiently large under our present circumstances. He was not altogether satisfied that the Institution could not be run for less money than it now costs. In fact, the expense of maintenance is rather more than the country should be called upon to pay. The cost per head per week is about $2.81. This he thought rather an excessive charge, and he believed the Institution could be well maintained for much less money. He was perfectly willing that the patients should have all the necessaries required, but did not think there food should cost so much. Some of the patients might, also, earn something by working on the land adjoining, and would probably be benefited in health thereby. They could easily raise all the roots required for the use of the Hospital. When the militia are on duty, it costs only 17½ cents per man per day to supply them with the very best food. He was surprised that the Government had taken no heed to the recommendation of the Superintendent with respect to means for extinguishing fires, in case the latter should break out. That official states in his report that no new patients have been admitted since the month of August for want of room; and that the present accommodation is wholly inadequate to meet the wants of the country, especially with reference to male patients. The Superintendent thinks a new wing to the building should be erected, but this is too much to expect from

the present Government. Hardly a week passes without applications for the admission of patients, and accommodation should be provided for them. When the number of people of unsound mind, for whom no provision is made, is considered, an indignant public will certainly protest against such a policy on the part of the Government. Why has not a boat been supplied for the use of the institution to rescue patients who go into the river? Several narrow escapes from drowning have taken place. The *Examiner* newspaper deserves credit for having brought this matter prominently before the Government. If any patient should be drowned, the blame would certainly be laid upon the Government, unless a boat is provided. He was glad that telephonic communication between the Hospital and the city had been established.

Hon. Mr. PROWSE did not understand why this discussion had been forced upon the Committee at the present time. The honorable members for Southport and West River should have been a little delicate in bringing on such a discussion. Had it not been for the investigation which took place by a Committee of the House, and the damaging report which they made, he (Mr. Prowse) believed the Asylum building would not be standing to-day, as it would have tumbled down. He, himself, had written some letters pointing out the course which the Davies Government should have pursued in reference to that matter. No wonder that they became unpopular and lost the confidence of the country. He supposed the honorable member for Southport remembered very well how very unwilling he (Mr. Beer) was to leave the Speaker's Chair. The honorable member will have to behave himself a great deal better than he has been doing of late before he will get back to it again. Were it not for the efforts of the Committee alluded to, we would not have such a building as we have at present. He was always of opinion that the large amount of money expended upon it was sufficient to provide accommodation for a much larger number of patients than the present building can contain.

Mr. BEER was surprised at the remarks of the honorable member for Murray Harbor, who was a member of the Davies Government, and who remained a member of it after the investigation alluded to had taken place. If the work was carried on in so inefficient a manner the honorable member must have been to blame for it. Can he justify his conduct? If there was anything wrong on the part of that Government why did not the honorable gentleman resign his seat? The honorable member's remarks in reference to his (Mr. B.'s) being in the Speaker's Chair were pointless, and were only intended to draw off the attention of the House from his own shortcomings. The return which was laid on the table of the House in reference to repairs made on the Asylum buildings was not the one he had asked for the other day. This return does not state what the money was paid for,—whether it was for labor or materials. He would therefore ask the honorable Commissioner of Public Works to lay on the table of the House the vouchers relating to the work.

Hon. Mr. FERGUSON did not know what particular functions his honorable colleague felt called upon to discharge. The honorable gentleman had asked why it was that the Government had not carried out the recommendations of the Superintendent of the Asylum, and voted the money necessary for that purpose? The Government are not bound to grant whatever sums of money are asked for by officials at the head of any public department, unless they see that it is really required. He (Mr. F.) supposed the honorable member wished to try his hand at taxation, as he was at present doing in another direction, and was endeavoring to induce the Government to come down with heavy expenditures without regard to the wishes of their constituents or the country. He thought he had a duty to perform with regard to his constituents, and to read, mark, learn, and inwardly digest what the Expenditure should be. The Government think it their duty to exercise the greatest possible care in dealing with this institution. It appears the honorable gentleman considers the patients in the Hospital for the Insane too well fed, because an expenditure of $17\frac{1}{2}$ cents per day was sufficient to keep each militiaman in fighting trim. The honorable member should remember that the Camp was not heated by steam, neither was an expensive building to be kept in repair for their accommodation. On making proper inquiry, he (Mr. Beer) will find that from 20 to 25 per cent. of the outlay is incurred in connection with the heating and repairs of the building. Patients require also to be clothed out of this money. Looking at these facts, he did not think the cost of maintenance was excessively high. This Institution is certainly not more expensive than others of a similar kind elsewhere. All supplies are puchased with the greatest possible care. The coal was not purchased by tender last year but it was procured on very advantageous terms. This was owing to the fact that year after year contracts for the coal supply had fallen into the hands of men who, notwithstanding the most strenuous efforts on the part of the trustees of the institution, did not supply the kind of coal for which they contracted. Last year, therefore, the Trustees pursued a different course, and it was the first time they received satisfaction in the supply of coal. The arrangement was made without regard to political patronage. It is a matter of satisfaction to the Government that all the supplies for the institution are furnished on strictly business principles. Although the expense of maintaining the institution is higher than they wish to see it, it is as low as they can expect to make it, having regard to the interests of the unfortunate inmates. If the recommendation of the Superintendent were adopted to-morrow, and the proposed cottage built for his

accommodation, the rooms vacated would not be suitable for the reception of patients, as they are much larger than if built expressly for that purpose.

Mr. J. R. McLEAN asked what was to be gained by having a report on the Hospital for the Insane if it was to be of no advantage to the Government? It appeared to him. that the want of accommodation for male patients is one of the most important questions to be settled in connection with this institution, for there are numerous instances where parties had been refused admission who should have been received had there been sufficient room for them. He knew one poor unfortunate man who was discharged and sent home to his people, who had to bear the expense of sustaining him. If there is not sufficient accommodation for male patients in the building, why do the Government not provide it ? The cottage proposed by the Superintendent should certainly be built. This would leave more room for patients, and would be a great advantage.

Mr. PERRY saw no charge for fish used in the Hospital for the Insane. It is strange that no fish is used there for there must be parties there who do not partake of meat on certain days of the week. If these persons are compelled to violate the rules of their Church in that respect, a great injustice is done them.

Hon. Mr. SULLIVAN, — These

persons are not responsible for their conduct.

Mr. PERRY,—Does the honorable Leader of the Government say he is not responsible for the state of matters alluded to?

Mr. FARQUHARSON said that the Government had been rewarding their political friends by giving them contracts to supply the coal for the public buildings without tendering therefor. A particular supporter of Dr. Jenkins at the last partial election for the House of Commons, in Queen's County, was rewarded in that way. This was a very suspicious piece of business. That gentleman obtained a contract last year for $3,800 worth of coal, without tendering for it, and had it weighed on his own scales. He believed that some of that coal laid for weeks and months on the wharf exposed to the weather. He, as one member of the House would protest against this.

Hon. Mr. CAMPBELL said that the honorable member for West River should be the last to find fault with the actions of the present Government in reference to the management of the Hospital for the Insane. Several repairs and alterations had been made in the building during the past year. Rooms in the attic were fitted up for the accommodation of patients. He believed that the Asylum had been managed by the Commissioners on proper business principles. Owing to the fact that inferior coal had been supplied to the Asy-

lum, year before last, truckmen had to be employed, at large expense, to put in an additional supply of superior quality. Having found that the Court House was supplied with a very inferior article, instead of the kind of coal contracted for, the Government compelled the man who put the coal in the vaults to remove the whole of it, which he did at his own expense. No better coal was ever put into the public building than that supplied during the past year by private contract. How was the supply of coal procured by the Davies Government in 1878? Was it tendered for? No. It was supplied by private contract. It appeared to him that what certain members of the Opposition want in brains, they make up in abuse of the Government. So far as the coal supplied to the Government, last year, was concerned they had full value for the money paid, which had not always been the case in former years. The contract was made without any reference to party politics. The young man who supplied the coal was found strictly honest in every respect.

Mr. FARQUHARSON,—How did the honorable the Commissioner of Public Works know whether he received the full quantaty of coal charged for, or not? It was impossible for him to say whether he did or not. This was the first time a contract of this kind was let in that way. The fact that a large quantity of coal had to be ordered to be taken out of the vaults of the Court House on account of its being of inferior quality had nothing to do with the matter of letting by tender. To enter into a private contract for a supply of coal to the extent of $3,800 was decidedly wrong, particularly during an election contest.

Mr. BEER contended that the Government were remiss in the performance of their duty in not obtaining the supply of coal for the public buildings by public tender He noticed that the coal supplied last year had cost forty-two cents per ton more than that of the previous year. By demanding and securing good and proper security, any party can be forced to comply with the terms of the contract. The very idea of purchasing a supply of coal otherwise than by public tender is reprehensible. He believed that about $20,000 in all had been expended, last year, by the Government in private contracts. Perhaps the amount was still larger. It appears that $535 was expended for milk, last year, for the use of the patients in the Hospital for the Insane. That would have gone a long way in keeping a number of cows. Again $602 were paid for potatoes, $82 for straw, and $122 for a waggon. He thought some explanation should be given regarding such expenditures.

Hon. Mr. FERGUSON said that with reference to the cost of coal for the public buildings during the past year, any person could see whether or not the price had been excessive. Almost every person knows the price of coal at the Pictou mines. In former years, when tenders were received it was found that they were actuaally below the amount for which the article tendered for could be supplied. Under such circumstances, it was clearly the intention of the tenderer to supply an inferior article. There is what is called "Bank coal," which was supplied year after year notwithstanding the efforts of the honorable the Commissioner of Public Works to secure the article contracted for. Such a result was inevitable when parties tendered for the supply at less than the cost price. More particularly was such the case in 1883, and the Commissioner of Public Works was under the necessity of insisting that a cargo of this inferior coal be taken out of the vaults of the Law Courts after it had been placed there by the contractor. The Trustees of the Hospital for the Insane and the Government made a close calculation, and found that money would be saved to the country by contracting with a reliable party to supply the kind and quantity of coal required for that Institution. They did so and the result has been eminently satisfactory. The extra sum paid last year, for coal, was for the quantity supplied to make up for the deficiency in the quality supplied during the previous year. Although the price paid last year was a little higher than that of 1883, the Government had the satisfaction of securing the coal contracted for, in good condition. The old Lunatic Asylum property still belongs to the Government, and a quantity of hay is cut and saved from the grounds every year. With respect to the waggon, the old one belonging to the Institution became unfit for use, and a substantial new one, which could be used either as a driving or express waggon, was purchased as advantageously as it could be secured for in Charlottetown. There was a small item for stable hire for the use of the Supervisor when he comes to town on official business.

Mr. SINCLAIR said that since August last, it appeared from the Report that no patients have been admitted to the Asylum for want of sufficient room, and yet no monies is to be expended this year for additional accommodation, This is a very serious matter. What is to be done in the case of those who apply or have already applied, for admission? Have the latter been sent back to the country to be cared for by their friends? The Government should surely provide the requisite accommodation. This matter should not be overlooked. It is not to be supposed that insane people must be cared for by their friends while the latter are contributing to the support of a public Institution like this. Accommodation must be provided for all insane persons who apply for admission to, and comply with the terms of the Institution. He hoped the Government would exhibit sufficient manhood to make such provision. He did not think the explanation respecting the supply of coal at all satisfactory. The safest and cheapest course is to let all such contracts by tender, under proper security. Under such circumstances, there can be no difficulty in compelling a man to fulfil the terms of his contract. He hoped the Government would not fail to make provision for the accommodation of a larger number of patients in the Building.

Hon. Mr. SULLIVAN did not state that the Government would make no repairs in the building used as Hospital for the Insane, this year. Repairs are needed every year, in that building, as well as in every public building. It will be necessary to make very considerable repairs in it, but they will not cost anything like the sum expended last year. The honorable member for Strathalbyn referred to the fact that officials at the Asylum last year were hampered for want of room for new patients. During the months of August and September, one or two patients were refused admission, not because there was no accommodation for them but because they were not considered fit subjects for admittance to the Institution. There is no need, at present, to refuse any fit subjects admission thereto. It is frequently the case that when persons are found to be troublesome at home their relatives think they should be admitted to the Asylum. As honorable members were perfectly aware every person who is a little silly is not fit to be admitted to that Institution. A doctor's certificate must first be procured. Unless this is produced no person has a right to apply for admittance. Unless something very extraordinary hap·pens, there is ample room in the building for all new applicants. He did not think there is any danger that any fit person will be refused admission during the year. Letting the coal by public competition is a very good method, but it sometimes happens that a better arrangement can be made with a known trustworthy person by private contract. The latter was the case last year, and the result justified the action of the Government with reference to the matter. It gave perfect satisfaction. There is nearly enough coal now on hand to last until next Autumn, or the end of the year; and the Government will not be under the necessity of purchasing a large quantity early in the season when vessels are engaged in other kinds of trade.

Mr. D. C. MARTIN said that the members of the present Government, when in Opposition, always contended that all public contracts should be let by tender, yet it appeared that during the past year contracts for Public Works to the extent of over $21,000 had been entered into without any public competition whatever! The argument advanced by the Govenment respecting the contract for supplying the public buildings with coal is childish and foolish. The honorable Commissioner of Public Works had a right to send a man to see that the proper kind of coal was being supplied and placed in the vaults, and not have waited until it was all in before making an examination. In his opinion,

the Government were not justified in pursuing the course they did in letting public contracts by private tender. The system was a bad one, and did not result in an economical use of the public funds.

Resolution put and carried unanimously.

Hon. Mr. SULLIVAN moved that "a sum sufficient" be granted and placed at the disposal of the Government for the consolidation of the laws of the Province; and for Legislation $12,800.

Mr. SINCLAIR wished to know whether this consolidation was intended to be only a sham, as had been the case for some years past.

Mr. FARQUHARSON had expected the Government would have had some policy to propound for the purpose of reducing the expense of legislation. No less than 43 men are now engaged in legislating for this small Province in the local House alone. He believed that the people were opposed to the expenditure of so large a proportion of the public money in this way, and he was prepared to reduce the cost of legislation, so far as his vote was concerned. The want of action with respect to this matter will cause a feeling against the Govenment when they appeal to the country.

Mr. J. R. McLEAN said that every member of the House and every man in the country knew that our laws are in a very mixed condition for want of consolidation. Amendment after amendment had been made to certain Acts, and magistrates find it almost impossible to decide what the law really is in certain cases. Even the lawyers themselves frequently give wrong opinions in important cases, owing to the condition of our Statutes It is almost impossible to find the true bearing of those statutes in many cases. If $5,000 or $6,000 were expended in the consolidation of our laws, it would be money well expended. But he believed that the legal fraternity are not desirons to have it carried out, as their interests lie in the opposite direction. With respect to the grant for legislation, he would like to know whether there is ever to be any reduction of the cost of legislation in this Province. The Government should devise some plan to bring it about. He wished to know what they intend to do about it.

Mr. SINCLAIR.—Do the Government intend to take any action in regard to the consolidation of the laws this year?

Hon. Mr. SULLIVAN said that the honorable member had a right to know whether or not the Government intend to take the action alluded to: but he had no right to attribute motives to honorable members.

Mr SINCLAIR,—If this vote for consolidation of the laws is only intended for a sham, it should not be passed. With reference to the vote for legislation, he thought it high time it should be reduced by passing such a measure as would

effect the object desired. He hoped the necessary provision would be made for this next year; and that the time will soon come when not more than half of the present grant will be found sufficient. He had long been of the opinion that two Chambers are not now required in the Legislature of this Province. He thought it would be necessary to have an amalgamation of parties in order to deal with this question. If the Government undertake to legislate upon it without regard to the Opposition, they will find themselves just as far from attaining their object as they formerly were. The other Branch of the Legislature must be consulted on the matter and a Committee of the best men of both parties appointed to make the best arrangement possible. It should not be a partizan affair. If ever the Government intend to take any action on this matter, they should do so next Session. There are 43 members in both Houses meeting day after day and doing little else than absorbing a certain portion of the public funds.

Mr. D C. MARTIN was sorry that no fixed amount was placed in the resolution for the consolidation of our Provincial laws, as it had become an absolute necessity that action should be taken in reference to this matter. Our laws badly need consolidation and revision. It appeared to him that this vote of "a sum sufficient" really meant that the Government intend to do nothing at all. The matter should be attended to at once. So far as the expense of legislation is concerned, it is now generally acknowledged that it is much too large for the work done. The House has been sitting over three weeks, and has only passed two or three small Bills beside the Acts of Incorporation. Some scheme should be devised and discussed to lessen the present cost of legislation in this Province,

Hon. Mr. FERGUSON supposed the Opposition desirous of a change in the management of public affairs. The Government made most strenuous efforts during their first Session to lessen the cost of legislation but were defeated by the Opposition Party, in reference to that matter. Time and again a measure having the same object in view was passed by this House and was defeated in the Council. When the Government found they could not carry either of their measures into effect, they proposed that both Branches be dissolved and an appeal be made to the people on the question; but the Opposition Party opposed it, although one of their number suggested it. When the Government appealed to the country in 1882, they were sustained; but the Council had a majority of Opposition members, and resisted every attempt to reduce the expense of legislation. However. the Government succeeded in reducing the total sum from $18,000 to $12,000 per annum, or nearly fifty per cent. One thing is clear, and that is, the Opposition have done all they could do to prevent the Government from carrying any measure through the

Legislature, having that object in view.

Mr. BEER moved that Mr. Speaker take the Chair and that progress be reported.

Motion put and lost.

Mr. BEER thought the Government should have introduced a measure having for its object the reduction of the cost of legislation. One-fourth of the present number of members could easily have performed all the works done during the present session in one-fourth of the time spent thereon. It is well-known that the Leader of the Government in the Upper House, when the Bill to abolish the Legislative Council was passed by this House, took effectual steps to defeat it. Why did not the Government call that honorable gentleman to account for his action on that occasion? Why did they not ask him to resign his seat as a member of the Executive? The fact that they did not do so showed their insincerity.

Hon. Mr. SULLIVAN said that the Honorable Joseph Wightman was Leader of the Government in the Upper House at the time alluded to by the honorable member for Southport. Now, that honorable gentleman recorded his vote in favor of the Bill for the abolition of the Council. The honorable member made a very ingenerous and improper charge against that gentleman, in asserting that he was insincere in his action, and his charge is without any foundation in fact. Mr. Wightman could give no better proof of his sincerity and earnestness in reference to the question at issue on that occasion, than by voting for the Bill introduced by the Government. But the Opposition in the Upper House voted against it and defeated it. All the objections and obstacles thrown in the way of the Government to prevent the passage of the Bill, were supported by the entire Opposition of both Houses. It is thus clear that the present complaints of the Opposition with reference to this matter are thoroughly insincere. The honorable member for Strathalbyn is, no doubt, laughing in his sleeves at the result of their action. However, the Government have enormously reduced the cost of Legislation, and have saved under that head alone no less than $25,000. He (Mr. S.) had several times voted in favor of reducing the allowance of members of this House to $100 each, but was opposed by the honorable member for Strathalbyn. If honorable members of the Opposition, who wish to reduce the cost of legislation, think they have not earned their sessional allowance, they need not ask for it at all. With reference to the consolidation of the laws, it is the intention of the Government to avail themselves of the present vote to have it carried into effect.

Mr. BEER said that the Government should introduce a Bill providing for Biennial Sessions of the Legislature. In some of the States of the American Union, such a law is in force.

Mr. J. R. McLEAN did not agree with the proposal to provide for biennial sessions of the Legislature. He did not believe than many people in this Province are desirous of abolishing the Legislative Council.

Hon. Mr. FERGUSON had good reason to believe that if the Government would come down with a measure to establish a system of biennial sessions of the Legislature, the Opposition would strongly oppose it. To show the great saving effected by the present Government in the cost of Legislation during the past six years, he would submit some figures showing their expenditure as compared with that of previous Governments from 1873 to 1878 inclusive, viz:

PREVIOUS GOVERNMENTS.

Expenditure for Legislation, 1873,	$18,098.18
" 1874,	18,255.58
" 1875,	18,218.80
" 1876,	16,202.98
" 1877,	17,099.62
" 1878,	18,118.12
A total of	$105,993.28

PRESENT GOVERNMENT.

Expenditure for Legislation, 1879,	$16,071.41
" 1880,	13,240.74
" 1881,	13,058.93
" 1882,	12,680.53
" 1883,	12,882.24
" 1884,	12,935.29
A total of	$80,869.14

Difference in favor of present Government, $25,124.14.

Had it not been for the action of the Opposition in defeating the Bill for the abolition of the Legislative Council, there would have been an additional saving to the country of at least $30,000. For the loss of this amount the Opposition are responsible.

Mr. SINCLAIR asked what right honorable members had to receive more than thirty pounds per year, when, before Confederation, that was the regular allowance for the session?

Mr. FARQUHARSON thought that the sessional allowance to members might be considerably reduced, and the general cost of legislation much lessened. If the Government are prepared to bring down a Bill for the purpose of reducing the cost of legislation, the Opposition will be prepared to support it, if it prove a suitable one.

Hon. Mr. CAMPBELL said that the honorable member for West River and his party were responsible for an expenditure of $28,000 which was altogether and unnecessary. But he (Mr. C.) never was in favor of reducing the sessional allowance below $200, as he had yet to learn that the country wants any member to do his work for nothing.

Resolution put and carried.

On motion, Mr. Speaker resumed the Chair, progress was reported, and leave given the Committee to sit again.

House adjourned for one hour.

I. O.

MONDAY, April 6.

EVENING SESSION

Mr. D. C. MARTIN in pursuance of a notice placed by him on the Order Book asked the honorable the Commissioner of Public Works if it is the intention of the Government during the next Summer to open a Road extending the Colville Road to Pinette Bridge in accordance with the prayer of the Petition of the inhabitants of the surrounding districts presented in 1883, or any portion of the said Road?

Hon. Mr. CAMPBELL said it would not be in the interest of the Public to make the expenditure necessary to open this Road. It would be in the interest of the public to finish the Colville Road and that would be done. It was not the intention of the Government to open the road through to Pinette Bridge.

Mr. D. C. MARTIN said he understood that the Honorable Commission of Public Works had promised to open this road to Pinette Bridge. If, however, half the road was opened this summer it would be better than none.

Mr. BEER asked the Provincial Secretarer and Treasury for the account of payments made from the 1st January, 1884, to the 31st of March, 1885, that he had asked for some days ago.

Hon. Mr. FERGUSON said the statement asked for by his honorable colleague had been laid on the table of the House some time ago.

Mr. BEER said the papers put on the table of the House by the Honorable Commissioner of Public Works did not contain the information that he (Mr. B.) had asked for.

Mr. PERRY said he wished to remind the Honorable Commissioner of Crown Lands that the return he (Mr. P.) had asked for some time ago had not yet been laid on the table of the House.

Hon. Mr. FERGUSON,—If the return asked for by the honorable member was so important, the notice asking for it should have been placed on the Order Book earlier in the session. The hands in the Land Office have been so busy preparing the returns asked for by the Opposition that this one had not yet been prepared. The one that had been asked for by the honorable member for Campbellton had been laid on the table of the House to-day. The others will be presented as soon as possible. The returns asked for are so voluminous that they require a great deal of work to prepare them.

Mr. BEER wished to bring to the notice of the Honorable Commissioner of Public Works that the statement laid on the table of the House showing the expenditure on Public Buildings did not contain the information asked for. The return asked for was a statement of the expenditure on these buildings from January 1st, 1884, to March 31st, 1885. If the statement could not be made out the vouchers would do as well.

Hon. Mr. CAMPBELL said he would give the honorable member from Southport the same answer he (Mr. C.) had given the honorable Leader of the Opposition the other day. These vouchers are in the care of the Clerk of the Public Works Department, and will be given to any honorable member who wishes to see them in that office. In adopting this course, he (Mr. C.) only followed the course Mr. Davies pursued when he was Leader of the Government. It is well-known that the auditor often had to go back over these vouchers when checking the accounts against the Government. As there was great danger of them being lost if they were laid on the table of this House, he (Mr. C.) was not justified in bringing them out of the office where they were deposited. Papers that may be of great importance in the future should not be allowed to get lost, and if laid on the table of the House some of these vouchers might get astray.

Mr. PERRY said that he had asked the Honorable Commissioner of Public Works, some days ago, to to lay on the table of the House a detailed statement of the number of bridges carried away in 1884 by freshets and storms, and the amount each bridge had cost to repair, and to whom sold, but no answer had been yet given to his question.

. Hon. Mr. CAMPBELL said the honorable member had all the information he had asked for, in the returns already on the table of the House. It was not to be expected that he (Mr. C.) could go to every supervisor in the Province and get an account from them of the bridges that had been carried away by freshets, distinct from ordinary repairs. Honorable members had any information about the expenditure of his department that it was in his power to give.

Mr. PERRY. — The Honorable Leader of the Government, in his Budget Speech, said that a large number of bridges had been carried away by freshets and storms, and that considerable expense was incurred in rebuilding them. Now the Honorable Commissioner of Public Works said he would not give us this information, and honorable members have no means of knowing whether many bridges had to be rebuilt.

Supply.

Hon. Mr. SULLIVAN moved that the House do now resolve into a Committee of the whole to consider further of Supply.

Mr. FARQUHARSON said, before Mr. Speaker left the Chair, he wished to make a few remarks. He (Mr. F.) did not want to make any very lengthy remarks, nor did he want to go back to the doings of the late administration as the Honorable Leader of the Government had done. When the present Government came into power they had made a great many promises of what they would do. They said they could do without the assessment Act, that Mr. Davies only wanted money for himself and his friends when he imposed that Act, and they also said Mr. Davies had an interest in the Asylum contract, and that the contractors for that building were connected with him. He (Mr. F.) charged the honorable member for Murray Harbor with having made these statements against the late Government. Was that honorable member prepared to prove the truth of these assertions? On account of these false charges, and because the present Government said they did not want any taxes—that they could make ends meet without them—the people had returned them to power. The statement that had been laid on the table of the House this year purporting to be the Public Accounts for 1884, did not reflect much credit on the Government. It clearly showed that they are unable or unwilling to do their duty in the manner they promised. In former years when there was a surplus from the previous year's account, this surplus would be included in the account of the following year, but last year, when as is well-known, they had a heavy deficit, it is not included in this year's accounts, and the Honorable Leader of the Government, in his Budget Speech, told them that there was a surplus of $700 or $800 on the transactions of last year.

In 1881 the honorable Leader of the Government said that any Government that would spend over $250,000.00 per year, would be spending too much money, and yet last year the Government spent $30,000.00, or $30,000.00 over that amount. Is this the way they kept their promises? There was a great cry raised because the Davies Government spent $14,000 without first obtaining a vote of the House, to Macadamize a road that has not cost the country anything since that time, yet last year the Honorable Commissioner of Public Works spent $16,800.00 more on bridges and roads than the vote of this House had authorized him to expend. In 1884 the the sum of $30,690.60 was expended on bridges, although only $22,000.00 were voted for this service. On roads, $23,622.97 were expended, notwithstanding the amount granted for this service at the late session of this House was under $16,000.00 Why were these large expenditures made? We find that over $20,000.00 has been spent by the Honorable Commissioner of Public Works in excess of the sum granted by this House. This large amount has been given to political favorites of the Government. The Government has a few pets both in town and country who are given large amounts by private contract that should be let by public tender. In the first place he (Mr. F.) would like to lay before the House a statement of the sums received by the Government during the past six years. The receipts at the Land Office have be as follows:—

1879	$44,812.72
1880	54,361.59
1881	64,831.75
1882	46,130.62
1883	51,350.03
1884	46,033.74
	$307,520.45

Even if the interest on the amounts due in the Land Office is deducted, which would not amount to over $135,000, the balance of $172,520.45 of capital that has been spent by the present Government while in power, is an average of over $28,700 a year. He (Mr. F.) did not think it right that this large amount should be expended when no extra expenditure is made for permanent Public Works. From assessments during the past six years the Government have received as follows:—

In 1879	$24,318.52
1880	24,923.57
1881	29,034.22
1882	3,663.59
1883	253.82
1884	
A total of	$82,193.72

Notwithstanding the present Government said that the Assessment Act was unnecessary; and that Mr. Davies should have done without it, we find, that while they have been in power, over $80,000 has been collected and expended from this source. They have also received large amounts in windfalls from the Dominion Government. What do these amount to? The Davies Government had the same chance of obtaining these payments if they had chosen to humiliáte thè Province as these honorable gentlemen had done. The Davies Government knew that we had claims on the Dominion Government, but they did not choose to ask for "payments on account" in the way the present administration did.

In 1879 the windfalls
amounted to		$39,700.52
1880	"	17,569.78
1881	"	4,436.78
1882	"	5,050.20
1883	"	
1884	"	52,222.19
A total of		$119,979.47

If the amount received at the Land Office, amounting, as he had shown, to $172,520.45, and the windfalls, $119,979.47, had been capitalized, it would now be $292,-499.92, the interest on which would be over $14,000 a year for all time to come. Instead of doing so the present administration had spent this money for ordinary expenditure, because they had raised a cry against the Davies Government for imposing the Assessment Act, and in consequence of which they rode into power. After spending nearly $300,000 of capital they will now have to impose twice the amount of taxation that was necesssary when the late Government managed the affairs of the Province. There is no doubt but the Government will have to impose direct taxation at an early day. He (Mr. F.) thought that the Government would have given some information respecting the manner in which our expenditure is to be met.

He did not justify all the actions of the late Government. No doubt mistakes had been made by that administration, but as we grow older we should get wiser, and the present Government should show what improvements they had effected. In 1879 the Government presented a statement to the Legislature showing that the Davies Government incurred a debt of $79,000. In it they included every claim they possibly could and left out many assets that should be credited to the late administration. The way the public accounts are now kept they are unintelligible to many people in the country. By the way the accounts are made up the debt at the 31st December last amounted to $53,931.70. This is the amount the present Government admit they are in debt. We find, however, that $4,500 was paid to the Local Banks for interest on over drafts. They say that only six per cent. interest was paid the banks. Will they admit that? The sum paid for interest shows that $75,000 had been borrowed from the banks for twelve months, and yet they ask us to believe that the Province is not running into debt. The Government said they had sufficient revenue, but we now find that last year we had to pay $4,500 for interest. Is that the way to manage the affairs of the Province? They are running the country deeply in debt, and yet they pretend to be the farmers' friends. He (Mr. F.) wished to show the House and the country that this administration is not doing as well for the Province as it should do. It is well known

·that they will lose one half of the $10,000 they say the old bank owed them, the old duty bonds were said ·to be no good in 1879, and ·yet the Government now uses them as· an asset for $5,849.14. They have· also· carried over an amount due by the Stock Farm which has not been included in the public accounts for last year.· This amount of · $652.89 should have been included in ·the liabilities of the Province. It is a most unjust way of keeping the public·accounts, when all the debts are not included. He (Mr. F.) supposed the Government kept a separate account in the banks for the Stock Farm. Was that the proper way to prepare a financial· statement? Putting in assets· that were worthless and leaving out debts that must be paid!

The Public. Accounts show a balance against the Province of	$53,931.70
Loss on account in the old bank $10,689.32, only worth 50%	5,343.66
Duty Bonds (worthless)	5,849.14
Amounts carried over belonging to the expenditure of 1884.	7,436.52
Due by Stock Farm	652.79
A total of	$73,213.81

due the 31st 'of December, 1884. The Teachers' Salary, due on- the 31st December, 1884, was $26,201.50, making $99,415.31, due at the end of last year.· If the statement was made up to·the 31st of March, 1885, when $24,000 additional had to be paid the teachers, we would

find that the Government owed over $113,000. Any man with credit can borrow money, as the Government are doing, to pay their running expenses, but when the farmers find out how the Government have been spending money on friends, instead of paying the debts they should pay, they will drive these men from power. The Government during the past year have spent over $25,000 on political favorites without so much as calling for tenders.

Hon. Mr. CAMPBELL,—Give us the items.

Mr. FARQUHARSON said he would give them the items, but could not do so as fully as if the returns asked for had been tabled at a proper time. In 1878 the Honorable Leader of the Government said as follows :—

Page 110. '' Hon. Mr. Sullivan said it was the first time the Leader of the Government in this Island had refused to bring down the vouchers, and if he would search the history of Legislation of every country, he would not find a precedent for such a refusal. There was no necessity that they should be lost as ·they should be left in charge of the Clerk of the House. It was very well to have the Public Accounts, but they wanted the vouchers to prove the correctness of the Public Accounts."

Notwithstanding the fact that these were the views of the honorable gentleman when in Opposition, he (Mr. S.) and his colleagues now refuses to lay these vouchers on the table of the House. He (Mr. F.) had a list of some amounts paid by the Honorable Commissioner of

Public Works for contracts let without tender or public sale, in 1884, chiefly to political friends.

Southport Ferry Wharf	$1,669.74
Rocky Point	1,056.37
Dredging at Georgetown	125.00
Hayden's Milldam	42.00
Cardigan Ferry Wharf	479.94
North Pinnette Bridge	775.40
Fox River Bridge	330.40
Coal	5,036,54
Provincial Building	3,465.90
Prince of Wales College	1,530.28
Hospital	1,630.13
Government House	934.83

A total of $17,076.53

This is only a part of the expenditure in this way. The whole amount during the past fifteen months will make about $25,000. Men were employed by the day with a supervisor over them, and another superintendent was paid for looking over him, and in this way the money was wasted. It is said that some men support a Government because they have a lively sense of favors to come, but as this large amount was given to one honorable gentleman to expend no doubt the Government will now be supported from a sense of gratitude. In this list we find the sum of $5,036.54 for coal. Will honorable members beleive that this amount was nearly all paid to men who were very active partizans at the late Dominion Election? It is the first time during his (Mr. F.'s) experience in the Legislature that public contracts were given to men who made themselves useful at elections. On the Provincial Building the sum of $3,465.90 was spent besides coal. Where did this money go? How was it expended? We find that W. E. Dawson got large sums of money from the Public Works Department. Over $1,395 were paid this firm in 1884 without tenders being called for. Perhaps the Honorable Commissioner of Crown Lands can explain why so much patronage was given Mr. Dawson! He (Mr. Farquharson) understood that the name of W. E. Dawson appears on some documents in the keeping of the Government.

Hon. Mr. Prowse,—The honorable member should explain what decuments he is referring to.

Hon. Mr. Sullivan said surely the honorable member for West River does not wish a false impression to go abroad about a private individual. He should answer the question of the honorable member for Murray Harbor.

Mr. Farquharson said he understood what he was talking about and would explain the matter in a way honorable members of the Government would not like. Another firm, Norton Bros., got over $500. On this building two firms received over $900 for hardware. Hermans & Son also got a large amount and he would ask any honorable member if value for this expenditure could be seen. The names of these firms are public property, for they have been receiving public money, and the country has a right to know where its money is going to.

Hon. Mr. Prowse,—What about

the name on the public document?

Mr. FARQUHARSON said he was sorry the honorable member for Kensington was not in his place, as he (Mr. F.) had a few words to say respecting the estimates of revenue that had been submitted by the Honorable Leader of the Government. These estimates admitted that our revenue would fall short about $45,000, which amount the Government expected to receive on account of our claim for winter communication. The present Government say we are a happy people, receiving more from the Dominion Government than we pay to them; but the honorable member for Kensington has dissipated that idea. In referring to our claims on the Dominion Government it should be remembered that when the House of Commons resumed the adjourned debate on Mr. Blake's proposed amendment to Sir Charles Tupper's motion, that the Resolution adopted in Committee of the whole, respecting subsidies to certain Railway Companies of Canada be now read a second time, and which amendment was that the following words be added to said motion:—"But this House feels bound to express the opinion that when Canada, (as proposed by said resolution) recoups one of the Provinces for part of the past local expenditure on Railways, should have regard to the past local expenditure in the other Provinces on Railways, almost all of which have been declared to be for the general advantage of Canada; and this

House regrets that the Government, while proposing a measure of relief to one Province, has not taken steps with a view to a fair and proportionate measure of relief in respect of local expenditure in the other Provinces." Notwithstanding the Honorable Commissioner of Crown Lands had told them that Mr. Blake had made no reference to Prince Edward Island when speaking on this subject, it could be readily seen that Mr. Blake's amendment was likely to give this Province some money on account of our having built the Railway at our own expense. Supporters of Sir John voted against the interests of P. E. Island on this occasion; and Macdonald and Hackett went with them. What can we expect when we have men representing us who would do so! It is said that he (Mr. F.) was crazy on the National Policy; but when the interests of the Province were being sacrificed, is it any wonder that men's minds should be excited? He (Mr. F.) believed we should follow the example of Mr. Fraser, of Nova Scotia, who had moved for separation from the Dominion. We were promised before we entered Confederation that the tariff would not be increased, but now our people have to pay heavy taxation through the goods they buy. We have to pay the Government nearly two cents a pound on sugar and an equally exorbitant duty on nearly all other goods. What do we get in return for paying these large amounts? Nothing that is in any way beneficial to our interests. Have any efforts been made to effect a treaty with New-foundland? It is well known that we will have to pay $1.00 a barrel duty on herring, and fifty cents a hundred pounds on dry fish after the 1st of next July, and the Local Government, as it is their duty to remedy grievances of this kind, should have brought the matter to the notice of the Dominion Government. But the Government will do nothing to advance the interests of the Province. They have never called the attention of Sir John and his Government to the large amount of money we have to pay the Custom Houses of the United States in order to sell our potatoes, horses and other produce. Our small traders buy their goods from Canada, but the Canadians do not want anything we have to sell. The present Local Government have not even attempted to show what a grievance this state of affairs is causing. We should legislate on questions of this kind instead of frittering away our time over petty local matters. When the present Government were elected they promised to be the friends of the farmers, but he (Mr. F.) would like to know what they had done to benefit our Agriculturists? Last year they put down $2000 in the estimates for the importation of improved Stock, but not one dollar had been spent for this purpose. He (Mr. F.) supposed it was spent for coal, hardware and stationery! Is that the way to use friends? There were several other matters that he had wished to refer to, but as he (Mr. F.) had not yet obtained the vouchers that were asked for, it

was impossible to finish the statement he intended. Honorable members have no means of knowing the policy of the Government on many important matters. It is time that the Land Office should be looked to. It should be closed at an early day. His honorable friend the member for Tignish had placed a notice on the Order Book in respect to this matter and it was time the question was discussed. The expense of maintaining this office in eating up the receipts. Last year nearly $6,000 were paid as expenses and yet the receipts are constantly decreasing. We have a long list of persons who have not paid the amount due the Land Office and among them we find the names of parties who are actually lending money. Precepts are issued against poor persons, but men who could pay are not forced to do so. Payment should be enforced when men are able to pay and the number of years in which nothing has been paid should not be the rule to follow with respect to the issuing of Precepts. The Government should allow a discount to all persons who paid in their amounts promptly. They accuse the Opposition of trying to prevent people paying the Land Office. It was not true. Every man indebted to that office should pay his money, but to close up the office a discount should be given to poor people in order to induce them to make their payments. He (Mr. F.) did not think there was any necessity of having a head for the Land Office. The present Commission-er may do as much as those who preceded him, but it is well known that the honorable gentleman is very often away lecturing and attending to other matters and the duties of his office can not be very onerous. The honorable gentleman should pay back the five dollars per day for the seventy-five days the honorable member for Tignish told us that the honorable member was absent from the Land Office. If he did so it would show that he was a "lover of his country" more than by giving lectures on that subject. We have to pay too many figure-heads. The trustees of the Asylum, although most of them are members of the Government, receive $250 each. Honorable members of the Government have no right to draw more than $1,300 a year. The honorable Leader of the Government should superintend all the offices and it would only be necessary to have one head for all the departments. We have competent officials in these offices and one person should be able to superintend all of them. It would be necessary to have an Engineer for the Public Works Department but his salary would be saved by the improved condition of the Public Works. The Opposition have no difficulty in showing how $20,000 can be saved in our expenditure each year. We have no need of a political Attorney General and by taking away the heads of all the departments considerable saving will be effected and increased efficiency will be attained in the management of our public business. Where is the money to come from

to pay all these officials? With a deficit of over $73,000 already although he (Mr. F.) was not a prophet, yet he would fearlessly assert that $100,000 will not pay our indebtedness next year. If they don't get more windfalls from Sir John the Province will be hopelessly in debt. No doubt, however, the "Chieftain" will be good to his friends, and he (Mr. F.) hoped they would get enough to pay their indebtedness. We find after all the promises the present Government made, that they could run the Government and make ordinary receipts meet ordinary expenditure, that they have spent $275,387 of what can justly be called capital. Even if they had continued Davies' Assessment Act they would still be $10,-000 or $12,000 behind each year. He (Mr. F.) challenged any person to dispute the correctness of the figures he had submitted, although some of them are not so complete, for want of the vouchers, as they might have been. The Government tell us that they have $24,-200 to get from the Dominion Government for which no doubt they will have to give a "receipt in full" this time. The Dominion Government gave them $53,000 last year on account of the "urgency of the case" and the Local Government will have to give a "receipt in full" for the same reason. We are told that our wharves are free, but he (Mr. F.) would like to know what rate of wharfage we will have to pay in the future. What arrangements did the Government make respecting the matter or did they neglect it ? The Commissioner of Crown Lands should give the explanations asked for, for he is constantly preparing figures. If they have any defense they should make it. But what defense can they make ? When they have run the Province into debt over $73,000 besides paying $4,500 for interest on other amounts of which we have no account, how are they going to pay their indebtedness ? Where is the money to come from ? Can they explain why $20,000 have been given to favorites without tenders being called for ? Why has $16 000 over what this House voted been expended by the honorable the Commissioner of Public Works in one year? Contracts for thousands of dollars are being let especially the one for Bridge at St. Peters Bay, which were never petitioned for ! Honorable members have for years been asking for new Roads and other Public Works in their districts, but can get nothing done. The people who ask least seem to fare off best and he (Mr. F.) would advise the people not to ask for anything while the present administration are in power.

Hon. Mr. SULLIVAN said he must remind the honoroble member that he had not given the explanation he (Mr. F) had promised in reference to the paper of Mr. Dawson that he said the Government held.

Mr. FARQUHARSON said he understood that Mr. Dawson's name was on the bond of a prominent official of the Goverament.

Hon. Mr. FERGUSON said he would, in the first place, refer to the statement just made by the honorable member for West River, respecting a bond which he says is signed by Mr. Dawson as security for the head of a department in the Government. He (Mr. F.) wanted to tell the honorable member and the House that Mr. Dawson is not security for any departmental officer, nor does his name appear on any bond held by the Government as far as I am aware. The honorable gentleman said it was on account of Mr. Dawson's name being on the same bond, that certain supplies for the Public Buildings had been purchased from that gentleman. This statement is in keeping with the general tenor of the honorable member's speeches. Even if Mr. Dawson was security for one of the officials of the Government, was that any reason why no supplies should be purchased from him ? Why should not some goods be purchased from Mr. Dawson when they are required, so long as no more was charged for them than what they could be bought for elsewhere ? The honorable member's conduct in thus dragging the names of gentlemen who are not in politics, and who are highly respected by all the community, into this debate, was most unwarrantable, and shows how far he is willing to go in order to try and damage his opponents. Three weeks had elapsed since this House met, and it is nearly a week since the honorable Leader of the Government made his Budget Speech, to which the honorable Leader of the Opposition replied. The honorable member for Tignish had been allowed to resume the debate on several occasions, and had been given every opportunity to bring all the charges that even he could imagine against the Goverhment. But when the honorable senior member for Charlottetown had answered the honorable member, the Opposition, considering "discretion the better part of valor," allowed the motion to pass, and the House to go into committee without further debate. They have now taken the extraordiary course of opening up the subject again, a course that was never adopted unless some new motion of extraordinary importance was submitted. It is no wonder the honorable member for West River suggests that the public departments should be run without heads. The Opposition is evidently being run in that manner. When the Assessment Act was repealed they said we were starving the public works of the Province; and recommended that assessment should be continued. Since hearing the Budget Speech of the honorable leader of the Government, a change has apparently taken place in their views. They find that taxation is not necessary, that no blue ruin is falling on the Province, and that the popularity of the Government is daily increasing; and they now say that the Government is spending too much money; but they have not one word to say about raising additional revenue by taxation. The Opposition are actually

becoming economical! Who ever heard of such a thing as the Grit party wishing to amalgamate offices and reduce expenditure? They are trying to steal the livery of the Government in order to ingratiate themselves with the country. The Opposition and their organ have been proclaiming that the Province is on the brink of ruin. He (Mr. F) had looked over the estimates of the Opposition for some years past, respecting the indebtedness of the Government, and he would read them to the House:

In 1879 the estimated
deficit was		$118,000
1880 "	"	56,000
1881 "	"	41,000
1882 "	"	24,000
1883 "	"	95,000
1884 "	"	85,000
Altogether		$419,000

Honorable members were aware that he (Mr. F.) had to arrive at these figures by approximation, for it was well known that no two members of the Opposition used the same figures when talking of the amount the Province was in debt in any year. Sometimes we find that their figures for a particular year vary all the way from $15,000 to $120,000. If these deficits had occurred; if the statements of the Opposition were to be relied on, the Government would now be over $400,000 in debt. There is no better way to show how unreliable are the statements of the opposition than to quote from their own speeches.

By the figures of the honorable member for West River, the debt at the end of last year was $73,000, and the honorable Leader of the Opposition said it was $85,000 ; but if their figures of previous years were worthy of the slightest consideration, the indebtedness of the Province would now be $419,000. He (Mr. F.) wished to show the House and the Country that the present administration were more economical in every department of the public service than any preceding Government By doing so, no reflection is cast on honorable members who had formed part of preceding Governments. When he (Mr. F.) showed that the present Government had made better and more economical use of the revenues of the Province, he was only doing his duty to his honorable colleagues, all of whom were alike entitled to credit for the record of the present Government. It is now twelve years since the Province entered Confederation and this term naturally divides itself into two periods of six years each. The present administration have held the reins of power during the latter period.

PREVIOUS GOVERNMENTS.

In 1873 expenditure was $401,661.92
1874   "   435,207.56
1875   "   395,277.43
1876   "   353,327.84
1877   "   381,632.13
1878   "   334,131.29

$2,301,238.17

PRESENT GOVERNMENT.

In 1879 expenditure was $313,845.00
1880   "   257,308.35

In 1881 expenditure was $261,275.51
1882   "   257,228.03
1883   "   270,477.40
1884   "   279,545.35

A total of $1,639.679.67

Saving effected by present Gov'ment $661,558.50

He (Mr. F.) might mention that he had given the figures as they appeared in the Public Accounts. The expenditure in 1878 did not include the $60,000 that was incurred in 1878, but which did not appear in the accounts of that year. This amount is included in the expenditure of 1879, making that year's expenditure greater by that amount, and in that particular the calculation is unfair to the present Government. Without allowing for this amount, which the present administration are not responsible for spending, we find that during the six years the present Government have been in power they have expended $661,558.50 less than was expended by their predecessors during a similar period of six years. In other words, for the last six years, over $110,000 a year has been saved to the Province !

Mr. SINCLAIR said the honorable gentleman's argument had no force, as a Conservative Government had been in power during part of the first period.

Hon. Mr. FERGUSON,—It did not matter what party was in power during the first period, the comparison was equally favorable to the present Government. When the Owen Government were in power there was money in the banks to the credit of the Province, and a demand was made by the people, that, as they were only receiving four per cent. for this money it should be put in circulation by building public works of utility. The excuse cannot be urged in favor of the Davies Government. Mr. Davies declared that the affairs of the Province were in a very bad state, and that it was necessary to resort to direct taxation. He (Mr. F.) did not use these figures to reflect on preceding Governments, but to defend the present administration and to show that they had spent $110,000 per annum less than their predecessors. The present Government are not responsible for passing the Education Act, but that Act has resulted in greatly increasing expenditure. The following statement shows what had been spent for education during the past twelve years, divided as before, into two periods of six years each :

PREVIOUS GOVERNMENTS.

Expended for Education

in 1873,		$59,194.83
1874,	"	61,787.11
1875,	"	60,481.51
1876,	"	60,550.38
1877,	"	80,813.60
1878,	"	65,550.13
A total of		$388,377.56

PRESENT GOVERNMENT.

Expended for Education

in 1879,		$91,007.87
1880,	"	96,213.81

1881,	"	96,489.46
1882,	"	97,411.77
1883,	"	101,193.41
1884,	"	105,185.09
A total of		$587,501.41

Showing an expenditure of $199,123.85 during the six years the present Government had been in power over what was expended for this service during a similar period by their predecessors. In comparing the expenditure of these two periods, you have to add this amount of $199,123.85 to the $661,558.50 of reduced expenditure, as it is an increase of expenditure the present administration are not responsible for. The honorable member for West River took credit to the late Government for building the Asylum. The present Government are not responsible for the excessive cost of that building, although they had to provide about $55,000 of the cost. The size of the building, and the expensive nature of its maintenance, were due entirely to the late Government. The following statement will show the expenditure for maintenance of the Asylum during the two periods as before :

PREVIOUS GOVERNMENTS.

In 1873 the sum of		$ 4,542.00
1874	"	7,462.82
1875	"	9,457.00
1876	"	11,781.14
1877	"	9,647.40
1878	"	10,189.26
A total of		$53,077.62

PRESENT GOVERNMENT.

In 1879 the sum of		$11,758.12

1880 the sum of	$15,030.96
1881 "	14.290.98
1882 "	18,508.67
1883 "	16,828.40
1884 "	19,034.25
A total of	$95,451.38

Showing that the present Government were called on to provide $42,373.76 for the asylum, over the amount spent by their predecessors during a like period.

There are some portions of every Government's expenditure which are not controllable, but there are other expenditures that are directly under the control of the Executive. Such is the expenditure for the Executive Council, which is largely made up of amounts paid members of the Government for mileage, &c. The following statement shows how the present administration have saved the people's money in this respect:—

PREVIOUS GOVERNMENTS.

The Expenditure of the Executive Council was:

In 1873 - - -	$1,578.31
1874 - - -	1,990.85
1875 - - -	2,212.17
1876 - - -	805.64
1877 - - -	2,860.32
1878 - - -	1,645.67
A total of - -	$11,092.96

PRESENT GOVERNMENT.

The Expenditure of the Executive Council was:

In 1879 - - -	$1,931.54
1880 - - -	753.83
1881 - - -	632.21
1882 - - -	403.34

1883 - - -	414.55
1884 - - -	348.14
A total of	$4,484.51

Showing a saving in favor of the present Government of $6,608.45 ! In Legislation the same system of economy had been inaugurated, although, owing to the action of the Opposition in the Legislative Council, as much had not been saved as the Government had hoped. The following statement shows, however, that even with the additional expense of an unnecessary Legislative Council, $25,124.14 had been saved during the last six years:—

PREVIOUS GOVERNMENTS.

Expenditure for Legislation, 1873,		$18,098.18
1874,	"	18,255.58
1875,	"	18,218.80
1876,	"	16,202.98
1877,	"	17,099.62
1878,	"	18,118.12
A total of		$105,993.28

PRESENT GOVERNMENT.

Expenditure for Legislature, 1879,		$16,071.41
1880,	"	13,240.74
1881,	"	13,058.93
1882,	"	12,680.53
1883,	"	12,882.24
1884,	"	12,935.29
A total of		$80,869.14

Difference in favor of present Government, $25,124.14. The Stock Farm also afforded a strong evidence of the good management of the present administration.

Dividing as before, the 12 years since Confederation, into two equal periods, we have the following comparisons:

PREVIOUS GOVERNMENTS.

Deficits 1873	$1,300.00
" 1874	5,368.95
" 1875	5,220.00
" 1876	1,640.00
" 1877	1,300.00
" 1878	1,500.00
A total of	$16,328.95

PRESENT GOVERNMENT.

Deficits 1879		$1,501.00
" 1880		Surplus
" 1881		do.
" 1882		390.70
" 1883		164.02
" 1884		98.60
A total of		$2,152.79
Deduct surplus, 1880,	$106.57	
" 1881,	214.68	321.25
A total of		$1,832.54

Difference in favor of present Government $14,496.41. Oh! but we are told the present Government have received large sums from the Land Office. Well, let a comparison for the two periods referred to be made in this respect also:

PREVIOUS GOVERNMENTS.

1873	-	-	$35,891.99
1874	-	-	44,848.46
1875	-	-	24,333.24
1876	-	-	41,122.79
1877	-	-	78,506.20
1878	-	-	54,379.42
			$279,082.80

PRESENT GOVERNMENT.

1879	-	-	$44,981.37
1880	-	-	54,200.45
1881	-	-	64,831.75
1882	-	-	46,130.62
1883	-	-	51,351.03
1884	-	-	46,033.74
			$307,528.96

The present Government only received $28,446.16 from the Land Office in excess of what had been received from the same source during the preceding six years. The receipts from lands were larger during the Davies administration than they have been since. No direct taxation had been imposed on the people of this Province for three years. The total amount of taxes collected for the last six years was about the same as the amount which the old Land Assessment would have yielded had it been in force. Dividing the twelve years since Confederation as before into two periods, we have the following comparison:

PREVIOUS GOVERNMENTS.

1873	-	-	$14,300.51
1874	-	-	14,992.53
1875	-	-	14,592.21
1876	-	-	14,074.38
1877	-	-	58,448.11
1878	-	-	38,834.69
			$155,242.42

PRESENT GOVERNMENT.

1879	-	-	$26,631.15
1880	-	-	26,800.85
1881	-	-	31,299.63
1882	-	-	3,960.37
1883	-	-	274.35
			$88,976.35

It will thus be seen that the present administration have raised $66,266.07 less revenue by taxation during the six years they have been in power, than their predecessors did for a similar period of time. Honorable gentlemen in Opposition have asserted that the present Government have withdrawn large sums from our capital at Ottawa. Nothing could be more incorrect than this. Not one dollar has been drawn by the present Government from amounts to our credit as capital at Ottawa except in the purchase of proprietory estates, the payment of expenses in connection with the Land Purchase Act, and in settlement of old claims for railway damages. The Government has, however, succeeded in collecting considerable sums from the Dominion on account of expenditure on piers and the maintenance of short term prisoners. These amounts were not obtained from capital. They were secured owing to the good management of the Government, and in most cases in spite of the Opposition who had not the brains to see that we were entitled to the money. The honorable gentleman for West River had endeavored to make a great ado because the present Government had let some small contracts without tender, notwithstanding that the present administration had let fewer contracts in that manner than any previous one, and had adopted the tender system for almost every contract that they enter into. It ill became the honorable member for West River to make reference to anything of this kind. Has he forgotten the transactions of the last two or three months during which he was a member of the "rump" of the Davies Government? Has he forgot the register grates that were sold to the Government by the firm of which the Provincial Secretary of that day was a member? This gentleman sold $800 worth of those grates, under the name of another firm, to the Government of which both he and the honorable member for West River were members. The honorable member had referred to some accounts for hardware that had been procured without tender; and yet he knew that these small articles are constantly required, and could not be bought in any other way than the one that has been adopted by the honorable the Commissioner of Public Works. The course the Opposition had adopted was a most extraordinary one. They allowed nearly three weeks to pass after the House had met, and then on the 27th March they came down from their caucus room, where they received instructions from outsiders and filled up the order book with questions asking for returns, which would keep all the clerks in the building busy for months in order to prepare them. Such questions as had been asked by his honorable colleague were never before placed on the order book.

Mr. BEER said the statement he wanted could not be asked for any sooner, as two or three weeks had elapsed after the meeting of the Legislature before the Public Accounts had been tabled.

Hon. Mr. Ferguson, said his honorable colleague was not correct in his statement. Every honorable member knew that the Public Accounts were laid on the table of the House earlier in the session than they had ever been before. The Opposition had delayed asking these questions until nearly three weeks had passed in order, no doubt, that it would be impossible for the Government to have these statements prepared before the end of the session, and then give them something to complain of. The statements asked for are, many of them, so ridiculous, involving so much labor, and of so voluminous a nature, that it was impossible to have them prepared up to the present time. The honorable member for West River is very much exercised in his mind in reference to the transfer of the wharves to the Dominion Government, and thinks the tolls should be fixed before the Government transferred them. Two years ago the honorable member for Springton made a speech when the resolution to go into supply was being debated, and the following is what he said on the wharfage question:

"Mr. Sinclair said we talk about the money which we have lost through the National Policy, which has worked detrimentally to the interest of this Province, but the loss in that way is not to be compared to the loss which will accrue to us through the pressure upon our trade by the heavy dues which will be demanded from our traders. If we murmur at the charge they will tell us that we ourselves allowed the same thing to be done. What would the wharfage fees for the Province amount to? We ship about 3½ millions of bushels of produce, which, at 1 cent per bushel amounts to $35,000. In addition to this there are other exports, and all the imports. In three years the Province will lose more than the whole amount which it will receive for those wharves and piers." Here is the calculation of the honorable member for Springton, that in three years we would pay more than we would receive for these piers from the Federal Government. Where do the honorable member's calculations stand now? He (Mr. F.) had shown how the calculations of the Opposition about deficits, had come to grief, and the hon. member is in no better position in respect to this matter. Over two years have passed, and not one cent of wharfage has been collected from these piers. Who is the blind financier now? The Dominion Government have passsd an order in Council fixing rates of wharfage to be collected and have adopted the same schedule of rates that was formerly in force in this Province. Thus all their alarm about this matter as well as their calculations of the heavy taxation our traders would have to pay, has proved baseless, and they are now left without any calculations that have even the shadow of a chance to become true.
G. F. O.

Mr. Beer said that if he had not been refused documents which he had a right to see, he would not have spoken on the present occasion. His honorable colleague had drawn some comparisons very favorable for the present Government, but the honorable gentleman should remember that during the six years after Confederation, the Government was in the hands of nearly the same men as at present, and therefore the shortcomings of that Government should be laid at the door of the present one. He maintained that although the present Government did not introduce the Education Act, they are responsible for the carrying out of its provisions. In fact, some of their members are responsible for the introduction of that Act. If the Government think there is money expended under the Act that should not be expended, they should take steps to prevent the waste, and to regulate the expenditure. They found fault with their predecessors for letting contracts without public competition, but we now find them making private contracts amounting to over $20,000. This is a state of matters which should not exist. On Government House alone $934.83 was expended last year without tender for any part of the work. He took exception to this. This Province has no right to provide a Government House for the Lieutenant Governor. That gentleman is a Dominion official, and if a Government House is to be provided, it should be done by the General Government. If the vouchers were before him he would enter into this matter more fully. He found, also, that the Government have actually been paying for Gas for Government House. The bill seemed to run from month

to month, making in all about $100. We have no right to pay that bill. The Leader of the Government had as much right to charge the Province with his private gas bill as the one alluded to. Talk about economy. He would like to see it practised in such matters as that. He could go through the whole of these returns and point out similar irregularities.

Hon. Mr. FERGUSON found that the honorable member's question was not put on the Order Book until 26th March, although the House met on 11th March.

Mr. BEER,—The notice was placed on the Order Book as soon as possible after the Honorable Commissioner of Public Works tabled his report. In fact, it was placed there before the report was actually tabled, for he waited until tired for that report; and he thought if he was ever going to receive the information sought for, he should ask at once. The report was not tabled until the 27th, or two weeks after the House met. The Honorable Commissioner of Crown Lands had gone back to the old story of the Register Grates for the Hospital for the Insane, which had done such good service in the days of old.

Hon. Mr. FERGUSON saw a large pile of those grates the other day, yet on hand.

Mr. BEER,—Are those grates to be kept there? Surely they must be of some value! He doubted if five of them could be found to-day. It appears that at the close of the year the Government owed the Banks no less than $56,952, and that they gave themselves credit for $493.02. They had no right to reckon the $493, on deposit in the Bank of P. E. Island, as they could not expect to collect it. As to the old duty bonds, they were long since looked upon as worthless.

Hon. Mr. SULLIVAN,—There is a fair prospect of collecting about $3,000 of the amount due on them.

Mr. BEER,—There was due the teachers, at the close of the past year, the amount of their salaries for three months. The surmise of the Honorable Leader of the Government that there will be a surplus of upwards of $8,000 at the close of the present year was not likely to be fulfilled. He hoped the documents which had been asked for would be furnished.

Hon. Mr. SULLIVAN,—The honorable member can see those documents in the public offices to which they belong, at any time he asks for them. In the House of Commons, the vouchers are never placed on the table of the House. It would place the Government in a false position if, in after years, those documents could not be found, as it might be said that they never existed at all.

Hon. Mr. CAMPBELL,—With respect to the alleged gas bill for Government House, it never existed. There are two lamps at the Guard House for the gas for which the Government have always paid, but they have paid for no gas used

at Government House. We own Government House and land, and it is the duty of the Government to keep the buildings in proper repair.

Mr. BEER thought $108 a large item for two lamps for the guard house.

Hon. Mr. CAMPBELL,—No gas bill was ever paid for Government House except when repairs were being made therein, when gas was required by the workmen, who were fitting it up for the present Governor. The honorable member for West River asserted that he (Mr. C.) spent $15,000 during the past year in the interests of his own constituents. Now, he (Mr. C.) was not aware that the electors of the first district had ever received any favors from the present Government. In fact, they never made demands upon the latter. There was a time when there was an immense over-expenditure, and when public contracts were let without tender or public sale, without even the sanction of their Government. He referred to the latter part of the term when the late Government were in power. The honorable member used all his influence to secure support for that Government and for the parties who managed the Public Works Department in that way. It is true that after the Estimates for last year were voted, he found that a large number of culverts had been carried away by the freshets of that year, and that it was necessary to have them repaired. There was no other course to pursue.

Perhaps the honorable member would have perferred to see them left as they were! So with the *Patriot* newspaper! But the Government choose to run the risk of receiving the sanction of the House and to make the necessary repairs to the culverts and roads. When they expended that money, they knew they could come down to the House with a perfectly honest account. What course did the Davies Government pursue in 1878 when they expended $35,000 or $40,000 over and above the amount appropriated by the House for a similar purpose? They wrote to the Supervisors to "draw slowly" until the close of that year. The honorable member was in that Government when they carried forward to 1879 on over-expenditure of upwards of $60,000. In fact, they hid up their over expenditure, so that it did not appear in the public accounts for 1878. The present Government did not pursue any such course; they opened no suspense account, but paid their bills. They paid every dollar justly due for work done in the Public Works Department, and trusted to the support of the House in what they did. He was prepared to justify every action in his department, and to show that all expenditures were properly made. The honorable members for West River and Southport were dishonest in the extreme in their representations. Were the ordinary expenditures for repairs ever let by tender under the late Government? They were not. He hoped he would never be small enough, or mean enough, to find fault with any Government for letting by private contract ordinary repairs on the Province Building, Normal School, Prince of Wales College, etc., and to endeavor to show that they had improperly expended the public money in that way.

Mr. FARQUHARSON,—If the Honorable Commissioner of Public Works can show that the previous Government expended $25,000 of money in the Public Works Department without tender or public sale, he (Mr. F.) would give in.

Hon. Mr. CAMPBELL said that in 1878 a larger amount was expended by his predecessor in that Public Works Department, not only without tender, but the work was given to that gentleman's political friends only. Never in the history of this Province was so much work done without tender, or public sale, as in 1878, and the honorable member for West River defended the action of the official right through to the last. In this statement he (Mr. C.) did not include repairs on any public building in the Province. He simply referred to public works let by private contract which had previously been let by tender. As to supplies for the department, he generally sent a man round to the hardware stores to ascertain where goods could be purchased at lowest figures, and patronized them only. He held in his hand a return of all the public works which had been let by the late Government under private contract only. Among these was the Southport ferry wharf. He knew how that work had been performed. Let any person attempt to pull out one stick of timber from it, and he will put out five pieces. For every dollar expended by the present Government on the work, they received full value for their money. Instead of neglecting the constituents of the honorable member for West River, he had probably over-stepped the mark in their favor. In the case of the Rocky Point Ferry, a certain amount of work had to be performed, and if he had had an honest contractor to deal with he would have had a much better job, but the reverse was the fact, and he had to fall back upon the securities. The person who finished the work proved to be a most estimable man, whose character is above reproach. The Cardigan ferry wharf was extended under the Supervisor, Mr. Flannagan, and never was public money more judiciously expended. North Pinette Bridge was almost entirely rebuilt in 1877, but last year he had to go over it again. A good, reliable, honest man was placed in charge of the work, and the money was most economically and properly expended. But there is still some work to be done thereon. He expected to make it a first class bridge for less than one-fifth of what a new one would have cost. So far as his (Mr. C.'s) own district was concerned, all the public works had been let by tender, except repairs which required immediate attention. Crapaud breastwork gave way owing to the fact that not a bit of iron was used in its construction. This work was constructed under the late Government. He went up and attended to it on Monday, and by Saturday night the road was made passable. If he had waited to let the work by tender, the howl of the Patriot newspaper would have been heard on the matter. That howl is now, however, one of the best certificates any public man in this Province can have. The improvements made in the grounds in front of the Provincial Building were made by the Government, because they had a just right to do so, in the face of the fact that the citizens had put their hands into their pockets and paid for planting and ornamenting the grounds around the building. So far as the purchase of the coal for the Asylum was concerned, he thought the trustees of that institution had acted wisely in securing it by private contract, without tender. In 1878 the coal for the Public Buildings was purchased in a similar manner. Instead of employing one man to make the ordinary necessary repairs to the public buildings, the late Government employed four men in 1877, one of whom received $1,190, the second $947, the third $277, and the fourth a smaller sum. The man employed by the present Government performed his work for the reasonable sum of $1.50 per day. In addition to all their other extravagances, the late Government employed an Engineer, at a large salary. In all, the Davies Government squandered $3,400 per year on the Engineer, Superintendents of Public Works and others; and yet the Opposition now make a dead set against the man who has honestly earned all the money he received. He would inform gentlemen on the other side that not a single account had been paid for work done by the Public Works Department that had not been scrutinized by himself. Not a dollar has been paid but what has been fairly earned. With respect to the register grates, the last time he counted them there were twelve of them unused lying in a heap. The honorable member for West River, endorsed their purchase without tender, not knowing whether or not they would ever be used. We have now an Attorney General who does all his own work without any assistance. The late Government had one who could go to Halifax to sell the interests of the Province, draw his salary, and pay another at the expense of the country to perform the work of his office while absent. In the Public Works Department, this year, some $6,000 less has been expended than was expended last year up to the same date, showing that a very small sum indeed has been carried forward from last year. The policy inaugurated by the Gavernment from the first they intend to pursue to the end; and, perhaps, the Opposition, if called upon to govern the country, will carry out the very same policy. But he believed that at the end of their present term, the Government will be returned to power, to carry out the same economical principles as they have, up to this time, established as part of their policy.

Mr. SINCLAIR said that the question now to be considered is as to what tack the Ship of State is on at present, and what harbor she is likely to get into. If the Government go on expending for the next twelve months at the same rate as at present, with no larger revenue to meet their expenditure, we shall be at least $100,000 in debt at the end of their term of four years Notwithstanding the sum received on account of the piers, the Government find themselves with a balance against them, according to their own showing, at the close of the past year, of $53,000. Instead, however, of covering with the piers money the previous indebtedness of the Province, they made it cover the expenditure of the past year only. If we have $100,000 of a deficit at the close of the year, how is it to be wiped out? He noticed in the *Herald* newspaper a very significant hint as to how the Government propose to do this, viz: by a draft on capital account. One thing is certain, and that is, the banks will not carry an overdraft of $100,000 from year to year at six per cent, interest; and it would be just as well to draw from our Dominion funds as to issue debentures for the amount. There is of course $24,000 to be paid us by the Dominion on account of the piers money, but there is no provision made for the payment of the interest on the overdraft at the Banks, although the latter will be much larger than was the case last year. No amount has been set down for the consolidation of the laws, which if carried out, will swell the total indebtedness. The estimated receipts for the year will be at least $20,000 short of the amount necessary to cover the expenditure. It appears that a less amount has been collected at the Land Office than was received up to this time last year. He felt certain that the receipts from that source will decrease every year. The Government have put down as receipts about $24,000 which does not form part of the ordinary revenue, so that, to-day they are running behind their ordinary receipts at the rate of $50,000 per year. Whatever government will succeed them, will, therefore, be compelled to adopt a different policy in that respect. No Government with such a policy could continue it and remain in power more than twelve months, as the banks would refuse to carry them any further. It was the duty of the Government to bring down receipts that will be likely to meet the estimated expenditure. The Superintendent of Education thinks there will be an increase in the expenditure for Education, but the Government suppose there will be a decrease to the extent of about $20,000. Then again, the Hospital for the Insane was unable to receive any new patients after the month of August, of last year, owing to the want of accommodation. This was a sad state of affairs. Even if the present Government do remain in power a few years longer, direct taxation is inevitable. It cannot be otherwise if we have no other receipts than those we now have. As for compensation for the loss sustained on account of the non-fulfilment of the Terms of Confederation, no Government can depend upon that, for revenue. He believed that the Government had forced their claim for compensation for our piers upon the General Government as strongly as they could, and gave them due credit for what they had done. There are other piers not yet taken over by the Dominion, and he hoped they would succeed in having the whole question satisfactorily settled. But the present Government would not have moved in that matter to any greater extent than any other Government had it not been for the action of the Supreme Court in the Holman-Green case. That decision was a timely one for them. As matters now stand, the prospect is pretty dark for the future financial position of this Province. If the present policy of running in debt is to be pursued a whole year longer, and it is found necessary to raise $100,000 by direct taxation, the country will have a very heavy burden to bear. Our revenue is falling away in several directions. Even the fees from the County Courts are diminishing. With what was done seven or eight years ago, we have nothing at all to do. The extravagance of previous Governments does not justify a like course at present. It is the duty of the Government to administer the affairs of the country in such a way that they can justify the course which they have pursued when they appeal to the people at the polls. Immediately after Confederation took place, the Owen Government had nothing to do, but to draw upon the funds lying in the banks. The Davies Government, also, had sufficient funds to meet the expenditure, having raised a portion of them by direct taxation. So far as legislation is concerned, all the measures passed by the present Government, which were really governmental measures, were not worth ten cents; and he maintained that the course they are now pursuing, in not making provision for past deficits, will very soon place the Province in financial difficulties.

Hon. Mr. PROWSE said that the honorable member for Strathalbyn at one time undertook to lead the Government in this House, and what was the result? If we are now getting into a dangerous position financially, into what kind of condition did we get into when the honorable member himself was responsible for the finances of the country? The honorable gentleman introduced into this Province a financial system unknown in this or any other country. Did he make any provision for the payment of the interest on the Railway Debentures when it became due? None whatever. Why did the then Government build the branch lines of railway? Simply to keep themselves in power! What provision did they make for the payment of the interest on the money expended on the branch lines? None. What provision did they make towards paying the capital when the debt fell due? None whatever. Talk about the banks refusing to credit the Government of that

day. No honorable member knows better than he, that the then Government acted dishonestly in reference to the whole transaction when they neither provided for the payment of principal nor interest. They declared that Messrs. Pope, Haviland, and Howlan had formed a railway ring, and had an interest in the construction of the railway. The Haythorne--Laird Government came into power under a promise to stop the construction of the railway; but instead of fulfilling that promise, they at once gave a contract for the construction of the branch lines to the very contractors whom they vigorously denounced only a few months previously. Yet this is the honorable member, forsooth, who now talks about economy and makes recommendations with reference to the management of the public finances! The course now pursued by the hon. gentleman was, certainly, the most astonishing he (Mr. P.) had heard of for a long time. Because the honorable member happened to see a paragraph in the *Herald* newspaper, stating that the Province had sufficient funds at Ottawa to meet all its liabilities, he jumps at the conclusion that the policy of the Government is to withdraw from capital to meet all past deficits. He really did not expect to hear from the honorable member so far-fetched a statement. He (Mr. Prowse) had charged the honorable member for West River with having given utterance to disloyal sentiments, but the honorable gentleman had not the manliness to make a reply. He would now charge that honorable member with being the greatest Fenian that exists to-day on the face of the globe. The honorable member stated that he wished thousands of Fenians would cross the United States border into Canada and take possession of the whole of the North-West; and that he himself, would like to be there with them to fire a shot! He would now put the question to the honorable gentleman as to whether he had made such a statement or not? Did the honorable member make that or a similar statement? Did the honorable gentleman not express the wish that thousands of Fenians would cross the border and take the great North-West of the Dominion? If so, the people of this country should beware of him. Why did the honorable member make that statement? For the purpose, no doubt, of encouraging the rebellion and entailing misery upon the country in order that the present Government may be ousted from power. The honorable gentleman cares not how much blood is shed and property destroyed, provided Sir John's Government loses the reins of power. The expressions made use of by the honorable member will be a lasting disgrace to him as long as his name is known in this country. It had been stated by the last speaker that the Government neglected their duty in not appearing before the Courts in order to have the question settled respecting our territorial rights in the shore fronts. The Government

did not desire to put in any claim to the shore fronts. They were of opinion that it was better for this Province for the Dominion Government to own the shore fronts, in which case the wharves or piers would belong to the latter for all time to come. As for himself, he never saw the decision of the Supreme Court on the Holman-Green case until he went to Ottawa. Even then, there was some difficulty in obtaining a printed copy of that decision. It has been affirmed by some of the Opposition that any member of the House who occupied a seat in the Davies Government, and afterwards resigned that seat should be held responsible for all the doings of that Government. With this statement he could not agree, for many things were done by that Government which he never agreed to. He had been challenged to state whether or not any member of the Davies Government had any interest in the contract for the erection of the Asylum Building. Well, he did not know that any of them had, or that they had not. There were certain things done by some of those members which made matters look very suspicious. When he found bills, for the benefit of the contractors, which had never been before the Executive Council, marked as passed and paid, he did not know what to say; but he thought men who would do that would do almost anything. One document, in particular, was refused the sanction of the Council, but was recorded on the Minute Book, on the same day, as having received that sanction. What about the Suspense Account and the Register Grates? - Fault had been found with the honorable the Commissioner of Public Works for expending money over and above appropriated for Public Works. He (Mr. P.) did not like to see the vote exceeded, but there are certain exceptional circumstances when the head of a depart ment is justified in doing so. For instance, a bridge breaks down, and a much frequented passage is obstructed. In such a case, the work should be repaired as soon as possible, and the Commissioner of Public Works should submit the matter to Parliament at the proper time. But honorable members all remember what a large amount was expended by the late Commissioner of Public Works a short time before the late Government went out of power, in macadamizing a certain road, without a vote of Parliament. He (Mr Prowse) would remark just here that he very much regretted having remained in the Davies Government as long as he did. The objectionable proceedings took place in April, and he resigned in the August following. The honorable member for Southport has found fault because certain vouchers were not produced and laid on the table of the House. To do this is decidedly objectionable, for if such documents happened to be lost, they could not be replaced. The Commissioner of Public Works has promised that any honorable member may go to the office of that department and look over any vouchers in the presence of the Secretary of Public Works. This should satisfy any reasonable person. The Leader of the late Government decided not to permit such a practice, as it was unsafe, and objectionable.

Mr. FARQUHARSON said that the Opposition merely asked for a copy of certain vouchers.

Hon. Mr. PROWSE said that this was the first time he heard the word "copy" used in connection with the matter.

I. O.

Mr. FARQUHARSON said that if there were any Fenians in Canada the honorable member for Murray Harbor was one of them.

Hon. Mr. PROWSE said he would ask the honorable junior member for Belfast, (Mr. Alex. Martin), to substantiate the truth of what he (Mr. P.) said respecting the matter. The honorable member was present at the time and heard what the honorable member for West River said.

Mr. D. C. MARTIN said honorable members of the Government are anxious to fas·en a charge of fenianism on honorable members of the Opposition They abuse the Patriot, that "despicable sheet" and endeavor to divert attention from the proper discussion of their misdoings. He hoped the House would take a proper course with respect to this matter and not allow outside issues to be dragged into it. The Government have a peculiar manner of justifying their public acts. They try to screen themselves by attacking their predecessors. They say the Davies Government ran the Province into debt. Last year they told us that the legacy of the Davies Government was the cause of their having to impose the Assessment Act for three years after they came into power, notwithstanding that the Auditor appointed by the present Government (W. C. DesBrisay) said there was $13,000 of a surplus when the Davies Government went out of power.

Hon. Mr. SULLIVAN said the assertion of the honorable member is not correct.

Mr. D. C. MARTIN,—The present Government said the Davies' Government were $60,000 in debt but such does not appear by the Public Accounts. Perhaps he (Mr. M.) did not understand these Accounts but he might be excused for not doing so when the *Examiner* newspaper which is well known to be inspired by the honorable the Commissioner of Crown Lands made the following statement in its issue of the 28th March, instant:

" A matter which requires attention! The Report of the Provincial Auditor on the Public Accounts for the past year is a creditable document *so far as it goes* but it is incomplete without a statement of the *Assets* and *Liabilities* of the Province on the 31st December, 1884. Perhaps there is a way of getting at the information from the Book itself—if so we would be obliged to any one who will furnish us

with the particulars for publication. The public want to know the exact position of the Province — what it has, as well as what it owes. If this information can not now be given a new leaf should be turned over at once. Stock should be taken and a value put upon every asset (great or small) owned by the Province or due to it. Its liabilities, if not now known should be ascertained immediately, and everything so arranged that at the close of each year, every person shall know just how the Province stands with its own people and the world at large."

This is a humiliating statement coming from a paper controlled by the honorable Provincial Secretary for the last six years. Either, the honorable Commissioner of Crown Lands, Provincial Secretary Treasurer did not understand these Accounts or else he did not let the readers of the *Examiner* into the secret. The Government are following the course they have adopted of spending of the money they are receiving from Ottawa. Is it wise to spend in one year $53,000 that was expended during ten years on public works? The $24,000 no doubt will be spent in the same way and at the end of a year or two this money will be all gone. We are spending the receipts of the Land Office in the same way and in a few years this source of revenue will be all used. The Land Office has closed 213 Accounts during the past year and only 103 new Accounts have been opened. How many precepts were issued in order to close these Accounts? We know that fifty farms had to be bought in by the Government, and, no doubt, many of these farms will remain unsold and be counted as assets in future statements. There are at the present time 5,569 open accounts in the Land Office but 4,877 accounts have been closed so that in future the revenue from this source will be decreasing. Deeds are not given until payment is made in full and in many cases this rule causes persons to mortgage their farms, so as to pay the amount due the Government The Government should pursue a different policy than that of using our capital for ordinry expenditure. The amount of subsidy from the Dominion Government only amounts to $168,967.67 per annum. In future the receipts from Public Lands should be capitalized and only the interest expended each year. By doing so, even after deducting one third from the amount due or likely to become due, we will have an income of nearly $24,000 per annum. This with the receipts from the Public Offices which last year amounted to $12,047·63 will make a revenue of about $204,000 a year. Any amount required for the Public Service in excess of this sum should be raised in some other way, than by depending on the Dominion Government for windfalls.

Mr. BLAKE said he did not intend to offer any very long remarks, as this irregular debate would be productive of no good. It only delayed the business of the country. We have had so many financial statements this evening that it is hard to tell in what position the finances of the Province really are. The last speaker had quoted from the *Examiner* newspaper, which had advocated the opening of a capital account for the Province. If this suggestion was adopted, it would show that we have assets much larger than our liabilities. We have heard a great deal about the debt of the Province, and dire prophecies of ruin overtaking the country. We have been told that the Banks will refuse to help the Government, and that our credit was completely destroyed. Honorable members, however, are getting so used to hearing the Opposition picturing the country as being in a dark and desperate condition, that they are getting very doubtful about crediting these assertions. When people tell a story very often they beleive it to be the truth, and that is the case with the Opposition. They have said so often that the country is ruined that now some of them actually believe it to be true. It is well known that when the present Government came into power there was a large indebtedness against the Province. There are many different statements as to what that indebtedness amounted to; but there can be no doubt that that indebtedness prevented the Government from repealing the Assessment Act when they came into power. The Government have been blamed by the Opposition for repealing the Assessment Act; and to listen to them one would imagine that the Assessment Act was a panacea for all the ills this Island is afflicted with. The present Government during the six years they have been in power have collected a little over $79,000 from Assessment on the people, whereas the late Government, in two years, collected over $90,000. The late Government, on account of the question that brought them into power, were allowed to impose the Assessment Act; and had they been careful and economical, they might have been in power to-day. But they did not act as they should have done and the fate that overtook them is well known. The present Government had promised to repeal the Assessment Act, if possible, and it is well known that they did so previous to the last election. At the last general election the people were told by the Opposition that the Government would reimpose the Assessment Act, as they could not do without it; but we know that such has not been the case. The present Government are determined to use every effort to carry on the business of the Province without direct taxation. If, by collecting the debts due the Province, and by carefully husbanding our resources, the Assessment Act can be done without, the Government will deserve the gratitude of the people. We know how the Government were treated by the Opposition in reference to the piers question. They were sneered at and told that they would 'get nothing. But the Government pursued the even tenor of their way and have already received $115,000 from the Dominion besides effecting a saving in our expenditure for public wharves of over $20,000 a year. This was a most creditable showing and so long as a similar policy is pursued, there will be no fear of them losing the support of the people, or of

their being drivn from power like the late Government. The people did right in driving the late Government from power, because they showed they had no feeling for the people. That no meetings had been held condemning the Government is one of the best signs of their popularity. In travelling through the country, he (Mr. B.) found that the people are well satisfied, for they say the Government are doing the best they can to keep off taxation. When the time arrives for the Government to go back to the people they will be returned to this House with handsome majorities, while many of the Opposition will be sent to look after their private business. When the question of the vote for the expenses of legislation was discussed last night, he (Mr. B.) found that the Opposition found fault with the Government for the expense of this service. It is to be regretted that the efforts of the Government in this respect had heretofore been unsuccessful. A great many of the members are only loafing about the House, and it is plainly evident that we are too much governed. If the pay of honorable members was curtailed so many of them would not be anxious to come here. But who is to blame in this matter? What was the course of the Opposition on this question? Every effort made by the Government to lessen the expenditure in connection with legislation has been opposed by the Opposition, who were jealous lest the Government should effect this reform. We find that a leading member of the Opposition, the

President of the Legislative Council said that the rights of the people would be in jeopardy if the Legislative Council was abolished. Through questionable means people were induced to vote for sustaining the upper chamber and the expense of maintaining it has continued. It would be useless losing time sending up a Bill for this purpose when every member of the Opposition, both in this House and the Legislative Council, would vote against it. He (Mr. B.) hoped that next session the reform would be effected. In reference to the speech of the honorable member for West River he (Mr. B.) had a few words to say. After noticing all the notices on the Order Book that had been placed there by the honorable member, it might be expected that some extraordinary " mare's nest " would be discovered to the discredit of the Government. But we find that the honorable member found nothing, and to vent his disappointment the honorable gentleman had inflicted a long speech on the attention of the House, whereby the business of the country had been most unreasonably retarded. He (Mr. F.) had dragged in the names of private gentlemen, such as W. E. Dawson, who is an estimable man, in order to make some political capital. There was no doubt but the articles purchased from this gentleman were obtained as cheaply as if procured by tender, as it is well known that prices were obtained by the Honorable Commissioner of Public Works from different persons before the orders were given and that thereby the lowest price would be quoted. Reference had also been made to Mr. Charles Lyons who is as respectable a man as any in the City, and he (Mr. B.) was proud to think that so worthy a citizen supported the Conservative Party. Fault had been found with the Government that coal had been purchased from this gentleman for the public buildings. But even the Opposition, after hearing the explanation of the Commissioner of Public Works must allow that the public interest was better served in this instance than it would be if the contracts had been let by tender. It could be easily seen that the contractor had only made thirty cents per ton on the transaction, and this was not a very large amount for the honorable member for West River to make such a fuss about. The principle of letting these contracts by tender is the proper one, but it is often found that the person having the lowest tender is not the best person to perform the work. He (Mr. B.) contended that when other things are equal the patronage of the Government should be given to their friends. The honorable Commissioner of Public Works had clearly shown that large contracts had been given to the friends of the late Government when that party was in power, and he (Mr. B.) did not blame the late Government for doing so. He (Mr. B.) could assure honorable members that he never knew of any instance in which the late Government purchased anything from their opponents if they could help it. Reference had been made to the Opposition the present Government had received while pressing the claims of the Province to a re-fund of the amounts expended for the construction of wharves and Piers. When he (Mr. B.) had been in Ottawa last year, Mr. Davies in his (Mr. B's.) hearing, —when this matter was discussed in the Dominion Parliament at Ottawa, when members of the Opposition asked why this money was granted—asked the Dominion Government on what grounds they based the granting of this money or on what part of the British North American Act was it founded. Mr. Davies had previously asked if a similar claim for the piers of New Brunswick would be acknowledged and said that it was only in order to take the Local Government who were friends of the Dominion Government, out of a muddle, that this money was to be refunded to Prince Edward Island. An action of this kind was calculated to prejudice our case in the eyes of the Dominion Government for Mr. Davies was representing an important section of the Province when he asked this question. When Mr. Davies did not get a satisfactory answer to his enquiries, he went on to explain why it was that the Island Government got into the muddle. We have been told that the Government would sell the rights of the Province in order to get themselves out of the difficulties they were in, but what do we find? We find that the Government did not sacrifice our interests, but have not only obtained the $53,222 that was first voted, but have also obtained an additional amount of over $24,-000. When the Opposition found that their tactics of endeavoring

to prevent the Province getting this money proved unsuccessful, they now say that they never opposed our obtaining it. The present Administration have succeeded in getting $80,000 and expect to obtain an additional amount before this matter is finally settled. This quite clearly establishes the fact that the Government have done everything they possibly could to further the interests of the Province and have shown themselves to be the best Government we have had since Confederation. He (Mr. B.) contended that the present administration is the only one that has done anything for the farmers of the Province. Not only have they kept the taxes off our farms, but in every possible way they have encouraged and stimulated the development of the agricultural interests of the Island.

Mr. A. MARTIN said as his name had been mentioned in connection with the statement made by the honorable member for West River, he (Mr. M.) wished to state what he heard that gentleman say respecting the Northwest rebellion. He (Mr. M.) had been present in the smoking-room of the House and heard the honorable member for West River give expression to the sentiments that had been related by the honorable member for Murray Harbor (Mr. Prowse). He (Mr. M.) was very much surprised to hear an honorable member of this House utter such sentiments. The honorable member for West River in course of a conversation respecting the unfortunate state of affairs produced by the misguided action of Riel said "that he (Mr. F.) hoped that a thousand or thousands of Fenians would pass over from the United States to join Riel and the insurgents." He (Mr. F.) further stated that he would not mind firing a few shots himself if he was there. He (Mr. M.) was very sorry to think that a person aspiring to occupy the honorable position of Leader of the Opposition in this Assembly, should so far forget what was due to the loyal people who had elected him to represent them, that he would give utterance to such treasonable and and traitorous expressions. It is no use for the honorable member for West River to try and wriggle out of what he had said. It would be far better for him to humbly apologize to the House for having allowed his partizanship to carry him so far beyond the bounds of decency. This whole debate to-night is attributable to the wild, rambling speech of this honorable member, and the intelligent people of this Province will severely censure the action of honorable members who deliberately obstructs the business of this Assembly. The honorable Commissioner of Public Works had given explanations of every transaction in connection with his department in a manner that was satisfactory to every unprejudiced mind, and the honorable member for West River will find that he cannot gain anything by trying to bully this House.

Mr. RICHARDS said he thought every honorable member should express his opinion on the manner in which the business of the Province was conducted by the Government. They had heard a great deal in reference to the finances of the Provinces and as every honorable member was no doubt, just as good a financier as the honorable the Commissioner of Public Works, no harm was done by discussing and criticising the actions of the Government. The important question to be considered is how much was the Province in debt on the 31st of December, last. By the Public Accounts we know that there was a balance due against ordinary revenue of $54,-000 and there is no doubt but over $20,000 should be added to this sum for amounts not included in that balance. These amounts added make $74,000 and the question naturally arises, how the Government intend to pay this large sum in addition to ordinary expenditure, with the revenue they say is at their disposal? How will they come out at the end of this year if matters are allowed to go on as they are doing? People in the country say they would rather pay a small tax than run the Province in debt and this is the policy the people wish the Government to pursue. At the first of next year he (Mr. R.) expected there would be a debt of $100,000 on the Province and we would like to know how this will be paid If the Government expect to receive a large amount on account of winter communication or on account of piers, they should let honorable members know it: but without assistance from these sources; there is no doubt but we will come out with a large deficit.

Hon. Mr. SULLIVAN said the honorable member for Biddeford said that at the end of this year he expects the Province will be $100 - 000 in debt   He (Mr. S.) would like to know how the honorable member's estimates were prepared? Supposing that the debt at the end of 1884 of $54,000 was admitted how would the additional $46,- 000 be incurred.

Mr. RICHARDS said that while the requirements of the public service were increasing, the receipts from the Land Office were decreasing; and that, no doubt, quite as large a deficit would arise this year as did in 1883.

Motion put and carried.

House in Committee of the whole.

Mr. BLAKE in the Chair.

Hon. Mr. SULLIVAN submitted the following resolution :

Resolved, That the following sums be granted, and placed at the disposal of the Government, for the following services, viz :—

Salary of Legislative
Librarian, $400.00
For purchase of books,
Legislative Library,   100.00

Mr. D. C. MARTIN said the Legislative Library was very inefficient. A Committee had been appointed to look after this matter, but nothing had been done. The Government should give more attention to an important matter like this,

and see that the many books which are required to complete works of reference are procured.

Hon. Mr. SULLIVAN said he was well aware that many people are of the opinion that they can manage everything much better than anyone else. When the Government came into power, they found the Library had been badly managed, and that a good many valuable books were missing. Honorable members, however, should remember that this is not a lending Library for the public, it only being a Library of reference for honorable members of the Legislature during the session. The small sums voted each year are for the purchase of books necessary for such reference. A considerable part of the amount expended last year was for the British Encyclopedia, a work published in separate parts, which had been purchased by a previous Government. Unfortunately the gentleman who for many years had been Librarian, died during the recess, and although for a number of years this gentleman had been unable to help in Library, yet he had given much valuable assistance in reference to the purchase of books. The present Librarian is an officient officer and no doubt will give that attention to the duties of his office that their importance requires.

Resolution put and carried.

Hon. Mr. SULLIVAN submitted the following resolution :

Resolved, That the following

sum be granted, and placed at the disposal of the Government, for the following services, viz :—

Printing and stationery for Lieutenant Governor's office $25.00

Mr. PERRY wished to know why the usual amount for the Private Secretary of the Lieutenant Governor, and also the gate keeper's allowance of $100, had not been included in this resolution. While considering that the Dominion Government had a right to pay these amounts, yet if they have not been paid by that Government the Lieutenant Governor should not be asked to pay them out of his own pocket.

Hon. Mr. SULLIVAN said,—Several years ago a number of honorable members of this House came to the conclusion that it was not the duty of this Legislature to pay the salary of the Lieutenant Governor's Private Secretary. It was thought advisable to make the change when it was not known who would be the next Governor, and last year the amount voted for this service was only sufficient to pay the salary to the 1st of July. This action was deliberately taken by the House last session and consequently the Government did not think it advisable to place any sum in the estimates this year for this purpose. If the acting Leader of the Opposition is of the opinion that this burden should be bourn by the Dominion Government, why should this Legislature be asked to pay even this small amount when

it is not their duty to do so ?

Resolution put and carried.

Hon. Mr. SULLIVAN submitted the following resolution :—

Resolved, That the following sums be granted and placed at the disposal of the Government for the following services, viz :—

Institution for Deaf & Dumb, Halifax	$300.00
Institution for the Blind, Halifax	200.00
Fire Department, Charlottetown	650.00
Fire Department, Summerside	150.00
Mrs. Mary Whelan	300.00
Unforeseen	1,000.00

Mr. PERRY said he did not understand the item "Unforeseen $1,000" whether it means unforeseen for the whole of the Estimates or for this resolution. He did not see the good of putting this item of $1,000 for unforeseen expenditures in this resolution, when the Government took on themselves to spend $30,000 over what this House authorized them to spend last year. He was surprised that the honorable Provincial Secretary-Treasurer did not ask the House for authority to pay the $53,000 that the Province is in debt, or at least to ask for liberty to make provision for paying the interest on it.

Hon. Mr. SULLIVAN said a similar item had been voted by this Legislature for years past and the honorable member himself has voted for a similar resolution without taking any objection to it.

Resolution put and carried.

Hon. Mr. SULLIVAN submitted the following resolution:—

Resolved, That the following sums be granted and placed at the disposal of the Government, for the following, services, viz:—

Maintenance of Poor House $3,500.00
Paupers   3,600.00

Mr. PERRY said he did not know why the Report of the Poor House Commissioners had not been printed. He (Mr. P.) found that half the people in the Poor House are from Charlottetown, and it looks as though this institution was intended for the support of the citizens of Charlottetown. As the institution is maintained by the whole Island, the Report should have referred to the fact that half the inmates were from Charlottetown. It costs nearly $4,000 to maintain this Institution and every district had as much right to send poor people to it, as the City of Charlottetown.

Hon. Mr. McLEOD said that the honorable member for Tignish had put a false construction on the Poor House Commissioners Report. The Report although not printed, is a very full one and contains all the information that should be included in it. Although many of the persons in the Poor House hail from Charlottetown, if the Report is examined it will be found that many of them formerly resided in other places. Many of the inmates were born in the old country and only lived for a short time in Charlottetown previous to being admitted to the Poor House. Instead of one half of the inmates of the Poor House, not 20 per cent. of them actually belong to the city. When persons are admitted to the Poor House, the master of the Institution asks them where they last resided and generally these persons say that it was in Charlottetown. In reality only fifteen of the present inmates were born in Charlottetown.

Mr. PERRY said that the honorable senior member for the City had given more information in a few minutes than was contained in the whole Report. But he (Mr. P.) was not sure that the information given was reliable, as the Report, which no doubt the honorable member himself had prepared, said differently. If it was known that these persons were only temporary residents of the City, it should be attended to in the report. The people of the Province pay for these services and want to know how the money is expended. In future the Comissioners should give a fuller Report.

Hon. Mr. SULLIVAN said that the Report was a very full one, in fact contained more information than former ones. He (Mr. S.) did not see what difference it made, if all the inmates of the Poor House were from Charlottetown. Personally he did not believe in the Poor House, as he believed it was money misapplied The institution never should have been started; but as it was in operation when the present Government came into power, they dould not throw out the poor people on the charity of the world. The Poor House Comissioners take the first applicants, who apply for admission when there is a vacancy, and have no right to reject any person who applies to them, provided he is a fit person for the institution. It would not make any difference if all the inmates were from Charlottetown. The fact of them being poor and unable to get support in any other way is the reason why they are admitted.

Resolution put and carried.

Hon. Mr. SULLIVAN submitted the following resolution : —

Resolved, That the following sum be granted and placed at the disposal of the Government, for the following services, viz : —

Public Postage　　　$400.00

Resolution put and carried.

Hon. Mr. SULLIVAN submitted the following resolution ; —

Resolved, That the following sums be granted and placed at the disposal of the Government, for the following services, viz : —

Salary of Provincial Secretary, Treasurer and Commissioner of Public Lands　　　$1,300.00
Salary of Assistant Secretary Treasurer　　　1,000.00

Printing and Stationery for Treasurer's Office　　200.00
Salary of Assistant Commissioner of Public Lands　　800.00
Salary of Draughtsmen　1,250.00
Salary of Clerks　　1,100.00
Expenses of Surveys　　300.00
Expenses of Collecting Tours　　250.00
Interest on purchase money Estates　　515.22
Printing and Stationery　200.00

Mr. PERRY said before this resolution is passed he wished to say a few words respecting the manner in which the Land Office is conducted. He (Mr. P.) did think that the Government would at this session, ask the House to make some radical changes in the management of that office, before asking for the large sum contained in this resolution. The report of the honorable Commissioner of Public Lands for 1884 says as follows: "During the year, 6,517 acres of land have been sold to 103 persons, for which the sum of $10,-060.47 has been agreed to be paid. The total quantity of land sold since 1855, when the Provincial Government commenced the purchase of Proprietary Estates, has reached 674,125⅝ acres, and 122,252¼ acres appear to remain still in the hands of the Department." There was not sufficient work done in this Department for the money paid for doing it. Have they got any plans in that office worthy the name of plans? They have not. Many of the plans are torn and almost illegible. He (Mr. P.) himself could draw all the Deeds issued by that office in one month. He expected that the honorable Commissioner would ask the House to give him leave to lessen the expenses of this Department. The receipts are falling off every year and yet the expenses are increasing There is one item of $300 for Surveys. Where are they to be made? The honorable Commissioner has not pointed out where one reliable Survey has been made. He (Mr. F.) promised to have the estates owned by remaining Proprietors surveyed, but he has not done so. Why does he not send surveyors and find out how much land they actually have in their hands. The report of this Department is very imperfect, like a great deal of the work done in that office. But it is no wonder work is badly done, for it is well known that the honorable Commissioner is away most of the time from his office, lecturing, canvassing and visiting schools. The honorable member has failed to do proper work in the Land Office, and even has to admit himself that it is not reliable. He (Mr. F.) has had the Government at his back to grant any money he requires and why is it that these Estates have not been surveyed. He (Mr. P.) also saw that $200 is charged for expenses of collecting tours. This appears to be a large sum for a few weeks travelling in the Fall of the year. He (Mr. P.) also found that there were a greater number of persons in King's County who have not paid the Land Office during the past ten years than in the West. How is that? How does the honorable gentleman expect to wind up the business of the office when he has fifty or sixty farms on hand for which he has no purchasers. The pamphlet published by the Government tried to blind people, in order to induce them to come from England to buy these lands, but it did not have the intended effect. He (Mr. P.) contended that this resolution asked for more money for the expenses of this department than the people were willing to pay. He believed the $200 asked for was more than was spent during the collecting tours. Not over twenty days are occupied with these tours, and as only two men are sent out from the office, and as the expense of travelling is not very great, being only $5.25 for a return ticket to Tignish, he (Mr. P.) could not see how so much was spent for this service, If we are going to lose $100,000 by keeping up this office would it not be better to give the amount to the poor people who are buying their farms? He (Mr. P.) hoped that next session at the furthest, the honorable Commissioner will prepare and bring down a report that will contain the information the country requires. We want to know all about these lands that are for sale. If a full description of them had been published in the pamphlet it would have saved the trouble of doing so now, but as that was not done, the only thing to do is to have them described in the report of the Honorable Commissioner of Crown and Public Lands for 1885.

Hon. Mr. FERGUSON said the hon.

orable member for Tignish had got off his usual speech attacking the Land Office and all connected with it. He (Mr. P.) could only be compared to a garrulous old woman who talks for talk's sake. He (Mr. P.) had promised his friends in Tignish that he would get the Land Office if he was elected, and during the first year or so afterwards he seldom came near the Land Office. But this session the first place he (Mr. P) made for, after arranging with his landlord, was the Land Office, no doubt to sigh over the thought that it was not for him. The honorable member thinks that there is not much work being done in that office because I am not always there. The Opposition seem very much annoyed at my going to meetings in the country when public questions are being discussed, but as I consider it my duty and the duty of every man in a public position to attend meetings of this kind, the complaints of the Opposition will not prevent my doing so. I have given good attention to the duties of the Land Office besides attending to the management of the Asylum the Stock Farm the Poor House and the Provincial Exhibition, and every honorable member knows that all these branches of the Public Service require to be well looked after, as well as the Department of which I am the head. The honorable member, however, did not attack the weakest part of the Land Office. Every one knows that when trade is good and business rushing, that a great deal of money is taken in

every business, but when times get dull and you commence to collect old debts, it becomes a much more difficult matter to get in money. And so it is with the Land Office. As the debts become older, the more difficult are they to collect. Some honorable gentlemen think that this office should be amalgamated with the Registry or some other office, but it is a fact that cannot be denied that there is actually more work in the Land Office at present, than at any former period. If such a course was adopted as the Opposition suggest, out of $500,000 now due the Land Office not over $100,000 would be collected. Deeds and titles to land are constantly becoming more complicated and more difficult to settle and the amount of work necessary to keep these matters straight, is something that the honorable member for Tignish has no conception of. The honorable gentleman complains of the expenses of the Land Office. One would imagine that the cost of the office had greatly increased when the honorable member makes svch an ado about it. He (Mr. F.) held in his hand a statement of this office during the last year of the Davies Government that he would read to the House.

PUBLIC LANDS OFFICE 1878.

The following amounts paid for Salaries of Officials	$5,600.00
Woodrangers, Repairs, &c.	211.13
Interest on Purchase Money	442.97

Collecting Expenses	234.16
Miscellaneous	32.50
	$6,520.76

This is what the Land Office cost in 1878 when Mr Davies was Leader of the Government. The honorable member says the amount for collecting Tours is excessive, as only a few weeks in the Fall was occupied with them. The time taken up by collecting tours is twice as long as stated by the honorable member. The route travelled was settled some years ago and takes five or six weeks each year. The amount in the resolution not only includes the travelling expenses, but also the hire or rent of a room at the several places where money is received in which to do business, besides horse hire and other expenses. The expenses last year for the Land Office were as follows:—

Salaries of officials	$3,150.00
Printing, &c., &c.	312.09
Woodrangers	112.50
Surveys	133.50
Expenses Collecting Tours, 1884	240.15
Interest of Purchase Money.	461.24
Miscellaneous	8 48
	$4,417.96

To which add half the Salary paid the Provincial Secretary Treasurer of $1,300 — 650.000

Making a total of · $5,067.96

as the whole expense of this Department for 1884. The amount to woodrangers is an old score that had been incurred some years ago, and which was found to be due the persons who received it. In reference to what the honorable member said about surveys it should not be forgotten that surveys were not made when they should have been, and it is very little use to spend money now in doing so. The honorable gentleman also tries to raise a sectional cry and said that larger amounts are in arrears in King's County than in Prince County, and yet that more money was received in Prince County. The honorable member does not seem to understand that the people in Prince County, especially those far west pay their instalments during the collecting tours, whereas the payments from King's County are often made in Charlottetown. He (Mr. F.) did not know whether he would hold the office for any length of time, but whoever has charge of this Department will have to look sharply after the amounts owing to it. The amounts due over ten years are increasing. No precepts were issued excepting where no payments had been made for ten years previously, but the fact could not be denied that great sums have been collected in consequence of the policy inaugurated by the Government in 1881, whereby all persons owing the Land Office were compelled to make payment of the money due that office. It is well known that it was this policy that caused the defeat of the honorable senior member for Murray Harbor in 1882 and that the honorable members for. Tignish and Campbellton were returned because they opposed that policy. The two latter gentlemen, however, have now become ashamed of the communistic principles which they formerly advocated, but they will find that what they said in 1881, 1882 & 1883, on this matter will meet them should they ever have to form a government. The firm action of the Government has made these assets valuable and the people approve of the way the office is managed. But, whoever, is in charge of that office one thing is certain, that a great many more precepts will have to be issued. Many persons are holding back their payments on account of the delusive hopes held out to them by some honorable members of the Opposition who thereby are doing the interests of the Province serious damage, and for which the people of the Province will, justly, hold them accountable.

Mr. PERRY said he did not get much information from either the report or the speech of the honorable Commissioner of Crown and Public Lands that he should not be so hard on a poor descendant of the Acadian people The honorable gentleman had given the House no information about anything, excepting that more precepts are to be issued. This plan was tried in Tignish before, at the last election, but it had no effect, and the Government did not gain anything by doing so. The report of this department did not contain anything like the quantity of information it should contain and what is in it is not correct, as almost every part of it contained doubts respecting the accuracy of what it said itself.

Mr. FARQUHARSON said all the returns and reports submitted by the government were full of errors. It was well known that the honorable Commissioner of Public Lands was not in his office half the time he should be and it is no wonder that the country's business is going to the dogs. He (Mr. Farquharson) expected that some policy would be formulated by the government this session respecting this department; but it seems that they are bound to do nothing but drift helplessly along, getting deeper and deeper into debt each year.

Mr. D. C. MARTIN said it was high time the government took hold of the Land Office in a proper spirit. Last year only 508 Deeds were executed and as there are five hands it that office, it was not two for them each day. They should do at least twelve every day when so many clerks are employed. It is true that they collected some money one month taking $5,000 and another $2,000; but it is scandalous to think that for so great an expenditure, over $4000 per year, so little work is done.

Resolution put and carried.

Hon. Mr. SULLIVAN submitted the following resolution :—

Resolved, That the following

sums be granted and placed at the disposal of the Government for the following services, viz :—

Salary of Provincial Auditor and Clerk of the Executive Council ... $1200.00
Printing and Stationery 250.00

Resolution put and carried.

Hon. Mr. Sullivan submitted the following Resolution : —

Resolved, That the following sums be granted, and placed at the disposal of the Government, for the following services, viz :—

Salary of Commissioner of Public Works $1,300.00
Salary of Secretary of Public Works 1,000.00
Travelling expenses of Commissioner of Public Works 300.00
Printing and stationery 500.00

Mr. FARQUHARSON said if the amount in this resolution is for the honorable member who made so boisterous a speech to-night, he did not deserve to get it. He (Mr. F.) did not consider the Honorable Commissioner of Public Works had earned his salary last year for he had allowed the expenditure to greatly exceed the estimates, showing that he (Mr. C.) does not know what public works are actually required. We want an Engineer to look after our Public Works, who could tell how much would be required in any one year. As the honorable Commissioner had been

giving away so much public money to his friends last year, he does not deserve to get any pay this year. The honorable gentleman made the worst record last year that he has done yet. He (Mr. F.) knew the Government all feel bad about it, but that will not bring back the money that was wasted.

Resolution put and carried.

Hon. Mr. SULLIVAN submitted the following resolution :—

Resolved, That the following sums be granted, and placed at the disposal of the Government, for the following services, viz :—

Ferry, Charlottetown, Southport, East and West Rivers, $1,700.00
Ferry, Georgetown and Montague, 2,400.00
Ferry, Summerside and Bedeque 1,450.00
Ferry, China Point 50.00
Ferry, Cranberry, Hills-boro River 45.00
Ferry, McCannell's or Hickey's, Hillsboro River 45.00
Ferry, Ellis River, Lot 14 85.00
Ferry, Walshtown 120.00
Ferry, Grand River, King's County 80.00
Ferry, Elliott River 95.00
Ferry, Cardigan 100.00

Mr. FARQUHARSON said that $95 for Elliott River ferry was not sufficient to enable a contractor to carry on this work efficiently.

Mr. ALEX. MARTIN said he wished

to call the attention of the Committee to the return lately placed on the table of the House, showing that over $124,000.00 has been paid for Southport Ferry during the past fifteen years, an amount which averages over $8,000 per year for that term. It is well known that as population and traffic increases, that the expense of maintaining this service will also increase ; and the Government would do well to take into consideration the best and cheapest way to give increased accommodation to the large and respectable country to the southward of that ferry. Especially as the people in that section of the Province have no accommodation from the Railway should this matter be considered. The Railway cost $3,250.000, and nothing has been done to compensate the people of Belfast and Murray Harbor for the disadvantages they suffer on account of having no connection with that means of easy communication. He (Mr. M.) believed that a survey should be held in order to ascertain the cost and feasibility of building a bridge across the Hillsborough. The ferry is now costing the average amount spent during the past fifteen years $8,000. It is believed that $5,000 is paid in tolls annually, which, added together, would be $13,000 that this ferry now costs the Province each year. He believed that this large sum would go a long way towards paying the interest on the cost of a bridge, and in his opinion the Government should ascertain what such a bridge could be built for. The people of that part of the Province had been

promised that if ever the branches were built, Belfast should have one also ; but it is well known that this promise has not been fulfilled. Another thing promised was, that one of the Thompson Road steamers would be sent to them, as it was better than a railroad. They had obtained none of these advantages that had been promised them, and as it was in the interest of economy, as well as in that of fairplay, the bridge across the Hillsborough should be built without delay.

Mr. D. C. MARTIN said he expected to have heard, ere this, from the Government whether they are going to do something to compensate the Belfast district for the loss of Railway accommodation. He (Mr. M) understood that the new boiler for the steamer "Elfin" was yet in Pictou, and in all probability would not be placed in that steamer in time for the opening of navigation. He would like to know what the Government intended doing in this matter. The question should be taken up at once. As the "Southport" runs to West River, if the "Elfin" is not in fit condition to run on Southport ferry that accommodation that the large interests at stake required would not be given to the people.

Hon. Mr. PROWSE said he sympathized with the honorable senior member for Belfast who finds that his honorable colleague has been too fast for him. He (Mr. P.) might tell the honorable member that the matter he (Mr. M.) is so anxious about is under the serious consideration of the Government and before next season the requisite accommodation for Southport ferry will be provided. The honorable member is very anxious to have large expenditures made by the Government, although he has been advocating that people in some sections of the Province should have the interest taken off the amounts they have agreed to pay for their Lands. No doubt the honorable member is quite willing that the people of Belfast should be taxed to help pay for this bridge for which his honorable colleague was so ably advocating, as taxation is what the Opposition are always praising.

Resolution put and carried.

Hon. Mr. FERGUSON submitted the following resolution:

Resolved, That the following sums be granted, and placed at the disposal of the Government, for the following services, viz:—

Rights of Way and New
Roads $5,000.00

Hon. Mr. FARQUHARSON said he would like to know if it was really intended to spend the amount in this resolution for this purpose, or was it to be like it was last year.

Resolution put and carried.

Hon. Mr. FERGUSON submitted the following resolution:

Resolved, That the following sums be granted, and placed at the

disposal of the Government, for the following services, viz:—

REPAIRS.

Hospital for Insane for repairs	$ 500.00
Provincial Building and Offices,	1,200.00
Government House,	500.00
Poor House,	100.00
Stock Form Buildings,	200.00

Resolution put and carried.

Hon. Mr. FERGUSON submitted the following resolution:

Resolved, That the following sums be granted and placed at the disposal of the Government for the following services, viz:—

Docks and Ferry Slips,	$ 3,000.00
Bridges, Queen's, Prince and King's Counties,	20,000.00
Rent of Slip, Pownal St. Wharf,	324.00
Roads, Culverts and Small Bridges, Queen's Prince and King's Counties	15,500.00
Salaries and Commissions of Supervisors,	3,000.00
Macadamizing,	2,000.00
Bushing Ice,	400.00
Miscellaneous and unforeseen,	1,000.00

Resolution put and carried.

Hon. Mr. SULLIVAN submitted the following resolution:

Resolved, That the following sums be granted and placed at the disposal of the Government, for the following services, viz :—

Packet Service, Charlottetown to Grand River, Lot 56,	$ 100.00
Packet Service, Wood Islands and Belle Creek and Flat River,	145.00
Packet Service, Murray Harbor,	150.00
Packet Service, Rustico, New London and Malpeque,	600.00
Coast and River Steam Service,	2,600.00
New Boiler for steamer " Elfin,"	2,600.00

Mr. D. C. MARTIN said that last session he had brought to the notice of the Government that the amount granted for Packet Service between Charlottetown and Wood Islands, Belle Creek and Flat River was insufficient, as it required two Packets to perform this service in a satisfactory manner. This year only the same amount is voted. He (Mr. M.) had no hesitation in saying that one packet can not discharge this service properly. He would suggest that $350 be voted for this service and would move an amendment to that effect. The people of this part of Belfast district have no railway or steamboat accommodation and the least they should get is good packet service. It is not asking the Government too much to subsidize two packets as the cost would not be over $300 or $350. The packet employed last year did not perform this service in a satisfactory manner and a change should be made this year.

Mr. A. MARTIN said he would like to see the Government increase the subsidy as the service was not very satisfactory last year. He hoped that two packets would be placed on this route; but as he understood the contract with the present contractor had been let for three years, it was very difficult to alter it just at present. No place had a better right to communication of some kind, than these settlements. He (Mr. A. Martin) was sorry he could not second the amendment proposed by his honorable colleague, as it was altogether irregular and contrary to the rules of Parliament for such a motion to be made at this time. His honorable colleague should know that such was the case and that it would put him (Mr. A. Martin) in a false position if he seconded the amendment.

Mr. D. C. MARTIN said he had no intention of putting his honorable colleague in a false position. He only wished to have justice done to the people of these settlements.

Mr FARQUHARSON said he had been talking to a person from the Belfast District who had been complaining of the insufficiency of the Packet service to that part of the Province. The honorable junior member for Belfast is going to vote against an amendment that will bring money to his own District.

Mr. ALEX. MARTIN said he did not say that he would do anything of the kind. He (Mr. A. Martin) would be only too glad to get what money he could for the Belfast District and to get every possible accommodation for the people who live there, but although one of the junior members of the House, he knew more of the rules of this House than to vote for a motion that was not in order.

Hon. Mr. CAMPBELL said the honorable senior member for Belfast has been acting a farce by making a motion which he knew would not be received. The honorable senior member has never come to my office once to enquire into this matter whereas the honorable junior member had been there several times to see if this amount for Packet service to Wood Islands, Belle Creek and Flat River could not be increased; but the Government did not see their way clear to granting the increase at present.

Mr. PERRY said the honorable member for Belfast was perfectly in order in making the motion that he (Mr. D. C. Martin) had done.

Hon. Mr. SULLIVAN said the honorable member for Tignish should know that an irregular motion can not be received by the chairman of Committee or even by the Speaker in the Chair. He (Mr. P.) also should know that May says that when the House is in Committee of Supply that no motion to increase the amount of sums granted by the House shall be accepted unless introduced by a member of the Government. He (Mr. S.) must assume that the honorable senior member for Belfast knew that

he (Mr. M.) could not present this amendment. If he did not know the rules of this House, and pleads ignorance, his constituents will not be well pleased to know that, although so much longer in this House, he (Mr. D. C. Martin) did not actually know the rules of Parliament as well as the honorable the junior member for his District.

Mr. D. C. MARTIN said he was sorry if he had overstepped the rules of the House; but as the motion had been made he would leave it with the Committee to deal with. Honorable members knew that last year he had spoken about this matter and the honorable Commissioner of Public Works had no right to say that he (Mr. M.) was acting a farce in bringing in this amendment.

Hon. Mr. PROWSE said he was surprised at the action of the honorable members for Tignish and the senior member for Belfast; but he (Mr. P.) was not at all surprised at the honorable member for West River, who will do or say anything. The honorable senior member for Belfast knew or should know that certain rules were adopted at the first session of this Parliament one of which his amendment was a direct violation of.

The chairman of the Committee having declined to accept the amendment, the Resolution was put and carried.

After some further time spent in Committee without debate Mr. Speaker on motion resumed the Chair, and the Chair-man reported all the Resolu-tions which have been agreed to in Committee and moved that the question of concurrence be severally put thereon to-morrow.

Motion put and agreed to.

House adjourned until ten o'clock, forenoon.

G. F. O.

TUESDAY, April 7.

Hon. Mr. FERGUSON, a Member of Her Majesty's Executive Council, presented to the House the Trea-surer's Accounts for the year 1884.

Ordered, That said Accounts be laid on the table.

An Act respecting the village of Kensington was read the third time and passed.

An Act to Incorporate the Caven-dish Hall Company was, also, read the third time and passed.

Hon. Mr. SULLIVAN, from the Committee on Expiring Laws, sub-mitted the Report of the said Com-mittee, and the same was received, read, and committed to a Committee of the whole House.

The House accordingly resolved itself into the said Committee.

Mr. JOHN McLEAN in the Chair.

Hon. Mr. SULLIVAN said that the Report sets forth that three Acts are about to expire. They are all private Acts. He was not aware whether the Good Templars re-quired their Act to be continued, but he knew that the Presbyterian Church at St. Peter's and Bay Fortune wished to have their Acts continued. He would therefore move the following resolution, viz.,

Resolved, That it is expedient to continue the following Acts :—

The Act of the Twenty-sixth Victoria, Chapter Twelve, intituled "An Act to Incorporate the Minister and Trustees of the Presbyterian Church at Bay Fortune."

The Act of the Twenty-sixth Victoria, Chapter Thirteen, inti-tuled "An Act to incorporate the Minister and Trustees of the Pres-byterian Church at St. Peter's Bay."

And the Act of the Twenty-seventh Victoria, Chapter Thirty-three, intituled "An Act to incor-porate the Grand and Subordinate Temples of the Independent Order of Good Templars of Prince Edward Island."

Resolution put and carried.

On motion, Mr. Speaker resumed the Chair, and the Chairman re-ported the resolution agreed to.

Hon. Mr. SULLIVAN moved that a Committee be appointed to pre-pare and bring in a Bill in accord-ance with the resolution.

Motion put and carried.

Ordered, That Honorable Mr. Sullivan, Honorable Mr. Gordon, and Mr. McKay do compose said Committee.

Hon. Mr. SULLIVAN from the last preceding Committee appointed, presented to the House a Bill to be intituled: "An Act to continue certain Acts therein mentioned." Said Bill was read the first time and ordered to be read the second time to-morrow.

Hon. Mr. CAMPBELL a member of Her Majesty's Executive Council presented petitions from inhabitants of King's, Queen's, and Prince Counties, praying for the opening of new Roads.

Hon. Mr. SULLIVAN moved the following resolution, viz : —

Resolved, That all the Petitions relating to New Roads be referred to the honorable Commissioner of Public Works, to take such action thereon as may be requisite.

Mr. PERRY said that the resolution was in accordance with the action of the House last session in reference to this matter, but every honorable member, as well as the honorable Commissioner of Public Works had an interest in it. Each individual member formerly had an opportunity of expressing his opinion respecting it, but by passing this single resolution, the Petitions were all to be handed over to the Commissioner of Public Works to be dealt with by him as he pleases. Those petitions were brought in only at the eleventh hour, instead of being laid on the table early in the session, to allow honorable

members an opportunity of examining them, and ascertaining whether the roads asked for were required or not. He did not know how many of those petitions came from his District, and he supposed other honorable members were much in the same position. Pressure is frequently brought to bear upon the honorable Commissioner of Public Works with reference to them, and no doubt he is influenced to a certain extent in that way. A road in his own District had been opened up in a place where it is not wanted, owing, no doubt, to political influence. He was not going to oppose the resolution, but he thought it a useless one. The petitions were introduced through the Commissioner of Public Works and were to be referred back to him! He thought such a course altogether unnecessary. He hoped this would be the last year in which such a summary mode of dealing with these petitions would be adopted.

Hon. Mr. CAMPBELL said that he had not these petitions in his possession so long as the honorable member for Tignish supposed. They had been received only quite lately. On Thursday last three of them came in. For some years the House went through the farce of appointing a Committee to examine the petitions for new roads, and to report to it such as they recommended to be granted. During late years, those petitions have all been referred to the Commissioner of Public Works, to be dealt with by him as he saw necessary. The result was that he carried them with him in his tours through the country, and in all cases examined the proposed routes for new roads. When that official was a mere figure-head, and remained in his office all the year round, such was not the case. Now, when he has to travel from East Point to North Cape, he has the best opportunity of judging where a new road should be opened. He is, of course, responsible to the Government of which he is a member, and to the House for his action with respect to those petitions. He did not think the honorable member for Tignish had any right to complain of the manner in which he had been treated. The honorable gentleman complained that a road had been opened in his district, where it was not wanted; and stated that a member knew the wants of his own district much better than the Commissioner of Public Works, with respect to such matters. He (Mr. C.) would now tell the honorable member that the road referred to by him has been opened up in the public interests, and that it is very necessary. The honorable gentleman had himself complained that some people had not access to their lands for want of a public road. Well, that road was opened for the purpose of affording access to certain farms, to which there was formerly no road. He believed that the interests of the country will be much better served by referring those petitions for new roads to the Commissioner of Public Works, than by dealing with them in any other way. Where he was convinced that a new road is really wanted, he had never refused to

attend to it; but this was a matter which must be authorized by an Order in Council. He felt certain no honorable member had any case to complain of since the petitions had been referred to him.

Mr. J. R. McLean said that under the old system honorable members had an opportunity of making such remarks on petitions from their respective districts for new roads as they thought necessary. Under the present system, they are entirely precluded from so doing. Why are these petitions brought down to the House at all, when they are merely handed back to the Commissioner of Public Works? There is no doubt that an influential man, who can tell a good story in support of his claim for the opening of a new road, can generally secure what he asks for. Honorable members of the House should certainly have an opportunity of expressing an opinion on petitions from their respective districts for the opening of new roads. He protested against the present summary way of dealing with those petitions.

Mr. Hooper did not think the honorable Commissioner of Public Works knew more about the wants of a District with respect to the opening of new roads than did its representatives. He felt certain that members knew those wants better than the Commissioner of Public Works. He asked the honorable gentleman the other day whether or not he received a petition from the inhabitants of a portion of his District for the opening of a new road in that locality. Now, he (Mr. **H.**) knew that only a few individuals were asking for the new road, and that the great majority of the people in that vicinity was opposed to it. He wished to know whether or not it was the intention of the Government to close up the old road. This was why he had asked the question the other day. He maintained that the old road could not be closed while nearly all the inhabitants of the neighborhood were opposed to closing it.

Hon. Mr. CAMPBELL had examined the route referred to by the honorable member for Morell, and found that it would pass through a large swamp and would require a Bridge. He bought and paid for the right of way.

Mr. SINCLAIR thought these Petitions should have been left in the custody of the Clerk, in order that honorable members might have access to them during the session. There are many proposed new roads, which the representatives for the various Districts will not know whether asked for or not. The Commissioner of Public Works should know all about these roads, but there is usually a good deal of favoritism about these matters, and honorable members wish to see justice done all parties. He knew that two short roads had been asked for in his District, but they had not yet been opened. If the Petitions are to be disposed of in this summary manner, members will not know what is to be done with the Petitions from their Districts. They had a right to be made acquainted with the action proposed to be taken with reference to those petitions.

Hon. Mr. SULLIVAN said that after the prorogation of the Legislature, these petitions will be placed in the office of the Department of Public Works, where the public may have access to them at all times. It seemed to him (Mr. S.) that was the proper place to deposit them, as the Commissioner of Public Works has better facilities for conferring with members from the country as to whether or not it is advisable to open a new road in any locality, than any one else. The honorable member for Strathalbyn seemed to be very suspicious, but he (Mr. S.) did not think there was any reason for it.

Mr. FARQUHARSON said that the honorable Commissioner of Public Works professes to know the wants of the people with respect to new roads better than their Representatives themselves, although there are roads upon which the honorable gentleman has never stepped. There seems to be no doubt that he (Mr. C.) has his political favorites and that they have an influence over him when asking for the opening of any new road. Last session $5,000 was voted for new roads and only $1,500 expended. When these Petitions are placed in the hands of the Commissioner of Public Works, it is frequently the last that is heard of the majority of them.

Hon. Mr. FERGUSON said that

any person at all acquainted with this Island must know that we are pretty well supplied with roads; in some cases with too many of them. There are yet places, however, where new ones are required. This is owing partly to the haphazard manner in which roads were opened up in the first instance. A Committee was formerly appointed to do the work, and it has been said that those who could influence the Committee received what they asked for. This went on until the Public Works Department was properly organized with a properly constituted head. He thought the course pursued last session was the proper one to follow. All the members of the House will have an opportunity to examine these petitions and to judge their contents before any action is taken by the Commissioner of Public Works. That official will take the responsibility of recommending what roads shall not be opened. Until two years ago the opening of a new road was not referred to the Executive Council at all; but at present no road can be opened without an Order in Council for that purpose. There are several reasons for adopting this system. Every representative of a district knows that he was sometimes pressed by political friends to do what he felt was not for the public interests to do with respect to the opening of a proposed new road. Under the present system only such new roads as are absolutely necessary for the public interests are opened up by the Commissioner of Public Works.

Mr. BEER said that there is no doubt that the system adopted by the House with respect to this matter was for many years only a farce. Roads that were recommended to be opened were referred to the Government, but the latter only opened such of them as they thought proper. He quite approved of placing all the responsibility in connection with the opening of new roads upon the shoulders of the Commissioner of Public Works. Still he thought the resolution rather hasty, as these petitions should have been allowed to remain on the table for two or three days in order that honorable members might have an opportunity to examine them. They could then be referred to the Commissioner of Public Works. There is a petition for a new road in a portion of his district to enable people to procure mussel mud for their farms. Another petition asks for a short road to shorten the distance to town, and to make the route easier than the one which now exists. It will reduce a distance of thirteen miles to eight miles, which is important. Other new roads are asked for, which he hoped would receive due attention at the hands of the Commissioner of Public Works.

I. O.

Mr. D. C. MARTIN said the Commissioner of Public Works had taken a singular position with respect to this matter. He (Mr. M.) would like to know what will be done with these Petitions. The least that should be done would be, that the titles of these Petitions should be read by the Clerk of the House. This House, should say what new Roads shall be opened. Petitions were sent in to the Public Works Department two years ago, but because some friends of the honorable Commissioner had spoken against them, nothing had been done. This had been the case with respect to the road at Village Green. Whilst many of the inhabitants were favorable to this road a few others were against it and in consequence nothing had been done. Whether the honorable Commissioner of Public Works should have such great power was a question that honorable members should seriously consider. The honorable gentleman had spent $775.00 in Belfast district last year and had given it all to political favorites. When an election is coming on the honorable Commissioner is very active in opening new roads, but at other times nothing will be done by this honorable gentleman. He (Mr. M.) thought the old plan should be followed, viz: that of referring these petitions to a Committee of the House on New Roads.

Motion put and carried.

Hon. Mr. SULLIVAN gave notice that to-morrow he would ask leave to introduce a resolution setting forth that no new matter on which a Bill may be formed shall be introduced into this House this session after Wednesday, April 8th instant.

Mr. J. R. McLEAN in pursuance of notice in the Order Book asked the honorable Commissioner of Public Works if it is the intention of the Government to repair the Souris Beach Road between Souris East and West previous to the opening of navigation.

Hon. Mr. CAMPBELL said he did not understand the question. The Souris Beach Road is in good order excepting where some drift sand had accumulated on it. He (Mr. C.) would like to know if the honorable member wished the Government to stop the drifting of the sand.

Mr. J. R. McLEAN said this Road was not in good repair as it was badly broken up. It should be made one of the best roads in the District as is was the most travelled.

Hon Mr. CAMPBELL said that the honorable member was violating the rules of the House by discussing the matter. He (Mr. C.) would give the honorable member an answer to the question in a proper manner when he (Mr. C.) was prepared to do so.

House adjourned for one hour.

G. F. O.

EVENING SESSION

City Bill.

On motion of Hon. Mr. McLeod the Order of the Day being read for the second reading of the Bill intituled "An Act to further amend the City of Charlottetown Incorporation Acts," the Bill was accordingly read the second time. .

Hon. Mr. McLEOD said in moving that the House do now go into the Order of the Day, it was customary to make some observations respecting the provisions of the measure under consideration. In 1876 a Bill had Passed the Legislature empowering the City Council of Charlottetown to impose a Personal Property tax. This measure did not work satisfactorily as the owners of real estate had to bear the greater Part of the burden. In 1880 another Bill was Passed imPosing assessment on real estate, but this Bill made no reference to assessment for Personal property. It has been construed by the Stipendiary Magistrate of the City that the latter Bill repealed the Act imposing assessment on personal Property. Although there was no intention of doing so when the Bill was Passed in 1880 and although the majority of the citizens are of the opinion that the whole assessment should not fall on real estate, yet for the last two years the Principal Part of the taxes collected by the city have been from the owners of real estate. This has had a bad effect when any desirable improvements are required. The owners of real estate having to pay all or the greater Part of the taxes collected, and have opposed any expenditure by which the taxation on their property would be increased, as they considered it unfair that real estate should pay for the improvements enjoyed by all classes of citizens.

It is only fair that all sources of wealth should contribute towards the revenue of the city. Taxes are collected for protection from fire, for Police services and 'many other Purposes, the benefits of which are enjoyed by the owners of Personal Property as well as by those who Possess real estate, and it is only equitable that Personal Property should pay a proportionate Part of these expenditures. It may be said that a Personal Property tax would allow the goods on the merchants' shelves to be taxed every year, although they might remain unsold from one year to another. He (Mr. McL.) did not see any force in the objection as the goods receive Protection from the fire m an. and Police force while in the Possession of the merchant or on his shelves. The Bill now introduced states in the first section that the City Council shall have Power to tax Personal Property, and this is the Principal provision of the measure. It is proposed to impose one third of one per cent. on Personal property, and three-fourths of one per cent. on real estate. The second section Provides that Commercial Travellers must take out a license before they will be allowed to sell goods in the city. This will Prevent Persons from the other Provinces opening shop and slaughtering goods to the great injury of the regular traders, without paying anything towards the cost of the City Government. Such persons are to be asked to pay a license fee. The 3rd Section is an amendment of the Act passed in 1880. That Act enabled the City Council to impose taxation on the property of corporations but made no provision for taxing the property of foreign corporations. Foreign corporations should be taxed as well as native ones and this section is an equitable one. This section also defines what personal property of such corporations is assessable. The fourth section defines what is personal property and how much of it is amenable to taxation. It also sets forth that a schedule of the different kinds of personal property shall be furnished to the ratepayers, who are required within 14 days to fill into it what property they own. If the assessors appointed by the City Council do not consider that these schedules are properly filled they can go to the premises of the ratepayer and assess the personal property. All personal property over $200 is liable for assessment. The fifth section provides the mode whereby the taxation on personal property shall be collected. The City Council have good machinery for collecting the taxes on real estate and this section provides similar machinery for personal property taxation. Some may think that the machinery provided by this section is too summary, but he (Mr. McL.) did not think the objection would hold good as real estate was just as valuable as personal property and the less expense incurred in collecting these taxes the better for all parties. A summary mode of collecting will cause less friction than if a more expensive way was adopted. If it is not at all desirable that expenses should be heaped upon the citizens even if they do not pay their assessments as promptly as they should. The sixth clause provides that the City taxes must be paid before the property can be sold by an execution out of the Courts or by a Bill of Sale. It often happens that merchants fail and their goods are sold by the Sheriff. This section says that if the City Assessment is not paid, that the Sheriff must pay it out of the proceeds of the sale. This lien on the goods begins when the Assessment list is returned by the assessors or by the rate-payer; but will not prevent the sale of the rate-payers goods in the usual way of business. Some might think that this section would prevent the sale of personal property until the civic assessment is paid, but such is not the case. It only provides that the civic assessment shall first be paid before property is sold by process of law or Bill of Sale. The 8th section provides that a poll-tax shall be paid by every citizen. This will divide the burden of taxation as many have neither personal property or real estate. The 11th clause proposes the amalgamation of two offices, viz: that of Secretary of the Board of School Trustees and City Clerk. The present Secretary of the School Trustees does the business of the School Board and the citizens desire that these offices be amalgamated as thereby a saving of $500 per annum will be effected. He (Mr. McL.) was doubtful if one man can perform these duties satisfactory, but the matter, no doubt, will be carefully considered in committee. The 12th clause provides that in case of an election for Mayor and City Councillors, when only one person is proposed for either of the positions, that no election shall be held for that Ward. The 13th clause provides that Foreign Fire and Life Insurance Companies doing business in the City shall take out a license to do so. The 14th clause relates to the collection of assessments. At present a list of defaulters is published in the *Royal Gazette* and one other paper published in the City. This section will give the City Council power to publish the list in one or more City papers only and it is considered that considerable saving will thereby be effected. The 16th clause changes the term of the School year so as to make it correspond with the end of the Civic year on the 31st of December At present $26,000 of an assessment is collected and it is found hard to make an estimate of the amount required for the year and it is considered desirable to have this change, so that the Council will be able to know the amount required for each year's expenditure. The 17th clause proposes to extend the jurisdiction of the Stipendiary Magistrate in actions for debt to the same sum to which Judges of the County Court have jurisdiction, that is from $80 to $150. Objection may be made to this clause because there is a Circuit of the County Court in the City where actions can be brought, but if the clause is adopted the fees of the Court will go to the City Treasury whereas at present these amounts go to the Provincial Treasury. Another clause provides that if a worthy first-class Hotel is started in the City that its proprietors shall be exempted from taxation for it for 15 years. The City Council have power under former Acts to exempt new industries from taxation, and have exercised it in one or two instances. If a hotel is built that will attract business to the City, it will be of as much benefit as any new industry. The 19th clause provides that the City Council shall have power to issue debentures to the same amount as those falling due. The large amount of $18,000 will fall due next year and it is considered desirable to give the City Council power to issue new debentures in place of those falling due; but this clause does not give the City power to increase the total amount of the debt. These are the principal provisions of this measure which he (Mr. McL.) trusted would be acceptable to the House. If any further explanations were desired they would be given in Committee.

Motion put and carried.

The House accordingly resolved itself into said Committee.

Mr. ALEX. MARTIN in the Chair.

The first clause being read by the Chairman,—

Hon. Mr. CAMPBELL said he had been thirteen years in the Legislature, and every year during that time the city had come to this

House with a Bill asking for improved legislation. As all persons are interested in the success of the capital of the Province, it no doubt is the duty of honorable members to carefully consider the nature of the measures presented for their approval, but these many amendments were costing the country a large sum. In 1876 a Bill came before this House containing a similar provision to what is included in this clause, and as that amendment has not been repealed or amended he (Mr. C.) contended that it is still in force. The fact was that it was found that the taxes imposed by the former Bill would bear heavily on the citizens, and it had to be dropped and a Bill taxing real estate was passed. It is very difficult to understand the provisions of this Bill. He (Mr. C.) was afraid they had a very mischievous tendency. With all due difference to the honorable senior member for the City, and City Council. He (Mr. C.) did not consider this Bill an advisable one. They should consolidate the statutes already passed, and have a Bill prepared and printed so that honorable members could once for all legislate on this matter. In this Bill they ask for provisions that only should be given to a legislature. They claim the privilege of taxing all sources of wealth and income. They had no right to impose taxation on Banks and Insurance Companies doing business in the City, and he (Mr. C.) did not consider the City Council should be empowered to do so. Another objectionable clause is the one asking power to tax commer-

cial travellers. These men do business all over the Island, and the corporation should not be allowed to tax them for coming into the City. The great objection to the Bill is that the Acts incorporating the City should be consolidated and printed, so that honorable members from the country can properly understand the nature of the Bill brought before them.

Mr. BLAKE said the Honorable Commissioner of Public Works did not understand the question when he said that the City Bills were costing the country a large amount. It did not cost much for the City Bills that were passed, but any sum expended for this purpose was greatly increased because the House so mutilated these Bills that after being passed they were of very little use. It was part of the duty of the Legislature to make laws for the City, as well as the country, and honorable members need not be surprised if the representatives from the City are asking for Bills of this kind. The Honorable Commissioner of Public Works need not be alarmed respecting the mischief that this Bill will do. The Bill has been carefully prepared and has been submitted at the request of the citizens of Charlottetown, expressed at a meeting held for the purpose of considering the clauses of this measure. The meeting was adjourned so that any objectionable features in the Bill as first prepared might be amended; and this Bill is now approved of by the citizens. The amendments proposed by this Bill, although apparently trifling, will remedy matters that have worked prejudicially against the interests of the City, and honorable members, no doubt, will be willing to pass such such laws as will tend to advance the interests of the capital of the Province. It has been found that an additional revenue of $10,000 will be required in order to carry on the business of the City properly. It has been found during the past that real estate paid a greater proportion of the amount of taxation than it had any right to do, and it is now considered advisable that any further taxation should be levied on personal property.

Last year the amount
raised by taxation was $26,000
From other sources the
revenue was   15.000
                           _____
Making a total of $41,000

These may appear large amounts to collect in one year in a city like Charlottetown, but it must not be forgotten that certain parts of the expenditure are uncontrollable. Education alone costs $9,635 which large amount has to be raised by the citizens of Charlottetown each year, in order to maintain the efficiency of the Schools in the city. It has been found that $33,000 has to be raised before any improvements can be made. The City owes a large debt and interest has to be provided each year. It was not necessary for him to explain how the debt was incurred, but the interest has to be met. An additional $10,000 is required this year and this Bill has been carefully prepared, so as to effect this purpose. The citizens themselves should be capable of framing a Bill to meet the requirements of the City, and as it did not tax any one outside of the city, he (Mr. B.) did not think the honorable Commissioner of Public Works should take such strong objections to it. Although he (Mr. B.) was a resident and representative of the City, he had an interest in the country and would not support any measure that would be prejudicial to the interests of the country, and he hoped that honorable members would not put any objections in the way of this measure which, no doubt, would be of great service to the citizens of Charlottetown.

Mr. SINCLAIR said he had no objection to granting what was just, but this measure was not a just one. The House had not been properly treated by the City. The Acts respecting the City should be consolidated and brought before the House earlier in the session, and not left until a day or so before the close, before they are brought up. He (Mr. S.) was quite willing to allow the citizens to tax themselves, but this Bill will allow the City Assessors to tax the produce of country dealers that may be stored in Charlottetown in transit. It will also lessen the price paid farmers by the merchant as the tax on personal property will include produce of all kinds. He (Mr. S.) contended that the Bill should have come forward earlier in the Session, and he was surprised the honorable members for the City had taken so long to get this Bill prepared.

Hon. Mr. McLeod said the honorable member for Springton could not refrain from having a slap at the representatives of the City. The Bill had been introduced as soon as it had been placed in the hands of the representatives and it was only in deference to the wish of honorable members who were desirous of perusing the Bill before it came up for discussion, that it had been deferred until the present time.

Hon. Mr. Campbell said he contended that the Bill introduced by the City this year should have consolidated the laws relating to the City. It is no use to say that honorable members understand this measure, and it is a most contradictory one. The City had large amounts of interest to pay that they should not have to pay if they had properly conducted their business. They pay large amounts for rents of schools and for interest on the cost of School buildings for which they borrowed money, instead of paying for them as people in the country had to do. The City is paying $4,500 for interest and rent that they should not have to pay.

Hon. Mr. McLeod said the honorable member himself is most responsible for this state of things and for the large expenditures on schools that necessitated it. Contrary to all precedent he (Mr. C.) put four men appointed by the Government on the School Board; and only three who were nominees of the City Council who have to meet the expenditure of these men. He says the Council has been extravagant, but it was not in their power to control the action of the School Board. If the City Council had power to control these expenditures, a different state of affairs would have been the result.

Mr. D. C. Martin said the City Schools are in a flourishing condition and are a credit to the gentlemen whose business it is to look after them. The House had not received the consideration it deserved with respect to this matter as only one copy of this Bill had been made. Several Acts are referred to in this measure and sufficient information respecting the Bill is hard to arrive at. In reference to the tax on commercial travellers it was well known that this tax cannot be collected in the other Provinces. There are also many clauses of the Bill that are objectionable especially the taxation on mortgages on property in the country. He (Mr. M.) would not support this measure.

Hon. Mr. Sullivan said that every year new amendments to the City of Charlottetown Incorporation Acts are presented to this Legislature. The people of Charlottetown or rather the various City Councils have not been able to make up their minds what they require to carry on their Civic affairs, and since 1855 nearly every session a Bill has been introduced into this House relating to the City. The honorable senior member for Belfast said he had been unable to find sufficient time to understand this Bill since it was introduced. When it is remembered that fourteen days have elapsed since this Bill was read the first time, it shows that either the honorable member had not been attending to his duties or that it took him a long while to understand anything. No honorable member can complain of not having had ample time to examine this measure. Several honorable members had asked that sufficient time would be afforded them to look over this Bill and it had not been brought up for discussion before this evening on that account. After having fourteen days to consider this Bill he (Mr. S.) must say that he was not wedded to its provisions. At the last election held in the City the gentleman, who had formerly held the office of Mayor, for some years was not re-elected, but another gentleman was chosen. The City had now a new Council, and he (Mr. S.) expected that the Bill they would prepare for the consideration of this Legislature would be more satisfactory than the one that is now presented. While he appreciated the efforts of the honorable members for the City, and in endeavoring to commend this measure to the favorable consideration of the House, they must not consider that honorable members should vote for every measure that the City Council of Charlottetown wishes to be made law. Honorable members should use their intelligence respecting all matters brought before them. We have been told that the City Council have consulted a great many per-

sons outside of the corporate body respecting this matter, but he (Mr. S.) did not think they should have done so. The City Council should themselves have taken the responsibility of framing this measure, and not have gone around the town consulting persons, many of whom no doubt, were actuated by selfish motives in giving the advice they did. Many of the provisions of this Bill were calculated to be very injurious, and he would like to show the Committee how prejudicially it would act in many cases. The Bill provides that no amount of personal property under $200 shall be taxed. Suppose a man has household furniture or other personal property to the amount of $500 he will be taxed for the whole amount, notwithstanding he had only $300 worth more than the person who was exempted. The tax should only be collected on the excess over $200 and not on the whole amount of the property. Another extraordinary provision is where a man doing business, will be taxed for every item of property he possesses and some of his property will be taxed twice. There is a tax on horses and carriages already, and yet this Bill provides that they shall again be taxed as personal property. He would also refer to another most improper provision which is embodied in this measure. Suppose a person lives just within the city limits, and has an office in the business part of the city, this person will be taxed. His neighbor, whose house happens to be outside of the limits of the city, but who also does business in an office in the city, will not be taxed. The Bill should provide that persons who live in the city, or do business therein, should be liable for taxation. Another extraordinary provision is the one which exempts mortgages on property within the city from taxation. One man invests his money in our Banks and his capital is taxed. Another who invests his capital in Mortgages, the safer investment of the two, is not taxed. Such extraordinarily one-sided provisions never came before this Legislature in any preceding Bill. Another provision asks this Legislature to set aside the Educational System that has been adopted by this Province. Who, he would like to ask, provides the means for carrying on the Educational System of the city? We all know that a large portion of these means come from the Government of the Province, and that being the case, the Government have a perfect right to have some control over the expenditure. It is quite proper for the City Council to be anxious to curtail the expenditure of all unnecessary amounts, but they have no right to impair the working of the Educational System. The City had an excellent School Board who do their work well, he believed, and who receive no renumeration for their services. These gentlemen have sent a resolution to the Government, stating that they do not consider it desirable to amalgamate the offices that this Bill provides for doing, viz,— the office of Secretary of the School Trustees and that of the City Clerk. The School Trustees have a Secretary who, for a long time, has been intimately connected with our School System, who has been a school teacher himself, who has given great assistance in regulating the system on which our schools in the city are conducted, and who is acquainted with the working of the School Law now in force in the city. The City School Board consider that the School Act could not be worked so satisfactorily in the city if this gentleman were discharged, and the office amalgamated with another. He did not think the citizens of Charlottetown will thank this Legislature for passing this Bill when they come to pay the expense of the litigation its provisions will incur. The tax on Commercial Travellers has been found to be *ultra vires*. It has been decided in cases of a like nature that have arisen in St. John and Quebec, that this tax can not be collected, and although the question had not been appealed to the highest Courts in the Dominion, there were grave doubts in the minds of many high legal authorities whether such a tax can be collected in any city. The tax on foreign banks is a similar provision, and if passed, will delude the citizens into believing that they had a source of revenue when they could collect nothing from it without litigation. It would cost the citizens thousands of dollars to decide questions of this kind, and it was very doubtful if such expenses should be added to the burdens of the city. He (Mr. S.) believed that the Acts at present in force are sufficient to raise all the revenue required for the legitimate expenditure of the city. The Act of 1876 imposes taxation on personal property, and although a question had been raised in the Stipendary Magistrate's Court whether taxes could be collected under its provisions, he (Mr. S.) thought the first section of that Bill set the matter at rest. Sec. 17 of that Act reads as follows:— "The term 'personal property' whenever mentioned in this Act, shall be construed to embrace and extend, not only to all property ordinarily included in the term, but also to to all shares or stock of any Banking or Insurance Company or other joint stock Company, and any assessment levied upon any such stock or shares shall be levied on the profits or premiums declared on such shares or stock for the year preceding, by such Banking or Insurance Company only, and not on the stock or share themselves." That section sufficiently defines personal property, for it is well known that goods, household furniture, horses, cattle, etc., are what is usually called property of this kind. The section in this Bill only puts that Act in operation, and is altogether unnecessary. The honorable member for Springton called attention to the fact that oats, potatoes and any other farm produce, in transit, in the hands of citizens, can by this Bill, be taxed. He (Mr. S.) understood that it is proposed to exempt oats from the operation of this clause, as they are a large export and often held in considerable quantities, but he did not know where the line is to be drawn. Why should the men who deal in oats be exempt from taxation when the men who deal in potatoes, turnips, eggs or sheepskins are taxed?

He did not hesitate to say that hardly a single clause of this Bill will be acceptable to the citizens six months after it is in operation, as it exempts some people, while making others pay more than a fair share. There is also another provision in this Bill that he must allude to as it was one the Government could not allow. This clause provides that an increased jurisdiction shall be given the Court of the stipendiary Magistrate. The jurisdiction of that Court is already too high, for the fees of the County Court for Queen's County are largely decreased on account of the power already given to the Stipendiary Magistrate. If this increase of jurisdiction is granted, the people in the country districts will have to make up the falling off there will be in the revenue derived from fees received at the County Court. The more fees that are collected in the City office of the County Court, the greater the revenue the Government will receive from this source and the result of passing this clause would be prejudicial to the interests of the Province and of the County in particular. With the exception of three clauses, there was nothing in this Bill that should be acceptable to the House. He was convinced that if the Bill was passed, the City would be appealing to the Legislature at its next session to amend it. It was not in the interest of either the country or the town to pass this Bill. Although last year he (Mr. S.) had to pay upwards of $200 for taxation on real estate in the city, he would rather continue to do so, than to pass, a Bill like the one under consideration.,

G. F. O.

Mr. BEER agreed with the honorable Leader of the Government that this Bill had been drawn up by a very cunning person with a particular object in view. That person was the City Recorder. Looking at the opposition shown to the Bill by his honor, it was surprising that the latter did not move that the Speaker take the Chair. The honorable gentleman blamed the City Council because they took the citizens into their confidence, and invited some half dozen of them to assist in devising some means whereby the City funds might be increased. Some public meetings were held, at which resolutions were passed upon which the present Bill was founded. If the citizens were agreed in reference to this measure, he could not see why the House should object to it. It would be better for the Legislature to pass one General Act permitting the citizens to tax themselves as they think fit for civic purposes. If the City is expected to run its own business, it should be allowed to assess itself as it thinks proper. He thought it best to read the Bill clause by clause, discuss it, and strike out what is deemed objectionable.

Hon. Mr. McLEOD said this discussion should have taken place when the Speaker was in the Chair. The Bill was prepared by the Stipendiary Magistrate. He did not think the objections which had been raised against it amounted to anything. As to the tax on Commercial Travellers, there is not a City in the Dominion, where there is not such a law in force, except Charlottetown. In the City of Quebec, there is a clause exactly similar, in force. It is a question as to whether or not the City has the power at present to tax Commercial Travellers. Objections have been raised to the tax on personal property, some maintaining that a man should only be taxed for the value of his personal property in excess of $200. Under this Bill, if a person owns $250 worth, he will be taxed for the whole amount. There is no tax upon money invested in mortgages in the City, because the lender may turn round and charge the borrower whose property is mortgaged, with the tax on the Interest, and as Real Estate is already heavily taxed, it should not be taxed a second time. The machinery for the collecting of taxes in the City has hitherto been found to be very defective, and needs improvement. This measure is intended to meet the want. This Bill does not touch the personal property of persons doing business as merchants or professional men in the City, but reside outside the City limits. A few words added to it will cure that defect.

Mr. FARQUHARSON said that so far as the Bill personally affected him, it made no difference to him if the Speaker resumed the Chair, and no report is made. This Bill has been introduced by Petition and has been endorsed by the citizens, who have carefully considered its provisions. If it does not conflict with any existing law, and does not injuriously affect any person outside the City, he did not think there should be much opposition to it. He could not see that it would affect the interests of country Districts. If it requires amendment in some respects, it is the duty of the House to make it what it should be, as far as this can be done. Some of the objections made to it by the honorable Leader of the Government are not very material ones. He thought the House might be guided to a considerable extent by the City of Halifax Bill, which has been working satisfactorily in that City. He hoped the Bill would be read clause by clause and fully considered. He was prepared to assist in amending it and rendering it workable.

Mr. SINCLAIR could not see why there should be a tax on the Income arising from mortgages on lands in country Districts, or in any place outside of Charlottetown. As a layman, however, he did not profess to understand this matter. He found that in collecting these taxes, power is given the assessors to push the notice into the hands of any person about the house or on the premises upon which the tax is to be levied; and that from that procedure there is to be no appeal. He thought this a pretty arbitrary course to pursue. He had no objection to giving the City any proper advantage, but the House should look into these provisions. It appeared to him

that a looser measure than this could hardly be framed.

Mr. BLAKE,—There is provision in the Bill for an appeal to the City Court within ten days after the notice of Assesment has been served. He was sorry to see the opposition to this Bill which had been manifested by the honorable Leader of the Government and the honorable Commissioner of Public Works, for it seemed to him that it would result in the loss of the measure. If this Bill is thrown out, there will have to be an additional tax on Real Estate in the City to the extent of about $10,-000. He hoped honorable members would consider the position in which the City is at present placed. The Act at present in force provides for an Income tax, but all Local Government and Dominion Officials are exempt, and the provision proved so unworkable that the whole tax was thrown upon Real Estate. He could not see that there is anything in this Bill that will impose any burden on country people. When the honorable Leader of the Government pointed out the defect, he should have suggested amendments, but he did not do so. It is impossible for any body of men to frame a perfect Bill or one that will meet the wishes of all the tax-payers. The citizens expect this Bill to pass, and he hoped that it would not be thrown out altogether, but that, if found necessary, amendmments would be made in it. It is true some are opposed to it, but it is impossible to please all. He did not know that there had been any lobbying with respect to it, although, in former sessions, that practice had been indulged in to a certain extent with reference to City measures. With respect to the cost of Education in the City, the Government pay the Teachers the Statutory allowance, but it does not provide the means for meeting the expenses of the Schools, which, in Charlottetown amount to about $9,500 per year, including Interest on School Debentures. As regards the tax on personal property, there must be exemptions somewhere, and the line must be drawn. The citizens and Council considered that the poor man who owns less than $200 worth, should be exempt from the payment of a tax on it. As, however, the tax on that amount would not exceed sixty cents, it was scarcely worthy of mention. He hoped the Bill would not meet the fate with which it had been threatened.

Hon. Mr. SULLIVAN said that the constituents of the honorable member who had just sat down, have no reason to find fault with him as he had done his duty with reference to this Bill. There is no appeal from the tax levied upon any citizen, under the provisions of this Bill to any independent tribunal. No doubt the Stipendiary Magistrate does his duty satisfactorily, but to place the matter on a proper footing, there should be provision for an appeal to some independent tribunal, apart from the City Court. He thought the Bill did affect the country Districts, for while mortgages in the

City are exempt, mortgages in the country are not exempt from tax. The Income of every citizen is taxed, derivable from every source. Under such a law, the holder of a mortgage in the City could turn round and charge the mortgagor with the tax on the mortgage. There is a provision in some mortgages now recorded in the Registry Office that in case an income tax is imposed in Charlottetown the borrower shall be compelled to pay that tax on the mortgage. The Representatives for the City are simply doing their duty in attending to the interests of their constituents with respect to this matter, and when the honorable junior member for the City says that the citizens are anxious that this Bill should pass, he means a Bill which will accomplish the object intended. He (Mr. S.) felt sure that the citizens will thank the House for rejecting some of the objectionable clauses.

Hon. Mr. PROWSE said it was no new thing to have Bills of this nature from the City of Charlottetown, near the close of the session. He always maintained that the City should have power to levy such taxes as it requires. It is now admitted by every person that the Income tax with the Real Estate tax is not sufficient to meet the requirements of the City. The condition of the side-walks is proof of this. He would withhold from the City no power to tax the citizens as it thought proper, but he could not allow it to impose a tax upon country people. Now, it had been pretty clearly shown that this Bill would operate in that way. The proposed tax on the Incomes of Banks is a very undesirable one. The experience of our Island Banks has been a sad one, and there is a difficuliy in making these institutions pay, here. A good deal of the stock in those Banks is held by persons belonging to country Districts, and he did not see why that Stock should be taxed by the City. The same remark would apply to other corporations in which country people hold Stock. If the City members would consent to exempt country Stock, &c., from taxes for the benefit of the City, they would have his support

Mr. RICHARDS thought all honorable members should do their duty with respect to this Bill as well as with reference to all other measures coming before the Legislature. It appears that if this Bill does not become law, a far heavier tax must be levied upon Real Estate, which is already sufficiently taxed. Some provision should be made to relieve the burden on the latter. An income tax is too inquisitorial in its nature, and is always objectionable Every other means should therefore be exhausted before resorting to it. Why not adopt some plan which will reach those who, to-day, pay no tax whatever? He did think that persons holding mortgages on property beyond the bounds of the City should be taxed, as this would really be a tax on other localities. If, however, the citizens are anxious for such a measure as this Bill, why not strike out its

objectionable features, and make it as workable as possible?'

Mr. FARQUHARSON understood that about $18,000 in debentures would fall due this year, and that if this Bill does not pass, a heavy direct tax must be levied to meet them.

Hon. Mr. McLEOD,—Why not pass those clauses to which there is no objection, and deal with the others afterwards? There is no reference to mortgages outside the city limits, but, if the House thinks it necessary, a provision will be inserted exempting them. The Bill had been allowed to lay over until now in order to give time for its full consideration. It was not intended to apply to martages at all, and if honorable members wish, a special provision will be inserted to that effect.

Mr. BLAKE said it was distinctly understood that this Bill would not affect mortgages on lands in country districts, and perhaps it would be well to make a special provision for their exemption.

Hon. Mr. SULLIVAN said that unfortunately the exemption of country mortgages had not been carried out in the framing of the Bill. It will tax incomes receivable from such mortgages, and, as he already stated, money lenders frequently make a special provision in their mortgages that all income tax on them shall be paid by the mortgagor. This Bill will, therefore, in effect, tax country people. The first clause is not objectionable in one sense, but in another sense it is, as it will commit the House to a tax on personal property. Further on, personal property is defined. In passing this clause, the House will be committed to the definition of personal property further on in the Bill. He thought it would be better to report progress, as honorable members needed some rest.

Mr. SINCLAIR,—It is not customary to report progress until one clause has been passed. Almost every clause in the Bill will require to be transposed. He was willing to go as far as was just and right in order to give the city what it wants. He thought it would be well for the introducer, who knows what the views of the House are, to prepare the necessary amendments, in order that when the House meets in the morning there may be no delay in dealing with them. The Leader of the Government had pointed out what are serious objections to the Bill, and amendments to meet those objections should be prepared to prevent delay. There are objections with reference to the use of the word "inhabitant" in one of the clauses; to the clause relating to the amalgamation of the Offices of Secretary of the City School Board ond Clerk of the City Council, &c. He thought the House perfectly willing to do what is right to meet the requirements of the City.

Hon. Mr. McLEOD said that a few words added to the various clauses would cure the whole matter. In passing the first clause, the House would not be committed to any provision contained in the Bill further on. Special provision can be made to exclude mortages both in town and country, from its operation. This clause merely gives power to tax personal property and Real Estate in the City of Charlottetown. Why not pass it.

Hon. Mr. SULLIVAN,—If it is agreed to amend the clause defining personal property, it would be as well to pass the first clause of the Bill.

On motion, the first clause was put and agreed to.

Second clause read.

Mr. BLAKE would like to have an understanding that this Bill will be considered fully before the close of the session. It must not be overlooked.

Mr. PERRY said there appeared to be no final decision on the part of the Supreme Court with respect to the Income tax. If the Corporation wish to have the clause passed, let them enforce its provisions at their own risk. They will not attempt to enforce it if they think it is *ultra vires*. The City is liable for a large amount of money and should have the means of raising money to meet their indebtedness, so long as they do not interfere with country people, and country rights.

Hon. Mr. CAMPBELL did not wish by any means to burk the Bill, but to give the introducer time to prepare his amendments to this clause·

Hon. Mr. SULLIVAN said there was no petition from the citizens asking for this Bill, and he was quite certain the City Council does not represent one-tenth of them. In fact, he was certain the City Council themselves are not aware of the contents of this Bill. There is no desire, however, to burk the measure. It is the wish of the House to meet the requirements of the city as far as possible. He thought progress should be reported in order to give the City Representatives a little further opportunity to carefully consider the Bill, and to prepare the necessary amendments. This was in the interests of the people of Charlottetown.

Mr. MATHESON thought all incomes derived from mortgages outside the city should be taxed. It appeared that the city will require all the money it can raise to meet the demands upon it. He, for one, had no objections to most of the sections of this Bill. It may require amendment in some minor points.

On motion Mr. Speaker resumed the Chair, progress was reported, and leave given the Committee to sit again.

On motion the 25th Rule of the House was suspended to enable a member to present a petition.

Thereupon a petition was present by Honorable Mr. Lefurgey, from the town of Summerside, asking for an amendment to its Act of Incorporation.

Ordered, That said petition be referred to a Special Committee to report thereon by Bill or otherwise.

Ordered, That the Honorable Mr. Lefurgey, Mr. Bentley and Mr. Gillis do compose said Committee.

Hon. Mr. LEFURGEY from the said Committee presented to the House a Bill intituled: "An Act to consolidate and amend the Acts incorporating the town of Summerside, intituled, 'The Summerside Incorporation Act, 1885,'" and moved that it be received and read.

Hon. Mr. SULLIVAN said that the Bill was one of extraordinary size and length, and as the Legislature will probably be prorogued on Thursday next, he thought it would be impossible to deal with this measure properly by that time. Beside this, the Council would require three whole days to deal with it. It might be well to read it a first time, but there is not sufficient time at the disposal of the Legislature to pass it.

Hon. Mr. LEFURGEY had only received the Bill quite lately, but he hoped it would be gone into. Summerside is the second town on the Island and should receive proper consideration.

Mr. PERRY said that it surely was not the intention of the honorable Leader of the Government to refuse to go into the consideration of this Bill without the consent of his friends in the Government. So far as he (Mr. P.) was concerned, he was quite willing to spend an extra day over it, for the benefit of Summerside. Prince County did not often trouble the House with Special Acts.

Hon. Mr. SULLIVAN said that the honorable member for Tignish was endeavouring to make a little political capital for himself in reference to this matter. The gentlemen who brought this Bill here, were informed that it was intended to prorogue the Legislature on Thursday next, that every means would be taken to push the Bill forward, but that if honorable members from the country would not remain in the House sufficiently long it would be impossible to pass it. He knew that the honorable member for Tignish absents himself seven or eight days at a time. The honorable senior member for Summerside only received the Bill to-day, and cannot be blamed for the delay in having it brought forward. Perhaps the town Council of Summerside is not to be blamed. He hoped there would be time to pass it, but he understood there was a large counter-petition against the passing of the Bill and asking that it be amended in many respects. But he had been informed that some of the proposed amendments had been accepted by the promoters of the Bill. If possible, the House would pass it, in order to meet the wishes of the people of Summerside.

Mr FARQUHARSON thought the House should go into the consideration of the Bill. He was quite willing to help it forward.

Mr. YEO thought the Bill should be duly considered, and hoped the Government would not throw it out.

The Bill was then read a first time, and ordered to be read a second time to-morrow.

Hon. Mr. LEFURGEY presented a counter-petition against the passing of the Bill, and the same was received, read and laid on the table.

Hon. Mr. LEFURGEY said that the Bill had arrived two or three days ago, but the Petition had not arrived until to-day. The counter-petition asks that the Bill be not passed until certain amendments to it are made. To a certain extent, those amendments have been made, but the whole of them have not been adopted. At a public meeting held in Summerside, a motion was made that the Bill be allowed to lay over until next session, in order that the people might see and understand its provisions, but it was not carried. A motion was carried to the effect that a Committee of seven be appointed to confer with the town Council, and have the Bill amended in such a way as to meet the views of those who signed the counter-petition. This work had been partially accomplished, and that Committee had handed the counter-petition to him, to submit the same to the House. This was how that petition came into his hands. Both petitions are before the House; and if the Bill is found to be what it should be, he supposed the House would pass it.

House adjourned uatil to-morrow forenoon at ten o'clock.

I. O.

WEDNESDAY, April 8.

MORNING SESSION.

Mr. SPEAKER in the Chair.

Supply.

Mr. BLAKE, from the House in Committee of Supply, reported 27 resolutions which had been agreed to in Committee, and moved that the question of concurence be now severally put thereon.

Motion put and carried.

Mr. BEER asked why the contract for Georgetown Ferry was increased from $2,000 to $2,400.

Hon. Mr. McDONALD said the amount for this service was voted last year before the contract was let. The former contract had been $2,800, and did not include the service of the steamer to Montague Bridge, which service the present contract included.

Said resolutions were accordingly read, and the question having been severally put thereon they were agreed to by the House.

Hon. Mr. SULLIVAN, Hon. Mr. Ferguson and Hon. Mr. McLeod were appointed a Committee to prepare and bring in a Bill in accordance with the resolutions.

Hon. Mr. SULLIVAN, from said Committee, presented to the House the "Appropriation Bill, 1885," which was received and read the first time.

Hon. Mr. SULLIVAN moved that the 10th Rule of the House be suspended in order that the said Bill be now read the second time.

Mr. YEO said he did not intend to object to the motion of the Honorable Leader of the Government; but the business of the House had been rushed through very rapidly during the last few days. He (Mr. Y.) did not think the Opposition had received the consideration they deserve, and many persons in his position would take advantage of the rules of the House to object to the 10th Rule being suspended.

Hon. Mr. SULLIVAN said he would like to hear of one single occasion on which every consideration had not been accorded the Opposition. When the question of winter communication was under discussion ample time was accorded the honorable gentleman and honorable members of his side of the House to fully discuss the matter. Last Saturday, when the honorable gentleman was absent from his place in the House, although the Government might have then proceeded with the business of the session, they did not do so. It is a chronic complaint with the Opposition every session, that due defference is not paid to them, notwithstanding the fact that every opportunity had been afforded them of finding fault with the actions of the Government. The House had remained in session all night so that a full discussion of the resolutions of Supply might take place and the honorable member had nothing to complain of.

Mr. YEO said the Opposition complained that nearly a fortnight had elapsed at the first of the session without anything being done. It was well on in the second week of the session before the Public Accounts were tabled, and the report of the Honorable Commissioner of Public Works was only tabled the day before the House went into supply. The whole business of the session is rushed through in one week, and honorable members have no chance to carefully consider the important matters on which they have to legislate. The Honorable Leader of the Government has asked me to point out an instance when courtesy was not extended to the Opposition. Honorable members do not forget that on last Thursday when His Honor the Lieutenant Governor came to assent to some Bills, the House was not notified until that gentleman was actually in the Library. In this way the business is rushed through without due consideration.

Hon. Mr. SULLIVAN said the honorable member had no right to charge the Government with the actions of the Lieutenant Governor. It was not known that His Honor the Lieutenant Governor was coming to assent to these Bills at the time he did. The hour that was intimated to His Honor by myself was not convenient to the Lieutenant Governor as he had other engagements; but at a later hour in the day, in order to oblige some parties, who were anxious to have some private Bills passed, His Honor came to the building. On this account the House did not receive the usual notice.

Mr. J. R. McLEAN said it was a pity that a better understanding did not exist between His Honor the Lieutenant Governor and the Government. It was not fair to honorable members that the House had not received longer notice of when these Bills would be assented to. It was very late in the session before the report of the Public Works Department had been tabled, and as this was the most important department to honorable members from country districts, it did not give them justice when so short a time was given them to consider it.

Hon. Mr. McLEOD said he understood that His Honor the Lieutenant Governor had sent a note to the Honorable Leader of the Government intimating that he would be present in the Library at 5.30 o'clock, p. m., on that day, but the note had not been received when His Honor arrived.

Hon. Mr. FERGUSON said the Opposition complain of the tardiness of the Government in submitting the Public Reports. He (Mr. F.) would like them to point out an instance when the Public Accounts were submitted within nine days after the meeting of the

House, as was the case this session The important question of winter communication was taken up at the earliest opportunity. The report of the honorable Commissioner of Public Works was ready in manuscript long before the House met, but, owing to press of work at the printing office of the contractor, it was not tabled as soon as the other public reports. He (Mr. F.) was astonished at this charge being made by the Opposition as the honorable member for Tignish had been allowed to adjourn the debate on the question of Supply three times. The Opposition not being prepared to carry on the debate, and the House having gone into Committee of Supply, the Government allowed the debate to be again reopened, although it was an irregularity and contray to the usage of Parliament. This complaint has become chronic with the Opposition although there is no foundation for it. They have to make some charges against the Government in order to try and offset its increased popularity.

Mr. FARQUHARSON said the Opposition had reopened the debate on supply on account of the action of the Government when they refused to consent to a motion of adjournment proposed by the Opposition. On that occasion he (Mr. F.) had only spoken as he had a right to do, and the Government could not claim that they had accorded the Opposition any courtesy. That debate had shown up some of the Governments misdoings and was time well spent.

Returns have been called for by honorable members of the Opposition that have not yet been laid before the House. It is due to the reputation of the honorable Commissioner of Public Works that these vouchers should be tabled before the close of the session. It seems that the business is to be rushed through, notwithstanding the Bills from the City and from Summerside have not yet been passed. He (Mr. F.) would like to see all Bills carefully considered before they are passed. The honorable Leader of the Government was surely in error when he (Mr. S.) said that all courtesy had been extended to the Opposition. Does he forget the day that the House was called to meet at ten o'clock forenoon and did not meet until ten o'clock afternoon? Was that courteous to honorable members who were kept waiting around this House all day before it pleased honorable members of the Government to attend in their places.

Motion put and carried.

On motion the Bill was read the second time and committed to a Committee of the whole House.

Mr. Blake in the chair.

After a short time spent in Committee, Mr. Speaker on motion resumed the Chair, progress was reported and leave given the Committee to sit again.

Mr. PERRY said he wished to draw attention to the fact

that fifteen days ago he (Mr. P.) had asked the honorable Commissioner of Crown Lands to lay on the table of the House certain documents relating to the Land Office. Now, at the very eve of prorogation, these returns have not been brought down. One of these questions was in reference to a rebate of rent on certain Lands owned by the Government and was a very important matter. The business of the session is not half through. The report of the Committee on Public Accounts has not yet been received and we do not know if it is yet prepared. We also want to know if any persons have attorned to the Government for the lands occupied by them and if any rent has been paid. We should know about these matters before the House is prorogued. Perhaps it will in these cases, be like the returns asked for from the honorable Commissioner of Public Works in reference to the Bridges carried away by storms and freshets last year. That honorable gentleman said that this information is contained in the supervisors returns; but it is not. They say they spent $10,000 on account of these storms and freshets and why have not the vouchers for these payments been laid before honorable members. He (Mr. P.) did not think such conduct was justice, let alone courtesy to the Opposition. No doubt, honorable members of the Government will say that the member for Tignish has too much curiosity; but he (Mr. P.) had not asked for anything but what he had a right to know.

Hon. Mr. FERGUSON said the honorable Leader of the Opposition complained that the Government had not treated honorable members on the opposite side with courtesy, but the honorable member for Tignish had not treated the Government with decency. The House met on the 11th of March and nearly three weeks afterwards, after holding caucuses upstairs at which all the friends of their party in town were consulted, the Opposition came down, and with the honorable senior member for Belfast at their head, placed a number of questions on the Order Book asking for returns from the Land Office which involved an immense amount of labor to prepare. Answers were prepared as expeditiously as possible and when the fact is considered that the questions asked by the honorable senior member for Belfast were precisely the same as those of the honorable member for Tignish, only in a little different form, it will be readily seen that these honorable members are not very anxious about obtaining information, but only wished to give so much work to the clerks in the Land Office, that it would be impossible to have it all accomplished at an early day. The statements asked for involved a great deal of work and have nearly all been laid before the House. In reference to one of the questions he (Mr. F.) might say for the information of honorable members that as much money has been taken in the Land Office this year since the 1st of April as was taken in the month of April last year. After waiting three weeks before putting these notices on the Order Book, the Opposition now complain that they are not brought forward and that the Government are holding back information. Honorable members know this to be entirely different from the facts of the case, but as the Opposition have no charge to bring against the Government, they are trying to make a little political capital out of it.

Mr. D. C. MARTIN said the report of the honorable Commissioner of Public Lands is very imperfect and honorable members had a right to receive answers to all or any questions they asked.

House adjourned for one hour.

G. F. O.

AFTERNOON SESSION.

On motion, the House resolved itself into a Committee of the whole, to take into further consideration the Appropriation Bill for 1885.

Mr. BLAKE in the Chair.

A clause having been read,—

Mr. BEER said that some time ago he asked Mr. James Brown, C. E., what it would cost to make a survey of the Hillsboro' River with a view to the construction of a bridge across the same, from Charlottetown to Southport, and received a reply stating that said cost would be $200. He (Mr. B.) used all the influence possible with the Government to engage Mr.

Brown to make the survey, and also to prepare an estimate of the cost of the Bridge, for he thought if it did not exceed $200,000 the money would be well expended on the work. We are now paying for a ferry steamer and for the wear and tear of the boat. The cost of the ferry for the past 15 years was considerable, and we shall shortly need one or two new boats. If a bridge could be built for the sum alluded to, the interest on the debentures to be issued for securing the money, would not exceed the present annual cost of the ferry. He was surprised that the Government had not taken action in reference to this matter. They should at once attend to it, and ascertain whether or not the work can be done for a price within our means to pay. The bridge would be a great benefit to all the inhabitants on the south side of the Hillsboro', and he hoped that we should soon have one.

Hon. Mr. SULLIVAN said that provision is made for the proposed survey, under the head of " Miscellaneous." One thousand dollars is voted for various services, among which will be the survey alluded to. He did not think it would cost anything like $1,000 or near $200. He was told by competent authorities that the survey could be made more easily after the disappearance of the ice than at present. It is the intention of the Government to attend to the matter as soon as possible.

Mr. BEER was glad to hear that the survey is to be made.

Hon. Mr. Prowse,—Is the honorable member for Southport afraid that the honorable junior member for Belfast has taken the wind out of his sails with respect to the proposed Hillsboro' Bridge? He (Mr. P.) hoped the day was not far distant when there will be not only a bridge across the Hillsboro', but a railway through the southern part of the Island. He could recollect the day when the honorable member would undertake the construction of a railway to the moon, in order to retain the reins of power, if required. The great Mogul declared that Belfast should have either a railway or its equivalent, but neither had ever been given it. The then Government were going to obtain road steamers to travel over the whole Island, where there was no line of railway, but they changed their minds, and endeavored to persuade their constituents that it would be quite sufficient if their representatives obtained a seat at the Executive Council Board.

Mr. Alex. Martin had asked for returns from the Honorable Commissioner of Public Works for the purpose of showing that the annual expense of running the Southport ferry was sufficient to pay the interest on the cost of a bridge; but the honorable member for Southport objected to the returns because they included the cost of the ferry steamers! He supposed that it was the intention of the honorable member to claim that he was the prime mover in this matter. It is clear, however, that the honorable member attempted, at first, to throw cold water on it.

Mr. Beer said that the idea would never have entered the head of the honorable member who had just sat down had it not been for his proposition. Not until he (Mr. Beer) read a letter from Mr. Brown, C. E., did the honorable gentleman once think of a bridge over the Hillsboro'. The honorable member then acted upon a hint given him from another quarter, and placed a notice on the Order Book asking for returns, etc., relating to the ferry.

Hon. Mr. Ferguson was exceedingly glad that his honorable colleague was taking some little interest in the constituents of both. In his own peculiar way the honorable member had been endeavoring to call attention to the cost of the Southport ferry. If the figures really were excessively high, the honorable gentleman should have left to others the task of pointing out the alleged facts, instead of doing so himself. The course pursued was a strange way to accomplish his professed object. The honorable member professed to be the only member who had any interest in the district, or attended to its wants. The Government took the weight of him much more accurately than he is aware of. So far as he (Mr. F.) is concerned, he would be delighted to give his influence in favor of having a proper survey of the route for the proposed bridge over the Hillsboro'. Any action taken with reference to this matter, should be taken with a clear conception of the cost of the work, so that the country may not be misled with reference to it.

Mr. FARQUHARSON was of opinion that this proposal would end in nothing but talk. It would be talked of until next election. It is so much buncome for a certain purpose. Perhaps the Government will propose a tunnel across the Straits, for a purpose. It would be equally as much to the point as in the present case. He (Mr. Farquharson) would like to see the ferry put on a good footing. He understood that the boiler of the "Elfin" is condemned, and that the iron for a new boiler is now waiting in Pictou for the opening of navigation. The boat will not be allowed to run with her present boiler, and how are the public to be accommodated while a new one is being made? He hoped the new one would be made before being brought over, and that there would be no delay in the matter. This bridge question should have been settled many years ago. The existing public works are not attended to, and yet the Commissioner of Crown Lands proposes a bridge across the Hillsboro' costing at least $200,000. The Government know well they have no means wherewith to undertake the work. It is like building a castle in the air.

Mr. J. R. McLEAN,—Are the people receiving all the accommodation to which they are entitled with respect to wharves? He thought not. The wharf on the Montague side of the Cardigan ferry is in bad condition, and should be attended to at once. He believed there are several other wharves in the same state.

Mr D. C. MARTIN hoped the Government would do justice to the Belfast District. He was glad his honorable colleague had brought the Bridge question before the House. He was sorry to see that no provision was made for a survey of the route for the proposed Bridge, unless the Government appropriate money for that purpose, without a vote of the House. As to the ferries, they should be at once made more efficient. The Elfin is almost unfit for service, and may not be used at all next Summer. The East and West River ferries do not pay at all, but the Southport ferry does pay a handsome return. He hoped the proposed Bridge would be built.

Mr. SINCLAIR thought a Bridge across the Hillsborough would be a vast undertaking for this Province considering its resources. A Bill was passed in 1873, for the Incorporation of a Company for the construction of Bridge across the Hillsborough, but after considering the matter very carefully, it was concluded that it would not be likely to pay the interest on the cost. At most, it would be used only seven months of the year, when there is no ice on the river. No Government with our present resources would undertake such a work as that. Unless the tolls were made very low indeed, the Bridge would be little used. With reference to the cost of the Branch lines of Railway, the Haythorne-Laird Government had no need to make any provision to meet it. All the expense they were required to meet, the first year, was the cost of the survey Before any provision was required to meet the interest, we entered Confederation.

Hon. Mr. PROWSE said that the Haythorne-Laird Government gave a contract for the construction of the Branch lines, without making any provision to meet the interest on the cost The result was, their Debentures went down in the money market. Their action showed that their charges against their predecessors were wholly unfounded. He did not find fault with them for building the Branch lines, but if the then members for Belfast had been honest, they would have put down their foot and said: " we must have a Branch line for Belfast and Murray Harbor." The honorable members for Strathalbyn and Souris agreed that the Railway meant Confederation. If so, they might aswell as not have made provision for the additional Branch to Belfast, &c. Instead of doing so, however, one of the members of the then Government accepted office in this building, another the office of Speaker. Another a seat at the Council Board, another the job of supplying Stationery at the rate of $10 per member to the Legislature.

Mr. J. R. MACLEAN said that the honorable member for Murray Harbor was well aware that the Railway meant Confederation, whether the Branch lines were undertaken or not.

Mr. BEER would like to know what provision is made for the Southport ferry while the new boiler for the *Elfin* is being prepared and placed in her.

Hon. Mr. SULLIVAN,—This is not the time to discuss these matters. These moneys have all been voted by the House in Committee of Supply. Provision satisfactory to the public will be made by the Government to meet the case referred to by the honorable member for Southport. Provision has been already made for the survey of a route for the proposed Bridge. A survey will be made.

Clause put and agreed to. Next clause read.

Mr. BEER objected to any expenditure whatever on Government House, as the Lieutenant Governor is an officer appointed by the Dominion Government. We have enough to do to provide for our own necessities. Let the Dominion Government attend to that matter. He would suggest to the Leader of the Government that when he next goes to Ottawa, he should demand all sums expended by the Provincial Government upon Government House since Confederation.

Hon. Mr. SULLIVAN,—Let the honorable member for Southport submit a resolution with respect to Government House, if he has serious objections to this vote. Perhaps he is not aware that Government House and farm are the property of this Province. Provincial property should not be allowed to go to destruction. Why should not the Lieutenant Governor pay for the use of that House, while he occupies the premises? The cost of keeping it in repair, however, is not worth discussing, as that is a matter which must be attended to.

Mr. BEER admitted that the public property must be kept in repair, but a large amount of money is expended for that purpose which we have no right to pay. No less than $108 was, last year, paid for gas for the use of the Keeper. He did not believe it was ever expended for that purpose.

Hon. Mr. CAMPBELL,—The money was paid for two street lamps at the Guard House at the entrance to the grounds.

Mr. BEER,—The City pays about $28 per lamp per year. How, then, can each lamp in this case cost $108.

Mr. SINCLAIR asked what this vote of $500 was to be expended for? The House, every session, votes hundreds of dollars for Government House. Honorable members should know what the vote is for.

Hon. Mr. SULLIVAN,—The stables belong to the Government as well as the House, and must be kept in

repair, and made to present a decent appearance. He thought the City should provide the gas for the entrance way.

Mr. J. R. MACLEAN,—There are several wharves not yet taken over by the Dominion Government, which should not be allowed by to go to destruction for want of repairs. The people residing in their vicinity are suffering for want of suitable wharf accommodation. When the Dominion Government refuse to repair those wharves, the Local Government in the interests of the Province should do so.

Hon. Mr. FERGUSON,—Were the Dominion Government to neglect the Light Houses or Post Offices, would it be the duty of the Local Government to step in and take charge of them? The Dominion Government declare there are more wharves on this Island than are necessary for the trade of the country, and therefore refuse to take them all over into their hands. He (Mr. F.) knew, however, of a case where the Opposition were afraid the General Government would step in and take charge of a wharf, and thus remedy a grievance. As to Government House, it must not be allowed to fall into a bad state of repair.

Mr. SINCLAIR wished to know how this vote is to be expended? The House had a right to an explanation, and to be informed what was to be done with the money. The property has surely been inspected, and an estimate made of the cost of making necessary repairs! The House has a right to be made acquainted with all the particulars.

Hon. Mr. CAMPBELL said that if the honorable member for Strathalbyn had been in his place when the resolution was passed in Committee of Supply, he would have received all the information asked for. The vote is for the purpose of keeping the out-buildings and houses in repair, and also the roof of the house.

Resolution put and carried.

Another clause read,—

Mr. SINCLAIR saw that a certain sum was voted for roads, bridges and culverts. He found that according to the report of the Supervisors, his district required $2,200 for bridges alone. At that rate the whole expenditure for this purpose in this Province will be fully equal to that of last year, viz., over $30,000. Now, he believed that the Supervisors had stated the truth, although party officials. There are no less than 40 broken down bridges in his district, the repairs of which will cost $2,200. If that district is in that condition, the whole cost of repairs for bridges must reach the sum expended last year. How is this amount to be met?

Mr. HOOPER remained in the House until two o'clock on the night of the seventh, and afterwards found that the remaining resolutions of Supply were voted later in the night. He wished on that occasion to speak with reference to one of those resolutions, but had not an opportunity, as he could not remain all night. He wanted to know whether or not a Bridge on the Cahill Road in his District, is to be repaired. The Milltown Road requires to be opened up. It is very much wanted, and he hoped it will be attended to. Not one of the wharves in the District is in a fit state of repair for the loading of vessels. A road in the back part of Lot 38 should be attended to.

Hon. Mr. SULLIVAN said that the wharves at St. Peter's Bay as well as all the other wharves on the Island belong to the Dominion Government, and the Local Government have nothing to do with them. It is the duty of the gentlemen who represent that district in the House of Commons to see that those wharves are attended to, and, if proper representations were made, he had no doubt the case would be met. The shore fronts on which those wharves are built all belong to the General Government, and the wharves are as much their property as the Light Houses along the coast. The Local Government have, therefore, no right to maintain and repair those wharves. With respect to the railway crossing, the Dominion Government is in the same position. It is their duty to provide all crossings of that kind. If they do not do so, they make themselves liable for trespass.

Mr. HOOPER was glad to hear

these explanations with respect to the wharves. What is the reason they were not allowed to go out of repair until about three years ago ? Has the Local Government no influence with the Dominion Government to have proper crossings provided over the Railway ?

Hon. Mr. SULLIVAN.—As the wharves belong to the Dominion Government, the Local Government have no right to spend the people's money on them. That is clear. The providing of proper railway crossings also belongs to them, and the same remark will apply in that case, as to the former.

Mr. MATHESON was of opinion that wharves which the Dominion Government refuse to take over should be kept in repair by this Province.

Hon. Mr. PROWSE thought the honorable member for Campbellton should use his influence and energy in inducing the representatives for Prince County to ask the Dominion Government not only to repair all the old wharves, but to erect new ones where required.

Mr. J. R. McLEAN thought the Local Government had a right to keep in good repair all those wharves which the Dominion Government have refused to take over. If they do so, there is no doubt they will be recouped for every dollar expended. Reasonable exertion should therefore be made by them in that direction. If not attended to at once larger repairs will be required, and in the mean-

while the people will be deprived of proper wharf accommodation. He wished to call attention to the fact that the Supervisors do not always expend the money where it is most required. They frequently take what was intended for road No. 1 and spend it on road No. 4. Large sums of money are expended by private instead of public contracts. These Supervisors also give contracts to their particular friends ; and the members for the district have no control whatever of them. This is wrong, and better regulations should be made.

Mr. D. C. MARTIN knew that there were certain important bridges in the course of construction in his district, and he hoped they would receive proper supervision. The position of a Supervisor is a very responsible one, and should be filled by a person in every way capable of discharging the duties pertaining thereto. He hoped that the work on the bridges alluded to would turn out to be first class in every respect.

Mr. PERRY was not much acquainted with the wharves at Alberton, but it is the most important shipping place in that portion of Prince County. These wharves, however, are in a very bad state of repair, and when merchants wish to use them for shipping purposes, they are obliged to patch them up for the occasion. When shipping facilities are not provided, trade must inevitably suffer. Through mismanagement and penuriousness on the part of the Government, the price of potatoes has been reduced. The refund for the wharves taken over by the Dominion should be sufficient to keep the wharves not accepted by it in good repair. Mr. Hacket had written from Ottawa. stating that he had not been able to induce the Dominion Government to take over the Alberton Wharf. Who owns that wharf? Has it no owner? The Local Government say they do not own it, and the General Government rufuse to take charge of it. He could not understand this. There is a road called Peter's Road, in his district, which has not been opened up its entire length. The money was voted for this work, but was never expended; and no recommendation is made to carry it out this year. There are four or five settlers who have no way of getting from the Peter's Road to Palmer's Road, although the distance is only fifty chains. The Honorable Commissioner of Public Works sold the job, but the work was never completed, and he (Mr. P.) contended that it should be finished without delay. The Supervisor should be compelled to attend to this matter, and to expend the money which had been voted for that purpose.

Hon Mr. FERGUSON said it was now well known that the Local Government had taken the stand that the wharves are the property of the Dominion Government, and that we have nothing whatever to do with them. The Federal Government have never denied that those wharves belong to them. They said they would send down an engineer for the purpose of re-porting what wharves are of Federal importance. The report has been made, and only certain wharves considered to be of Federal importance have been taken in charge by the General Government. The Local Government has maintained its own ground, and their view has been accepted in regard to the question. It is contended by the Dominion Government that more wharves were built than were really necessary. It is now for the people through their representatives to convince them that several wharves not taken by them are necessary for shipping purposes. Last year, an important wharf in his (Mr. F's.) District was omitted and he suggested to the people to petition that it be taken over by the General Government. They did so. But the organ of the Opposition took the matter up and declared it was only a dodge, and that person who took charge of the matter was only a henchman of his. Many of the people therefore refused to sign the Petition; but what was the result of its presentation? The wharf was taken over by the General Government. If similar steps were taken with respect to the Alberton and other necessary wharves, there is little doubt they would be taken over by the Dominion Government. If the people want to use certain wharves not accepted by the General Government, let them petition accordingly. Instead of advising the people to pursue that course, the Opposition abuse the Local Government for not spending money upon works that do not belong to them, but to the Federal Government.

This is the work of a non-patriotic Party which is always contending against the rights of this Island. The same party tried hard to weaken our case at Ottawa, with reference to the Piers, and said the Government were trying to extort money from the Dominion that did not belong to us. Even now, it is easy to see the plan these gentlemen are pursuing, is of the same nature. Anything that would operate against the influence of the Local Government, they are prepared to support. Why do they not complain that the Local Government do not rebuild the Post Office, Building ? They have just as much right to do so as to say that the Local Government should rebuild the wharves. The fact is, they do not want a single wharf taken over by the General Government. He had good reason to think there was incomplete and inaccurate information supplied to the Engineers, in order to prevent us from receiving our rights from the Dominion Government in reference to the wharves. He believed the same principle is acted upon by the Opposition from the Atlantic to the Pacific Ocean. In place of loyally supporting the Dominion Government in putting down rebellion, they express sympathy with the rebels. Anything at all against the country to displace the party in power! In Halifax, the other day, every hinderance was thrown in the way of men volunteering to go to the North-West to put down the rebellion. This is in line with the conduct of the Local Opposition in this Island with respect to the piers question, and all others.

Mr. PERRY, — The honorable Commissioner of Crown Lands has declared that the Government will have nothing to do with repairing the wharf at Alberton, and that the people there have accommodation at the wharf. Such is not the case. Although a dispute is going on with respect to the ownership of the wharves, this is no reason why the people should not have the wharf accommodation they require for the shipment of their produce. It appears, however, that no shipping facilities are to be afforded them by the Local Government, no matter how much they may suffer for want of them ! If a wharf, not taken over by the Dominion Government, tumbles down, the Local Government will be held responsible for the loss to the Province. If our trade is really increasing, the people should have more wharf accommodation.

Mr FARQUHARSON said that an additional article appeared in last night's " Examiner," intended to injure him. He attributed it to the honorable member for Murray Harbor, the Commissioner of Crown Lands or the junior member for Belfast. Such attacks did not affect him in the slightest degree, and he would treat them with silent contempt. He thought he was sufficiently well known, to be able to take this course. Those attacks will react upon the heads of the authors.

On motion Mr. Speaker resumed the Chair, progress was reported, and leave given the Committee to sit again.

A message was received from the Legislative Council, stating that they had passed certain Bills.

On motion of Honorable Mr. Sullivan, the amendments made by the Council to the Bill to be intituled "An Act to incorporate the P. E. Island Agricultural Mutual Fire Insurance Company," were read the first time, and ordered to be read the second time to-morrow.

House adjourned for one hour.

I. O.

EVENING SESSION.

Public Accounts.

Mr. BENTLEY, from the Special Committee appointed to examine and report on the Public Accounts for the year 1884, submitted the report of said Committee, and moved that it be received and read.

Resolution put and carried.

Ordered, That the report of said Committee be referred to a Committee of the whole House to-morrow.

Mr. BENTLEY moved that the standing Rule of the House relating to the introduction of new matter be suspended to enable a member to present a petition.

Motion put and carried.

A petition of William Phelan, P. P., J. S. Cameron, D. F. Macdonald and others was presented to the House by Mr. Bentley, and the same was received and read ; setting forth that the petitioners are desirous of being incorporated with others who may become members of the association, under the name of the Temperance Alliance of King's County.

Ordered, That the said petition be referred to a Special Committee to examine the same and report thereon, by Bill or otherwise.

Ordered, That Mr. Bentley, Mr. John McLean and Mr. A. Martin do compose the said committee.

Mr. BENTLEY, from the last preceding Committee appointed, presented to the House a Bill as prepared by the Committee to be intituled "An Act to incorporate the Temperance Alliance of King's County," and the same was received and read the first time.

Ordered, That the said Bill be referred to the special Committee appointed to report on every private Bill, to examine the same and report thereon.

Hon. Mr. SULLIVAN moved that the House do now resolve itself into a Committee of the whole to further consider the Appropriation Bill, 1885.

Motion put and carried.

Mr. BLAKE in the Chair.

The clause relating to the vote for Docks, Ferries, etc., being read,—

Mr. BEER said that previous to the adjournment of the debate on this clause, his honorable colleague (Mr. Ferguson) had addressed the Committee, and had travelled from P. Edward Island to the Northwest, denouncing the Opposition in order to give them a lecture on loyalty. He (Mr. B.) could not agree with the statements of the honorable member that the Opposition, not only in this House, but in the Dominion Parliament, are disloyal. The honorable gentleman gave as proof of the disloyalty of the Opposition, that, whereas eight Lieutenant Colonels, who were members of Parliament, and members of the Liberal Conservative Party, had offered their services to the Government, and were prepared to go to the front, not one member of the Opposition party had followed their example. He (Mr. B.) would like to ask the honorable member to name one member of the Opposition in the House of Commons who is a Lieutenant Colonel in the Militia.

Hon. Mr. FERGUSON said he did not say that these gentlemen were Lieutenant Colonel. He said that grit members of Parliament refused to pair with members of the Conservative Party, who wished to join their regiments and go to the front with them.

Mr. BEER said it did not become the honorable gentleman to accuse honorable members on this side of the House of disloyalty. Some few years ago he (Mr. B.) held a meeting at Stanhope, where young men in that vicinity were asked to join the Militia, and this honorable gentleman sprung to his feet and told the young men not to do so. Was that loyal conduct? This resolution asks for a large amount of money for roads and bridges, but nevertheless he (Mr. B.) did not think it contained a sufficient sum for the amount of work that has to be done on these public works. Although about the same amount, $15,500 was voted last year for roads, yet we know that the honorable Commissioner of Public Works spent $27,000 for this service. How is it that so much less will be sufficient this year? He (Mr. B.) knew that the expenditure last year did not put the roads in any too good repair. Some roads were so bad that the people could not haul their produce to market. Petitions have been presented to the Government asking for repairs to roads, and the answer given was that no money was obtainable for such work. What is the use of placing in this clause an amount that will not cover the expenditure? When it took so much last year the Government will require just as much this year. The time has arrived when we should have some other way of voting amounts for these services. The Honorable Commissioner of Public Works should have an idea of what amount is necesary, and should not ask a little over half what he actually spent, as was the case last year. The amount asked for is not sufficient. One Supervisor asks for $1,200 for his district; and there are thirty-five districts, all of which require nearly the same expenditure, how can the honorable gentleman expect to perform the work required with so small a sum as he has placed in this clause. He (Mr. B.) contended that the amount for roads was not sufficient, and if we live to meet here another session he will find that the amount has been largely exceeded.

Hon. Mr. PROWSE said the honorable member for West River had said some things to-day that he (Mr. P.) did not expect any loyal man would say; but there were some facts that the honorable member tries to suppress. He (Mr. P.) did not intend to refer to the sentiments that had been expressed by the honorable member in the smoking room of the House; but he (Mr. P.) had scarcely commenced speaking on the question of Supply, when the honorable gentleman interrupted him and referred to him (Mr. P.) as a traitor to the Davies Government and a dangerous person. Since the time he (Mr. P.) had left the Davies Government there had been several elections throughout the Province and the country has decided who are the traitors. The honorable member for West River had no right to designate him as a traitor because he (Mr. P.) left the Davies Government. If he had not done so he would have been a traitor to his constituents. He

knew this was a sore spot with the Opposition for it is well known that the withdrawal of the Conservatives from the Davies Government, showed the people that something was wrong. The honorable member for West River must have valued his services very highly for he (Mr. F.) was paid $1,600 a year, besides $200 as sessional allowance for doing the work I did when I was in the government A man's guilt as a traitor is sometimes valued by the amount of money he received for betraying his friends and at this rate the honorable member was a greater traitor to the people, than I ever was to the Davies Government. The honorable member has not attempted to deny or explain the disloyal sentiments he made use of this year, but attempted to mitigate the indignation of honorable members by saying that the conversation was private and secret and that the honorable junior member for Belfast and I had entered into a conspiracy to endeavor to damage his (Mr. F's.) character. He (Mr. P.) indignantly denied the imputation that he had been carrying on a private or secret conversation on any question. The words were not said in joke, but were spoken as emphatically as the honorable gentleman could speak. It shows the bad position in which the honorable gentleman knows he has placed himself when he (Mr. F.) has to refer to some private matters by telling which, Mr. Davies acted very uprofessionally. He (Mr. P.) had only done his duty, when he brought the matter before the House as no hon.

orable member should be allowed to make use of such expressions with impunity.

Mr. YEO said he was not going to speak of Fenians or of the Riel rebellion. He was sorry the amounts for Roads and Bridges were so small, so much less than was expended last year. It is well known that the amount voted for this service, is much less than what they require. One supervisor asked for $2,050, another for $1,-300 and all that is placed at the disposal of honorable members is about $400 for each district. In the 2nd district of Prince County nearly all the unoccupied Land is owned by the Government and nothing will be required for rights of way, therefore new roads should be opened where they are so urgently required. Many such have been brought to the notice of the Government and great injury is done both to the People and the Province, when no roads are opened to this property. There are several Bridges in that District that require a large outlay. Especially one in Lot 13 which is nearly impassable. The wharves there are also fast going to decay. Every year these works require some repairs and if not attended to will go down altogether. The wharves not taken by the Dominion Government will soon become useless, unless the Local Government give them some attention. It is a good thing that the Government have received so much from the Dominion for wharves taken by them; but the Government should have brought to the notice of the Dominion Government, that if the other wharves are not taken charge and repaired, that a much greater amount will be required to put them in a state of repair. Either one Government or the other will have to maintain these works and it is an unfortunate state of affairs, that while this dispute is pending, the people will be greatly incommoded. As far as the amount for bridges is concerned, it is well known that already several large contracts have been let, and he (Mr. Y.) feared that the sum in the estimates will be insufficient to meet the requirements of the year. There are many new roads much needed in the 2nd district of Prince County and he (Mr. Y.) hoped the Government would use every exertion to have them opened and completed this season. In looking over the public accounts he (Mr. Y.) found that Prince County did not fare off very well last year.

Queen's County received
for Bridges $17,982.34
King's County   "   7,131.84
Prince County   "   5,576.42

As there are three honorable gentlemen from Prince County at the Council Board, he (Mr. Y.) was astonished that they have not seen justice done to Prince County.

Queen's County received
for Roads $3,798.30
King's County   "   2,460.95
Prince County   "   1,667.40

He (Mr. Y.) did not know why Prince County had received so small a share of the public money last year. If it could be shown that a greater expenditure was not needed, there would be some excuse for this great difference, but, it is well known, that such is not the case, and there is no reason why Prince County should not receive as much as either of the other countries.

Hon. Mr. CAMPBELL said honorable members of the Opposition are pursuing a most unusual course. They have not only asked for explanations of these amounts when these resolutions were going through Committee; but they now ask the Commissioner of Public Works to go over the same ground and repeat the answers he had previously given. The honorable member who spoke last was absent when these items were discussed although, as the representative of an important district, it was his duty to have been in his place in this House. The honorable member for Springton said that he had looked through the Supervisor's returns and found that some of them asked for as much as $2,200 and as there were 35 Districts, that the amount in the estimates was totally insufficient. The honorable gentleman should remember that the district to which he had referred had a large number of Bridges in it and was not a guide to the whole amount required. The honorable member holds up the largest amount asked for by any Supervisor in the Province and wished it to be accepted as the average amount required. If honorable members will take the trouble to add together the amounts asked for in the Supervi-

sor's returns, they will find that they only amount to $42,000 for the 35 districts, whereas the sum in the estimates for these services amounts to $44,000. Last year several large and important Bridges had to be built and up to this time of the year, contracts amounting to $11,000 over what has been let this year, had been contracted for. It does not follow because expenditures on Public Works of this kind are large one year, that they shall be equally heavy the year following. In fact the very reverse is often the case. The honorable Leader of the Opposition took exception to the amount expended in Prince County. If the honorable gentleman will look in the Public Accounts of the first year or so after he (Mr. C.) had charge of this department, he (Mr. Y.) will find that large amounts were spent in Prince County. Last year one very important bridge had to be built in Queen's County that cost such a large sum of money; but this year up to this time Prince County has the lead in the amount of work contracted for, as only small contracts have been let in Queen's County. We had a peculiar season last year. A great many small bridges were carried away, a circumstance which no one could have foreseen. Honorable members will find that while $86,000 is considered sufficient for the Public Works department for the present year, that $90,000 is provided in the estimates. He (Mr. C.) could show where $11,000 less than last year will be required. The Commissioner of Public Woks may have to overrun his estimates in some places ; but he knows that he will have to account to the independent members of this House if he does so. There was not one dollar unpaid by the Public Works department of amounts justly due at the end of the year, although honorable members said there was nearly a rebellion up west on this account. The honorable Leader of the Opposition had alluded, no doubt, to the road over which he (Mr. Y.) drove me last year. This road which he (Mr C) had agreed to open, if it did not cost over $200, was sold for a much greater sum, while he (Mr. C.) was Commissioner of Public Works he would allow no ring to rob the country and consequently he had dissapproved of the sale made by the supervizor, and had not paid the parties who were trying to get more money than they earned. This, no doubt, is the rebellion that that the honorable member alluded to. It is true that last year he (Mr. C.) had spent some thing over the amount voted last session, but if he had pursued the course adopted by the Honorable Leader of the Opposition, and the honorable member for West River, when they were members of the Government, these amounts would be included in the " Suspense Account." If these public works had not been repaired it would have given the *Patriot* a chance to publish one truthful statement respecting the condition of the roads and bridges of the Province. He (Mr. C.) took the honest course of spending these amounts, and had been justified in doing so by this House. If we have an ordinary season, he (Mr. C.) believed he could carry on the public works of the Province efficiently for the amount asked for.

Mr. YEO said he had not alluded to the road the honorable Commissioner had just spoken of. It is true he (Mr. Y.) had driven the honorable gentleman to see this road, but he did not know what instructions the Supervisor had received. He (Mr. Y.) did not know anything about the sale until asked by the honorable Commissioner of Public Works to inquire into the matter. The sale was attended by fifty persons or so, and he (Mr. Y.) understood that the contract was sold very low. Only a short time was allowed to complete the work and yet these men have not been paid for their labor, which is a hardship. He (Mr. Y.) was glad to find that so small an amount has been contracted for this year, and he hoped that the roads he had spoken about would be attended to without delay.

Mr. BEER said he was not convinced that the sum in this clause was sufficient. The Supervisor's return that he (Mr. B.) had alluded to was one of three in his own district. The honorable gentleman said that the amount asked for was for large bridges in that district, but he (Mr. B.) only found small bridges asked for in this estimate. The honorable gentleman said he had not paid out so much as he did at this time last year, but he (Mr. C.) did not tell us how much he owed on these contracts.

·· Hon. Mr. CAMPBELL said the Public Works Department always pay their bills when due.

Mr. BEER said the men have not been paid for working on Southport Wharf.

Hon. Mr. CAMPBELL said these men are paid every Saturday, and he challenged the honorable member to name a man who had not been paid.

Mr. BEER said that it will be found at the end of the year that the amount asked in this clause will be insufficient to meet the wants of the Province.

Mr. FARQUHARSON said he had nothing to say in reply to the honorable member for Murray Harbor, excepting to say that he (Mr. F.) knew nothing about "suspense accounts," and the Honorable Commissioner of Public Works does not know what he is talking about when he alludes to such things.

Hon. Mr. CAMPBELL,—I have the "Suspense Account" in my desk. Do you want to see it?

Mr. FARQUHARSON said the honorable Commissioner of Public Works tells us that he has contracted for $11,000 less for public works this year than he did last year. He (Mr. C.) did not tell us about the thousands of dollars spent for day's work of political friends. It was unbecoming for

him (Mr. C.) to speak so loud when, during the last fifteen months, he had spent $25,000 on political favorites. He (Mr. F.) supposed that these amounts were not called contracts, although the money is charged in the Public Accounts. We cannot get vouchers for these expenditures, although the present Leader of the Government denounced such practices when Mr. Davies was Leader of the Government. The Honorable Commissioner of Public Works tried to frighten honorable members by saying there were 2 600 road orders to look over. He (Mr. C.) does not know what is doing in his office, only what his subordinate tells him, and yet he has as much loud talk as if he knew all about it. Honorable members are held responsible by their districts respecting these expenditures, and yet we have no control over this department. He (Mr. C.) tells us that $17,000 over what was voted was spent last year. and we have to ratify it without knowing how or why it was spent. There is no use in forty-three men coming here to look after these matters when one man can upset all they do. He (Mr. F.) would not altogether condemn the statute labor, but the way it was performed it did very little good to the roads. A certain amount of work should be performed in July, and the roads should then be sold in sections, each of which should be kept in a satisfactory condition. Rains cause holes in the Roads the day after the Statute Labor is performed and they are left in that way until the next year. A small amount of work properly done would keep our roads in much better order.

Hon. Mr. CAMPBELL said no matter how often the honorable member for West River is contradicted he (Mr. F.) maintains what he first asserts. He (Mr. F.) has shown that he neither knows his duty as a representative or a member of the Government. He denies knowing anything about the 'suspense account,' notwithstanding he was a member of the Government when the celebrated letter was written to Supervisor's to "draw slowly." If he (Mr. F.) did not know anything of this, he should have known about it. The honorable member reiterates his assertion that I spent . $25,000 without public sale although he knows he can not prove any such thing. It is true some amounts were paid without being tendered for; but these amounts were for supplies which always have been procured in the same way. The honorable member had asked for a return showing how much had been spent without tender, but was much disappointed to find that only $4,000 had been expended in this way, outside of what was required for public buildings. Honorable members knowing that he (Mr. F.) can not substantiate any of the wild assertions he makes, and knowing that a man who would use such treasonable language as he (Mr. F.) has used, is not to be relied on, should pay little heed to what he says. Judging from his actions he (Mr. C.) considered it hardly safe to

trust him (Mr. F.) in the Public Works Jepartment. The Opposition are welcome to any information that is contained in the Public Works department. The honorable member for West River said it was altogether likely that this money had been paid, and that the government had divided the spoils with their political friends. He (Mr. C.) could tell them that if 'dividing the spoils' in this way had been practised by the Government when he (Mr. F.) was a member of it, that they had no such men in the Gtvernment now. He (Mr. C.) had offered to single out vouchers for any part of the expenditure and place them under the custody of the Secretary of the Public Works department, who was the proper officer to have charge of such papers, and it was the only way such vouchers could be preserved. When the Public Works department offers the Opposition all the information they ask for, they refuse to go and see it for themselves.

Mr FARQUHARSON said the explanation of the honorable Commissioner of Public Works was not satisfactory. He (Mr. F.) contended that thousands of dollars are omitted in the returns that have been tabled. We have asked for copies of these vouchers, but they will give us neither copies nor the originals. Honorable members have no right to go to the Public Works office to look for information that should be on the table of the House.

Mr. SINCLAIR said he wished

to make a few remarks about the salaries of supervisors. The sum of $15,500 is voted by this clause for roads, culverts and small bridges and $30,000 for supervisors. The wharves have been taken off the hands of the honorable Commissioner of Public Works, the large contracts are sold and an inspector put over them, and to pay one-fifth of the amount granted for this service to the supervisors for selling the contracts, seems to be a large sum to expend. As far as he (Mr. S.) could see there is only $68,169 voted by this clause for public works, and as the vote of $86,000 last year was so much exceeded, he could not understand how the honorable Commissioner of Public Works can expect to go over the Public Works of the Province with this amount.

Hon. Mr. CAMPBELL said the Supervisors are allowed $50 each for the expenditure of a certain amount of money, usually called the Road Scales. They receive 7½ per cent. on all sums they expend over these amounts. There is a reserve of 20 per cent. of the Road Scales to keep the roads in repair besides about $5,000 that is kept for repairing casual damages that occur. The Supervisors have considerable trouble in attending to their duties and the amounts they receive is not out of proportion to the work they have to do.

Clause agreed to.

The clause relating to Packet Service being read.

Mr. D. C. MARTIN said this clause contains an item for Packet Service between Charlottetown, Wood Islands, Flat River, and Belle Creek. Last year only $145 was granted for this service, an amount totally insufficient, as the work can not be performed for that sum. The amount expended last year was $188 and at least $300 should be granted this year, as $145,00 will not pay any person to perform this satisfactory manner. He (Mr. D. C. M.) trusted that the service will be better performed this year or that the honorable Commissioner of Public Works will carry out his privilege of spending more money than is voted, and give an increased subsidy for this service.

Hon. Mr. CAMPBELL said it was the fifteenth time the honorable senior member for Belfast had spoken about this matter. It seems to be the only question in which he (Mr. D. C. M.) is interested. The honorable member had displayed great ignorance of parliamentary usage when he had last spoken on this matter, and should be ashamed to resort to such tactics in order to damage his colleague. The honorable junior member for Belfast had told the honorable member on that occasion, that he was making a motion that was against the rules of parliament, and that he (Mr. D. C. M.) was only using clap-trap in trying to press it. He (Mr. C.) was proud to think that a supporter of the Government, who had only been one session in this House, should have shown so much greater acquaintance with the duty of a representative than the honorable senior member for Belfast. At the request of the honorable junior member for Belfast, the packet was allowed to go to Flat River ; and the honorable senior member would not have made such an ado about this matter, if he (Mr. D. C. M.) did not know that he had neglected the interests of his constituents at previous sessions. The Government have given $2,600 for increased packet service to Belfast, but the people of that district need not thank the honorable senior member for it.

Mr. D. C. MARTIN said that notwithstanding all the Honorable Commissioner of Public Works had said, he was willing to risk getting the popularity the Government were trying to take from him. Any motion is constitutional when it is carried and the chairman by refusing to put the motion, had prevented a vote being taken on it. The amount granted for this service is insufficient ; and although the Government may refuse it now, the time is not far distant when this service will be properly performed.

Hon Mr. FERGUSON said the honorable member relied on this question of packet service to carry the candidate of his party at the late election in the Belfast district, and it was made the war cry of the Opposition at that time. The honorable members raised this war cry at Wood Islands, but did not try it after the meeting at Belle Creek. This was a small way to try and injure an opponent, and

he (Mr. F.) was surprised that the honorable member would try to have himself advanced in the district by such means. Any advantages his district will receive are largely due to the exertions of his colleague (Mr. A. Martin). Knowing that the amount of this vote could not be increased through his exertions, he (Mr. D. C. M.) tried by this clap-trap to increase his popularity.

Mr. FARQUHARSON said the meeting at Belle Creek was strongly in favor of getting this packet service improved. The honorable Commissioner of Public Works was the servant of the House, and he had no right to insult and abuse honorable members of the Opposition for asking questions about his (Mr. C.'s) department. He (Mr. C.) had been backed up by the honorable Commissioner of Crown Lands, and it was not the treatment that should be accorded to the representatives of the people. The boiler for the steamer "Elfin" was still in Pictou, and he (Mr. F.) predicted that there would be trouble and delay in the spring on this account. The people of East and West Rivers will be deprived of ferry accommodation, and the Government should be censured for not having this boiler on hand in time.

Clause agreed to.

The clause respecting printing of Folio and Sessional Laws being read,—

Mr. BEER said that formerly the item miscellaneous in this clause was only $200, instead of $400 as at present. He had been told that the amount for the survey of bridge across the Hillisborough was included in the estimates. Perhaps this will account for the increase in this item.

Hon. Mr. SULLIVAN said that if the honorable member had been in his place, he (Mr. B.) would have known that the amount for this survey had been passed already.

Clause agreed to.

The clause respecting importation of stock being read,—

Mr. SINCLAIR said he understood the Honorable Commissioner of Crown Lands was a Commissioner of the Stock Farm, and he (Mr. F.) should give honorable members some information respecting what stock it was intended to import.

Hon. Mr. FERGUSON said it was the intention of the Commissioners of the Stock Farm to import two Clydesdale mares and a Clydesdale stallion. These are all the animals that it is intended to import this year.

Mr. SINCLAIR said the amount in the clause was too small to import three animals of the kind specified. We have been importing some good animals, and it would not be wise to bring any but good ones to the Province. It would be better to pay $1,000 or $2,000 for first-class animals than to get poorer ones at a lower figure.

Hon. Mr. FERGUSON said he agreed with the honorable member for Springton, that the animals imported by the Government should be good ones. The last Horse that was imported in this way had proved an excellent animal, and this horse (Barrister) only cost a little over one third of the amount in the estimates. As mares can be bought cheaper than stallions, he (Mr. F.) had no doubt but that three first-class animals can be obtained for the amount in this clause.

G. F. O.

Mr. J. R. MACLEAN said that if it is the intention of the Government to import two mares and a stallion, he wished to know whether the latter is to be sent to King's County.

Hon. Mr. FERGUSON. Yes.

Mr. BEER said that $2,000 was voted last year for the importation of improved stock, but none was sent for. Some good stock is very much required at the present time. If the Government intend to keep up the present high character of the Stock of this Province; they must import more pure bred animals than they have hitherto done. We have some very good stock on the Farm, but it needs to be replenished to be kept up to the mark. He was sorry the Government had not availed themselves of last year's vote to procure some superior stock.

Clause agreed to.

Next clause respecting allowance to members of the House and for stationery read and agreed to.

Clause relating to allowance to members of Legislgtive Council, and for stationery, was read.

Mr. BEER thought that by this time the Government would have succeeded in abolishing the Upper House. It seemed strange to be called upon to again vote this amount.

Clause agreed to.

On motion, Mr. Speaker resumed the Chair, and the Chairman reported the Bill agreed to, without making any amendment.

Ordered, That the Bill be engrossed, and that it be read the third time to-morrow.

Hon. Mr. MACDONALD from the Committee on Private Bills and to whom was referred the Bill to be intituled: "An Act to incorporate the Temperance Alliance, King's County," reported the said Bill was of a private nature and liable to fees, and recommended that $12 be charged.

Mr. SINCLAIR thought the charge very high for so short a Bill.

On motion, the report of the Committee was agreed to, and it was,—

Ordered, That the said Bill be read the second time to-morrow.

On motion of Hon. Mr. McLEOD, the House went into Committee of the whole to further consider the Bill to be intituled: "An Act to amend an Act to incorporate the City of Charlottetown."

Mr. ALEXANDER MARTIN in the Chair.

Second clause relating to Commercial Travellers and Agents, read and agreed to,—the blank being filled up with $100.

Third clause, relating to a tax on personal property read.

Hon. Mr. McLEOD moved that the word "thirty" be struck out and "twenty" inserted in lieu thereof. When the Bill was last before the House, there was some objection mrde to the use of the word "inhabitant" in this clause. Some persons residing just outside the City do business in it, and it is thought their personal property should be taxed. He would, therefore move that after the word "City" the following words be added to this clause: "or belonging to any person having an office or store in the said City, or practising a profession in said City."

Clause, as amended, agreed to.

Fourth clause read.

Hon. Mr. McLEOD moved that in the 24th line, the same words as in the former case, be inserted after the word "City." It was thought by some of the Committee appoited to prepare this measure, that mortgages from country people would not be liable to a tax, under its provisions. This clause does not specially exempt such mortgages, and in order to make sure work of it, he would move that after the word "Charlottetown," the words "or in any part of this Province," be inserted.

Clause agreed to.

Fifth clause relating to the Schedule of Real and personal property, &c., read.

Clause agreed to, with Blank. On motion that the Blank be filled up with "$200."

Mr. D. C. MARTIN said that a person assessed for $250 worth of personal property would be compelled to pay tax on the whole, while the one who owned $199 would escape the tax altogether. If a man owns $500 worth, $200 of it should be free of the tax, and the balance should be assessed.

Clause agreed to.

The sixth clause was read.

Hon. Mr. McLEOD said that the same mode of valuing Real Estate as at present, is here provided for. The Assessors make their valuation, and the person taxed has ten days in which to appeal against the tax, to the Stipendiary Magistrate. The latter after hearing all the evidence, either refuses to reduce the amount or makes such a reduction as the case requires. He knew of no individual case of hardship under this rule, which is now in operation. He did not know why any different mode of collecting the personal property tax should be adopted.

Mr. SINCLAIR thought the notice of Assessment should be served upon one of the householders instead of upon any inmate found on the premises.

Hon. Mr. McLEOD,—That provision is in another clause. If the person who has appealed against the Assessment made upon him does not appear, judgment goes by default against him.

Clause agreed to.

Seventh clause read, and agreed to.

Eighth clause read.

Mr. D. C. MARTIN thought this clause rather sweeping in its nature.

Hon. Mr. McLEOD said that it merely makes the Sheriff responsible for arrears of taxes due on personal property which he has seized and sold.

Clause agreed to.

Ninth clause read, and agreed to.

Tenth clause read, making provision for poll tax. The blank

having been, on motion, filled up with "Two Dollars," the clause was agreed to.

Eleventh clause read providing that the City Clerk shall be, by virtue of his office, Secretary of the School Board.

Hon. Mr. McLeod said that the Committee appointed by the Council were not posted with respect to the duties of the Secretary of the School Board. He, therefore, wrote a letter to the Chief Superintendent of Education asking whether the proposed amendment would operate against the successful working of the School Act in the City, and received the following reply, viz:—

Charlottetown, April 7, 1885.

Hon. Neil McLeod,
          M. P. P., &c. &c.,

Dear Sir:—I am in receipt of yours of the 6th inst., relative to the proposal to amalgamate the offices of the Clerk of the City Council and Secretary of the Board of School Trustees. The proposed change, in my opinion, would not work satisfactorily. The duties of the two offices would frequently conflict: besides, the Secretary of the School Board should have some knowledge of Educational affairs Whatever his competency in other respects, unless he understands the working of the City Schools, he can be of little service to the Board of School Trustees.

No serious objection occurs to me against the proposal to change the school year. As far as I can

judge, it would be well to give effect to the wishes of the City Council in this matter.

              Yours truly,
                    D. Montgomery.

As he agreed with the opinion contained in that letter, and as the Superintendent of Education was fully competent to judge as to the best course to pursue in this matter, he (Mr. McLeod) would move that the clause be disagreed to.

Mr. Farquharson said that the School Board disapproved of the amalgamation of those two offices.

Hon. Mr. McLeod moved that the clause be substituted by another giving the City Council power to amalgamate the two offices of City Clerk and Clerk to the Stipendiary Magistrates Court, if they choose to do so. The City Council can appoint as many clerks as they please, as assistants, in case they may find it necessary to do so. The Secretary of the School Board is required to visit the Schools during School hours, but the City Clerk could not attend to that duty.

Mr. Beer said that this clause was inserted in the Bill on the score of economy. It was the opinion of a number of persons that the three offices could be filled by one person. It had been suggested by some that the Clerk in the Education Office could also perform the duties pertaining to the office of Secretary of the School Board. Whether such was the case, he did not know.

Mr. FARQUHARSON was always under the impression that two of the three offices alluded to, could be filled by one person. He would vote for the resolution, and hoped the City Council would have power to appoint an Assistant Clerk, if necessary. He thought this amalgamation should be made compulsary.

Motion put and carried.

Twelfth Clause read,—

Hon. Mr. PROWSE thought the principle of dual representation should not be admitted in Parliament. The interests of the City conflict with those of the Country, and he was not sure that the interests of both are properly protected, by permitting the Mayor of Charlottetown to hold a seat in this House.

Mr. BEER,—Let the hon. member move that no member of the House shall be eligible for the position of Mayor. He was glad to hear the honorable member is not a monopolist.

Hon. Mr. FERGUSON thought the suggestion of the honorable member for Murray Harbor a very good one, for his honorable colleague had deserted him, and had addressed himself to the interests of the city, instead of those of the country. as those interests were identical with his (Mr. Beer's) own. The honorable member's heart is in the town, and he had not been working with him (Mr. F.) as he should have been. The

interests of a representative should not be divided in that way, and he hoped the matter would be remedied.

Mr. BEER was glad to know his honorable colleague thought his undivided attention should be given to the district represented by both. When asked to run for the office of Mayor, he stated that if he found the two positions conflict in any way he would look after his country district first, and the city afterwards.

Hon. Mr. PROWSE thought provision should be made in this clause to prevent this dual representation, as the honorable member was the Tory member for the City and the Grit member for the country district.

Clause agreed to.

The 13th, 14th, 15th and 16th clauses were severally read and agreed to.

The 17th clause having been read,—

Hon. Mr. McLEOD said that this clause would extend the Jurisdiction of the Stipendiary, and would deprive the County Courts of some of their work.

Mr. FARQUHARSON said that the City Court meets monthly, while the County Courts meet but four times per year. He was in favor of this clause, and thought provision should also be made for the Stipendiary's adjudicating in cases amounting to $150 instead of $80 as at present.

Mr. D. C. MARTIN was opposed to the extension of the Jurisdiction of the Stipendiary Magistrate, not that justice would not·be administered as well as at present, but he objected to the principle in itself.

On motion the clause was disagreed to.

The remaining clauses of the Bill were severally read and agreed to.

On motion, Mr. Speaker resumed the Chair, and the Chairman reported the Bill agreed to with certain amendments.

Ordered, That the Bill be engrossed, and that it be read the third time to-morrow.

On motion of Honorable Mr. McLeod, the 25th Rule of the House was suspended to enable a member to present a petition, and thereupon he presented to the House a petition from Geo. Lawson, Wm. Shaw and others, praying for the incorporation of a Company to be styled the "Presbyterian and Evangelical Protestant Union Publishing Company."

On motion said petition was referred to a Committee, to report thereon by Bill or otherwise.

Ordered, That Honorable Mr. McLeod, Mr. A. Martin, and Honorable Mr. Prowse do compose said Committee.

Hon. Mr. McLEOD, from the said Committee, presented to the House a Bill to be intituled: "An Act to Incorporate the Presbyterian and Evangelical Protestant Under Publishing Company," and, the same was received and read the first time and referred to the Private Bill Committee to report thereon.

Mr. BENTLEY moved that the Bill to incorporate the King's County Temperance Alliance be now read a second time, and said that its object is the promotion of Temperance and the enforcement of the Scott Act. It makes provision for officers to transact its business. Any resident of King's County may become a member by the payment of a small fee.

Motion put and carried.

The Bill was accordingly read the second time, and committed to a Committee of the whale House. The House accordingly resolved itself into the said Committee.

Mr. ALEX. MARTIN in the Chair.

The Bill was read, clause by clause, and agreed to without debate.

On motion, Mr. Speaker resumed the Chair, and the Chairman reported the Bill agreed to, without any amendment.

Ordered, That the Bill be engrossed and read the third time to-morrow.

The "Appropriation Act, 1885,"

was, on motion, read the third time and passed.

Hon. Mr. FERGUSON, from the Private Bill Committee, reported that the "Act to Incorporate the Presbyterian and Evangelical Protestant Union Publishing Company" was of a private nature and liable to fees, and recommended that $15 be charged.

On motion, the report was agreed to.

On motion of Honorable Mr. McLeod, the Bill was read a second time, and committed to a Committee of the whole House.

The House accordingly resolved itself into the said Committee.

Mr. JOHN MCLEAN in the Chair.

After a few minutes spent in Committee, without debate, Mr. Speaker, on motion, resumed the Chair, and the Chairman reported the Bill ogreed to, without amendment.

Ordered, That the Bill be engrossed.

An Act to continue certain Acts therein mentioned, was, on motion, read the second time, and committed to a Committee of the whole House. The House accordingly resolved inself into the said Committee.

Mr. JOHN MCLEAN in the Chair.

After a short time spent in Committee, without debate, Mr. Speaker, on motion, resumed the Chair, and the Chairman reported the Bill agreed to.

Ordered, That the Bill be engrossed, and that it be read the third time to-morrow.

The House, having sat until after midnight, adjourned until ten o'clock on the forenoon of the 9th inst.

I. O.

THURSDAY, April 9.

Mr. SPEAKER in the Chair.

On motion of Mr. Bentley the 10th Rule of the House was suspended in order that the Bill intituled "An Act to incorporate the Temperance Alliance of King's County" should be read the third time.

The Bill was accordingly read the third time and passed.

On motion of Honorable Mr. Sullivan the Bill intituled "An Act to continue certain Acts therein mentioned" was read the third time and passed.

On motion of Honorable Mr. Sullivan, the Order of the Day for the second reading of the amendment of the Legislative Council to the Bill intituled "An Act to incorporate the Prince Edward Island Mutual Fire Insurance Company" was read. The said amendment was accordingly read the second time and referred to a Committee of the whole House.

Mr. HOOPER in the Chair.

Hon. Mr. SULLIVAN said the amendment was to change the term for which policies were issued by this Company from five years to three years. As it was considered a good amendment he (Mr. S.) would support it.

Mr. BENTLEY said the petitioners must have had some reason for placing five years in the Bill.

Mr. J. R. MCLEAN supported the amendment.

On motion Mr. Speaker resumed the Chair, the Chairman reported the amendment agreed to.

On motion of honorable Mr. Sullivan the tenth rule of the House was suspended in order that the amendment to the Bill intituled "An Act to incorporate the Prince Edward Island Mutual Fire Insurance Company" should be read the third time.

The amendment was accordingly read the third time and passed.

Ordered, That a message be sent to the Legislative Council intimating that said amendment had been passed by this House.

On motion of honorable Mr. Sullivan the order of the day for the second reading of the Bill intituled 'An Act to consolidate and amend the Summerside Incorporation Act' was read.

Hon. Mr. SULLIVAN said he had moved that the order of the day respecting this Bill be read in order to give the honorable member who had charge of this Bill an opportunity to explain the nature of it. He (Mr. S.) did not know whether it was advisable to pass this Bill, as it was a very long one and may contain provisions that would be injurious to the people of Summerside. A petition for and one against this Bill has been presented to the House. Perhaps it would be better to defer the consideration of this Bill until next year when more careful consideration will be given it, than if it is rushed through at the end of the session. If the Acts at present in force are examined, they will be found to contain the provisions this Bill asks for.

Hon. Mr. LEFURGEY said that this Bill was only handed to him the day before yesterday. It was a very long measure and would require a great deal of careful consideration. The Town Council of Summerside had presented a printed Bill at the meeting held in that Town for the purpose of considering the measure that would be applied for, and he (Mr. L.) and the Law Clerk had been comparing that printed Bill and this one together and had found some discrepancies between them. One important clause, viz: that granting power to issue debentures is in the written Bill and was not in the printed one that was submitted to the meeting that he had referred to. A petition was got up by some of the residents against this. Bill, and a telegram had been sent to him (Mr. L.) asking that the Bill should not be passed until the Petition was received. It is an important matter for the town of Summerside that the several Acts incorporating it should be consolidated and he (Mr. L.) was desirous that such a measure should be passed. He did not, however, wish to pass a Bill that would not meet the views of the majority of the Citizens. He (Mr. L.) had suggested to the Chairman of the Town Council that this Bill should lie over until next year and if their Acts required any amendments for School purposes that such a Bill could be passed this session. He had been looking with the Law Clerk over the Acts incorporating Summerside but did not find the defects the Town Council complains of. These defects must be in their own by-laws which they could remedy themselves. In order, however, that we may see if by amending this Bill, we make it acceptable to the people of Summerside he (Mr. L.) would move that the Bill be now read the second time. He considered it was his duty to go into this matter and he hoped honorable members will give that careful consideration to its provisions, that the importance of the Town of Summerside had a right to receive.

Mr J. R. McLean said he was disposed to give the people of Summerside every consideration and was most anxious to have this Bill passed. The honorable senior member for that Town had only explained this Bill (which is a very long one, indeed,) in a very superficial manner, and as it was now so late in the session, it will be very difficult for honorable members to give an intelligent vote on the important matters contained in it. He (Mr. J. R. McL.) had been talking to gentlemen from Summerside who had signed the Petition in favor of this Bill, who were now sorry for doing so. As the Bill is so long it should have been brought in earlier in the session. It would be better to let it stand over until next session as this had not been done.

Dr. GILLIS said a great many City Bills came into this House late in the session, but this Bill came so very late, that it will not be either convenient or possible for us to pass it intelligently. It appears to be a very long Bill for governing a small town like Summerside. The Declaration of Independence or the terms of Confederation did not occupy more pages of foolscap. He (Dr. G.) had been told that this Bill did not ask for any more powers than have already been granted to the Town Council, and considering that it is so late in the session, in the interest of the citizens of Summerside, he believed it would be better to defer the consideration of this matter. If, however, honorable members are willing, he (Dr. G.) would be very glad to spend a few days to consider this Bill and have it made the law.

Hon. Mr. McLeod said he had overhauled this Bill with the

Law Clerk, but owing to its very great length, he was not in a position to advise its adoption. It provides for the election of Wardens of the Town and contains the same provisions for doing so, as are contained in the Dominion Election Laws. This is too cumbersome a method for a Town like Summerside. This Bill came from the Wardens of the Town and there is no evidence that it contains what the people of Summerside require. If it was considered that the old acts worked unsatisfactorily, this measure should have been presented earlier in the session. He had a great desire to pass this Bill and had examined it privately, but after doing so would not advise the promoter of it, to have it passed.

Hon. Mr. FERGUSON considered this the most formidable Bill that had come before the House since he had been in it. The meeting held in Summerside with reference to this matter, did not come to any decision. The printed Bill was submitted to the meeting; but he (Mr. F.) understood that this Bill now presented is different from the printed Bill. It is impossible to tell whether, if it was passed, it would be acceptable to the people of Summerside. If the Bill had come in earlier during the session and had been discussed, an expression of opinion would have been elicited in Summerside; and the House would be in a position to make the measure as perfect as possible. Under the circumstances he (Mr. F.) considered it desirable that the Bill should be withdrawn.

A consolidation of the Acts incorporating the town is a wise provision, but it should have been presented earlier during the session.

Motion put and carried.

On Motion of Honorable Mr. LeFurgey the House resolved into a Committee of the whole.

Mr. HOLLAND in the Chair.

Mr. HOLLAND said he had great objections to taking the Chair on such a Bill. He did not consider it advisable to pass this Bill, especially as so large a petition had been presented against it.

Hon. Mr. PROWSE said he thought the Bill should be read all through by the Chairman before it was discussed clause by clause.

Mr. PERRY said it was contrary to the practcie of this House to adopt such a suggestion. The honorable member for Murray Harbor should not try to throw cold water on a Bill from so large and respectable a town as Summerside.

Hon. Mr. PROWSE said the honorable member for Tignish misrepresented the facts. The " Telephone Bill "had this session been read all through before being discussed. The honorable member had no right to misrepresent him (Mr. P.) and say he was trying to throw cold water on this measure.

Mr. J. R. McLEAN wished the introducer of the Bill to give some further explanations about it.

Mr. SINCLAIR said that neither of the honorable members for Summerside seem to be very favarable to this Bill. The petition against it was a good reason for delaying the matter, and he (Mr. S.) did not see the use of losing time over it. If the honorable members for Summerside are satisfied that it is not in the interests of their constituents to pass this Bill; the Committee will delay it. The introducer of the Bill should let the Committee know what he thinks of this Bill.

Hon. Mr. LEFURGEY said he was not the father of this Bill. He had been comparing it with the printed Bill and found it was not the same. He (Mr. L.) considered that when a Bill was printed and submitted to a meeting of those interested, that no material change should be made in it. The Town Council want to get a Bill they can understand, as at present one clause of the Laws clashes with another On comparing this Bill we found that part of the amendments asked for by the petition against it had been included in it. He (Mr. L.) was not altogether satisfied with the Bill, but he was willing to go into the matter, and make it as workable as possible. He had no desire to prevent the passing of this Bill, but he did not wish to pass a measure that might act injuriously on his constituents. This Bill may not be as good as what we have now, if it is not carefully considered.

Mr. J. R. McLEAN said the honorable member had the Bill in Committee, and would have to make seme move, either to go ahead with it or to move that it be deferred until next session. As the honorable member does not seem very well prepared to explain the Bill, perhaps it would be better to defer the matter.

Hon. Mr. LEFURGEY said he thought he could explain the Bill. Whether his explanations would be satisfactory to honorable members he could not say ; but he would do the best he could.

Mr. BEER said it was quite proper that the Bill should be put through this year, as no doubt the town of Summerside required this measure.

Mr. BENTLEY said it was unfair to ask the members for Summerside to explain all this Bill at one sitting. It was nothing but justice to go into the Bill and discuss it as it proceeded. Why did not the honorable member for Souris make a motion to defer the consideration of the Bill if he does not approve of it ? The Committee should consider the clauses of the Bill, and if advisable they should be passed.

First section read.

Hon. Mr. CAMPBELL said he looked upon Summerside as his County Town, and he had a great interest in any matter affecting its welfare. As he had a great desire to get this Bill passed, he would move that Mr. Speaker take the Chair, the Chairman report that some progress had been made, and ask leave to sit again.

Motion put and carried.

Hon. Mr. FERGUSON, a member of Her Majesty's Executive Council, presented to the House a statement showing the names of persons who have not attorned, and also a statement showing amount that had been received by the Department of Crown and Public Lands for rents.

Ordered, That said papers do lie on the table of the House.

Mr. BLAKE, in accordance with notice placed on the Order Book, asked the honorable Commissioner of Public Works to lay on the table of the House a statement showing the amounts paid John P. Nicholson during 1884.

Hon. Mr. CAMPBELL said the statement was being prepared and would be laid on the table of the House as soon as possible. As the vouchers had all to be gone through, it would take some little time to prepare it.

House adjourned.

G. F. O.

AFTERNOON SESSION.

Mr. SPEAKER in the Chair.

On motion, the 25th Rule of the House was suspended, and the "Act to incorporate the Presbyterian and Evangelical Protestant Union Publishing Company" was read the third time and passed.

The same rule having been suspended, "An Act in further amendment of An Act to Incorporate the City of Charlottetown" was also read the third time and passed.

Hon Mr. FERGUSON, a member of Her Majesty's Executive Council, presented to the House:—Statement, Public Lands Department, showing estimates of lands unsold, the townships in which such lands are situated, and the probable deficiency in acreage in certain estates

Ordered, That said returns do lie on the table.

On motion, the House went into Committee of the whole on all matters relating to Roads.

Mr. JOHN MCLEAN in the Chair.

After some time spent in Committee, without debate, Mr. Speaker, on motion, resumed the Chair, and the Chairman reported certain resolutions agreed to.

On motion, the House went into Committee of the whole, on all matters relating to paupers.

Mr. BENTLEY in the Chair.

After some time spent in Committee, without debate, Mr. Speaker, on motion, resumed the Chair, and the Chairman reported certain resolutions agreed to.

On motion of Honorable Mr. Lefurgey, the House went into Committee of the whole to take into further consideration "An Act to amend the Act to incorporate the Town of Summerside."

Mr. HOLLAND in the Chair.

Mr. J. R. McLEAN said that the honorable senior member for Summerside, in the forenoon, gave the House to understand that he would explain this Bill, and thus give honorable members an opportunity to discuss it more intelligently than they otherwise could.

Hon. Mr. PROWSE suggested that the Chairman read the whole Bill as distinctly as possible, in order that the House might better understand its provisions.

Mr. BEER thought the Bill should be considered clause by clause as usual.

Mr. D. C. MARTIN did not know much about this Bill, and he doubted if the introducer himself did. He thought the whole Bill should first be read, before the House could pronounce an opinion on it.

Mr. YEO thought each clause might be explained by the introducer, to enable the House to understand it. Too much time would be consumed in reading through the whole Bill before going into it clause by clause.

Hon. Mr. LEFURGEY said it would require a great deal of time to read and explain the whole of this Bill, and to compare it with the Act now it force. Besides this, he was a layman, and not as well posted as some other honorable gentleman.

Hon. Mr. FERGUSON said that the words used in this Bill were very large,—jawbreakers from the beginning to the end.

Mr. BEER was fully prepared to give the Bill due consideration, even if two days more were required to do so.

The first clause was then read.

Mr. J. McLEAN said that there was a strong petition against this Bill, and looking at that fact, and that it was now too late in the session to give it due consideration, he was opposed to any action being taken on it, at present.

Mr. RICHARDS said that the gentleman who brought down the Bill, the other day, had taken a good deal of trouble about it, and the town Council had held meetings and spent a great deal of labor about it. He understood that many of the amendments asked for in the petition, are now embodied in the Bill. The Summerside members ought to know more about it than any one else. It appeared that the Act now in operation is almost unworkable.

Mr. YEO thought it would be dealing in too summarily a way with this Bill for the Speaker to take the Chair without any report from the Committee. The Opposition were prepared to remain and give it due consideration. He had to confess he did not know what the people of Summerside require, but he thought they were pursuing the proper course in consolidating the various laws passed for the regulation of their affairs. He would be guided very much by the action of the Summerside members on the matter. If the Bill had been printed it would have been much easier to consider it.

Hon. Mr. ARSENAULT would like to see Summerside receive such a law as will meet its requirements; but it is now almost too late in the session to give this measure such consideration as it demands. In fact, there are only a few hours left of the session, and nearly a whole week is required to deal with this Bill in a proper manner. It should have been sent here much earlier in order to receive proper attention from both Houses. He did not think the people of Summerside would expect the House to sit a week longer, solely for the purpose of passing the Bill, especially as half their number is opposed to its provisions. Let the Bill be sent in good time next session, and it will receive the fullest consideration. A great many amendments are asked for, and they must be dealt with very carefully. The House had not time to go into it this session, and he thought the Bill would not spoil if laid over until next year. It would then receive all the consideration it deserved or required.

Mr. SINCLAIR thought it would be wrong to throw out the Bill in the manner proposed. He did not know what it contained, but he would be willing to remain until it is properly considered. The people of Summerside have certainly taken the right course in asking for the consolidation of the various Acts passed for their benefit. The House should hear it read, and know what it contains.

Mr. JOHN MCLEAN said that amendments are asked in no less than eleven paragraphs in this Bill, and 200 residents of Summerside do not want to have it passed as it now stands, no matter how excellent it may be on the whole a measure.

Hon. Mr. FERGUSON said that in the interests of the people of Summerside it would not be wise to go into the consideration of this Bill at the very close of the session, as it would be impossible to give it that attention that it should have. Amendments are asked for, and it would be the duty of the House to examine them thoroughly and insert such of them as it approved of. The people of Summerside cannot be supposed to be acquainted with all its provisions, because it has never been published. If passed under present circumstances, it cannot be free from blunders and imperfections. It would be better to allow it to lie over, and during the recess the people there can become further acquainted with it, and, if necessary amend it.

Mr. SINCLAIR thought the least the House should do was to take the Bill up clause by clause, and, if necessary to amend it. It should not be thrown out without a knowledge of its contents.

Mr. FARQUHARSON said that the Bill should be thoroughly examined, and if not found objectionable, it should be passed. Unfortunately the Summerside Bills generally came in near the close of the session, and there was not time to deal with them in a proper manner. He would be largely guided in dealing with this matter, by the action of the honorable senior member for Summerside. He wished to know the provisions of the Bill. It should not be thrown out in the summary manner proposed.

Hon. Mr. FERGUSON,—The honorable members for Summerside are, themselves, at a loss as to the best course to pursue. It is impossible that they could be posted in reference to the provisions of so lengthy a Bill as now before the House. Even if the House went into its consideration, it would be impossible to perfect it and make it what it should be, at this late date in the session.

Mr. J. R. MACLEAN thought Summerside was entitled to all due respect, and that the House should go into consideration of the Bill clause by clause. He would move that the Chairman read the Bill through, before doing so.

Mr. GILLIS said that the Bill had only been prepared a short time ago, and it had, consequently, come in at a very late hour in the session. A Bill of this nature entails upon those who prepare it, a very large amount of work; and as this one was very large, it would be almost certain to contain errors and inconsistencies which would require correction. He would like to see the Bill very carefully considered and passed, but he did not wish to see it rushed through the House in a hasty, slip-shod manner, as the result could not be satisfactory. If the House would devote sufficient time to the Bill, he would assist in making it as perfect as possible, otherwise it would be useless to attempt to make it what it should be. People on both sides of politics had signed the petition, for the Bill, and others, on both sides, the one in opposition to it. Of one thing he felt sure, and that was, none of them would be satisfied with an inferior measure. If the Bill is to be dealt with by the House at all, sufficient time must be devoted to it. If this could not be done, it would be better to allow it to lay over, as he did not know that it is very urgently required. He understood from the Chairman of the Town Council, that they did not want any additional power to that which they had already possessed under the existing Act. He had to confess he had not had time to study the provisions of this Bill as he desired to do. In his opinion, not less than 26 hours should be devoted to its consideration by the House. This would be in proportion to the length of time given to other measures. If the House did not mean to do full justice to the Bill, he would rather see it laid over until next session, for, in the interests of the people of Summerside, it should be carefully weighed and compared with the law now in force, before being passed.

Mr. J R. MACLEAN thought the Bill should be read over from first to last, before being considered.

Hon. Mr. LEFURGEY thought the Bill should be read over again in order to understand the bearing of the various clauses upon one another. It should also be compared with the existing Act, in order to see its relation thereto and to see that it contains all the necessary amendments. The petition against it, asks that it be not passed, unless all the amendments proposed in that petition be first inserted. Some of those amendments have already been embodied in the Bill, while others have not. There are 70 names for the Bill as it stands, and 270 against it, unless amended. Beside this there are some changes petitioned for which are unnecessary. Some of the clauses in the Bill are not required, and he would like to see them struck out altogether. In fact, it would be better not to pass the Bill at all, unless it is very carefully considered by the House, as it is a very lengthy and bulky one

Mr. J. R. MACLEAN moved that the Chairman read the whole Bill in order that the House may see what it contains.

Hon. Mr. ARSENAULT asked what would be gained by reading over the whole Bill. It was plain that the House could not give the requisite time to its consideration to do it justice. While it is being read, many members will be reading the newspapers.

Mr. D. C. MARTIN said that the proposal to allow the Bill to lay over until next session, was a very unfair one. As far as the Opposition were concerned, they were perfectly willing to go into its full consideration. Surely its introducer desired to have it passed by the House! He (Mr. M.) thought there was plenty of time to give it all the attention it required.

Mr. BLAKE did not wish to see the Bill dealt with in a summary manner; but as the House is going to rise to-morrow, it is impossible to give it the consideration which it really requires. It must be important to the well-being of Summerside or it would not have been sent here. Looking at the fact that there is a petition against it, more care than otherwise would be necessary in dealing with it. The only course to pursue is to allow it to stand over until next session, if the members from Summerside are willing to do so. It should be printed for the perusal of the people of that town. If the House attempted to deal with the Bill, as matters now stand, justice to it would not be done.

Mr. YEO did not like the idea of throwing out the Bill without knowing its contents. On the other hand, there does not seem to be sufficient time to deal with it in a proper manner. To pass it without the fullest consideration would be a farce.

Hon. Mr. FERGUSON,—The Bill contains 170 clauses, and it would take some days to engross it, not to speak of duly considering its provisions. As the House is to rise to-morrow, it is impossible to go on with it.

On motion, Mr. Speaker resumed the Chair, without any report from the Committee.

On motion, the House went into Committee of the whole to take into consideration the Report of the Committee on the Public Accounts.

Mr. J. R. McLEAN in the Chair.

First clause, relating to the receipts for 1884, read and agreed to.

Second clause, showing surplus on the year's transactions, of $735.88, read.

Mr. FARQUHARSON did not think this clause sufficiently clear. It is too non-committal in its statement. He wished it to show whether the balance of $53,931.70 is a debit or a credit. He took exception to this clause on that ground. A report of this kind should contain clear and explicit statements. This clause should be amended and made more complete.

Hon. Mr. FERGUSON thought the statement alluded to by the honorable member for West River was as plain as it possibly could be. In fact, any person could understand it. It is clear that the balance of $53,931.70 is not alluded to as a surplus. If it was intended to be reckoned as a surplus, the $735.88 would have been added to it, instead of being subtracted from it.

Mr. YEO thought this paragraph most ingeniously drawn up. It should show the balance against the Province for the two previous years so plainly that there could be no mistake.

Mr. BENTLEY said that the clause was as large as it was possible to make it. It states distinctly that the surplus on the transactions of 1884, viz., $735.88 is deducted from the balance of $53,931.70, leaving $53,195.82. The Committee did not attempt to hide anything, as they had nothing to conceal, and considered the suggestion of the honorable gentleman, the member for West River, entirely out of place. Any person could see from the paragraph that the balance alluded to was composed of the deficits of previous years. But the Committee scarcely expected the honorable member to sign the report, as one of its members, for he would, of course, take some slight exception to it. The one taken was, certainly very small indeed.

Mr. FARQUHARSON said that the Committee on Public Accounts

were supposed to be the joint authors of their report; but this report was drawn up and completed before he was asked to give any opinion with reference to its statements. The second paragraph did not meet his views, and he refused to sign it. He wished to see it amended, in order that it might be made clearer.

Mr. ALEX. MARTIN said that the objection made to the second paragraph of this report by the honorable member for West River was quite in keeping with his (Mr. F.'s) previous tactics with respect to other matters during the whole of the present session. The honorable member was only trifling with the question now before the House. Quibbling was the honorable member's forte. No honorable member of the House understood the matter but the honorable member himself, according to his own showing! It was about time for him (Mr. Farqueharson) to turn over a new leaf, and not take up the time of the House with such trifling remarks.

Mr. SINCLAIR said that if the honorable member for West River had been treated by the Committee as had been alleged, he did not wonder the honorable gentleman was not satisfied. It appears the Government members of that Committee prepared the Report, signed it, and then threw it to the Opposition members for their signatures. The latter had a right to expect better treatment than that. The $53,222.19 received from the General Government, as a refund for the Piers, should not

have gone to the Revenue Account for the past year. It had been stated by the honorable Leader of the Government, in 1884, that this refund would go to cover the debt, of the previous years. Instead of this, it is put down as Revenue for last year. This was not keeping faith with the House, and the deficits of previous years and the interest thereon are not provided for.

Hon. Mr. FERGUSON said that the honorable gentlemen of the Opposition are always complainers. Their dignity and privileges are interfered with on every side. Because this Report was prepared by the Chairman of the Committee, and presented to them for signature, the two Opposition members of that Committee have a grievance. They well know that it is the custom for the Chairman of the Committee on the Public Accounts to draw up the Repotr and to submit it to the other members; but they complain that the Opposition members should have been asked to assist in drawing it up. If the Report is correct, it is only wasting time to find fault with it The Opposition do not complain that this paragraph is not correct, but that it is not clear enough. As had been already stated, there is not a schoolboy in the country who could misunderstand the tenor of the clause. No one would think of deducting a surplus from a surplus but from a balance unpaid. The very fact that it is deducted from a balance shows that the latter is against the Province. It makes no difference what the Piers money is deducted from, the deficit against the Province remains exactly the same.

Mr. BEER said that it was not the custom for the Chairman of the Committee on Public Accounts to prepare the Report without the aid of the other members of that Committee. He maintained that the course pursued by the Chairman of this Committee was an insult to the members of the Opposition who were in that Committee. In 1879, the honorable senior member for Georgetown signed a Report on the Public Accounts recommending that the amount of the old Duty Bonds be written off, and not reckoned of any value as assets. But he (Mr. B.) observed that they still remain among the assets of the Province, although completely worthless. He maintained that the real debt of the Province is not clearly shown in this Report. As to the cash remaining in the Bank of Prince Edward Island, it is not worthy of mention. The Chairman of the Committee had not, by any means, pursued the proper course towards the Opposition members of it.

'Hon. Mr. McLEOD thought this a very unimportant complaint on the part of the Opposition members of the Committee. The Opposition had acted like a lot of old women in the course they had pursued with reference to this Report. It is well known that the value of the deposit in the old Bank of Prince Edward Island cannot be ascertained until the affairs of that Bank are wound up. There is no doubt that asset is good for the full amount. The right of the Crown has priority over the rights of all other creditors, and the Committee was perfectly justified in putting down the full amount of that deposit, as an asset of the Province. The Lieutenant Governor represents Her Majesty the Queen, and the claim of the Government has priority over those of all other creditors of the Bank. There is no doubt about that.

Mr FARQUHARSON said that the Chairman of this Committee was also the Chairman of the Committee of Public Accounts in the session of 1879, and at that time compared ordinary revenue with the ordinary expenditure. This course was not pursued in the present instance. This year, the honorable member put down as ordinary revenue the amount received as compensation for the Piers. Now, that sum could not be reckoned, properly, as ordinary revenue. On the other hand, there was no extraordinary expenditure during the past year. The honorable gentleman should have stated that the ordinary revenue did not meet the ordinary expenditure by about $50,000 or $60,000, and that the Committee regretted that such was the case. The real facts of the case should have been stated in the Report as clearly as possible.

Mr. BENTLEY said that the honorable member for Southport appeared very much disturbed because he (Mr. Beer) did not assist in the preparation of this Report. Would it not be believed that the honorable member for Southport and the honorable member for West River were both invited to name an hour to meet with the Committee for the purpose of consulting together on the matter? The other members of the Committee were prepared to meet them to receive suggestions and to discuss the various points with them, at any hour they would name. The honorable member for Southport referred to the Report for 1882. Did the honorable gentleman sign that Report. No. The honorable member offered quite a number of suggestions, and after all did not sign it. The present Committee wished to present this Report to the House on Thursday, and met together on the forenoon of that day, expecting the Opposition members to join them, but they did no put in an appearance until aftereleven o'clock, long after the hour named. When the honorable member for Southport came in, and took his place in the House, the Report was submitted to him, but he refused to sign it. Under such circumstances, it was unlikely the Committee would delay their work. Notwithstanding the fact that he signed it before presenting it to the Opposition members, they would have altered it or amended it, if they had any good reason for doing so at the suggestion of the two honorable gentlemen referred to. But those honorable members did not offer a single objection except the one

made by the honorable member for West River, and which the honorable gentleman had now stated in his place in the House. They suggested nothing whatever. If they were dissatisfied with the present report, why did they not bring in a minority report? They have, however, found very little fault with the report, and that little is entirely groundless.

Mr. BEER,—The report for 1882 was such that he could not sign it. There were statements made in it to which he strongly objected. He was present in his place all day on Wednesday, and nothing was said to him on that day about any meeting of the Committee. After the Government members had signed it, however, they brought it to him for his signature, and as he could not agree with some portions of it, he refused to append his name to it.

Hon. Mr. FERGUSON found that only on two occasions since the present Government came into power, had the Opposition members of the Committee signed the report on the Public Accounts. The usual course pursued in reference to this matter is for the Chairman of the Committee to prepare the report, and then to ask the other members to sign it. If this report was faulty, and such as should be amended, it would have been quite easy to have a meeting of the Committee to consider the matter, and to make the necessary amendments. It appears that the Opposition members were asked to name a time for meeting with the other members of the Committee, but that they did not do so. In past years, when a differemce of opinion arose between the Government members of the Committee and those of the Opposition, the latter brought in a minority report. Why did not the Opposition members pursue that course in the present instance? They had three members out of the seven appointed on the Committee, which is an unusually large number. Instead of blaming the Government members, the Opposition should have acknowledged their courtesy in the treatment they had received. It is clear that the latter do not wish to meet statements made over their own signatures. They refused to sign this report because it did not make the balance against the Province large enough to suit their views and purposes. The objections made by them against the report are frivolous in the extreme. The Chairman of the Committee made them a most courteous offer, but they refused to avail themselves of it.

Mr. FARQUHARSON had offered to meet with the Committee if the Chairman would show in the report the exact indebtedness of the Province on the 31st December, 1884. He considered the old Duty Bonds of no value, and that they should no longer be put down as a h asset. He would allow fifty cents on the dollar for the deposit in the old Bank of P. E. I., and no more. There was a sum owing at the close of 1884 for unpaid accounts, and also a quarter's salaries due the teachers for the same year, all of which should be charged against it. According to his calculation, the actual indebtedness of the Province on the 31st December, 1884, was $99,415.31.

Mr. BEER said that during almost every session three members of the Opposition had been appointed on the Committee on Public Accounts, so that the present case was by no means exceptional in that respect.

The remaining clauses of the report were then severally read and agreed to.

On motion, Mr. Speaker resumed the Chair, and the Chairman reported the report agreed to, without any amendment.

A message was received from the Legislative Council, stating that they had passed the Act to incorporate the Charlottetown Water Works Company, the Act to Incorporate the Temperance Alliance of King's County, and An Act to further amend An Act respecting to the Garnishment of Debts—with an amendment.

On motion of Honorable Mr. Sullivan, the said amendments were read the first time and passed, and ordered to be read the second time to-morrow.

House adjourned until to-morrow forenoon, at ten o'clock.

I. O.

FRIDAY, April 10.

Mr. SPEAKER in the Chair.

Hon. Mr. CAMPBELL presented the return asked for by the honorable junior member for Charlotte town, respecting the amount paid John P. Nicholson in the year 1884.

Ordered, That said return do lie on the table.

Mr. SPEAKER read to the House a message which he had received from His Honor the Lieutenant Governor, intimating that His Honor would be in the Legislative Council Chamber this afternoon at three o'clock, p. m., for the purpose of proroguing this session of the Legislature.

On Motion of Honorable Mr. Sullivan the House resolved into a Committee of the whole to take into consideration an amendment made by the Legislative Council to the Bill intituled "An Act to further amend the Act respecting the Garnishment of Debts.

Mr. BLAKE in the Chair.

After some time spent in Committee without debate on motion,—

Mr. Speaker resumed the Chair, and the chairman reported the amendment agreed to.

On motion of honorable Mr. Sullivan the 10th Rule of the House was suspended in order that the amendment to the Bill intituled "An Act further to amend the Act respecting the Garnishment of Debts" should be read the third time.

The amendment was acordingly read the third time and passed.

Ordered, That a message be sent to the Legislative Council intimating that said amendmment had been passed by this House.

A message was received from the Legislative Council with amendments to the Charlottetown Incorporation Act 1885. Also intimating that the Legislative Council had passed the Bills intituled "An Act to incorporate the 'Presbyterian and Protestant Union Printing and Publishing Company' and the "Appropriation Act 1885," without any amend-ment.

Mr. BENTLEY submitted the following resolution:—

Resolved, That a Committee be appointed to prepare an Address to be presented to His Honor the Lieutenant Governor, thanking His Honor for the various communications and messages received from him during the present session.

Motion put and carried.

The following Committee was appointed, Mr. Bentley, Mr J. McLean, Hon. D. Gordon.

Mr. BENTLEY from the foregoing Committee presented to the House the draft of an Address as prepared by the Committee as follows:

To His Honor the Honorable Andrew Archibald Macdonald, Lieutenant Governor of Prince Edward Island, &c., &c., &c.

MAY IT PLEASE YOUR HONOR:

The House of Assembly most respectfully thank your Honor for the various communications and messages sent to the House by Your Honor, during the present session, and also for the readiness with which your Honor has complied with the wishes of the House in furnishing such information as they have required.

On motion the same was received, read and agreed to.

Ordered, That the Address be engrossed.

Ordered, That the same Committee be appointed a Committee to present the Address to His Honor the Lieutenant Governor.

Mr. JOHN MACLEAN submitted the following resolution:

Resolved, That a Committee of three be appointed to examine and report upon contingent Accounts for the present session.

Motion put and carried.

The Committee was appointed as follows:

Mr. John McLean, Mr. Bentley, Mr. A. Martin.

On motion the Standing Order was enforced, when all strangers withdrew.

G. F. O.

AFTERNOON SESSION.

The Chairman of the Committee appointed to report on the Contingent Accounts of the House for the present session, presented to the House the Report of said Committee.

Ordered, That the said Report be now committed to a Committee of the whole House.

The House accordingly resolved itself into the said Committee.

Mr. BLAKE in the Chair.

After some time spent in Committee, with closed doors, Mr. Speaker on motion, resumed the Chair and the Chairman reported that the Committee had gone through the Report, paragraph by paragraph, had amended and adopted the same, and the Report so amended, being again read at the Clerk's table, was agreed to by the House.

Mr. YEO in accordance with notice previously placed by him on the Order Book, asked the honorable Leader of the Government what action had been taken on a petition from Archibald McMillan of Summerside, asking the Government to refund a certain sum of money paid by him to the Government on account of a grant of a certain portion of the foreshore in

Summerside Harbor

Hon. Mr. SULLIVAN said that in the month of February, 1879, when the late Government were in power, the grant of a portion of the shorefront at Summerside was made to Archibald McMillan. Since that time, the shorefronts have been found to be vested in the Dominion Government, and they alone have power to make such a grant. The Dominion Goveenment have, however, expressed their willingness to confirm all such grants made by the Local Government, and if Mr. McMillan will apply to them his grant will no doubt be confirmed.

Mr. BENTLEY from the Committee appointed to wait upon His Honor the Lieutenant Governor with the Address thanking him for the various communications and messages to the House during the present Session, reported to the House that their Address had been presented th His Honor.

Hon. Mr. SULLIVAN in pursuance of a notice placed by him on the Order Book, rose for the purpose of moving a resolution, which would explain itself, and is as follows:

Whereas, During the present session of the General Assembly this House did join with the Legislative Council in a testimonial to Her Majesty the Queen, praying Her Majesty's most gracious intervention in order to obtain from the government of Canada a fulfillment of the terms upon which this Island entered the Confederation in respect to communication with the mainland, and also the payment of compensation to this Province for the loss sustained by its people in consequence of the failure of the Dominion Government to carry out the said terms, and a joint address of both Houses has been adopted, requesting His Honor the Lieutenant Governor to forward the said memorial to His Excellency the Governor General for transmission to Her Majesty the Queen,—

And Whereas, Since the adoption of the said memorial and address an insurrection has unfortunately been incited in the North-west Provinces, whereby not only the peace and welfare of the Dominion have been disturbed, but the lives and property of its citizens are endangered, while some of Her Majesty's subjects have met their death in bravely endeavoring to uphold the authority of the British Crown.

And Whereas, This House recognizes the paramount obligation of the General Government to suppress lawlessnes and rebellion, and it is the imperative duty of every British subject to assist the constituted authorities in the restoration of quietness and good order, and in the maintenance of the Queen's supremacy.

Therefore Resolved, This House unwilling to embarass the General Government while occupied with matters of such weighty moment to the Empire, and looking to a speedy termination of the insurrection, desire to postpone for the present the carrying out of the constitutional means by which it seeks to redress a grievance of the people of this Province, and request His Honor, the Lieutenant Governor, not to forward the same memorial until such time, during the approaching Legislative recess, as, in the opinion of his advisers, shall be deemed opportune."

The object of the resolution is to place in the hands of the Government authority from the Legislature to have the Address to Her Majesty the Queen on the matter of Winter Communication with the mainland, forwarded at a time, which, in the opinion of the Government, will be considered an opportune occasion. Just now, the Dominion Government are engaged in suppressing a rebellion in the North-West, and it is easily seen that this is not a time when a question like this could be brought before them or the Imperial Government, with that success which is desirable. This resolution merely requests that it shall be in the power of His Honor the Lieutenant Governor to have the Address forwarded at a suitable time for transmission to Her Majesty. The Rebellion in the North-West has assumed proportions much greater than were at first expected, but it may be suppressed within a very short period. The Local Government have been expecting, from time to time, that the rebellion would come to an end, and therefore could not earlier submit this resolution to the House. He felt sure

that the Resolution will commend itself to the judgment of every honorable member of the House. Instead of weakening our claim, it will really strengthen it. The people of this Province are a loyal people, and do not desire to take advantage of an insurrection in the North-west to press upon the Dominion Government their claims in respect to the nonfulfilment on the part of the latter of the Terms of Confederation. Our claims will be pressed when both the Dominion and Imperial Governments have an opportunity to give them full and fair consideration. The Local Government will have to exercise their judgment as to a fit and proper time to have the Address forwarded. By the resolution, that time is limited to the recess, and some time during that period the Government will be bound to have the Address transmitted to the Queen. He thought nothing would be gained by sending it to the proper quarter at the present time. The Dominion Government would not allow it to go to the foot of the Throne without some explanation of the course they have pursued, as was the case in reference to our claim on account of the Fishery Award. They invariably take such action, in such cases. If the Address were to be forwarded without any such provision as is made in this resolution, it might remain in the hands of the Dominion Government for three months, before being transmitted to the Queen, so that we shall lose nothing in regard to time; and the Legislature will perform an Act which the Imperial Government will consider a graceful one, in the face of the attempt now being made in a distant part of the Dominion, to subvert the authority of Her Majesty.

Mr. YEO was somewhat surprised at the action taken by the honorable Leader of the Government in moving this resolution. The House is to be prorogued today, and yet his honor has brought down this very important matter, to be decided upon without delay. Every honorable member of the House regrets the insurrection in the North-west, but it was going on when the Address to Her Majesty was first proposed and passed. It is scarcely fair to ask the House to take such action as is now proposed on the very eve of the prorogation. Some time has elapsed since the Address was adopted, and the Government have had ample time to consider this question, and should have brought it to the notice of the House before this. If there was anything in connection with this matter which would throw any obstacle in the way of putting down the insurrection, the House would not desire to press it just now, but he did not see that such was the case. It is well-known that some unfortunate men, last winter, suffered so severely that some of them will probably carry the effects of their sufferings to the grave. It is therefore necessary that steps should be taken to improve the means of Winter Communication, without delay, in order to be ready for next season. The House had

heard a good deal about loyalty from members of the Government ranks, but it did not come from them with very good grace. There has been a good deal of lip-loyalty on their part. Honorable members have a duty to perform towards their constituents, and he thought that in passing the Address to Her Majesty the Queen, they have only been doing their duty. He saw no reason for delay in forwarding it to the proper quarter. If forwarded at once, it might be delayed at Ottawa a little while, but not very long.

Hon. Mr. SULLIVAN said that the Rebellion has assumed very much larger proportions than were ever expected, and it appears to be increasing, instead of diminishing. Under these circumstances, the Government delayed the present action until the very last moment. If the insurrection were stamped out, it would be unnecessary to pass the resolution at all. It seemed to him the duty of the Legislature to make such a request as this, as it did not properly belong to the government to do so. He did not think there is the slightest use in sending forward an Address of that kind until the Rebellion is put down.

Mr J. R. McLEAN said that while he sympathized with parties in the North-west who are suffering from the actions of the rebels in the present insurrection, he could not see that the proposed delay in forwarding the Address to Her Majesty would prove to be of any advantage to the people in any part of the Dominion. There is no good reason to think that if the Address is forwarded through the Governor General to the Queen, it would at all interfere with the action of the Dominion Government in suppressing the rebellion. The time has arrived when action should be taken to fulfil the Terms of Union in reference to Winter Communication with the mainland of the Dominion, and the sooner the better for all concerned. He would, however, agree to support one portion of the resolution, but not the whole of it, in its present form. He could not see that, if forwarded, it would inconvenience the General Government in the slightest degree, and it would be unwise to retard the progress of this question just now.

Hon. Mr. FERGUSON said that the resolution is not in the interests of the Dominion Government only, but in our own interests as well. In taking this step, we place upon record our desire to put down the rebellion, and show our sympathy with the General Government in the action they are taking. If we send up this Address for transmission to the Queen, just now, we shall find that the Dominion Government are so much engrossed with the suppression of the insurrection, that they will be unable to deal with it for some time to come. It does not pay to trouble a man who is too much engrossed with other business to attend to our case, until an opportunity occurs for so doing. It may be said that we are presenting an Address to the British Government, and not to

that of the Dominion. That is true, but there is no doubt that our application to the Home Government will be referred back to the government of the Dominion for friendly settlement. We should be in a position to show that all we have done has been done in a friendly way and in a proper spirit. Taking this view of the matter, he thought the resolution would very much assist our case, and the very fact that it has been passed, will dispose the Dominion Government to look into the whole question and probably settle it without any further delay. Sympathy with the general government in a time of trouble, such as this is, will find an echo in the hearts of the people all over the Island, and he felt confident the resolution would have the support of the House.

Mr. PERRY would be sorry to see the Dominion Government put to any inconvenience by our present appeal to Her Majesty the Queen, but the insurrection was in full blast when the Address was first proposed, and also, when it was passed, and it appeared to him the House was now asked to undo what it had already done. Honorable members are asked to throw cold water on the request they have made that the terms of union with the General Government be fulfilled. They are asked to pass a resolution requesting His Honor the Lieutenant Governor not to forward the address to the Queen, until the Local Government are pleased that he should do so. Is there any guarantee that the Government will have it forwarded when the rebellion is suppressed in the North-west? Honorable members should remember the nearly fatal accident on the Straits last winter and do nothing which would leave us in the same position during another season. If the honorable leader of the Government would move for an Address of sympathy with the Dominion Government in stamping out the insurrection, he (Mr. P.) would support them in it; but he could not stultify himself in the manner now proposed. He would utterly refuse to do so. The Opposition should be given time to submit a resolution embodying their views in reference to this question. They had not been fairly dealt with in respect to it.

Hon. Mr. FERGUSON seconded the resolution submitted by the honorable Leader of the Government.

Mr. SINCLAIR said that this matter had been sprung so suddenly upon the House that there was scarcely time for honorable members to make up their minds in reference to it. He did not think the Dominion Government were so much involved in the work of suppressing the rebellion that they had to neglect their other duties. There is a prospect of a great war between England and Russia which may occasion another delay. He thought we had suffered long enough, and if we are now going to back down, after all, and this action is published in every newspaper in the Dominion, it will have the appearance of our being very lukewarm in reference to the whole matter. Our action in appealing to Her Majesty the Queen, is one of vast importance to the people of this Province, and he thought this resolution, if passed, would do us a great deal of harm. He could not see that the rebellion had anything at all to do with our case. We are only asking that the compact entered into at Confederation be carried out. It would be very wrong for us to back down from the position we have taken, as to do so would cause great delay. It is our duty to press our demand for our rights, instead of taking this course. We have been treated very badly for a long number of years, and it is high time we should have our rights. We have no communication with the mainland except by means of open boats, in which the lives of our people are endangered. No further delays should be permitted. We are not justified in pursuing the course now proposed, and it is not calculated to secure for us any favor whatever. If the resolution would have the tendency to hasten the granting of our unquestioned rights, he would support it, but he could not see that it would. There is too little time left for the proper consideration of this matter. He did not see the notice of it on the Order Book yesterday, and was quite unprepared for it. To spring it upon the House, without proper notice, was very unbecoming. He did not feel like backing down from the position already taken by the House with respect to this matter.

Mr. YEO quite agreed with the remarks of the honorable member who had just resumed his seat. He did not wish to take up time with any further remarks, but would move that all that part of the Resolution after the word "whereas," be struck out and the following inserted in lieu thereof, viz: "While the present insurrection in the North-West Territories is much to be regretted—this House is nevertheless of the opinion that the matter of Winter Communication is of so much importance to this Province that it would not be advisable on the part of this Legislature to request to His Honor the Lieutenant Governor to withold the transmission to Her Majesty the Queen of the Address of both Houses of the Legislature of this Province respecting Winter Communication." The matter had been sprung upon the House so suddenly that honorable members of the Opposition had no time whatever to consider it. He could not see the pressing necessity for proroguing the House to-day. A few days would be well spent in discussing a question of this kind. He noticed, by late telegrams, that the Premier of the Dominion was of opinion that the Reports in reference to the insurrection have been very much exaggerated. If such was the case, it would only be a loss of time to pass this resolution.

Mr. PERRY seconded the amendment.

Mr. BEER did not want to embarrass the Dominion Government at the present time, as it is the duty of every loyal citizen to assist in putting down the rebellion. At the same time, if the Government had any intention to move a resolution such as this, they should have taken action at a much earlier period in the session. The House would then have been in a position to give the matter its undivided attention. He could not see that the Address to the Queen would interfere the least with the action of the Dominion Government in restoring order in the North West. They will have ample time to consider it after it is sent on for transmission to Her Majesty. He thought it likely that the rebellion would soon receive its quietus, and that there was no necessity to pass this resolution.

Mr FARQUHARSON did not think it at all necessary to take the action now proposed by the Government. It is probable that the rebellion will be brought to a speedy termination. The House should not stultify itself in passing such a resolution as the one moved by the Leader of the Government. The Address to the Queen had been passed unanimously, and should be transmitted to Her without delay. We have already suffered too much from the non-fulfilment of the terms of union.

The amendment having been put, the House divided as follows:

YEAS: Messrs. Yeo, Perry, Beer, Richards, Hooper, Matheson, Farquharson, D. C. Martin, Sinclair, J. R. MacLean, McLaren.—11

NAYS : Hons. Sullivan, Ferguson, MacLeod, Arsenault, Campbell, Lefurgey, MacDonald, Messrs. Holland, Bentley, J. MacLean, McDougall, Gillis, Blake.—13

So it passed in the negative.

The main motion was then put and carried unanimously.

Hon. Mr. SULLIVAN moved that a Committhe of seven members. be appointed to prepare An Address to His Honor the Lieutenant Governor, in accordance with the resolution.

Ordered, That the Hon. Mr. Sullivan, Ferguson, Lefurgey, Arsenault; Messrs. John McLean, Blake.

Hon. Mr. SULLIVAN from said Committee presented to the House the Draft of an Address, as prepared by them, and the same was received, read, and agreed to by the House.

Ordered, That the same Committee that prepared the Address be appointed to wait on His Honor the Lieut. Governor with the same.

Mr. FARQUHARSON according to previous notice given by him on the Order Book, asked the honorable Commissioner of Public Works whether it was the intention of the Government to repair the wharves on West River, at McEwen's Shore and at McEachern's this summer.

Hon. Mr. CAMPBELL,—It is not the intention of the Government to repair any wharves except those at which the Ferry Boats will touch.

Mr. PERRY said he rose for the purpose of moving a resolution, providing for an amalgamation of the Land Office and the Registry Office, with the view of closing up the former altogether. He had intended to move this Resolution earlier in the session, but had not an opportunity to do so. It is well-known that the cost of maintaining the Land Office is much greater than the Province should be called upon to bear, and the sooner it is closed the better for the tax-payers. The first step to take should be to wipe off all the Compound Interest on Interest due the Government from, those purchasing the freehold of their farms. The Compound Interest has, in some cases, accumulated to such an extent that the poor, unfortunate tenants cannot pay the amounts due for their lands. We know that many farms, upon the owners of which Precepts were served, and the lands sold, are still in the hands of the Government. In other cases, the amount of the arrears is more than the farms are worth. If the Land Office is kept open for 20 years longer, no less than $120,000 will be lost to the country in sustaining it. It is therefore better to wipe off the Compound Interest and reduce the price of bog and other poor land, than to keep up the Land Office. Simple Interest is sufficient for any tenant to pay.

A Message from His Honor the Lieutenant Governor by the Usher of the Black Rod, stating that His

Honor commanded the immediate attendance of this Honorable House at the Bar of the Council Chamber.

Accordingly Mr. Speaker and the House went up to attend His Honor, when His Honor was pleased to assent to a large number of Bills passed by both Houses during the session.

His Honor was then pleased to make the following Speech to both Houses, viz:

Mr. President and Honorable Gentlemen of the Legislative Council.

Mr. Speaker and Gentlemen of the House of Assembly.

The diligent attention which you have bestowed upon the business brought under your consideration enables me, after an unusually short session, to relieve you from further attendance upon your legislative duties, and I desire to express to you my acknowledgments for the various measures which you have passed in the interests of the Province.

I feel confident that you will join with me in deploring the unfortunate outbreak which has occurred in the North-west Territories, and that you will unite in the heartfelt prayer that peace and good order may be speedily restored; so that Canada may continue to pursue her path of progress and prosperity.

Mr. Speaker and Gentlemen of the House of Assembly.

I thank you for the supplies you have voted for the maintenance of the public service, and which, I beg to assure you, it will be the constant aim of my government to dispense with economy and care.

Mr. President and Honorable Gentlemen of the Legislative Council.

Mr. Speaker and Gentlemen of the House of Assembly.

The joint address which you have adopted to Her Majesty the Queen, praying Her intervention to secure from the Dominion Government a fulfillment of the Terms of Union in respect to communication with the mainland as well as for compensation for loss sustained by reason of past neglect in the matter, I shall duly forward in accordance with your desire; and I sincerely hope that your appeal may result in the removal of a long standing grievance, and one from which the Province has suffered most acutely.

In now taking leave of you, I earnestly pray that during the recess a kind Providence may direct and bless your individual labors, and those of the people whom you represent, so that happiness and prosperity may abound in our Island home.

The President of the Legislative Council then said that it is the will and pleasure of His Honor the Lieutenant Governor that this General Assembly be prorogued and that this General Assembly is accordingly prorogued.

ISAAC OXENHAM,
GEORGE F. OWEN, } Reporters.

INDEX.

Lightning Source UK Ltd.
Milton Keynes UK
UKHW010757261118
332983UK00009B/672/P